2nd edition

Maththatmatters

a teacher resource linking math and social justice

by David Stocker

CCPA Education Project

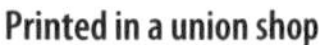

Printed in a union shop

As with many CCPA Education Project publications, **maththatmatters** gets to the very root of what education is about: facilitating positive social change. David Stocker's groundbreaking work provides educators and students with complete and thoughtful lesson plans, designed for grades 6-9, using math to teach about social justice in a way that is both accessible and powerful. We are extremely excited to have had the opportunity to work with David and to help make his materials available to a wider audience. Comments, suggestions and updates to the author are welcome.

Dirk Van Stralen has created a design and layout for **maththatmatters** that exceeded all expectations, and was a joy to work with throughout this process. To find out more about his work, please contact him at dirk@telus.net or visit www.dirkvanstralen.com.

Many thanks to the Canadian Auto Workers—and their longstanding commitment to public education--whose financial assistance helped make this book a reality.

Patricia McAdie, Larry Kuehn, Bernie Froese-Germain, Satu Repo and John McClyment have each contributed significantly to the long publication process. Their advice, support, patience and commitment is always greatly appreciated.

The CCPA Education Project would also like to express sincere and ongoing appreciation to its network of research associates and other supporters who so generously give of their time, energy and expertise. Thanks also to the CCPA staff: Melanie Allison, Bruce Campbell, Anskia DeJong, Trish Hennessey, Kerri-Anne Finn, Ed Finn, Jason Moores, Ellen Russell, Jennie Royer, Tim Scarth, Scott Sinclair, Diane Touchette, and Armine Yalnizyan.

About the CCPA Education Project:

The CCPA Education Project was established in 1996/97 to monitor corporate intrusion in public education: since that time, the mandate has broadened to include examination of other issues including standardized testing, vouchers and tax credits, user fees and fundraising, education funding, and post-secondary education. In September 2000 the CCPA began publishing the popular quarterly education journal *Our Schools / Our Selves* (established in 1988). *OS/OS* continues to be a forum for debates and commentary on a wide variety of education-related topics including: technology in the classroom, commercialism in schools, high stakes testing, curriculum design, women in the trades, education privatization, early childhood education, the school choice movement, safe schools, peace education and inclusive classrooms.

About the author:

David Stocker lives with his partner Kathy, their son Jazz, and soon a new baby, Kio. He has been a teacher for ten years at City View Alternative School in downtown Toronto. Its mission is to deliver a social justice, action-oriented program to grade seven and eight students.

About the illustrator:

Zenith Chance is a Canadian Chinese designer who loves his Art and Design. He spends days designing sportswear and nights drawing cartoons.

Comments, suggestions and updates to the author welcome:

dstocker@cyberus.ca

Printed in Canada

The main aim of education should be

to produce competent, caring,

loving, and lovable people.

Nel Noddings

If we are to reach real peace in this world

and if we are to carry on a real war against war,

we shall have to begin with the children.

Mahatma Gandhi

Orwell was wrong.

It's not Big Brother we have to fear.

It's Huxley's Brave New World

Wherein the truth drowns

In a sea of irrelevance.

Paraphrased from Neil Postman

★ Acknowledgements

Anthony Azzopardi, in his opening address to a group of math educators commented that one of the reasons we do mathematics is "to make the invisible visible." I couldn't agree more. In the past five years, a number of people have been instrumental in bringing the typically invisible to my attention and patient while we figured out just how mathematics could help people enter into important discussions about social justice issues.

In the early days, I am grateful for having met with Don Fraser, Gord Doctorow, John Clarke at OCAP, Peter Rosenthal, and Anna Willats. Greg deGroot-Maggetti, Chris Kubsch, Lynn Strangway, Mary Lou Kestell, Gord Perks and Sarah Winterton, Terezia Zoric, Richard Shillington, Linda McQuaig, Tim McCaskell and Charles Poynton all had important things to say, leading me to better and better places. Satu Repo, editor emeritus of *Our Schools, Our Selves* and Erika Shaker at the Canadian Centre for Policy Alternatives have also both been early supporters of my work, and I thank them for the opportunity to have a national voice in *Our Schools, Our Selves*. Thanks to Melanie Alison who has given so much to the project.

Many thanks to the Weisbaums, Sharon, Elli and Harry for so many things, but particularly the generous contribution of their time in the production of the **maththatmatters** video has meant a great deal to me. Sam Gindin at York University made several donations to the project, both from his extensive resources and his words of wisdom about the need for critical mathematics on the **maththatmatters** video.

It has been heartening to meet so many teachers and teacher candidates from around the province who have been so actively engaged during my workshops on the book. The comments and suggestions of many of those participants have inevitably shaped my ideas as the book was being written. It was encouraging to meet so many mathematicians at the CMESG working group on Peace and Mathematics. Sandy Dawson and Arthur Powell were skilled facilitators and Doug Franks, Francisco Kibedi, Dave Wagner, Peter Brouwer, Peter Taylor, Geoff Roulet, Stewart Craven, Joel Yan, Ann Kajander and Ralph Mason were then and in some cases continue to be a source of encouragement. Thanks to friends at OISE, Kathy Bickmore, Margaret Wells, Ron Lancaster, John Duwyn, Cathi Gibson-Gates, Nancy Steele, Indigo Esmonde and Bev Caswell.

Zen Chance was kind enough to donate his time and energy to the task of illustrating each of the fifty lessons, and didn't give up on me as I pestered him throughout the year. Dirk Van Stralen has been the force behind the design and layout, and has been enthusiastic throughout the process.

Being surrounded with supportive friends and family has its benefits. For their thoughtful contributions I'd like to thank Sam Zomparelli, Bryce Hartnell, JuJay Djang, Lisa and Denise Hansen, Ryan Andersen, Sarah Evis and Bob and Valerie Witterick. Antonino Giambrone, Anne McKenna, Colleen Costa, Nancy Steele, Biljana Svilaric and Maria Pasquino are the most exciting people to go to work with each day and a constant source of feedback and encouragement. Kevin Stocker and Helen Koutoumanos have shared their thoughts with me along the way, as well as the occasional osteopathic treatment and several fine meals. Many thanks to my parents Bob and Diane. Their child-raising laid the foundation for my interest in social justice.

Two special thanks are in order. The students of City View, past and present, have always cheered me on with their questions and comments. The attention they've given to the lessons we've piloted in class is evidence to me that 13 and 14 year olds are up for a challenge and will give back far more than you'd expect if you let them. They are my hope that the world will change for the better.

My partner Kathy has been an unending source of support to me throughout the past five years. Her careful attention to so many aspects of the book, the editing and formatting, the creative work with the quotations, the development of the workshop and covering off my responsibilities as I was away running them, have made **maththatmatters** undeniably richer. But this book emerged both directly and indirectly out of our day to day discussions about the world, which always push me to think more carefully and in ways I've never considered. I watch as she talks eloquently and with conviction about my work to others and am reminded again and again how very lucky I am to have met this woman and to have her in my life.

"It takes small things like a math book to make big changes."

Xochil

students speak

contents

Answers, activities & discussion notes

Introduction

Nel is sitting in my grade eight mathematics class with her hand raised confidently in the air. It's June and the classroom feels like a tropical jungle.

"David," she says, "just for the fun of it I've listed two full pages of occupations that require no use of mathematics beyond the simplest arithmetic. I'll bet good money that I don't need algebra for my next 80 years on the planet."

Snickering from the class.

"How many of you feel this way?" I ask, a single drop of sweat sliding down the side of my face.

Three quarters of the class cautiously raise their hands.

I try not to appear nervous but the jungle air is constricting my lungs. Chairs scrape. Even those who were carving words of farewell into the desktop look up expectantly. I move to block the door. Too late. Nel has started a revolution.

> "Nico can put the distance between Pluto and Mars into scientific notation but he can't explain the magnitude and impact of the U.S. military budget."

> "Keigan can calculate the circumference of Bippy the Hamster's running wheel but she doesn't understand how many innocent people fall within the impact zone of today's nuclear missiles."

Open any of the math textbooks or glance through the professional magazines and you will see that Nel has an excellent point. Middle school is a wasteland of pizza party math, where youth are meant to gleefully calculate the number of possible outfits they can select for the party, and delight in figuring out the volume of the pizza box, how many slices each should get and how much it will all cost.

There are activities to measure flag designs and calculate the radius of wheels. Students are asked to compare the height of the CN Tower to that of Death Valley. Is that toaster marked $29.95 fifteen or eighteen percent off of the original price? How many fries fit in the regular sized serving container? What if I super size-it?

Speaking with parents and teachers everywhere, educator and author Alfie Kohn asks the following question: Which is larger, 4/11 or 5/13? The answer, he says, if you're thinking from the students' point of view, is '**who cares**?'[1] And so, too, with fries and flags, toasters and towers: *who cares*?

There are two intertwined problems at play here. The first is that most people understand that there is a correct answer to Alfie's fraction question and, as a result, have come to believe that all we have to do is 'pour' into students 'the way to do it' and presto, they can do math. Paulo Friere describes this as the "banking concept" of education. Teachers act as experts and "deposit" truth into students, who are passive depositories. The first problem thus has to do with the *process* of math instruction, or perhaps the process's philosophical underpinnings.

Friere notes that "whereas banking education anesthetizes and inhibits creative power, problem-posing education involves a constant unveiling of reality. The former attempts to maintain the *submersion* of consciousness; the latter strives for the *emergence* of consciousness and *critical intervention* in reality."[2]

1 Kohn, Alfie. *The Schools Our Children Deserve.* Houghton Mifflin Company, New York. 2000. p. 141.
2 Freire, Paulo. *Pedagogy of the Oppressed.* Continuum. New York. 1986 p. 68.

"Whoa...!" some teachers respond. "Hey, now. 'Submersion of consciousness'? 'Critical intervention in reality'? I thought this was math class, where we figure out how many cups of flour we need for our tortillas!"

Which brings me to the second problem and the reason for this book, the problem of *content*. As teachers came to realize that the more relevant the material to the student, the better it's learned, we ended up with pizza party math. Objects in students' real lives could be used to "do math upon". Surely, however, there is more to real life math than rummaging around in kitchen closets to measure the volume of the Twinkies box or the can of Ravioli. We must distinguish between using things in the world around us to do math, and using math *to understand the world around us*. One is deceitfully artificial, a straw man. The other is dangerous, for it encourages people to think, and possibly, to act.

> "Vivian can develop the formula for finding the area of a parallelogram but she can't compare the rate of people per square metre in a homeless shelter to the same rate for a home in Rosedale."

To restate: **relevant** content is that which will engage the learner in their social reality. Now if you're thinking about the vast majority of people on the planet, social realities tend to be awash in inequity and injustice. Fortunately, there are many opportunities to address that injustice, as long as you're learning about the issues in the first place. **Maththatmatters** is a group of assignments designed to bring that content into the classroom.

There are two main objectives for this text. The first is to offer math activities that can be used to teach and reinforce the math skills that teachers are required to have their students learn. A text that does not address the skills outlined in curriculum documents is a text destined for a dusty shelf.

The second is to provide content that captures and increases student interest in justice, fairness and kindness, replacing purposeless content that furthers no student's ability to engage with their social reality.

I take it as a given that there are expectations, *copious* expectations in fact, that teachers are bound to address, and so I would be remiss if general curriculum strands were not linked and listed at the beginning of the book for easy reference. These allow the person using this resource to *substitute* portions of their existing program for **Maththatmatters** assignments and feel confident that the students are practicing the required skills. To put it another way, these assignments are not intended to be heaped on top of the mountain of work that already exists on your plate.

> "A'amer can calculate how likely it is that he'll roll a sum of four with two dice but he can't explain the chances of reaching age four in Sudan."

Maththatmatters questions the value of the content in our current texts and resources. If we want to encourage students to make the world a better place for everyone, to think in terms of possibilities, it not going to happen easily if we spend classroom time with pizzas and ravioli cans.

The assignments examine the here and now; for example, child abuse in "Breaking the Silence", and more distant issues that may still shape our day to day lives; for instance, the General Agreement on Trade in Services in "GATS Terrible!!" No lesson is meant to be the definitive word on the subject: all lessons are meant to fall under a general social justice perspective or umbrella.

In *Manufacturing Consent*, Noam Chomsky talks about the idea of "intellectual self-defense", which has to do with helping people to have the cognitive skill to protect themselves from deception. My hope is that the topics listed above will contribute to intellectual self-defense, but above and beyond students having a capacity to do mental Judo to protect themselves, I'd like them to think about how we might make the world better for others.

I

O

D

L

A

12

• Child & youth advocacy math • Monopolies math
• Social policies math
• Elections math • Union math • Politics math • Trade math
• Marketing math • Crime math • Pride math
• Poverty and hunger math • Sweatshop math • Public relations math
• Gender equity math • Accessibility math • First Nations Justice math
• Immigration math • Corporation math • War math • HIV/AIDS math
• Mental health math • Capital punishment math • Racial profiling math
• Violence math • Harm Reduction math • Environment math
• World math • Finance math • Privitization math • Patent rights math
• Healthcare math • Activist organizing math

Social JusticeMath

"To say that all students must somehow be prepared for the privileges and responsibilities of democratic citizenship seems right, but what role does mathematics play in this?"[3]

Nel is back again, prodding me to explain how, exactly, math can be used to engage more fully in a democracy.

"Have you seen the Wal-Mart commercial?" I ask.

3 Noddings, Nel. http://www.ed.uiuc.edu/EPS/PES-yearbook/92_docs/NODDINGS.HTM July 23, 2003.

"You mean the one with the bouncing yellow cartoon face, carrying a bow and arrow and wearing a Robin Hood hat?" she replies. "He leaps around the Wal-Mart store shooting arrows at the posted product prices, knocking them lower and lower."

"That's the one. What do you know about Robin Hood?"

"He steals from the rich to give to the poor." The deep irony of a Wal-Mart-created Robin Hood washes over me.

I prod. "How does a store afford to give us all of those deals? Surely the owners of Wal-Mart don't want little Robin roaming around cutting away at their profits...?" We're about to get into difficult questions that have very complicated answers- many that require mathematical thinking.

"Antonino can figure out his daily paper route salary using an algebraic equation but he can't use a pattern to show how violence on television and aggression in the world are related."

Numbers are used all of the time to manipulate people. Numbers used in marketing tell half-truths, or really, very narrow slices of truth. All parts of the political spectrum produce statistics to advance their own agendas. Crucial patterns and relationships (studied in what we call algebra!) are routinely hidden from view. In a democracy, and in the social justice movement in particular, mathematicians of all ages will be required to continually point out how numbers are *repeatedly* used to *facilitate oppression*, and more importantly, how numbers can be used to promote honesty, equity, fairness and kindness.

Although some people give their perfunctory "moo" at election time, really it's difficult to participate meaningfully in a democracy if you don't understand the issues upon which you are voting. I'm speaking broadly now: voting includes the choices we make as consumers, choices we make around how to spend our time, the community projects that we're involved in, the emphasis that we place on particular social issues over others, and the boxes that we tick at the polls. Voting in ignorance is like trying to pick out a thoughtful gift for a stranger: you might get lucky, but probably not.

"Ramona can sketch the front, top and side views of a cube but she can't use angles to interpret a boundary dispute between the provincial government and a First Nations community."

In a system of education, and specifically math education, that focuses so much of its time and resources on skills based education, memorization, regurgitation, standardized testing and reams upon reams of math problems whose content is immaterial, we miss a huge opportunity. We miss the opportunity to engage students in democratic process and increase their interest in social justice advocacy. To interact with students as if they are empty vessels to be filled with facts and figures is to "disconnect...students [from their] social realities and from issues of equity, responsibility, and democracy."[4]

Math is a particularly useful language to use when talking about quantity and quality, about relative relationships, about connections and probabilities. Math is excellent for describing similarities and pointing out differences, tracking trends and describing patterns. We communicate ideas to others whether we describe and explain our world using bar graphs or body language. And certainly, questions of how much, how often, how similar and how different can be questions of justice.

The difficult thing about these lessons is that the questions that they raise are rarely captured with simple answers. In pilot lessons we moved toward better understandings of the topic using math, without ever completely understanding. Such though is life.

---

4 Macedo, Donaldo. *Chomsky on MisEducation*. Rowman and Littlefield Publishers, Lanham Maryland. 2000, pp. 4-5.

Rather than using content and questions that lead the learner to simple numerical answers, devoid of real meaning, many of these assignments are designed to get students and teachers to ask more difficult questions, like the following:

- Who's perspective is this? What influences and shapes the person with this perspective? *Cui bono*? Who benefits? Is there a conflict of interest?
- What information is missing and why is it missing? Might missing information lead me to different conclusions?
- Do I trust the truthfulness of the information before me? Why or why not? What proof do I have?
- What do opponents of this perspective say?
- Do all perspectives carry the same value? Which ones are more compelling and why?
- How might I further complicate my thinking about this?
- Whom does this perspective or situation hurt? How does this affect me personally?
- How might I have some personal responsibility for this situation? What can I do to make it better? What has already been done to make it better with which I can connect?

"You, yourself can learn. Teach them about equity and justice so that some day they will teach their children about what they've learned and then the world will be a more peaceful place."

Zack

students speak

These are topics that can link with learners' growing sense of global awareness and optimism. And ideally they provide ideas to connect to an immediate community where possibilities for action exist. Talk without action is the fastest way to create cynics.

These assignments touch on topics like abuse, capital punishment, childhood death due to poverty, suicide and racist government policies. They look at genocide and the appropriation of Native land. The workings of greed and deception are served up for investigation. This work is not what I call "cotton candy equity" (looks big and impressive, but not much substance).

But far from creating a deep cynicism, **Maththatmatters** is meant to promote intelligent skepticism. Friere writes, "Problem-posing education is revolutionary futurity. Hence it is prophetic (and, as such, hopeful)...it affirms [people] as beings who transcend themselves, who move forward and look ahead...for whom looking at the past must only be a means of understanding more clearly what and who they are so that they can more wisely build the future."[5]

Molly in grade eight, expresses her hope and optimism at the end of one of her assignments. "As a final thought, I don't think this is going to be solved by next year, or the year after. In fact I don't even think it'll be solved in ten years, but, if we keep on working, we'll eventually figure it out." And if Molly and other students are thinking in those terms, we're moving in the right direction.

Throughout the process of writing this book teachers have generously shared with me some of their concerns. Perhaps you will identify with some of them.

---

5 Freire, Paulo. *Pedagogy of the Oppressed.* Continuum. New York. 1986 p. 72.

"I can't add more on top of my math course, because there's no time– I have to report on over 100 expectations, all in 10 months. Already I have to move at the speed of light to cover the basics."

"We can't make the world better if we're living in a bubble."

Tessa

students speak

Maththatmatters assignments are meant to gradually *take the place of components of your program*. Many of the standard intermediate level expectations can be assessed using these activities (teachers have reassured me that they can easily modify them for lower and higher grade levels).

For the tentative at heart, it's possible to start by introducing as few activities as you wish: perhaps only one in the first term to see how it goes. When you get a sense that you can speak to the expectations and generate assessment material (and more importantly that the students enjoy the assignments), you can supplement more activities.

"Real life math you can actually do something with."

Keiran

students speak

Many of the activities also include expectations from more than one "strand". What this is meant to do is demonstrate to learners that often skills (and knowledge) are far more intertwined than we make them out to be. What this means for you as a teacher is that a single assignment might generate multiple bits of assessment for a report card. For your convenience the strands have been listed in the next section.

"I don't know anything about social justice issues and advocacy– how could I possibly facilitate math classes on patriarchy, homophobia, and the workings of multinational corporations? That's way out of my league."

"It just makes more sense to learn about things that matter."

Zoe

students speak

These activities are meant as an invitation to you to step down from your role as the expert and to engage with the students as a learner yourself. In this context it is *preferable* for you to say, "I don't know the answer." What *is* required of you though is that you help people to ask probing questions. Your role is as a problem-poser. "How will we figure this out together?"

Each assignment begins with some written background information that is meant to spark discussion. The background is not a Ph.D. thesis, it's only a little part of a story. It is usually, however, enough to begin to explore the topic with the group together without having to do any research before you start. The information in each assignment will not only provide opportunities to do math to understand the topic, but will also naturally create questions that have answers that are not provided, and this may lead students to follow those pathways. Whether further information is found in a library book, on the Internet, or by talking with Aunt Olivia, the class as a whole contributes to a broader understanding of the topic in a follow up class or classes. You determine how much time to follow those pathways.

To reiterate, you don't need to know anything about social justice, you must only have an interest in asking questions. Friere would say that the traditional relationship between teacher and student is reconstructed so that "both are simultaneously teachers *and* students."[6]

"Aren't these assignments going to be out of date fairly quickly, with all of the real-life numbers and statistics that you use?"

Some of the lessons are a look at a particular time period, for example the economics of what was going on in Canada in the 1990s. Or how Chinese immigrants were treated in the early 1900s. But it's true. Some lessons are time dated and the patterns will change. Of course this is an opportunity to get students to look at when the data was generated, ask whether or not they think it's changed at all (and in which ways) and find a way to update the numbers on their own.

I'm afraid that the students won't learn the math skills as well. I know if I give them a drill sheet that I can tell quickly at the end that they either have the skills or they don't.

Although the curriculum is ten kilometres wide and about one centimetre deep, many educators (supported by substantial research) now realize that effective learning requires depth and that if you spend time to develop it, *the results far surpass skimming the surface*. Steven Zemelman and his colleagues note "covering less in more depth not only ensures better understanding, but increases the likelihood that students will pursue further inquiry of their own at later times."[7]

But let's not forget the issue of content. Remember that **Maththatmatters** is concerned with a *particular sphere of knowledge*, because you can still have a constructivist classroom where students are actively finding the volume of a pizza box. In the end, thinking about things that have real meaning is more likely to promote learning.

> "You do the math because you're curious- is it really true that needle and syringe exchange programs reduce HIV infection? Seriously? But wait, looking at this graph, it might mean this! No one's really curious about the fate of pizza slices, I mean, it just ends up being: who cares? Does this matter? What the hell? Why am I doing this?"
>
> Tessa
>
> **students speak**

What do I do with a classroom of students who function at different ability levels?

The very nature of open-ended assignments is that students can work to their own ability level. Students who complete the same assignment rarely hand in the same responses, and the variety of thought can become the starting point for classroom discussion.

The material seems biased to me– sort of Left leaning. That doesn't seem to be neutral and objective. It's too political.

---

6 Freire, Paulo. *Pedagogy of the Oppressed*. Continuum. New York. 1986 p. 40.
7 Zemelman, in Alfie Kohn, *The Schools Our Children Deserve*. p 143.

All material carries bias of some sort. Really the question is whether or not we want to spend time educating for peace and social justice. If we do, let's admit that bias and get to work.

Getting students to be sceptical of any teacher or person that claims that they are neutral or objective is important. We all bring to our classrooms and our lives a perspective on the world. Students are buried in math classrooms that avoid these subjects like the plague: how can that be neutral and unbiased? Of course it can't.

> "Now's the time to learn."
>
> Kathryn
>
> **students speak**

I'm worried that the principal or the parents will get upset. I'm not sure how much I want to rock the boat– it's my neck on the line.

There is undoubtedly the possibility that you may raise eyebrows with some of these lessons. Of course, this is one of the goals of education- to challenge people to think beyond what they're used to, beyond their comfort zone. Although it may not be easy, I always suggest to the teacher participants in my workshops that we, as members of a generally privileged profession, have an obligation to use our privilege to make the world better. And that means taking a stand when it's not popular.

At the end of the day, each of us will decide how far to push the envelope based on our own unique circumstances. But let's not make decisions based on convenience or on assumptions about how others will react. There are 50 lessons in this book- choose ones that you believe are reasonable starting points and progress as you become more comfortable. Let's not forget as well that we can engage parents in discussions that will create parent advocates- an easier job when what you're trying to teach has clear value. Engaged and excited students will help put parents more at ease as well.

> "Actually, I have never understood math better. Not only do I understand the general skill, I can also begin to understand the world better. And if I understand the world better I can change things. And knowing that is one of the best things in the entire world. There is no way to describe that feeling."
>
> Xochil
>
> **students speak**

David, you work at an alternative school devoted to social justice. Everyone is on board....parents, principal, staff and students. It's not the same at my school. I'd be alone doing this work.

To my way of thinking this is all the more reason that you should give these lessons a try. Students who don't see their reality within the classroom are isolated and at risk. Imagine their surprise and interest when you start to talk about things that actually matter to them.

Building networks is important. Another teacher or two who can be convinced to give a few lessons a try will be very helpful. Asking other subject area teachers what topic they're working with and then integrating a related math lesson has been very successful for me. And although I do work at an alternative school, I still need to advocate for this approach to parents. They've never experienced these types of math lessons and so must have an opportunity to wrestle with the idea of linking math and social

> "Schools need to teach this stuff, children can't be hidden from the world. Explain to them that this is important, that by doing this you are helping children understand the world around them."
>
> Sasha
>
> **students speak**

justice. Most parents want what's best for their children... it's a matter of helping them to see that this is clearly more helpful than the usual math materials.

If you have more questions now than you did when you began reading this resource, that's probably a good thing. Experimenting with the assignments in approach and focus has been, for me, the best way to make math classes more interesting. And relevant.

It's time to say good-bye to pizza party math. Good luck.

Simple Simon

Simple Simon
Met a high man
In the government
Said Simple Simon
To the high man
"How are taxes spent?"

"Billions," said the high man
"For an antimissile system
That's bound
To be obsolete
Before it ever
Gets off the ground."

"But that's ridiculous!"
Said Simple Simon.
"If people knew,
They'd make a fuss."

"True," said the high man,
"And when you take into account
That for just about half that amount
Everyone could have a decent job
And a house in a decent neighborhood."

"Fantastic," said Simple Simon.
"I don't believe it."

Said the high man,

"Good."[8]

---

8 Eve Merriam, *The Inner City Mother Goose*. Simon & Schuster Books for Young Readers. New York. 1996, p. 15.

Lessons Overview

Lesson	Pages	Mathematics Strand					Justice Topic									
		Number Sense	Measurement	Geometry and Spatial Sense	Patterning and Algebra	Data Management and Probability	Class/Poverty	Gender	Race	Age/Youth	Media	Ability	Workplace	Big business	Sexuality	Civics / Community
1 Super Size-It? Really?	27	•			•	•		•	•	•			•	•		
2 Get Tough On Youth?	32	•			•	•			•	•	•					•
3 Who Runs The Show?	37	•				•	•	•		•			•	•		•
4 In The Zone	42	•			•		•	•	•	•			•	•		
5 None Is Too Many?	46					•			•							
6 Pride And Progress	50	•				•								•	•	•
7 Roasted	55	•			•	•	•							•		•
8 Side-Lined	59	•					•	•		•						•
9 Poor Sport	63				•	•		•		•		•				•
10 Darth Vader Has Arrived	67	•			•	•	•	•	•	•				•		•
11 Some 'Fare' Better Than Others	71	•				•	•					•	•	•		
12 War Within	76	•			•	•	•	•	•	•					•	•
13 Disabled By Prejudice	80		•	•	•		•	•	•			•	•			•
14 Too Close For Comfort	83		•	•	•		•						•			
15 Our Home And Native Land?	86	•	•	•	•		•		•	•				•		•
16 Larger Than Life	91	•				•	•	•	•	•					•	
17 Do You Have Confidence In Those Results?	95	•					•			•	•			•		•
18 The Weekend's Here	98				•	•	•	•	•	•		•	•	•		
19 Is Justice Blind?	103	•				•	•		•	•				•		
20 Driving While Black	106	•			•	•	•		•	•						•
21 Making A Killing	113	•		•	•	•	•							•		
22 Correlated Or Causal?	115	•			•	•				•	•			•		
23 Rule Of Thumb	119	•				•	•	•		•						•
24 Kidfluence	123	•	•		•	•				•	•			•		
25 Linked, Organized, Informed	127	•			•	•	•							•		

Lesson	Pages	Mathematics Strand: Number Sense	Measurement	Geometry and Spatial Sense	Patterning and Algebra	Data Management and Probability	Justice Topic: Class/Poverty	Gender	Race	Age/Youth	Media	Ability	Workplace	Big business	Sexuality	Civics/Community
26 Going For Probable Silver	133				•	•	•									•
27 Welcome To The Club	135	•				•	•							•		•
28 What Big Feet You Have	140	•	•	•	•		•							•		
29 Blunt Force Trauma	144					•	•			•			•			
30 Totally SAP-ped	147	•			•	•	•	•	•	•			•	•		•
31 What's A Gerrymander?	151	•														•
32 Coming Clean?	155	•		•				•		•	•			•		
33 A Little Goes A Long Way	158		•	•	•									•		
34 The Return Of Tobin Hood	162	•	•		•	•	•	•	•	•		•		•		•
35 Buying Your Eyes	166	•	•		•	•				•	•			•		
36 Oink, Oink!	169				•	•	•				•			•		
37 The Winner Takes It All...?	173	•						•	•				•			•
38 "GATS Terrible!!"	178	•	•		•		•							•		•
39 Breaking the Silence	181					•		•		•					•	
40 Mad	184	•			•	•	•	•		•		•				•
41 Media Monopoly	188	•				•	•	•	•		•			•	•	
42 Sick And Tired	191	•				•	•							•		•
43 The Poverty Of Distribution	193				•		•							•		
44 Just Desserts?	196	•				•	•	•		•		•	•	•		•
45 If Syrup Costs 2 Cents A Cup...	199	•		•	•	•	•				•			•		
46 Healthcare For The Masses	203	•			•		•	•	•			•		•		
47 Sheltered From The Storm?	207	•		•	•	•	•		•			•				•
48 Clear Sight	212	•								•	•			•		
49 The Last Spike	215	•					•	•	•				•			
50 Your Title Goes Here	219	•	•	•	•	•	•	•	•	•	•	•	•	•	•	•

Lesson Descriptions

Lesson Title	Lesson Location	Here's what it's about...
1 Super Size-It? Really?	27	Injuries abound in the fast food industry, minimum wages are the order of the day, and not a union is in sight... "would you like to super-size that?"
2 Get Tough On Youth?	32	We're too easy on youth! The crime they commit is out of control, and the Youth Justice Act has no teeth! At least that's what you'd think if you read the newspapers. But is any of it true?
3 Who Runs The Show?	37	Capitalism's principal actors are corporations, and there are now more than 40,000 of them worldwide. Considering that 53 of the top 100 economies in the world are these transnational businesses, we may want to ask whether the rules of the game are in our best interests...
4 In The Zone	42	More than 25 million people in developing countries work in export processing zones (EPZs), where goods are produced en masse, wages are dirt cheap, and heaven help the employee who raises an eyebrow.
5 None Is Too Many?	46	The Canadian government shut its borders to Jewish immigrants during World War Two. Was this intentional policy, or statistical glitch? Look at the numbers of immigrants we've let in during the past 130 years and decide for yourself...
6 Pride And Progress	50	Gay rights have come a long way in the past twenty years- in some areas of the world more than others. Much remains to be done, but here's a look at slowly shifting attitudes.
7 Roasted	55	Coffee drinkers of the North and coffee farmers of the South are linking up through a system called Fair Trade. Here's a look at how Fair Trade helps reduce poverty, protect the environment, and rattle the monopoly that a few wealthy farmers and businesses hold in the industry.
8 Side-Lined	59	How are poverty lines determined? Why can't anyone agree on where the poverty line should be set? Absolute poverty and relative poverty- what's that mean? And what impact does poverty have on people's health?
9 Poor Sport	63	You've heard them all- competition is fun, competition produces skill mastery, competition is biologically natural, competition is motivating: unfortunately, extensive research contradicts all of these ideas. Surprised? Good. Take a look.

Lesson Title	Lesson Location	Here's what it's about...
18 The Weekend's Here	98	A short history of unions, including the shift to a shorter workweek. And a look at how productivity increases and averages can hide what's really happening in the workplace.
19 Is Justice Blind?	103	How fair is the death penalty? A close look at the arguments against capital punishment and at those people most affected.
20 Driving While Black	106	The Toronto Star's series on racial profiling by the police rocked the community and led people to ask: "exactly why are people who are black treated differently than people who are white?" Statistics were scrutinized...here's a part of the story.
21 Making A Killing	111	During the Cold War years, the United States and Russia raced to build enough nuclear weapons to destroy the world many times over. Nuclear disarmament has been happening, but not without setbacks and not without groups standing in the way.
22 Correlated Or Causal?	115	How closely are TV violence and viewer aggression related? Does one cause the other? You may be surprised!!
23 Rule Of Thumb	119	An old British law enabled husbands to beat their wives with a stick, as long as it was less than the thickness of their thumb. Today, domestic violence continues and the need to address it is pressing. Math can help. Here's how.
24 Kidfluence	123	Canadian children and youth spend 1.8 billion dollars of their own money and influence their family's spending of ten times that amount. That's why marketing directly to children and youth is so important- but is it ethical?
25 Linked, Organized, Informed	127	The explosion of computer technology has provided activists with powerful tools- tools to store and retrieve huge quantities of information (in databases), tools to communicate globally, and tools to organize resistance action quickly and effectively.

Lesson Title	Lesson Location	Here's what it's about...
26 Going For Probable Silver	131	Harm reduction is an approach to (typically) drug problems that emphasizes reducing harm, rather than the 'war on drugs' zero tolerance approach. With the controversy around safe injection sites for drug users, it's important to know why harm reduction is so valuable...
27 Welcome To The Club	135	How different are the economic fortunes of the top ten percent of Canadian society and the bottom ten percent? Does a rising tide lift all boats, or sink the ones tied to the docks?
28 What Big Feet You Have	140	The Recycling Council of Ontario has developed a questionnaire to measure your ecological foot print: a measure of the impact your lifestyle has on the planet. Here's your chance to see how your foot size compares...
29 Blunt Force Trauma	144	People say that standardized tests are a way to make the education system accountable to the public, but the research tells a different tale....
30 Totally SAP-ped	147	The World Bank and the IMF give loans to developing countries to pay back their debt, but only on the condition that they restructure their economy through a structural adjustment program (SAP). Who benefits?
31 What's A Gerrymander?	151	What does a salamander have to do with voting? Are voting boundaries set in stone? Or can they change? For whom can they change...and why....
32 Coming Clean?	155	Selling products is an art, but sometimes it's sneaky. Here's a look at how a slight change in product can lead to a big change in profits. Also, some questions about why cleaning commercials look like they're right out of the 1950s.
33 A Little Goes A Long Way	158	When we talk of chemical disasters that lead to toxification of the environment and danger to people, are we asking the bigger questions? Why do these things happen, and can they be prevented?

Lesson Title	Lesson Location	Here's what it's about...
34 The Return Of Tobin Hood	162	Tobin Hood? Don't you mean Robin Hood? What's an economist by the name of James Tobin got to do with redistribution of wealth? And why is it causing such a stir in Europe?
35 Buying Your Eyes	166	Who would turn down free TVs and computers for public schools, especially those in need? Unless they weren't really free...
36 Oink, Oink!	169	North Americans consume at an unparalleled rate compared to other areas of the world...a look at how 5% of the world's population uses a great deal more than 5% of its resources.
37 The Winner Takes It All...?	173	There are many different ways to structure a voting system- the first past the post system ignores all of the votes except for the winner's. Proportional representation voting, on the other hand, includes all of the votes. Here's a look at why that matters.
38 "GATS Terrible!!"	178	The General Agreement on Trade in Services (GATS) is a prescription by the World Trade Organization for the privatization of public services, like health care. Here's what happens when essential services are turned over to the business world, where profit is king.
39 Breaking the Silence	181	Children and youth often don't talk about abuse that they have experienced or are currently experiencing. Here's a look at why that's the case, and why some make the courageous step to speak out.
40 Mad	184	Mental illness: nobody ever talks about it, and yet most of us will know someone or be affected by it personally during our life. It's a complicated topic, and rather than ignore that it's an issue, let's talk about why it matters and how people get help.
41 Media Monopoly	188	It used to be that many different businesses owned the media: but that's all changed now. The material that reaches the public is in the hands of a very few people: here's why we lose out when some voices disappear.

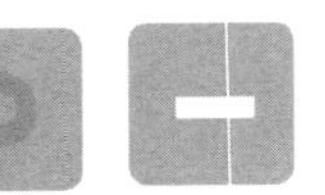
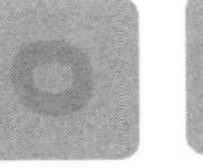

Super Size-It? Really?

"Food is an important part of a balanced diet"

– Fran Lebowitz

The fast food industry has exploded since its humble start as seasonal drive-in restaurants. Encouraged by the huge increase in car owners, flashy drive-in restaurants with carhops grew rapidly through the 1940s, until the McDonald brothers tried something radical in 1948: the restaurant kitchen could now function as a high speed assembly line.

Workers no longer needed experience and special skills: everything was simple, and as the years progressed, automated. The market for fast, cheap food led to the emergence of Dunkin' Donuts in 1948, Kentucky Fried Chicken in 1952, Burger King in 1953, Taco Bell in 1962 and Wendy's in 1969, all of which contribute to a culture of conflict between the expense of labour and the bottom line profit for **stakeholders**.

The fast food industry invests a lot of energy and money **lobbying** governments to limit new worker safety laws, food safety regulations and **minimum wages**, all of which cut into profit margins. There are about 15,000 McDonald's in North America. Two Canadian teens, backed by the Canadian Auto Workers, were able to organize the first ever union in a McDonald's in 1998.[9] Only 14,999 to go...

9 www.americanedu/TED/bigmac.htm

Why do you think that fast food restaurants would be so opposed to unions that there is a complete absence of them in the fast food industry?

A study is done on injuries on the job in fast food restaurants: burns, strains, and falls are amongst the most common, but an interesting pattern emerges, captured in the table below.

	Fast Food Chain A	Fast Food Chain B	Fast Food Chain C	Fast Food Chain D
Number of Adult Workers Injured Per Year	224	87	123	68
Number of Teenage Workers Injured Per Year	448	174	246	136

1. What is the relationship between the number of adult workers and the number of teenage workers injured in these fast food chains? Create an algebraic equation to describe the relationship.

2. What reasons can you think of that might lead teenagers to experience more injuries in comparison to their adult counterparts? Explain two.

3. Why is it unlikely that you would get a table with results exactly as they are above?

4. In the United States, approximately 100,000 adults are injured on the job every year.[10] How many teenage workers are injured each year? Show how you can use your algebraic equation, even if you can do the work in your head.

5. "In 1998 more restaurant workers were murdered on the job in the United States than police officers."[11] This amounted to about four or five **homicides** a month. What conditions do you think contribute to this phenomenon? List three.

6. Annual sales of fast food in the United States are $107,778,072,000.[12] What is this number in words? In scientific notation? What can you compare this number to so that it makes a little more sense? Annual sales of McDonald's food in Canada are approximately $1.65 billion.[13] Put that number into standard form and scientific notation.

7. Minimum wages are the most many fast food workers can expect. Unfortunately, the minimum wage in the States at the end of the 1990s was worth 27% less than at the end of the 1960s.[14] How can the following situation be possible?

---

10 Schlosser, Eric. *Fast Food Nation*. Houghton Mifflin, New York: 2001, p. 83.
11 Schlosser, Eric. *Fast Food Nation*. Houghton Mifflin, New York: 2001, p. 83.
12 *Good Food News, Food Share*, www.foodshare.net, Vol. 15 #18, 2001.
13 Fox, Jim. McD in Canada readies mini-store for towns nationwide, *Nation's Restaurant News*, May 2000.
14 Schlosser, Eric. *Fast Food Nation*. Houghton Mifflin, New York: 2001, p. 73.

Year	Minimum Wage	Worth
1968	$5.67	$5.67
1998	$6.35	$4.14

8. If you are an **employer** hiring staff in Canada, it is required that you contribute 20% on top of a worker's salary for **benefits**, if they work 40 hours a week or more. If a 40 hour a week, full year salary at minimum wage is $15,000, how much will the employer have to pay?

9. What is an easy strategy for an **employer** to avoid having to pay the extra 20%?

10. The graph below looks at the **median** weekly earnings of full time workers wage and salary workers in 2003, comparing workers who are unionized and those who are not.

    a. What percentage do unionized workers earn over non unionized workers as a whole? Show your work.

    b. Which group is best helped by the presence of unions, as a percentage of their non-unionized counterparts? Show your work.

    c. Make another comparison of your own using the graph.

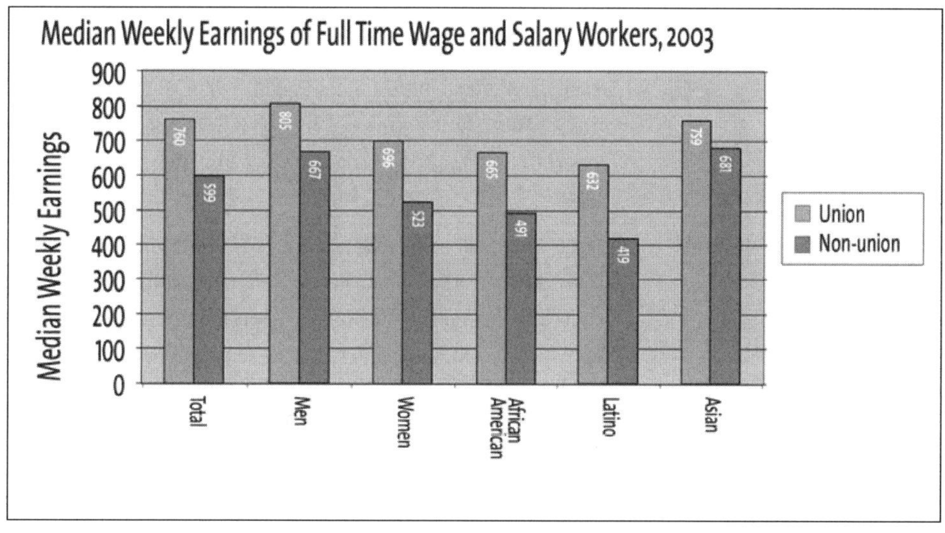

Source: U.S. Department of Labor, Employment and Earnings, January 2004. Prepared by the AFL-CIO

d. Graph the unionization rates in the following industries:

Industry	Unionization Rate
Educational services	68.9%
Public administration	68.5%
Utilities	68%
Health care occupations	52.9%
Agriculture	3.5%
Scientific and technical services	4.6%
Management occupations	8.5%

Source: Perspectives on Labour and Income, August 2005, Statistics Canada, p. 19.

e. The highest unionization rates are found in the public-sector- government, Crown corporations, and publicly funded schools and hospitals. The lowest unionization rates are found in the private sector. Why do you think this happens?

Obesity is a serious problem in Canada. It is linked to cancers of the colon, stomach and breast, heart disease, infertility and strokes. Although it hasn't been conclusively proven, and is likely to be denied by the fast food industry, the trends suggest a relationship between fast food diets and the rate of obesity.

11. The amount of money spent on obesity-related health care issues is approximately $240 billion dollars a year in the United States. The money **consumers** spent on weight loss plans is greater than $33 billion a year. Write both numbers using standard notation and scientific notation.

12. If you were writing a newspaper article to convince people how much obesity costs, which format would you use, standard notation or scientific notation? Why?

13. The in house garbage created by McDonalds each day[15] is represented by the following table. Write an algebraic equation for the amount of garbage created by McDonalds, determine how much garbage is produced each year based on your equation, and figure out how many elephants it would take to equal that mass of garbage.

Number of days	1	2	3	4
Kilograms of garbage	1.2×10^6	2.4×10^6	3.6×10^6	4.8×10^6

15 www.foodshare.net Good Food News Vol. 5 #18, 2001.

Food for thought...

A single fast food hamburger contains meat from dozens or even hundreds of different cattle.[16]

- Educate yourself so that you know your workplace rights
- Support union organizing
- Invite a union **activist** to visit the classroom
- Reading suggestion: *Fast Food Nation*, by Eric Schlosser
- Eat less fast food
- Organize healthy food for your school during break time
- Get out and be physically active

---

16 Schlosser, Eric. *Fast Food Nation*. Houghton Mifflin, New York: 2001, p. 204.

Get Tough On Youth?

"News, far more than art, is artifact."

– Marshall McLuhan

Youth are out of control. The **Youth Justice Act** is too lenient. We need to crack down on this growing epidemic of youth violence against people and property. We need to get tough. Or so the **media** would have us believe. But are all of these things really true? Are *any* of them true?

A study of 800 Canadian newspapers found interesting patterns. Although violent crime accounts for approximately 11% of all crime in Canada, a full 25% of criminal justice stories had to do with **homicide**, and more than 50% contained elements of violence. Three major papers in Toronto found that 94% of crime stories about youth were about violent offences compared to the less than 25% of Ontario youth cases involving violence. When questioned, editors acknowledged that they "typically only report the worst types of crime and the worst cases of those crimes."[17]

Since most people get information about the justice system from media sources, these stories can trigger anger and desire for **retribution** in the public, which result in disproportionately punitive responses to youth crime.

17 John Howard Society of Alberta, 1998. "Youth Crime in Canada: Public Perceptions vs. Statistical Information".

Why do you think that papers report the worst cases of the worst types of crime?

1. Take this quick quiz yourself, or quiz a family member who hasn't read the introduction to this lesson. The answers are on the next page, so don't look.

i) Canada's crime rate in 2002 was:

  a. 25% higher than in 1979
  b. 10 % higher than in 1979
  c. 5% higher than in 1979
  d. About the same as in 1979

ii) The murder rate in Canada has increased since the death penalty was abolished.

  a. True
  b. False

iii) The rate of property crime committed by youth in 2002 was:

  a. The lowest that it has been in 25 years
  b. Up 5% from 2001
  c. Up 10% from 2000
  d. At an all time high, up 15% from 2001

iv) The total number of cases processed in youth court between 1991/92 and 2002/03 has:

  a. Decreased 20%
  b. Decreased 5%
  c. Increased 5%
  d. Increased 20%

v) Which of the following lines on the graph represent the trend in the number of youth incarcerated between 1994/95 and 2001/02?

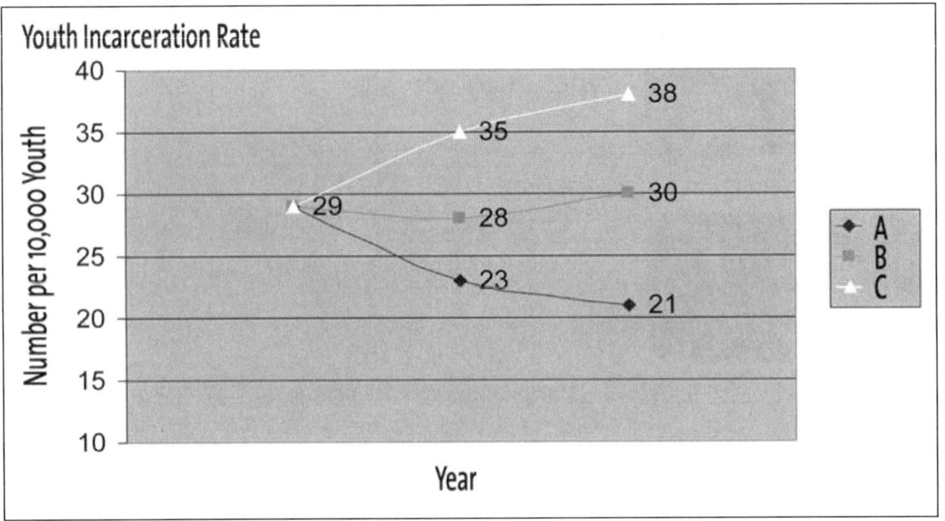

Answers:

i) Canada's crime rate in 2002 was about the same level as in 1979. The crime rate has been falling since the early 1990s.[18]

ii) False. The homicide rate has been relatively stable since 1976.[19]

iii) The lowest that it has been in 25 years.[20]

iv) Decreased 20%, primarily due to a 47% drop in the number of crimes against property cases.[21]

v) Line A represents the decline in the youth incarceration rate from its peak in 1994/95 to the year 2001/02.[22]

2. Roughly speaking, one young person is charged every week to ten days for a homicide offense in Canada.[23] Write an algebraic equation and solve for the number of youth charged per year in Canada. If you assume that everyone charged is guilty (which is a stretch), do you think that this number is more or less than the number of adults convicted of homicide?

3. Adults are responsible for roughly 590 homicides per year in Canada[24]. What percentage does that make youth homicide as a total of the whole?

4. In 1994, an **Angus Reid** poll showed that 92% of respondents wanted to change the Young Offenders Act so that trying youth in adult court would be easier, and 89% "were in favour of boot camps for youth."[25]

---

18 Wallace, Marnie. "Crime Statistics in Canada, 2002" Statistics Canada, *Juristat* Vol 23 #5.
19 Roberts, Julian. *Public Knowledge of Crime and Justice: An Inventory of Canadian Findings*. University of Ottawa, p. 2.
20 Wallace, Marnie. "Crime Statistics in Canada, 2002", Statistics Canada, *Juristat* Vol 23 #5.
21 Robinson, Paul. "Youth Court Statistics, 2002/03" *Juristat* Vol. 24 #2 Statistics Canada.
22 Marinelli, Julie. "Youth Custody and Community Services in Canada, 2001/02". *Juristat* Vol 24 #3.
23 John Howard Society of Alberta, 1998. *Youth Crime in Canada: Public Perception vs. Statistical Information* www.johnhoward.ab.ca/PUB/C16.htm.
24 Ibid.
25 Ibid.

The following table is based on the real life relationship between the rate of adults **incarcerated** and the rate of youth incarcerated in Canada in 2000-2001.[26] Figure out the algebraic relationship that describes the pattern.

	Region One	Region Two	Region Three	Region Four
Rate of Adult Incarceration	346	567	245	144
Rate of Youth Incarceration	1003	1644	711	418

Across Canada as a whole, the sentenced incarceration rate of detention for adults in was 46per 100,000. What was it for youth?

5. Different youth face different experiences with the justice system in Canada. What does the following graph[27] suggest about how Aboriginal youth experience the system?

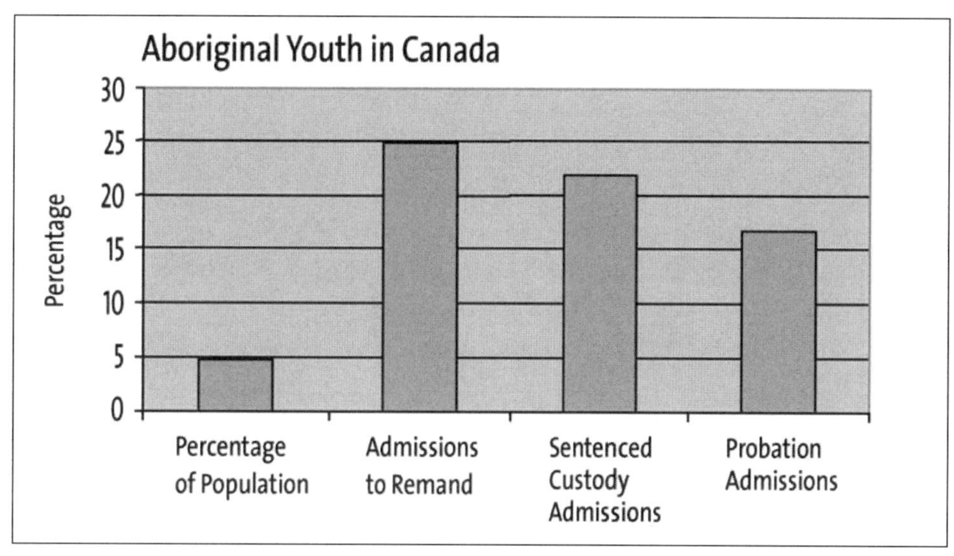

6. Circle the word that best matches what you think will happen at each stage of the youth crime issue:

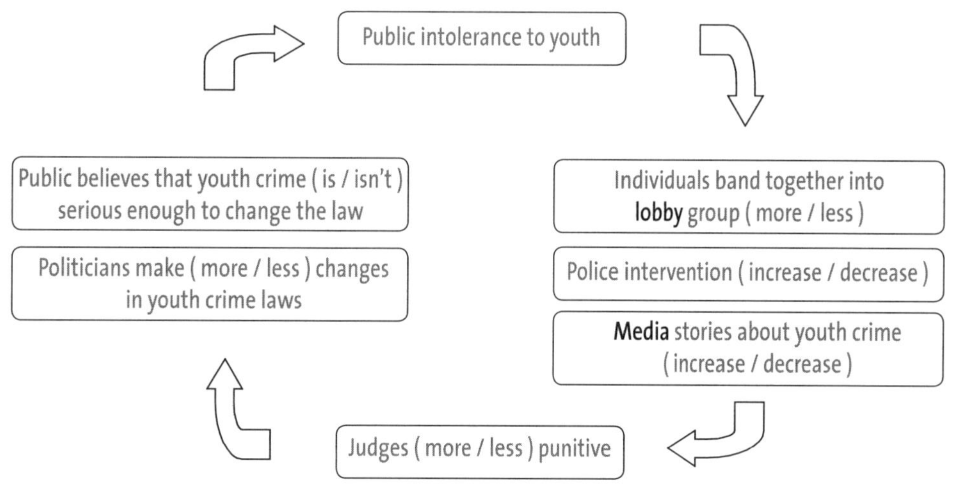

26 http://www.statcan.ca/english/preview/85-002-XIE/P0070385-002-XIE.pdf

27 Marinelli, Julie. "Youth Custody and Community Services in Canada, 2001/02". *Juristat* Vol 24 #3

7. A $300,000 Federal grant was given to revitalize an apartment complex in the Jane and Finch area of Toronto. The money helped to support a youth day camp, after school programs, employment and job skills training, police partnership projects and a community centre with computers, a garden and tennis courts. Putting youth in prison can cost up to $100,000 per youth per year.[28] Discuss these two figures.

- "It has been found that persons who are more informed about criminal justice issues tend to have more rational and less **punitive** convictions than those that have limited knowledge."[29] In challenging false perceptions about youth crime, it is crucial that **advocates** for youth address the very real fear that people feel.
- Call or write to your local newspaper when the stories that you see about youth crime seem **sensationalized**. Introduce statistics to support your views.

---

28 "Project targets kids to battle crime". *Toronto Star*. July 5, 2002, B1, 5.

29 John Howard Society of Alberta, 1998. *Youth Crime in Canada: Public Perception vs. Statistical Information* www.johnhoward.ab.ca/PUB/C16.htm

Who Runs The Show?

The Golden Rule: Those with the gold rule.

In the mid eighties there were about 7000 **transnational companies**, businesses working on a global scale to make profit. Now there are more than 40,000.[30] Any limits to economic growth, including environmental standards, worker protection, and trade barriers are influenced by these businesses.

Because they have so much money, transnational corporations (TNCs) exert more pressure within the global economy than national governments.[31] In fact, 53 of the top 100 economies are TNCs. Governments who want businesses to invest in their countries end up competing against each other by cutting labour costs, slashing environmental standards, decreasing **corporate** taxes and lowering **social spending**.[32]

At home in Canada, the top 150 corporations are represented by the Canadian Council of Chief Executives (CCCE) who call themselves a "not-for-profit, **non-partisan** organization of **CEOs**". While representing less than one hundred thousandth of the voting population, these people administer over 2.3 trillion dollars in **assets** and account for 72% of the **private sector GDP**.[33] And that's a lot more influence than most of us have.

---

30 Langille, David. *Exposing the Facts of Corporate Rule: A Handbook on How to Challenge the Big Business Agenda*, Centre for Social Justice, 1991.
31 Ibid., p 5.
32 Ibid., p. 4.
33 www.ceocouncil.ca May 16, 2004

How do environmental standards and worker protection lower the competitiveness of a business?

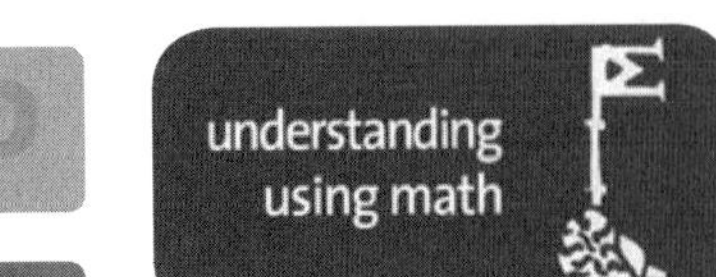

1. The following statement appears on the CCCE website:

   "Corporate taxes are the single most damaging form of tax to economic growth. Significant cuts in corporate taxation therefore could be a critical source of competitive advantage in attracting investment and jobs."

Look at the following bar graph that shows historical trends in taxation and answer the following questions.

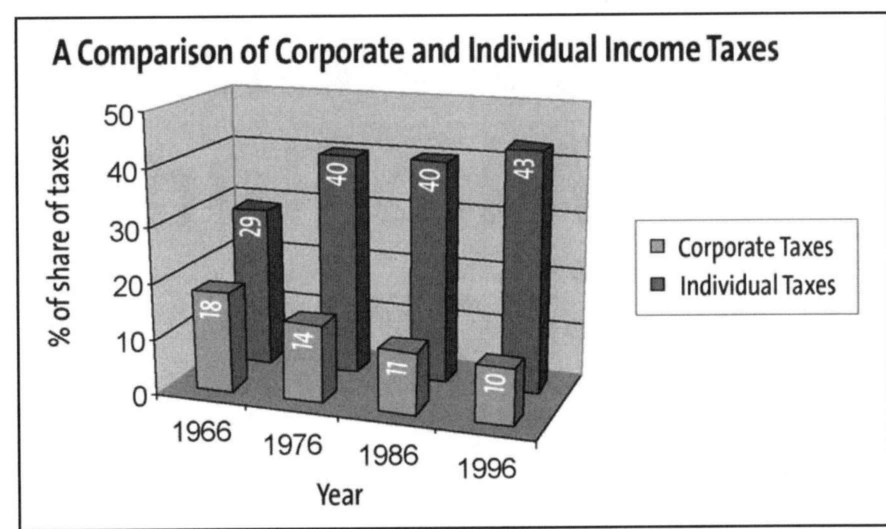

   a. Would these trends be desirable for businesses?

   b. Are these trends desirable for individual tax-payers?

   c. What is happening to the tax base that can be used to support **social programs**?

   d. Discuss the issue of lowering corporate taxes as a way to keep a competitive advantage in attracting investment and jobs.

2. Each year around April you may notice your parents or guardians becoming anxious about completing their tax report and paying anything that they owe. Corporations, however, are allowed to move their tax payments forward ("defer") each year, essentially avoiding payment.

This money does not end up going to government coffers. Look at the following two tables and make four comparisons of your choice.

Corporation	Deferred Taxes Owed[34]	As of
Alcan Aluminum	$966,000,000 (US)	1996
BCE Inc.	$2,049,000,000	1996
Bell Canada	$2,133,000,000	1996
Canadian Pacific	$1,377,300,000	1996
Chrysler Canada	$997,000,000	1996
Imperial Oil	$981,000,000	1996
Pan Canadian Petroleum	$1,002,100,000	1996
Petro Canada	$793,000,000	1996
Seagram Company	$2,461,000,000 (US)	1997
Shell Canada	$762,000,000	1996

Project	Cost per year
One fifteen bed women's shelter plus a community outreach program for a total of 300 clients.	$600,000
Build 1000 subsidized apartments to house one quarter of all women and children in Toronto shelters.[35]	$14,200,000 (1 time cost)
Build 100 new outdoor basketball courts.[36]	$500,000 (1 time cost)
Youth drug and alcohol prevention programs for 650 students.[37]	$135,000
Tutoring, youth leadership, counselling for women and children, spring and summer camps and after school programs for a combined total of 442 (mostly) youth.[38]	$469,000

3. Fifty three of the world's largest 100 economies are now corporations.

    a. Transfer the following GDPs and Company Sales into scientific notation. Is there any benefit to working with very large numbers in scientific notation? Are there any drawbacks? What are they?

34 Centre for Social Justice. *Exposing the Facts of Corporate Rule.* p.17
35 www.pjac.ca
36 www.pjac.ca
37 Lidia Monaco, St. Christopher's House
38 Lidia Monaco, St. Christopher's House

b. Make at least two comparisons using the numbers in the chart.

Country or Company	GDP or Company Sales[39]	Scientific Notation
Canada	$542,954,000,000	
China	$522,172,000,000	
Mexico	$377,115,000,000	
India	$293,606,000,000	
Mitsubishi	$184,510,000,000	
General Motors	$168,829,000,000	
Denmark	$146,076,000,000	
Ford Motor	$137,137,000,000	
Turkey	$131,014,000,000	
Saudi Arabia	$117,236,000,000	
Norway	$109,568,000,000	
Israel	$77,777,000,000	

4. The CCCE's website posts the following statement:

"At the federal, provincial and municipal levels, it is vital to ensure that each tax dollar spent on social services has the greatest possible impact. To this end, governments must work together more effectively, especially in improving accountability for the resources allocated to social programs."

Look at the graph. Discuss the statement above with respect to the numbers below.

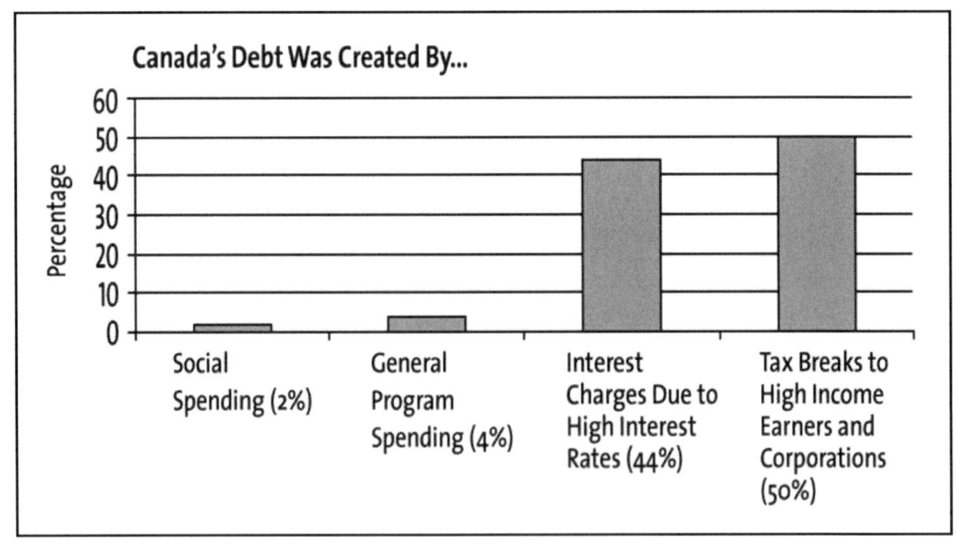

[40]

39 Centre for Social Justice. *Exposing the Facts of Corporate Rule*, p. 7.
40 Langille, David. *Exposing the Facts of Corporate Rule: A Handbook on How to Challenge the Big Business Agenda*, Centre for Social Justice, 1991.

5. While big business continues to make huge profits, some have also downsized their workforces. Compare the profits to the number of employees that have been fired in the years between 1997 and 2002.

Corporation	Profit (2002)	Employees (1997)	Employees (2002)	Employees Net Change
Stelco Inc.	$14,000,000	11,732	9,749	
Canadian National Railway	$571,000,000	24,081	22,114	
Bank of Montreal	$1,400,000,000	39,515	33,000	

a. Fill in the net change in the number of employees working for each corporation.

b. Do huge company profits necessarily protect workers from being laid off?

Food for thought...

There are more than 80,000 corporations in Canada that make profit and yet pay no income taxes at all.[41]

- The Canadian Centre for Policy Alternatives maintains a website with information on business, **labour** and government issues. Stay up to date at www.policyalternatives.ca.
- Invite in a local politician to talk about corporate tax laws and **deferral** of taxes.

41 Languille, David. *Exposing the Facts of Corporate Rule: A Handbook on How to Challenge the Big Business Agenda*, Centre for Social Justice, 1991.

In The Zone

"Governments need armies to protect them against their enslaved and oppressed subjects."

– Leo Tolstoy

It's your first day of work. You arrive at 6 am and file past the two men armed with machine guns and then pass through the barbed wire gates to take your place in huge shed-like buildings amongst hundreds of other workers making shoes, shirts, toys and electronics for people in Canada and the United States.

You share your workspace with women producing goods at hundreds of machines. Since you call the Philippines home, you remember the number of workers in these buildings used to be 23,000 across the country in 1986. Now it's more than 400,000. Nearby in China, it's more than 17 million.[42]

Governments want these businesses to stay- perhaps they will take root and become an integrated part of the country, providing jobs and technology. Kindly, these governments have created huge **tax breaks** to lure in foreign business, pushed **regulations** to all time lows, maintained a **minimum wage** lower than the real cost of living, and offered up their military to ensure that nobody gets any funny ideas about starting **unions**.[43]

It's 8 pm. You can go home now, after collecting your $1.70 for the day. It's been a short day, really. Only 14 hours. If you were in China you'd be here for another 4 hours, until midnight. Welcome to the **export processing zones (EPZs)**, also known as **sweatshops**.

---

42 Klein, Naomi. *No Logo*. Alfred A. Knopf Canada, 2000, p. 205.
43 Ibid., p. 206

The big **multinational corporations** don't own the factories in export processing zones: the factory owners bid against each other to work on contract. What benefits does this offer a multinational?

1. The **Chief Executive Officer (CEO)** of Disney was making $9,783 an hour in the late 1990s. A Haitian worker making Disney products made 28 cents an hour.[44] How long would it take one worker, working 70 hour weeks, to make how much the CEO earned in one hour? In your life, when would this worker have had to start their 70 hour weeks, to earn $9,783?

2. "All 50,000 workers in the Yue Yen Nike Factory in China would have to work for 19 years to earn what Nike spends on advertising in one year."[45]

   a. How many years would a single worker have to work to match the funds Nike spends on advertising in one year?

   b. Put that number of years in perspective: what was happening in the world when that worker started his or her job?

3. You are the leadership at a big multinational company, who has factories in Canada, the United States and Germany. The following chart lists the average salaries and number of workers that you employ.

   a. Figure out how much you are paying your **labour force** currently.

   b. Find out how much you would save per hour, per 40 hour week, and per year if you fired all of your staff, closed down the factories in Canada, the U.S. and Germany, and opened a factory in an export processing zone, paying the same number of workers 30 cents an hour and making them work 70 hours a week.

	Average salary per hour	Number of workers
Canada	$11.42	800
United States	$10.56	1,450
Germany	$12.45	760

44 Klein, Naomi. *No Logo*. Alfred A. Knopf Canada, 2000, p.352
45 Ibid., p. 352

4. Big companies have to spend large amounts of money for "fixed costs": including machinery, buildings, and vehicles.[46] In order to pay for these expenses, circle the trends (↑ means increase, ↓ means decrease) that you suspect will occur:

Amount of products produced:	↑ or ↓
Speed that **employees** work:	↑ or ↓
Wages:	↑ or ↓
Employee **benefits**:	↑ or ↓
Push to open new markets:	↑ or ↓
Amount of advertising:	↑ or ↓

5. If 236 million workers are employed in the garment industry worldwide and 75% are women,[47] how many women work in the garment industry?

6. Sometimes when people talk about sweatshops and export processing zones, they fail to realize that a large number of workers here in Canada are **exploited**. One group, called **home workers**, sew clothes for large retailers and designer labels in their own homes, often making less than minimum wage, working 70 hours per week, and having no access to **Employment Insurance, Canada Pension Plan**, or vacation pay. They number 8,000 mostly **immigrant** women in Toronto alone![48]

   a. If the **employer** pays the home worker by the hour, at $5.50 per hour, what is the algebraic equation that describes their pay?

   b. How much would a home worker be paid for a 70 hour week?

   c. If the employer pays by the piece of clothing (14 cents a piece), what is the algebraic equation that describes the pay of the home worker?

   d. Pretend that the home worker can make an average of 42 pieces of clothing per hour. Use your equation to figure out their average hourly wage. Which is better in this case: being paid by the piece or being paid by the hour?

   e. The employer approaches the home worker with a contract for shirts, but says he can only pay 12 cents per piece. If this worker does her average 42 pieces per hour, what is her weekly pay, and how does it compare to when she was paid by the hour?

   f. What will the worker have to do to match her former weekly salary, when she was paid by the hour (how many more pieces will she need to make per hour and per week)?

---

46 *Worldwatch 2004* Report, p. 14.
47 *The Labour Behind the Label Issue Sheet*, Maquila Solidarity Network, p. 1.
48 www.unite-svti.org April 16, 2004.

g. Can you think of another drawback to working for pay based on the number of garments you produce rather than an hourly wage?

7. A pair of Nike shoes can be made for about $5 and sold to the public for between $100 and $180.[49]

   a. What is the algebraic equation that describes the difference in sale price and the cost to make the shoes per pair of shoes sold? Use the average shoe price. Why is this difference not all profit?

   b. If a single shoe store sells 30 pairs of Nike shoes on a Saturday in the mall, how much money was generated above the cost to produce the 30 pairs of shoes?

8. Workers in Haiti making Disney shirts earn about 20 cents per hour. One shirt that they make sells for $10.97 at Wal-Mart.[50] How long would a worker have to work to pay for this shirt at Wal-Mart?

Food for thought...

A **tax holiday** is where a multinational corporation does not pay any tax at all. It's a policy meant to lure companies to the country to do business. In the Philippines in a town called Rosario, only 30 of the EPZ's 207 factories pay taxes. At the end of the tax holiday they close and reopen as another company to avoid paying taxes.[51]

- UNITE has a Canadian website at www.unite-svti.org/ that has sweatshop information. The United Students Against Sweatshops website is also useful.
- Order a "Stop Sweatshops: An Education/Action Kit" for your classroom ($12.50) from www.maquilasolidarity.org. Within it are action kits on building company profiles and organizing a sweatshop fashion show.
- Invite a home worker to visit your classroom and talk about the at-home industry.
- Watch the documentary "Mickey Mouse Goes to Haiti"
- Be careful about what kind of clothing you buy!

---

49 Klein, Naomi. Nologo. Alfred A. Knopf Canada, 2000, p. 372.
50 Ibid., p. 353.
51 Ibid., p. 209.

None Is Too Many...?

"Washing one's hands of the conflict between the powerful and the powerless means to side with the powerful, not to be neutral."

– Paulo Friere

In 1939, the ship St. Louis, carrying 907 Jewish **refugees** from Europe was not allowed to dock in Latin America, the United States, or Canada. Canadian Prime Minister Mackenzie King said that the refugees were not a Canadian problem, and so the ship returned to Europe, condemning to death at the hands of the Nazi regime many of the passengers.[52]

Mackenzie King and **Immigration** Minister Frederick Blair had been at the forefront of new immigration policies adopted in the 1920s that sorted incoming peoples based on their desirability. Chinese, Japanese and Jewish immigrants found themselves at the bottom of the ladder, a product of the prevailing racist attitude of the times.[53]

In 1933 Toronto, a baseball game in Christie Pits Park between an all-Jewish team and a team from St. Peter's Church erupted in violence after a **swastika** was unveiled in the stands.[54] Although this type of outright **fascist** behaviour remained "marginal and marginalized,"[55] it wasn't until 1952 that immigration laws removed the racial categories that had served to prevent Jews seeking asylum in World War II from reaching Canada. During the war, a senior Canadian official was asked how many Jews would be welcomed to Canada after the war. His response was "None is too many."

52 www.whitepines.com.
53 Ibid.
54 www.bnaibrith.ca/institute/millenium.
55 Ibid.

Look up Mackenzie King in Encarta (www.encarta.msn.com) and read his biography. Look carefully at his achievements in the early 1920s and during World War II. Does the bibliography talk about his immigration policies or the St. Louis situation? How is King portrayed? Why do you think he is portrayed this way?

1. Open a spreadsheet program and using the following chart as a model.

Canadian Immigration 1860-1993	
Year	**Number**
1860	6000
1861	14000
1862	18000

Use cells B139 and B140 to have the spreadsheet program calculate the mean and the median for the data.

There are 134 years, so entering numbers manually will take a long time unless you try this simple trick. Enter the year 1860 and 1861 in cells A4 and A5 respectively. Then highlight both cells using your mouse. After highlighting, you will notice a small black box in the lower right corner of the 1861 cell. Click on that box and drag it downwards until you see the year 1993. Your "Year" column is now complete.

The number column will take some time. Use the chart on the last page of this assignment to fill in the number of people who immigrated to Canada for each of the 134 years. The numbers have been rounded to the nearest thousand. Your chart will end as follows:

1991	231000
1992	253000
1993	254000
Mean	
Median	

2. What is the "**range**" for this set of data?

3. Range gives you an idea of how **variable** the data is. In other words, a low range means that more or less the same numbers of people were let into Canada each year. A high range means that there was a lot of variability. Do you think the range is fairly high, or fairly low? Explain your answer.

4. Try to think of one factor that might make immigration variability the way it is in the chart. Describe your idea.

5. What is the **mean** for this set of data?

6. The median value is where half of the numbers are above the **median**, and half are below. What is the median for this set of data?

7. Create an XY Scatter graph, connecting the points with a line. Paste the graph into your spreadsheet and print out both to submit with your report. Don't forget titles and labels.

8. With the exception of the start of the immigration data in the 1860s there is one particularly low region on the graph. Identify the years.

9. Out of 134 years of immigration, how many and in which years did Canada let in less than or equal to 10 000 people?

- Take a look at an immigration timeline at: http://cbc.ca/newsinreview/ dec97/gypsies/none.html.

Food for thought

"The admission of refugees perhaps posed a greater menace to Canada in 1938 than Hitler did."

– William Lyon Mackenzie King, Prime Minister of Canada

"During the twelve years of Nazi terror, from 1933 to 1945, while the United States accepted more than 200,000 Jewish refuges; Palestine, 125,000; embattled Britain, 70,000; Argentina, 50,000; penurious Brazil, 27,000; distant China, 25,000; tiny Bolivia and Chile, 14,000 each, Canada found room for fewer than 5,000."[56]

---

56 Abella, Irving and Harold Troper. *None is Too Many (Canada & The Jews of Europe, 1933-1948)* Toronto, 1982.

Reference Chart

Year	Number	Year	Number	Year	Number	Year	Number	Year	Number	Year	Number
1860	6000	1883	134000	1906	212,000	1929	165000	1952	164000	1975	188000
1861	14000	1884	104,000	1907	272000	1930	105000	1953	169000	1976	149000
1862	18000	1885	79000	1908	143000	1931	28000	1954	154000	1977	115000
1863	21000	1886	69000	1909	174000	1932	21000	1955	110000	1978	86000
1864	25000	1887	85000	1910	287000	1933	14000	1956	165000	1979	112000
1865	19000	1888	89000	1911	331000	1934	12000	1957	282000	1980	143000
1866	11000	1889	92000	1912	376000	1935	11000	1958	125000	1981	129000
1867	11000	1890	75000	1913	401000	1936	12000	1959	107000	1982	121000
1868	13000	1891	82000	1914	150000	1937	15000	1960	104000	1983	89000
1869	19000	1892	31000	1915	37000	1938	17000	1961	72000	1984	88000
1870	25000	1893	30000	1916	56000	1939	17000	1962	75000	1985	84000
1871	28000	1894	21000	1917	73000	1940	11000	1963	93000	1986	99000
1872	37000	1895	19000	1918	42000	1941	9000	1964	113000	1987	152000
1873	50000	1896	17000	1919	108000	1942	8000	1965	147000	1988	162000
1874	39000	1897	22000	1920	139000	1943	9000	1966	195000	1989	192000
1875	27000	1898	32000	1921	92000	1944	13000	1967	223000	1990	241000
1876	26000	1899	45000	1922	64000	1945	23000	1968	184000	1991	231000
1877	27000	1900	42000	1923	134000	1946	72000	1969	165000	1992	253000
1878	30000	1901	56000	1924	124000	1947	64000	1970	148000	1993	254000
1879	40000	1902	89000	1925	85000	1948	125000	1971	122000		
1880	39000	1903	139000	1926	136000	1949	95000	1972	122000		
1881	48000	1904	131000	1927	159000	1950	74000	1973	184000		
1882	112000	1905	141000	1928	167000	1951	194000	1974	218000		

Pride And Progress

"If you're teaching astronomy and you hide 10% of the stars and planets, astronomy itself doesn't make sense."

–Les Parsons

In November of 2003 the Legislative Assembly of Nunavut passed the Human Rights Act, making it the final Canadian territory to ban **discrimination** on the basis of **sexual orientation**.[57] Canada along with Australia, New Zealand and a number of European countries, is a pioneer in some senses, **advocating** for lesbian, gay, bisexual, and transgender/transsexual (LGBTT)* peoples' rights.[58]

Other places around the world are less tolerant of **homosexuality**. Albania, Bangladesh, Congo, Lebanon and Liberia claim that homosexuality does not even exist in their societies, and in dozens of countries being gay is illegal.[59] **Sodomy** laws in 13 U.S. states were only struck down in June of 2003.[60]

In the struggle to promote human rights, Mary Schneider reminds us not to "**succumb** to a **rhetoric** of victimology", treating people who are **oppressed** as victims. LGBTT youth do indeed face big struggles against **bigotry** and discrimination, but, noting their "powerful and creative **resilience**" and resistance, some people suggest that really, LGBTT people can develop some incredible skills.

*A more inclusive acronym is LGBTTIQQ2S, the final letters standing for Intersex, Queer, Questioning and Two-Spirited.

---

57 Redding, Andrew. "Sexual Orientation and Human Rights in the Americas", *World Policy Reports*, Dec. 2003, p. 86.
58 Seager, Joni. *The State of Women in the World*, 1997, Penguin Group, pp. 24-25.
59 Ibid. p. 25.
60 Redding, Andrew. "Sexual Orientation and Human Rights in the Americas", *World Policy Reports*, Dec. 2003, p. 86.

Which leaders in your community do not support equal rights for LGBT people? Why do you think that this is so?

understanding using math

1. Using a **spreadsheet** program, produce a pie graph based on the following data on social attitudes towards homosexuality in the mid-1990s.[61]

Countries that are very tolerant	12
Countries that are somewhat tolerant	28
Countries with general social disapproval	69
Countries that are hostile	60
Unclear/no data	10

   a. Make one observation based on your pie graph.

   b. How much do you think that this has changed in the past ten years and why do you think that?

2. A 2003 Gallup Poll in the United States found the following results:[62]

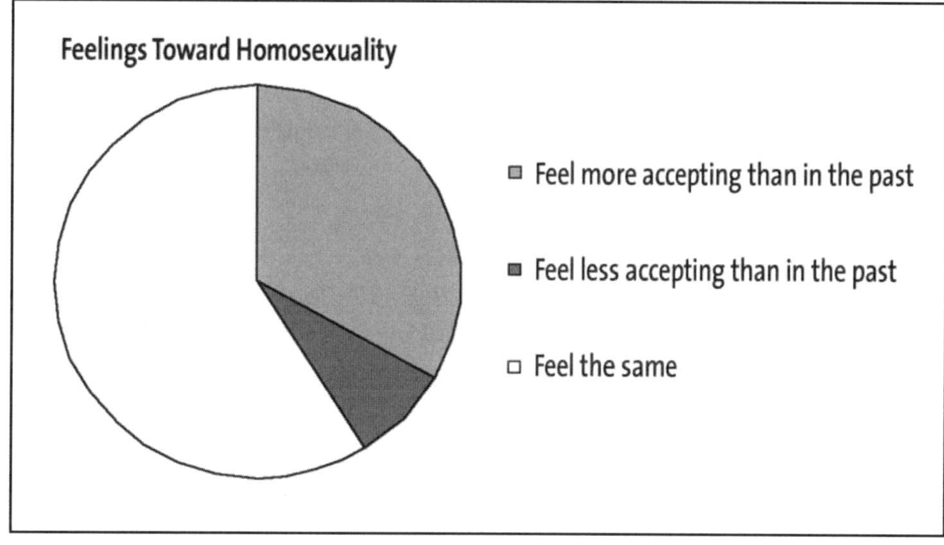

   a. **Speculate** as to why there are approximately four times as many people who feel "more accepting than in the past" versus "less accepting than in the past".

   b. What do you need to know about the "Feel the same" category to get a better understanding of social acceptance of homosexuality?

3. A poll asking Canadians whether they support or oppose allowing gay and lesbian couples to marry was conducted in August 2003 and February 2005.[63] Here are the results.

61 Seager, Joni. *The State of Women in the World*, Penguin Group, 1997, pp. 24-25.
62 Redding, Andrew. "Sexual Orientation and Human Rights in the Americas", *World Policy Reports*, Dec. 2003, p. 87.
63 EKOS Research, *Toronto Star*, February 12, 2005 A4.

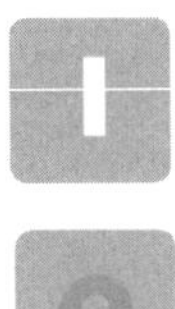

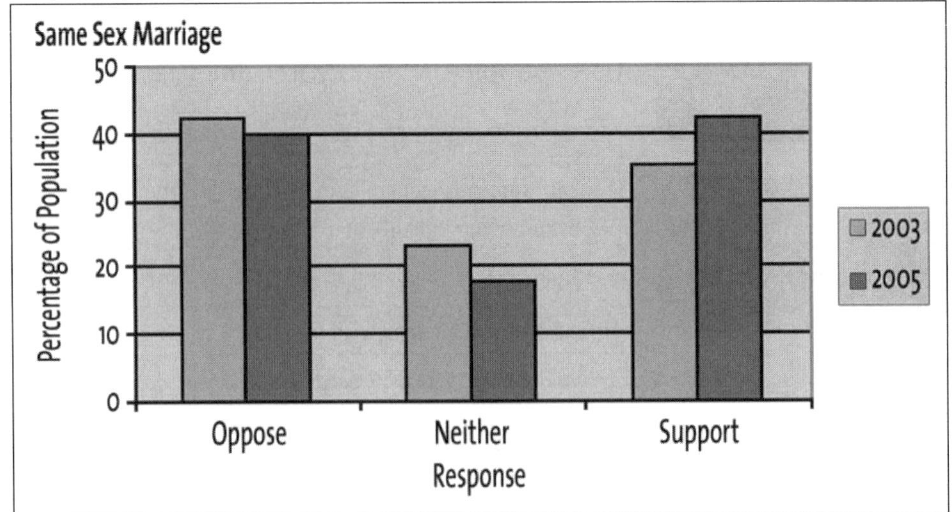

a. By what approximate percentage has support for gay marriage increased in the past two years?

b. From the following groups, decide who you think supports gay marriage more and why:

- Women or men
- Francophones or Anglophones
- Younger people or older people
- People with more education or less education
- Liberals/Bloc/NDP or Conservatives

4. Look at the following graph and explain what you think is happening and why, and what implication you think that will have for the future.[64]

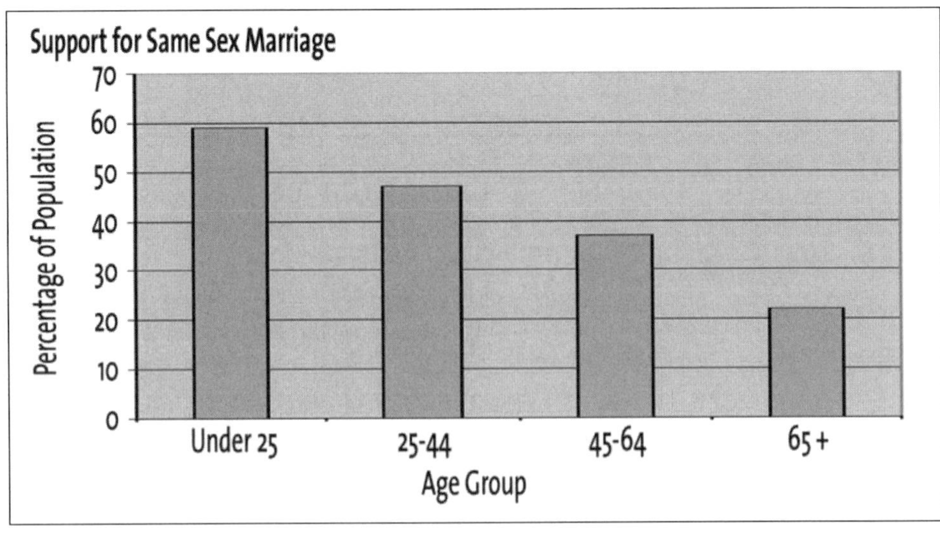

64 *Toronto Star*, February 12, 2005 A4

5. In Canada's 2001 Census, 6,685 same-sex Toronto couples registered as permanent partners, which is about one fifth of the total across Canada.[65] Approximately how many same-sex couples registered on the 2001 census?

6. Sometimes obscured by the same-sex marriage debate is the very real economic advantage of being married: **tax deductions, pension** benefits, **health insurance**, and inheritance benefits are just a few. An **Ipsos Reid** poll in Canada and a **Gallup** Poll in the U.S. found the following support for same-sex marriage:[66]

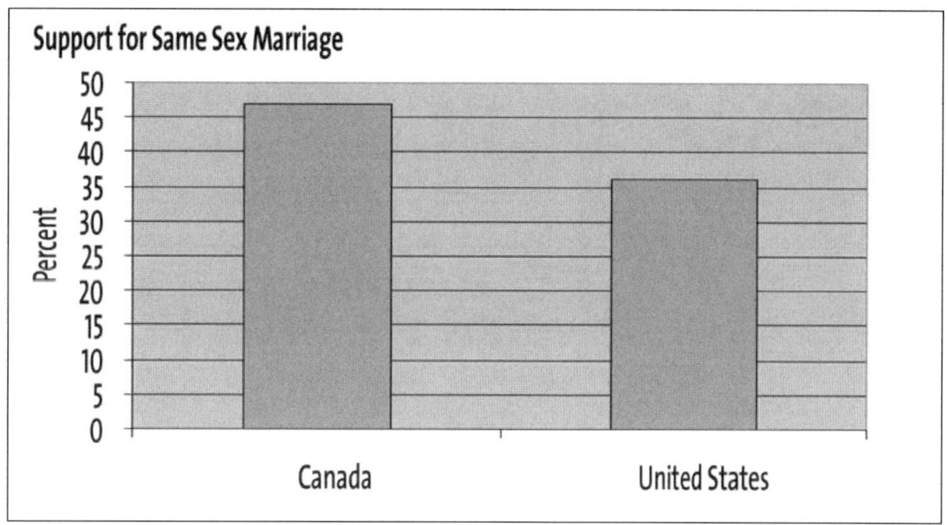

Speculate as to why there is a difference between Canada and the United States. What further research could you do to clarify the reason?

7. Not to be left out of the growing acceptance towards the LGBT community, businesses are realizing the money that this portion of society spends. Studies have been done and have found that because people who are gay tend to have fewer dependent children, they also have higher **disposable incomes**. The gay community also tends to be better educated than the general population. Here are some of the other results:[67]

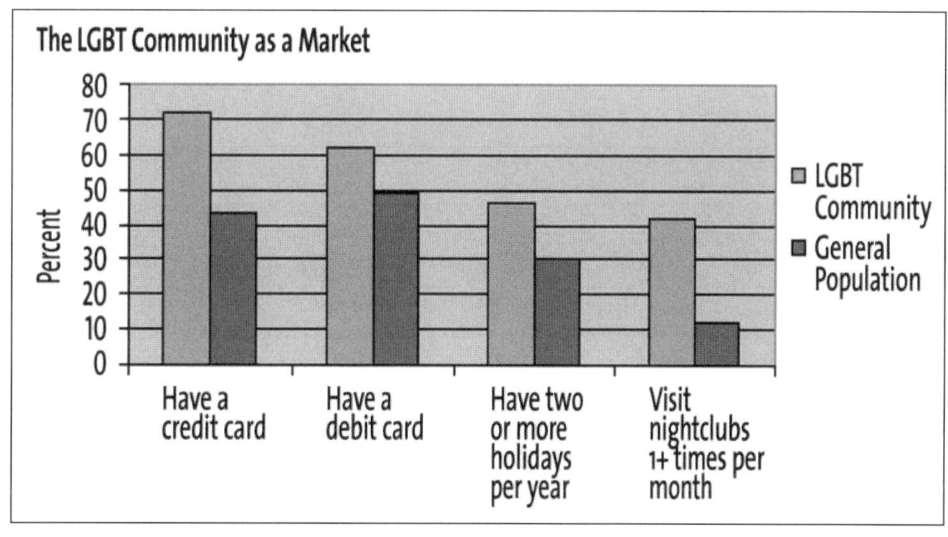

65 http://www.csudh.edu/dearhabermas/gaymarrbko3.htm
66 *CanWest News Service*, April 17, 2004.
67 www.gaytoz.com/bHomo_Economics.asp

a. Does anything in this particular graph prove that the LGBT community (in this case from a 2000 London, England sample) has more money to spend?

b. What might businesses do to increase their profits based on the above results?

c. Does this study suggest that businesses, over time, will promote acceptance of **diversity**?

make it better

- Have your teacher order a copy of the poster advertising the Lesbian Gay Bi Youth Line by calling 416-962-2232 x 2.
- Check out the Oasis online magazine: news and entertainment written by and about **queer** youth at www.oasismag.com.
- Show **solidarity** with LGBT students by organizing a **pride day** at your school. Resources at www.pflag.ca may be helpful.

Roasted

"That the poor are invisible is one of the most important things about them. They are not simply neglected as in the old rhetoric of reform; what is much worse, they are not seen."

– Michael Harrington

Maria is one of 25 million coffee farmers in over 70 developing countries. She earns $3 a day, three times as much as workers in Vietnam, producing coffee beans for wealthy countries of the North. She gets sprayed regularly with pesticide that's put on the crops. She lives in a tiny house with a dirt floor, without plumbing and electricity. She earns too little to afford medical care or nutritious food. Meanwhile, Phillip Morris, Sara Lee, Nestle and Proctor and Gamble make record **profits** from the labour.[68]

The prices for coffee on the world **market** are extremely **volatile**, and while **production costs** for the farmers can range from 60 to 80 cents per pound,[69] the going market rate has fallen as low as 24 cents a pound.[70] To survive, coffee farmers switch to more profitable but ecologically devastating practices, like clear-cutting land to grow coffee in the sun (shade coffee prevents soil erosion and supports many animal species).[71] Other farmers decide to grow coca and poppies instead (to make cocaine and opium), reaping the financial benefits of the drug trade.

Fair trade is a movement to pay workers of the South a fair rate for their products and to encourage

68 Profit Addicts Brewing Misery in the Third World, *Revolutionary Worker* #1110 July 15, 2001, p. 1, 5.
69 www.witherspoonsociety.org/coffee_production.htm
70 http://www.natcath.org/NCR_Online/archives/122702/122702k.htm
71 Hudson, Ian and Mark Hudson, *How Alternative is Alternative Trade?* Jan. 2003, p. 7.

ecologically sound farming practices. Labelling of fair trade coffee began in Holland in 1987[72] and as **consumers** of the North began to question the damage that their coffee drinking was causing, the demand for ethical coffee options has slowly increased.[73]

opening question

Oxfam, a development agency, has stated that low market prices for coffee will put millions of coffee farmers into extreme poverty, "with devastating consequences for health, education and **social stability**."[74] Why do you think that social stability would be affected?

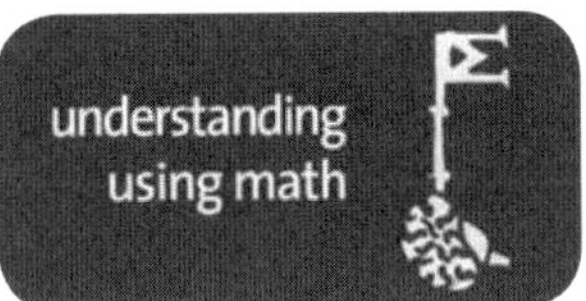

1. The rules of the fair trade movement are as follows:

    - Farmers are guaranteed a minimum price for their coffee of $1.26 per pound no matter how low the world market prices fall.
    - When the world market prices go above $1.26 per pound, farmers working under fair trade get a **premium** of 5 cents per pound above the world prices for regular coffee and 15 cents per pound for organic.[75]

    a. Use the graph below and create a new graph line that represents what farmers under fair trade agreements would have received.

    b. Volatility means big changes in short time frames. Which times represented high volatility in the coffee market?

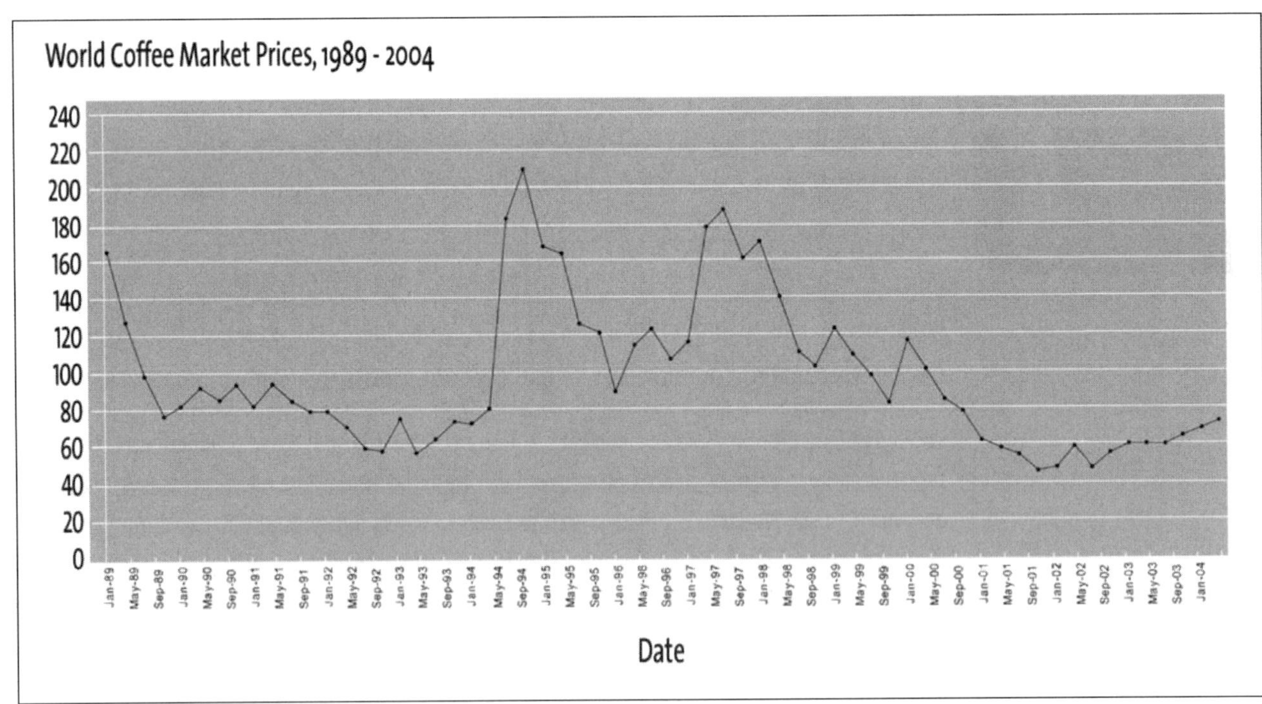

72 www.fairtradetoronto.com

73 www.transfairusa.org

74 Profit Addicts Brewing Misery in the Third World, *Revolutionary Worker* #1110 July 15, 2001, p. 1.

75 Hudson, Ian and Mark Hudson, *How Alternative is Alternative Trade?*, Jan. 2003, p. 10.

c. Use your line from part (a) to explain how that volatility is moderated in fair trade agreements.

d. Draw in the **best fit** line for the original graph and the best fit line for the modified data from part (a). What is the difference?

2. The following two tables show the relationship between the number of plants that can be grown for each **hectare** of land.

   a. Write an algebraic equation for each relationship.

   b. Write an algebraic equation for the relationship between the number of plants that can be grown in the sun compared to in the shade.[76] Discuss **profitability** based on this equation.

Number of hectares (shade grown)	10	15	20	100
Number of plants	20,000	30,000	40,000	200,000

Number of hectares (sun grown)	5	12	18	25
Number of plants	35,000	84,000	126,000	175,000

   c. Coffee plants grown in the sun produce higher **yields** of coffee beans. Discuss what impact this has on your conclusion from part (b).

3. It takes approximately 2,500 coffee cherries to make one pound of coffee. If you buy 2 kilograms of coffee, how many coffee cherries are in your purchase?

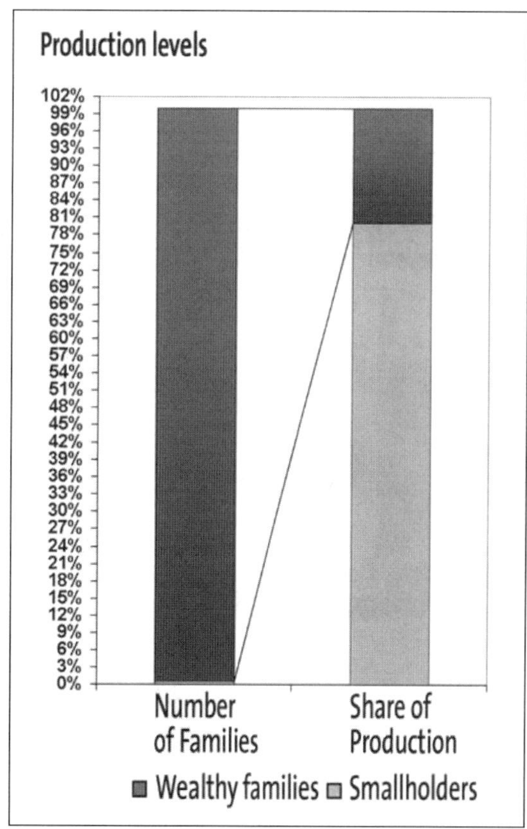

76 Hudson, Ian and Mark Hudson, *How Alternative is Alternative Trade?*, Jan. 2003,. p. 8.

4. One third of the 25 million coffee farmers run small operations, using two to five acres of land.[77] What is the number of small operation farmers?

5. The "Production levels" graph on the previous page describes the coffee situation in Guatemala. If you were trying to describe (to a student in grade three) what is happening, what would you say? Be specific. If the number of wealthy families is about 250, how many smallholders are there?

6. The following table shows the amount of fair trade coffee purchased in the United States between the years 1999 and 2003.[78]

Year	Millions of pounds of coffee	Percentage increase over the past year
1999	2	
2000	3.69	
2001	7	
2002	9.8	
2003	18.7	

   a. Complete the third column of the table.

   b. What is the average increase in sales over the entire period?

   c. What would you predict the sales for 2004 to be? Explain your reasoning.

   d. In 2001, fair trade coffee in the United States represented 0.35% of the coffee market.[79] How much coffee was not fair trade coffee in 2001?

- For a history of coffee, see "Profit Addicts Brewing Misery in the Third World" at http://rwor.org/a/v23/1110-19/1110/coffee.htm.
- Only purchase coffee with the Fair Trade label.
- Ask your local stores to offer Fair Trade products, like tea, coffee, sugar and bananas.
- You can find all Canadian fair trade licensees at http://www.transfair.ca/index/shtml.

77 www.fairtradetoronto.com
78 www.transfairusa.org "Fair Trade Market Achieves Record Growth in 2003", March 2004.
79 Hudson, Ian and Mark Hudson. *How Alternative is Alternative Trade?* Jan. 2003 p. 3.

Side-Lined

"We don't want a bigger piece of the pie – we want a different pie."

– Winona La Duke

The amount of annual income below which a person or family is considered to be living in poverty is called the **poverty line**. Not surprisingly, people do not all agree where the poverty line should be set. Even Canada's **federal government** has five different ways to measure the poverty line!

One approach to determining the poverty line is to say, "OK, let's figure out what basic goods and services are required for someone to physically survive and see how much that costs per year." This is called the **Consumption Basket Measure**. As you can imagine, people will disagree over what to put in the metaphorical basket: some will consider very few things, like food and shelter, while others may include transportation, school supplies, and access to communication and media.

Some poverty **advocates** say that unless you consider other factors beyond physical survival, such as social and emotional well-being, poor people will stand out and feel **deprived**. So poverty is not absolute: it is relative to the society in which the person finds him or herself. Finding the **average** or **median** income of a society may give you a better sense of what people need. This is called an Equity Based Measure.

What does it mean to say that the experience of being poor is relative to the community in which you live? Is the Consumption Basket Measure an absolute or a relative measure of poverty? How about the **Equity Based Measure**?

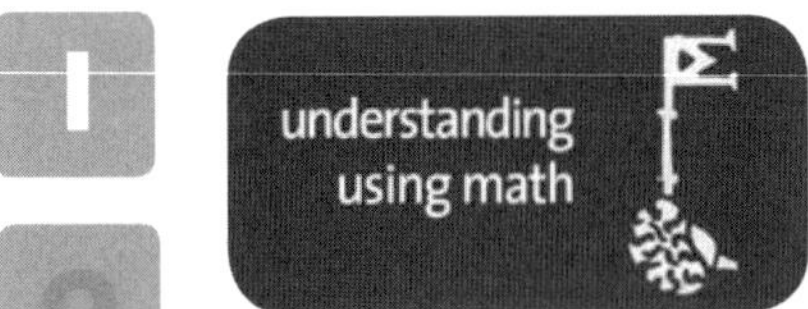

Some measures of the poverty line combine the Consumption Basket and the Equity Based measures. A good example is Statistic Canada's **Low Income Cut-Offs (LICOs)**. The following chart shows some examples of different measures and the poverty line that they set.[80]

	Type of Poverty Line	Amount
Consumption Basket Measures	Social Planning Council of Metro Toronto	$44,668
	Market Basket Measure	$26,899
	Fraser Institute	$18,603
Mixed Consumption and Equity Measures	Low Income Cut Off (after tax) (LICO)	$29,163
Equity Based Measures	Low Income Measure (after tax) (LIM)	$23,804
	CCSD Lines of Income Inequality	$33,912

1. Three consumption basket measures are listed in the table. What measure is the most restrictive (in other words, which basket has the fewest items)? Which measure is the most inclusive (has the greater number of items)?

2. One year, Canada's poverty rate was calculated, using the Market Basket Measure, to be 12%. In the same year, the Low Income Cut Off calculated the poverty rate at 17%. If you assume Canada's population is 30 million people, what number of people were considered poor by each standard? Show your work.

3. What is the **Fraser Institute**? If you used the Fraser Institute poverty line to calculate how many people in Canada are poor, would there be more or less poor people than if you used the Low Income Cut Off? Explain. Why would they set the poverty line so low?

4. Why might someone want the number of people considered to be poor to be a lower number? (Or phrased another way, where might money allocated to **social services** that help people who are poor be redirected to?)

Canada's economy experienced strong economic growth between 1997 and 2000, yet the number of people who relied on a **food bank** during those years increased 9.4%. In fact, between the years 1989 and 2000 there was a 96% increase in the number of Canadians using food banks.[81]

5. The number of people who relied on food banks in 1989 was 378,000.[82] How many people relied on them in 2000? Show your work.

---

80 deGroot-Maggetti, Greg. *A Measure of Poverty in Canada: a guide to the debate about poverty lines.* March 2002. http://cpj.ca/pjrc/research/02_poverty.pdf, Jan. 13, 2004.
81 Canadian Association of Food Banks www.cafb-acba/about_facts_e.cfm
82 Ibid.

6. By the year 2003, the number who relied on food banks was 778,000.[83] What percentage increase is this over 1989 levels? Show your work. In 2005 the number using food banks was 118% more than the 1989 levels. How many were using food banks in 2005?

7. In 1989 one in seven kids was poor in Canada. By 1999 one in five children was poor. In 2003 one in four children in Canada was poor.[84]

   a. What is the increase in the chances of being poor between 1989 and 2003 as a percentage?

   b. Discuss how the 2003 figure masks poverty rates in particular populations by comparing the poverty rate for each group in the following table.

Poverty rates, children age 0 – 14 years:[85]

Total	Aboriginal	Visible Minority	Children With Disabilities
23.4%	52.1%	42.7%	37%

The following graph was produced by the Canadian Council on Social Development, using a National Longitudinal Survey of Children and Youth (1994-95).

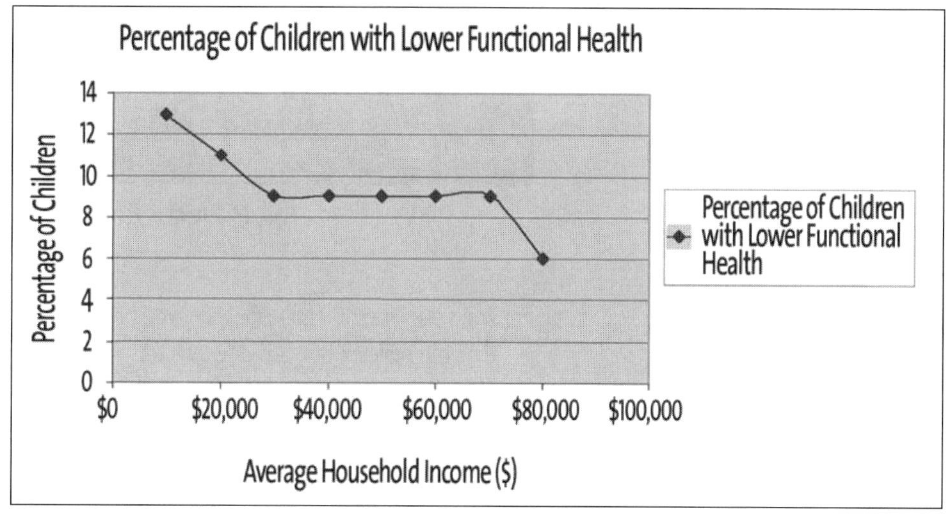

8. What happens to the number of children with health problems as the household income increases?

9. If the percentage of Canadians who are children is roughly 25%, what is 13% of 25%? (In other words, how many children live in a household with an average annual income of about $10,000) What is 9% of 25%? (In other words, how many children live in a household with an average annual income between about $30,000 and $70,000) Show your work.

10. Mark five different poverty lines on the above graph (exclude the LIM line).

11. If the Fraser Institute measure of poverty is used, and better assistance is provided to those below that particular poverty line, what will happen compared to if you used the LICO poverty line (speak specifically of children's functional health). Approximately what is the difference in the number of children served by each measure of the poverty line?

---

83 Canadian Association of Food Banks www.cafb-acba/about_facts_e.cfm

84 Casey Elaine, "Child Poverty Spreading Fast in GTA: Report", *Toronto Star*, A1, 8 June 30,2003.

85 Campaign 2000, *Putting Promises into Action, A Report on a Decade of Child and Family Poverty in Canada*, May 2002, p.10.

12. A strong **correlation** exists between inequality and poor health.[86] Does this statement suggest that we consider relative levels of poverty or absolute levels of poverty? Explain.

13. Although most people use poverty lines to describe how bad the level of poverty is, the most current thinkers say that the *number* of people below the poverty line tells you nothing about *how far* into poverty they are (in other words, how far from the poverty line). A different way of measuring poverty, called the **poverty box**, is now being used and takes both problems into account. Look at the following poverty boxes for three different cities:

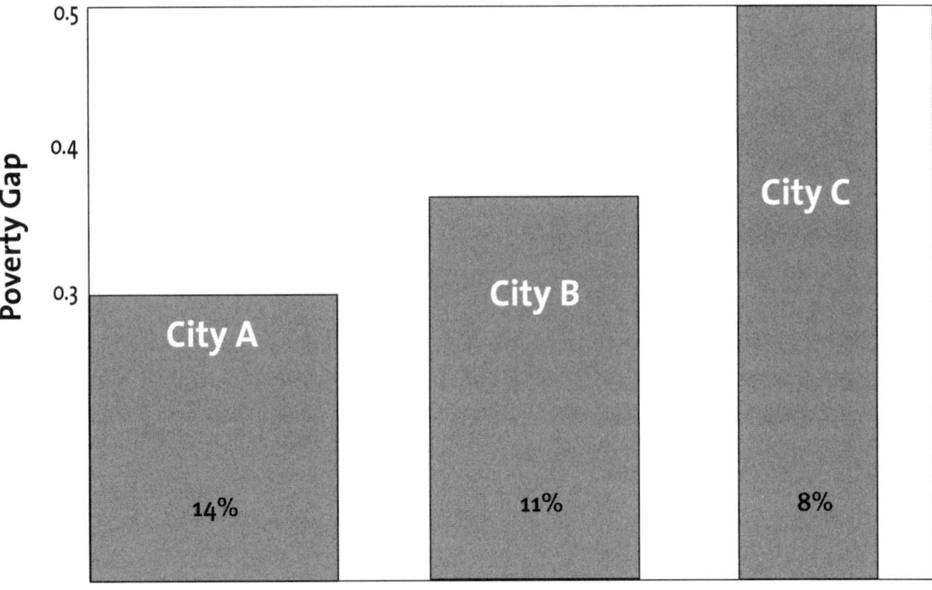

c. Rank the cities in order from the worst levels of poverty to the least worst. Remember that the poverty box takes two factors into account: the number of people below the poverty line (called the "poverty rate") and the average distance those people are from the poverty line (called the "poverty gap").

d. What mathematical quantity are you calculating to find the level of poverty for each city?

e. Use the three cities to explain how, if you only use poverty rates, you can be misleading about how big or small a problem poverty really is.

- Volunteer one day a week for four weeks at your local food bank.
- When you food shop, buy an extra bag of food for a food bank.
- Learn about **Campaign 2000**, the promise the Canadian government made in 1989 to end child poverty by the year 2000. How have they done? What remains to be done?

86 deGroot-Maggetti, Greg. *A Measure of Poverty in Canada: a guide to the debate about poverty lines.* March 2002. http://cpj.ca/pjrc/research/02_poverty.pdf , Jan. 13, 2004.

Poor Sport

"The true mission of American sports is to prepare young people for war."

– U.S. President Eisenhower

If you live in North America, it's likely that you've heard a number of things about competition. There is widespread belief that competition is natural, that it promotes skill and self-esteem, and that it's fun. Oddly enough, in study after study, these deeply held beliefs have turned out to be tentative at best, and often totally wrong.

The evidence comes from hundreds of research papers. Some telling comments:

> "Superior performance not only does not require competition; it usually seems to require its absence."[87]
>
> Competition has been shown to lead to "depression, extreme stress and relatively shallow relationships."[88]
>
> A study of more than 1,200 teenage athletes found that "winning" "had the weakest relationship with sport enjoyment."[89]
>
> "There is a remarkable correspondence between competitiveness in a society and the presence of clearly defined "have" and "have-not" groups."[90]
>
> On the other hand, cooperation is positively **correlated** to many indicators of psychological health, "such as emotional maturity, strong personal identity, and basic trust in and optimism about other people."[91]

---

87 Kohn, Alfie. *No Contest: The Case Against Competition*. Houghton Mifflin 1986, p. 47.
88 Ibid., p 115.
89 Ibid., p. 243.
90 Ibid., p. 38.
91 Ibid., p. 108.

Why do you think that in one study children rated as "highly competitive" were found to have lower empathy scores than children rated as relatively less competitive?

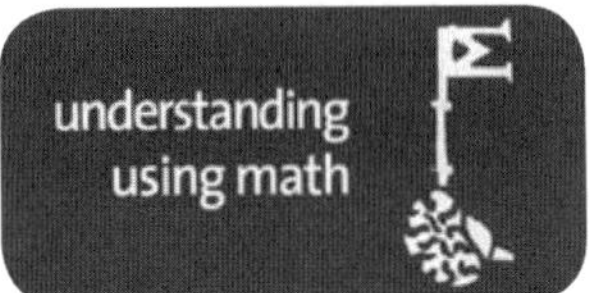

1. Play the Prisoner's Dilemma game.

You will need a group of three people. Two members of your group are suspects, picked up by the police because they believe that you are both involved in a robbery. The police separate the two suspects and **interrogate** them (once you've read the rules, send one person to another room).

A deal is offered. If suspect A gives evidence against suspect B, suspect A goes free and suspect B goes to jail, and visa versa. If both suspects give evidence against each other, both go to jail. If both suspects do not offer evidence both go to jail but based on less evidence, and so the jail time is less. The point system is as follows:

	Points for you	Points for the other suspect
You turn your partner in by giving evidence while your partner doesn't turn you in	5	0
Your partner gives evidence against you but you do not turn in your partner	0	5
Neither of you turn each other in	3	3
You both turn each other in	1	1

The third person in your group will go back and forth between the two suspects and record their "move". That person tells each suspect the outcome of the last "move" before recording each suspect's next move. The goal is to maximize your points in ten rounds of play. After each 10 rounds, rotate players.

2. Debrief the Prisoner's Dilemma game.

   a. What was the maximum score that you were able to get?

   b. What strategy did you use to maximize your score?

   c. What happened in the rounds following a round where one suspect gave evidence against another who did not give evidence?

   d. Compare your scores with those of your classmates. Who got the highest scores and what was their strategy?

3. Competition happens in all sorts of ways. Sometimes the amount of "air time" people have excludes the contributions of others. In one study of conversations between men and women, 96% of the interruptions were men breaking in on women.[92] How could you conduct a similar study of your own without letting the participants know what you were doing? Conduct the study and share your results with the class. What do you think this means? Is it important? Why or why not?

92 Kohn, Alfie. *No Contest: The Case Against Competition*, Houghton Mifflin 1986, p. 177.

4. A meta-analysis is a review of research that has already been done. One hundred and nine studies were compared looking at achievement in cooperative settings versus achievement in competitive settings. These are the findings:[93]

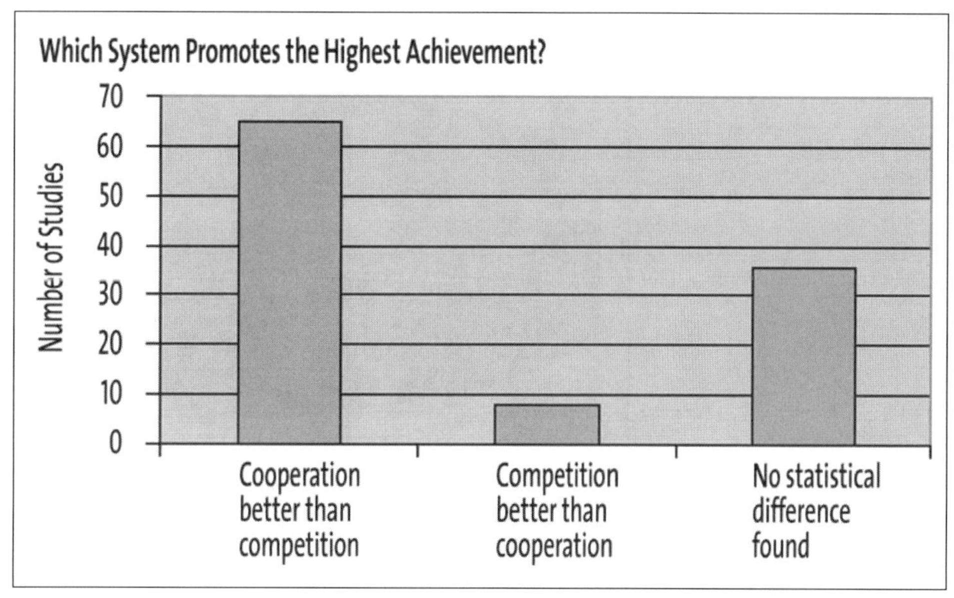

a. Why do you think that cooperation leads to higher achievement far more than competition does?

b. The cases in which competition led to higher achievement tended to be simple tasks. How might you explain this finding? What implication does that have on learning in a classroom?

5. Terry Orlick at the University of Ottawa led a group of children, from pre-schoolers to second-graders, in cooperative games and later looked for incidents of cooperative behaviour when the children were left to play by themselves. The following numbers **mimic** Orlick's results.[94]

	Child A	Child B	Child C	Child D
Cooperative behaviour before cooperative games	4	6	10	2
Cooperative behaviour after cooperative games	14	21	35	7

a. What algebraic equation describes the increase in cooperative behaviour after being exposed to cooperative activities as compared to before?

b. What does this suggest about the nature of cooperation?

93 Kohn, Alfie. *No Contest: The Case Against Competition*, Houghton Mifflin 1986, p. 48.
94 Kohn, Alfie. *No Contest: The Case Against Competition*, Houghton Mifflin 1986p. 38.

5. In a large review of the research comparing competitive and cooperative arrangements on self-esteem, a fair number did not find a **statistically significant** difference, but of the studies that did find a difference the following pie graph has something interesting to say:[95]

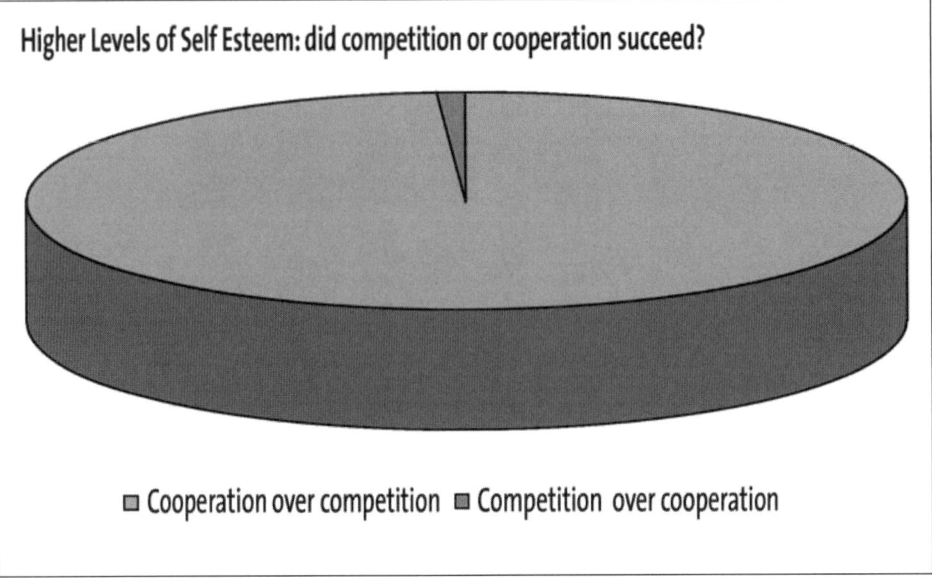

   a. What do you think is the ratio between the two categories?

   b. What **implication** does this have for sport and recreation programs in general?

Food for Thought

High standardized test scores of 5th and 6th graders are negatively correlated with competitiveness.[96]

- Just for fun, you can play the Prisoners' Dilemma at www.serendip.brynmawr.edu/playground/pd.html.
- Try to develop a cooperative activity for your gym class. It should be both challenging and fun. Ask your physical education teacher if you can try it out.

---

95 Ibid. p. 203
96 Kohn, Alfie Kohn. *No Contest: The Case Against Competition*, Houghton Mifflin, 1986, p. 53.

Darth Vader Has Arrived

"It will be a great day when our schools get all the money they need and the air force has to hold a bake sale to buy a bomber."

– Women's International League for Peace and Freedom.

The United States has been developing a missile defence program in order to defend itself against missile attacks from enemy countries. In late 2001, the States pulled out of the **Anti-Ballistic Missile (ABM) Treaty** which had prevented Russia and the U.S. from developing defensive systems that would benefit one country over another in the event of nuclear war. The logic went as follows: if both countries were defenceless against attack, neither country would attack, for fear of **retaliation**. Governments called it the **Mutually Assured Destruction** scenario (or **M.A.D.**).[97]

Canada is being asked to join this missile defence program. We should ask questions. Are there countries with the missile technology that can reach the U.S.? The CIA reports that the only two that are capable (Russia and China) are unlikely to attack[98] for fear of massive **reprisal**. Are intercontinental ballistic missiles really the greatest type of threat? Can defence systems work accurately? And, crucially, there is the question of cost. How much have taxpayers already contributed to this project, and what are future anticipated expenses? Is this the best use of our money?

---

97 Shah, Anup. http://www.globalissues.org/Geopolitics/ArmsControl/StarWars.asp. April 1, 2004.
98 Shah, Anup. http://www.globalissues.org/Geopolitics/ArmsControl/StarWars.asp. April 1, 2004.

Who would directly benefit from an allocation of government funds to make a missile defence system?

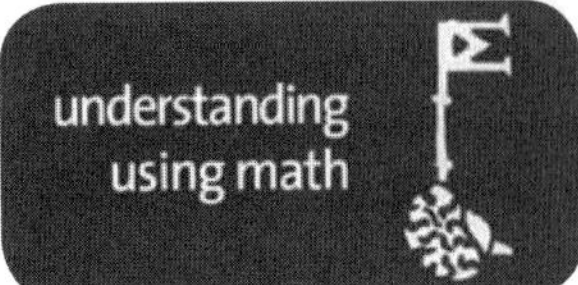

1. The **United Nations General Assembly** regularly passes resolutions on many different issues. Although they are non-binding, they can give you a sense of where governments stand on particular issues. In November 2001, the UN called on Moscow and Washington to make the ABM Treaty stronger. Here are the outcomes of the vote:[99]

In favour	Opposed	Abstentions
79	5	62

What percentage of the countries voted in favour of protecting the world from nuclear missiles? What does that tell you about international support for the ABM Treaty?

2. Another United Nations General Assembly vote called on countries to "maintain the highest possible standards of security, safe custody, effective control and physical protection of all materials that could contribute to the **proliferation** of nuclear and other weapons of mass destruction in order, among others, to prevent those materials from falling into the hands of terrorists."[100]

In favour	Opposed	Abstentions
139	3	19

The three opposing votes were from the Federated States of Micronesia, India, and the United States. If you turned the above table into a spinner, what is the probability that if you spun that spinner you would end up on an "Opposed Vote"?

3. Why would a country vote against the control of nuclear weapons?

4. A UN text calling for the "peaceful use of outer space and the prevention of an arms race there" was presented with the following results:

In favour	Opposed	Abstentions
156	0	4

   If the above table was turned into a spinner, what would the probability be of spinning a vote in favour of the resolution? What would the probability be of spinning a vote opposed? An **abstention**?

5. Part of the technical problems of a defence system is that a single missile can carry multiple warheads. If each missile can carry five warheads, how many targets would a defence system have to deal with if 25 missiles were deployed? If 60 missiles were **deployed**? What algebraic equation describes this pattern?

---

99 Shah, Anup. http://www.globalissues.org/Geopolitics/ArmsControl/StarWars.asp, April 1, 2004
100 http://www.un.org/News/Press/docs/2001/ga9983.doc.htm *Need for Disarmament Progress as Contribution to Anti-Terrorism Report* Fifty-sixth General Assembly Plenary 68th Meeting (AM)

6. Decoys can also be used. Let's suppose that each missile can carry five warheads and can be accompanied by 20 decoys. How many targets would a defence system have to deal with if 25 missiles were deployed? If 40 missiles were deployed? What algebraic equation describes this pattern?

7. A test-run of the defence system was conducted on the Cook Islands on July 7, 2000. It failed. But the event cost $100 million.[101] If American dollars are worth 1.3 times more than Canadian dollars and a four year university degree in Canada costs $40,000, how many students could have a free university degree with the money from this one military experiment?

8. The costs involved with creating a defence system include research and development, set-up, operation, and maintenance. The Center for Arms Control and Non-Proliferation, and Economists Allied for Arms reduction have suggested these costs would range between $800 billion and $1.2 trillion. Take the average of these two numbers, and use that money to solve as many of the problems below as you can.

   Write out the costs in both scientific notation and standard notation, so that you can more easily compare the numbers. The first cell has been done for you. Then decide how many years you'll fund this project, and the resulting cost. Tally your cost column - make sure you come in on budget.

Item:	Additional $ per year required[102]	# of years	Cost
Reproductive health care for all women	1.2×10^{10} or 12,000,000,000		
Elimination of hunger and malnutrition	1.9×10^{10} or		
Universal literacy	5×10^{9} or		
Clean drinking water for everyone	or 10,000,000,000		
Immunize every child	or 1,300,000,000		
		Total Cost:	

(If you went over your budget a bit, it's OK, because the States have spent $122 billion between 1957 and 1999 on missile defence[103] which wasn't included in your budget)

101 Wallace, Michael. *Ballistic Missile Defense: The view from the cheap seats*, WagingPeace.org (Nuclear Age Peace Foundation)

102 *Worldwatch Report* 2004 p 10.

103 Shah, Anup. http://www.globalissues.org/Geopolitics/ArmsControl/StarWars.asp, April 1, 2004

9. If the problems in column 1 of the above table were dealt with, what could you argue about the need for missile defence systems?

Food for thought...

In a nationwide poll conducted in February of 2005, 54% of those surveyed opposed Canada's participation in building missile interceptors as the United States intends.[104]

make it better

- Sign the declaration against missile defence at www.peacenow.org.
- Check out the Canadian Peace Alliance/L'Alliance Canadienne Pour La Paix" at http://www.acp-cpa.ca/en/index.html. It is an umbrella organization for peace groups throughout Canada. Use the site to locate a local peace group, and explore the Take Action section for good ideas.

104 Campion-Smith, Bruce. Missile support plummets. *Toronto Star* February 12, 2005, A4.

Some 'Fare' Better Than Others

"If we are going to end welfare, the rich should be the first to lose it."
– Mac Morgan

Welfare is the system through which those who are most in need receive income support from the government. For some, welfare may call to mind people who need some assistance because they have been fired or laid off, or people who have a disability that prevents them from working. For others, it brings to mind **stereotypes** and **prejudices**: "those people who cheat the system- who don't work and instead live off of my tax dollars."

Do corporations get welfare payments when the going gets rough? Well, actually, the government does provide huge sums of financial support that some call "**corporate welfare**". When governments reduce the amount of **taxes** that corporations have to pay, it's much like giving them multi-million dollar gifts. Sometimes corporations receive full **tax exemptions**- "tax holidays" where they pay no tax at all. Governments also make a generous donation to corporations by freezing **minimum wages**, using laws to pass along savings in **labour** expenses.

In Canada, the group that represents our top 160 corporations is called the **Canada Council of Chief Executives (CCCE)**. Although most people have never heard of the group, they run the show- and some of these corporations pay as little as 2% income tax.[105]

105 Poster – Jesuit Centre for Social Justice

Why would the government collect only 2% income tax on a corporation that made hundreds of millions of dollars in profit, while a worker who earns $40,000 might pay 35% in **income tax**?

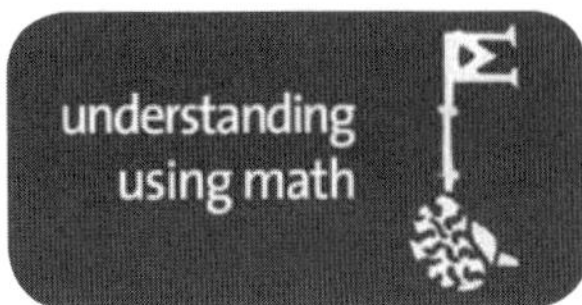

1. The following pie graphs show the amount of money the Canadian government received from corporate taxes in 1955, 1983 and 1998.[106]

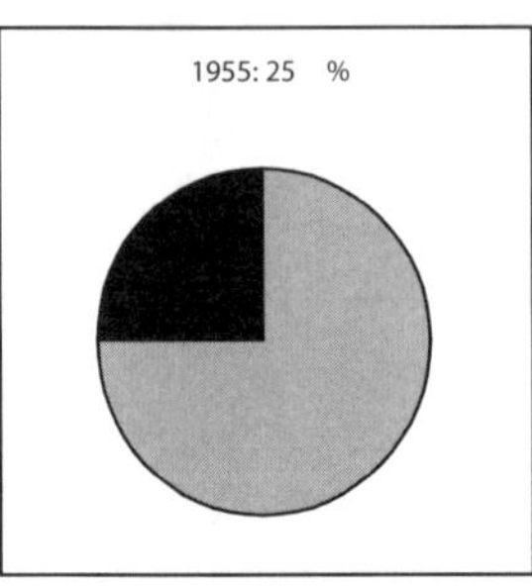

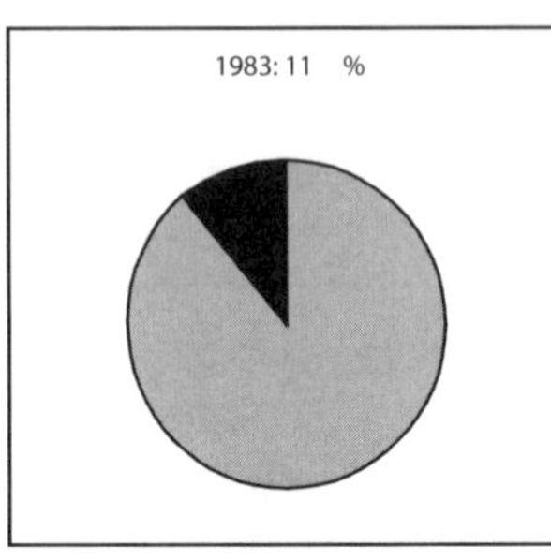

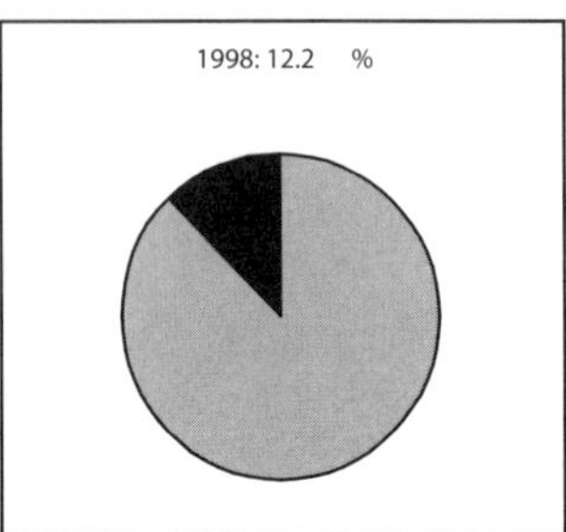

Where must the government be getting the money that it no longer gets from corporate taxes?

2. As of January 1, 2004 a Federal tax on large corporations dropped from 0.225% to 0.2%, and the amount of money the corporation had to make before it paid this tax jumped from $10 million to $50 million.[107]

    a. Explain what the savings would be for a corporation earning $60,000,000 with the federal tax reduction.

    b. Explain how a corporation earning $36,000,000 benefits and by how much.

3. In some Canadian provinces, corporations can be exempt from paying taxes for ten years, and sometimes longer. Let's say the regular tax rate is 25% and a corporation makes an average of $100,000,000 per year. Over the span of a ten year **tax holiday**, how much money would this corporation avoid paying?

4. In contrast, take a look at the following chart of welfare incomes for different types of families, in comparison to the **poverty line**.[108]

    a. If you were a person with a disability on welfare, which province from the list below would give you the least support?

    b. If you were a single parent with one child, which province would give you the least support? The most support? Does that support reach the poverty line?

---

106 Klein, Naomi. *No Logo*. Alfred A. Knopf Canada, 2000, p. 472.
107 www.pwcglobal.com April 25, 2004, p. 26.
108 http://www.ccsd.ca/factsheets/fs_ncwpl01.htm *Canadian Welfare Incomes as a Percentage of the Poverty Line by Family Type and Province*, 2001 Canadian Council on Social Development, using National Council of Welfare, Welfare Incomes 2000-2001, Spring 2002.

	Total Income	Poverty Line	Total Welfare Income as % of Poverty Line
		Newfoundland	
Single Employable	3,276	16,167	20%
Person with a Disability	8,902	16,167	55%
Single Parent, One Child	14,670	20,209	73%
Couple, Two Children	17,474	30,424	57%
		Quebec	
Single Employable	6,415	18,849	34%
Person with a Disability	9,314	18,849	49%
Single Parent, One Child	13,318	23,561	57%
Couple, Two Children	16,919	35,471	48%
		Ontario	
Single Employable	6,829	18,849	36%
Person with a Disability	11,763	18,849	62%
Single Parent, One Child	13,828	23,561	59%
Couple, Two Children	18,330	35,471	52%
		Alberta	
Single Employable	5,030	18,849	27%
Person with a Disability	7,596	18,849	40%
Single Parent, One Child	11,619	23,561	49%
Couple, Two Children	18,395	35,471	52%

Note: "Total welfare income" includes all income from basic social assistance, additional benefits, Canada Child Tax Benefit, Provincial/Territorial child benefits, the federal GST credit and Provincial/Territorial tax credits.

5. The **Daily Bread Food Bank** attempts to raise awareness of the issues facing Toronto's poor, by challenging corporate, political, media and artistic people in the community to live off of a welfare budget for a week.

    a. If your family lives in **social housing**, circle the column in the following table that applies to you to figure out your weekly allowance. Also, count yourself amongst the lucky few to find a subsidized place to live- as of 2003 there was a waiting list of over 66,000 people for social housing in Toronto (up 35% from 49,000 people in 1998).[109] Fill in the final two rows of the chart.

---

109 http://www.tcf.ca/vital_signs/vitalsigns2003/housing.html

	Single person, and one child	Couple and one child	Single parent, two children	Couple and two children
Monthly Income	$660	$768	$784.50	$1178
Minus Rent	$297	$262	$301.50	$760
After Rent Income				
Income for 7 days				

b. If you live by paying rent or a **mortgage** in the private rental market, circle the column that applies to you from the following chart. Fill in the final two rows of the chart.

	Single person, and one child	Couple and one child	Couple and four children	Single parent, two children	Couple and two children
Monthly Income	$957	$1030	$1533	$1086	$1178
Minus Rent	$700	$690	$1000	$710	$905
After Rent Income					
Income for 7 days					

c. From your weekly income, you would have to subtract any of the following items that apply to you (the bolded items are mandatory).

Telephone	$6.60 basic service, plus more for additional services like call waiting and long distance.
Cable	$6.12 basic service, plus more for digital cable or specialty channels.
Internet	$? Deduct your weekly internet service charge.
Laundry	$2.00 per load in the house, or $1.25 if you let the clothes air dry.
Transportation	$2.75 per trip on the TTC, or all gas, parking and leasing costs.
Personal products	$1.05 per person for one week worth of soap, shampoo or shampoo and conditioner, and deodorant. If you use other products make the extra deductions
Household products	$1.10 per person for one week's worth of toilet paper, dish soap, and laundry detergent. Fabric softener, bleach and household cleaners are extra.

d. What amount of money are you left with for the week, at this point?

e. All food purchases then have to come out of your budget, as do newspapers, magazines, gifts, diapers, school trips, school supplies, coffee, and over the counter medicine. The expenses not included are clothing, prescription medicine, child care, pet supplies, and household furnishings.

Food for thought...

"We have moved into an era where we are called upon to raise certain basic questions about the whole society. We are still called upon to give aid to the beggar who finds himself in misery and agony on life's highway. But one day, we must ask the question of whether an edifice which produces beggars must not be restructured and refurbished."

– Martin Luther King

- Challenge people on the stereotype that the poorest people in our society feed off of the system for free.
- Read what the Daily Bread Food Bank thinks should be done at http://www.dailybread.ca/pdf/blueprint.pdf.

War Within

"It's time to make the connection between debt relief and epidemic relief. If the international community relieves some of their external debt, these countries can reinvest the savings in poverty alleviation and AIDS prevention and care. If not, poverty will just continue to fan the flames of the epidemic."
– Peter Piot, Executive Director of UN AIDS

Acquired Immunodeficiency Syndrome, or AIDS, is caused by the Human Immunodeficiency Virus (HIV) that targets the body's **immune cells**. The impaired immune cells are then unable to fight off other bacterial and viral infections that most of us deal with easily. So, for example, people with HIV are 800 times more likely than the general population to develop active **tuberculosis**.[110]

HIV/AIDS is not just a disease of sex workers and injection drug users, although unprotected sex with multiple partners and the use of dirty needles that carry the virus are high risk behaviours. HIV/AIDS affects both men and women, rich and poor; however, because "**poverty**, underdevelopment and **illiteracy** are among the principal contributing factors to the spread of HIV/AIDS"[111] rich and poor are infected at different rates. As with all sexually transmitted diseases, facts, myths and rumours all combine to set a deadly stage for infection.[112]

---

110 *State of the World Population 2003, Making 1 billion count: investing in adolescents' health and rights* UNFPA 2003, p. 25.
111 Ibid, p. 23.
112 Ibid, pp 23-25.

In many places in the world, young women tend to have sexual relations with older men, who may already be infected. In societies where young women have very little power, their ability to negotiate the use of condoms is compromised. Even talking about sex is rare in many countries. And knowing about HIV/AIDS does not necessarily mean that people know about or will take preventative measures.

Because this **pandemic** is created by many social, biological, religious and economic factors it will take knowledgeable and skilled people to stem the disaster.

Why do you think that poverty, underdevelopment and illiteracy contribute so much to the spread of HIV/AIDS?

1. The following table demonstrates the relationship between the number of youth infected with HIV and time in seconds.[113]

Number of youth infected with HIV	20	30	35	50
Time in seconds	280	420	490	700

   a. What is the algebraic equation that describes the number of youth infected with HIV over time?

   b. Use your equation to calculate how many youth a day are infected with HIV.

   c. How many youth are infected each year with HIV? Relate that number to something that you are familiar with.

2. The following table demonstrates a pattern between per capita income and infection rate:[114]

Increase in per capita income	$4,000	$5,000	$7,000	$8,000
Decrease in infection rate	8%	10%	14%	16%

   a. What is the algebraic equation that describes the relationship between per capita income and infection rate?

   b. If a government could increase its per capita income by $3,000, what would happen to the rate of infection in the country?

   c. Why do you think poverty is linked to infection rate?

---

113 *State of the World Population 2003, making 1 billion count: investing in adolescents' health and rights* UNFPA 2003, p. 23.
114 Ibid, p. 23.

3. Biologically speaking, women and men have different risks associated with unprotected sex, captured in the following table.[115]

Number of young men infected	8	11	23	25
Number of young women infected	24	33	69	75

   a. What is the ratio of infection rate for women compared to men?

   b. Why do you think that this is so?

   c. Does this mean that young men can be less careful about unprotected sex?

4. Look at the following graph about the modes of HIV infection and make two conclusions based on the data.[116]

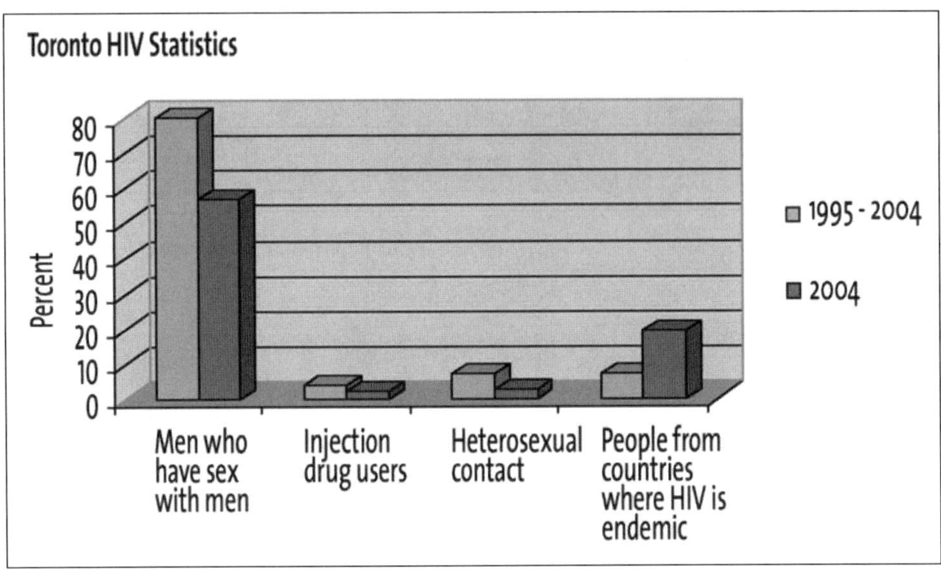

5. Use the information in the following table[117] to create a **spreadsheet** and a graph of your choice to demonstrate a comparison of your choice.

People Infected with HIV			
Region	Young Women (%)	Young Men (%)	Total
Sub-Saharan Africa	67	33	8,600,000
North Africa and the Middle East	41	59	160,000
East Asia and the Pacific	49	51	740,000
South Asia	62	38	1,100,000
Central Asia and Eastern Europe	35	65	430,000
Latin America and the Caribbean	31	69	560,000
Industrialized Countries	33	67	240,000
World	62	38	11,800,000

---

115 *State of the World Population 2003, Making 1 billion count: investing in adolescents' health and rights* UNFPA 2003, p. 23.

116 http://www.actoronto.org/website/home.nsf/pages/hivaidsstatsto

117 *State of the World Population 2003, making 1 billion count: investing in adolescents' health and rights* UNFPA 2003, p. 23.

Food for thought...

In 2003, in the **developing world**, less than 5% of the people who needed anti-retroviral drugs to treat HIV had access to them.[118]

"I believe that this could very well be looked back on as the sin of our generation. I look at my parents and ask, where were they during the civil rights movement? I look at my grandparents and ask, what were they doing when the holocaust in Europe was occurring with regard to the Jews and why didn't they speak up? And when we think of our great, great, great grandparents, we think, how could they have sat by and allowed slavery to exist? And I believe that our children and their children, 40 or 50 years from now are going to ask me, what did you do while 40 million children became orphans in Africa."

– Rich Stearns, President of Word Vision, US

- Go to the website www.stopthinkbesafe.org and play *STD Invaders*.
- Invite a public health nurse or a person living with HIV/AIDS into your classroom to answer questions about sexually transmitted diseases and HIV/AIDS.
- The Stephen Lewis Foundation helps to support people living with HIV/AIDS. Their website is www.stephenlewisfoundation.org.

118 Ibid, p. 27.

Disabled By Prejudice

"I think we can't go around measuring our goodness by what we don't do....I think we've got to measure goodness by what we embrace, what we create and who we include."

– Pere Henry, in the movie *Chocolat*

In the 1960s, huge peoples' movements erupted: African-Americans fighting for their **civil rights**, women demanding equality of the sexes, people speaking more openly about gay rights and hundreds of thousands of peace **activists** demanding an end to the war in Vietnam. In the 1970s, a group called the Coalition of Provincial Organizations of the Handicapped was founded to represent and give national voice to 30,000 Canadians with disabilities.[119]

Studies repeatedly show that people with disabilities face significant barriers to participation in our society. Difficulties with public transportation and access to public buildings contribute in no small part to higher levels of **poverty** and unemployment, more experience of violence and abuse and poorer access to health care services.[120] But while physical accessibility is a barrier, studies have shown that attitudes toward people with disabilities are the most significant contributor to unemployment and underemployment.

---

119 http://www.ccdonline.ca/FAQs/history.htm Council of Canadians with Disabilities

120 Steinstra, Deborah and Enza Gucciardi. Disabilities. *Ontario Women's Health Status Report, 2002* pp. 146-161.

Designing our environment to be **inclusive** takes creativity and some foresight, but surprisingly little money. A study of new buildings in the United States demonstrated that modifications cost less than 1% of the total costs, and adapting existing workplaces for people with disabilities averaged $100 per person.[121] If the physical accessibility is the easy part, it seems like we need to focus on not being disabled by our own prejudices.

Can you think of which groups of people within the category of "people with a disability" would face additional barriers? Explain your reasoning.

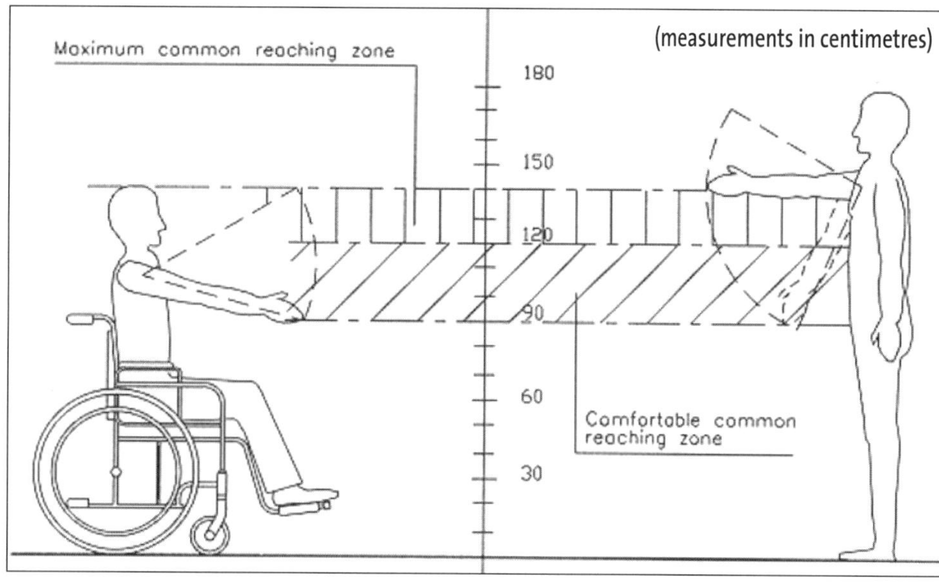

122

1. What is the common reaching zone height for a person who is standing and a person who is using a wheelchair?
2. What height is the comfortable common reaching zone?
3. What types of things in a school setting would typically be higher than the common reaching zone that would have to be modified?
4. The slope of a ramp for a person using a wheelchair needs to be such that for every rise of one centimetre, there should be 12 cm of ramp length.[123] Write the algebraic equation for ramp length related to ramp height.
5. No ramp should be longer than 9 metres in length without a landing.[124] How high will the ramp be at the 9 metre length?
6. Find a set of stairs leading into your school and calculate the height from the street level to the top of the stairs. Then calculate the length of the ramp required for that set of stairs.

---

121 http://www.facs.gov.au/internet/facsinternet.nsf/0/169b63db5bfae742ca256c78002005b3?OpenDocument
122 http://www.un.org/esa/socdev/enable/designm/AD5-02.htm
123 Strickland, Susan and Craig Birdsong, *Simple Home Modifications for the Disabled*, 2001, http://health.medscape.com/cx/viewarticle/202952
124 Ibid.

7. Draw an accurately scaled picture of the entrance to your school and draw in an access ramp based on the length in the last question. The width of the ramp should be 91.5 cm.

8. Some design criteria state that due to weather conditions the ramp should be 20 cm for every rise of 1 centimetre.[125] Is this more or less steep than the 1:12 ratio in the previous questions? How much more or less steep?

9. How long would the access ramp to your school have to be with the 1:20 ratio?

10. The minimum width for a hallway is 91.5 cm. and 81.3 cm for a door.[126] Are the doors and hallways in your school accessible for someone who uses a wheelchair?

11. The minimum width of a hallway for one **ambulatory** person to pass a person using a wheelchair is 123 centimetres. Are the hallways sufficiently wide enough in your school?

12. The space required for a person using a wheelchair to do a full 360° turn is a circle with a diameter of about 1.5 metres. What is the area of that turn space and could it be accommodated within your classroom?

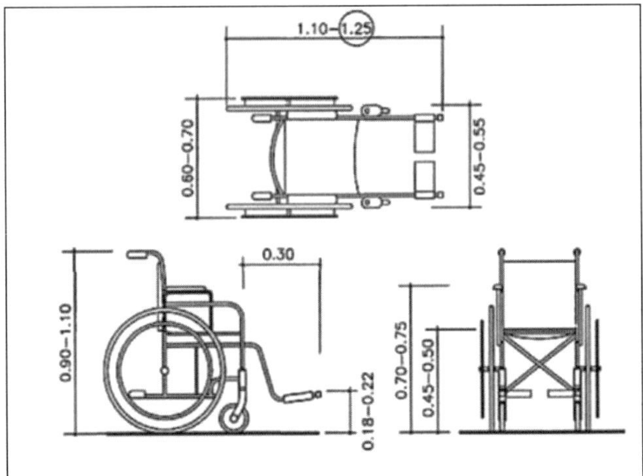

13. Use this diagram of a wheelchair[127] to design a work-space table that would accommodate a person using the chair. The measurements are given in metres, and where a range is given, it indicates the variance in different models of chairs. Draw your table from the two side views.

14. Has anyone noticed that these questions all have to do with physical access barriers, rather than barriers caused by people's prejudices? Have a discussion about why the physical barriers are less important than overcoming people's prejudices.

- As a class, brainstorm and identify organizations in your community that contribute to the advancement of rights for people living with disabilities. Invite someone in to speak about access in your city.

- Visit a local organization that lobbies for the rights of people with disabilities. What are the issues that are most pressing? How does one help?

---

125 Strickland, Susan andCraig Birdsong, *Simple Home Modifications for the Disabled*, 2001, http://health.medscape.com/cx/viewarticle/202952

126 Ibid.

127 http://www.un.org/esa/socdev/enable/designm/AD5-02.htm

Too Close For Comfort

"There are many shelters that do not meet the UN standards for refugee camps in terms of public health measures."[128]

Tuberculosis (TB) is a disease caused by the bacteria Mycobacterium tuberculosis. One third of the world's people are infected and each year two million people die from the disease. But tuberculosis does not infect people equally: people who live in **poverty** are more likely to contract the illness.

Homeless shelters are places where people can go to seek warmth, sometimes food, and a bed or, more usually, a sleeping mat for the night. They are run by **non-governmental organizations (NGOs)**, funded by the government and private donation. Government cuts to funding, less **affordable housing**, increased powers to landlords to set the cost of rent and evict tenants and low or frozen **minimum wages** all contribute to **homelessness** and cause the number of people using shelters to increase.[129]

Sometimes people who are homeless choose to sleep on the streets even though it is very cold and there are spaces in the shelters. One reason is the possibility of getting sick from sleeping in very close quarters. The distance between sleeping mats can be as small as 36 centimetres and most shelters are consistently over 90% full.

128 *TB or not TB? There is no question.* June 2003 Report of A Public Inquiry into the State of Tuberculosis Within Toronto's Homeless Population p. 1-16 www.tdrc.net/TB_Report.pdf Tuberculosis Action Group TBAG p.6
129 Ibid.

Can you think of other possible reasons why people might choose the streets over the shelters?

understanding using math

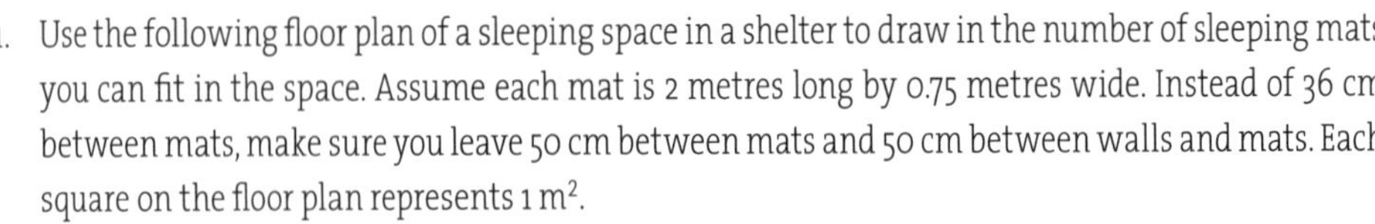

1. Use the following floor plan of a sleeping space in a shelter to draw in the number of sleeping mats you can fit in the space. Assume each mat is 2 metres long by 0.75 metres wide. Instead of 36 cm between mats, make sure you leave 50 cm between mats and 50 cm between walls and mats. Each square on the floor plan represents 1 m^2.

2. Calculate the total available floor space (this time, include the washroom area and the entrance).
3. Calculate the rate of people per square metre in this shelter. The **United Nations** sets the standard for space per person in refugee camps at 4.5 to 5 square metres per person. How does the rate for this shelter compare?
4. Calculate the rate of people per washroom in this shelter.
5. Calculate the floor space of your living space in square metres.
6. Calculate the rate of people per square metre in your home.
7. Call a local real estate agent and ask them what the typical square footage is for a house in a wealthy area of your city or town. Assume a family of four lives there. Calculate the rate of people per square metre in that house.

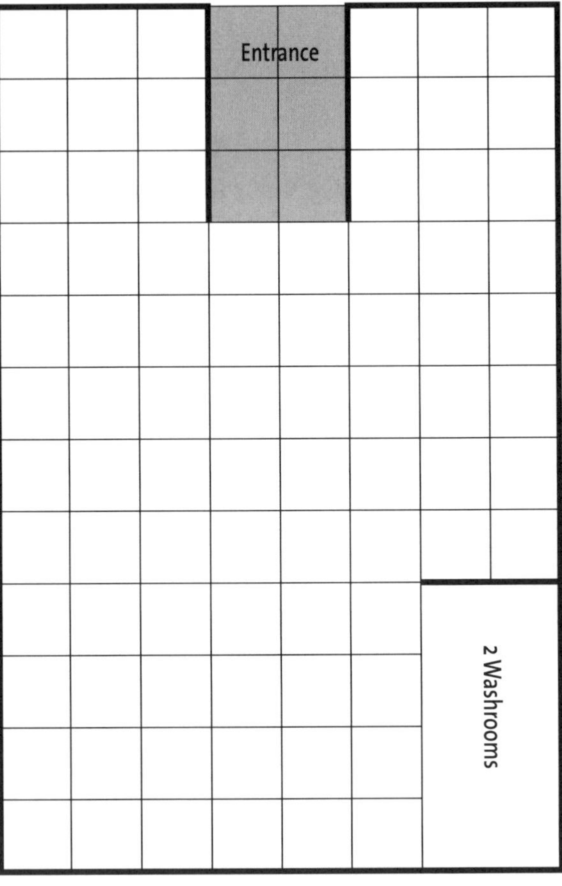

Part of the problem of shelters is what is called **forced migration**. In a program like Out of the Cold, the shelter location is different each night of the week, so people must always be on the move. This is called **transience**. Other shelters have maximum stay lengths, such as two weeks. The combination of close human contact and increased transience can make the spread of disease easier, and tracking the disease more difficult.[130]

130 *Gimme Shelter! Homelessness and Canada's Social Housing Crisis*, Nick Falvo, Centre for Social Justice May 2003 The CSJ Foundation for Research and Education

8. Imagine a person using the shelter system contracts the disease influenza. Due to transience and crowding in shelters, look at the spread of disease in the following chart.

Time, in days	Number of People Infected
0	1
1	2
2	4
3	8
4	
5	
6	
7	
8	
9	
10	

a. Complete the table. State the algebraic equation for this pattern.

b. Graph the results, using time in days for the x-axis and the number of people infected for the y-axis. What kind of growth is this?

c. If the disease was really this contagious, and nothing was done to prevent its spread, how many days would it take for 10,000 people to be infected?

d. What kinds of things cause the spread of disease? What implication does this have for the shelter system?

- Have a shelter worker visit your class to talk about the system in your city or town.
- Visit the National Coalition on Housing and Homelessness and sign the endorsement for a housing solution that works.
- Order and view "Shelter from the Storm" by Michael Connolly and "Street Nurse" from the Toronto Disaster Relief Committee.

Our Home And Native Land?

"The story of modern America begins with the discovery of white man by the Indians"
– Marshall McLuhan

In 1492, Christopher Columbus sailed across the Atlantic Ocean in search of a different trading passage to the riches of India. The fall of Constantinople to the Turks in 1453 was making European trade with Asia difficult, because the Turks now controlled the trade route.

On October 12th, Columbus landed in the Caribbean, on the island of Guanahani. The event would go down in history textbooks as "the discovery", but the death and torture that would be unleashed by Europeans across the continent is perhaps more accurately characterized as **genocide**. Millions of Native Americans would die in the coming centuries.

The first American Indian reserve was created in 1758, followed shortly by the British Proclamation of 1763, informing settlers that they were not to inhabit lands west of the Appalachian Mountains. However, the Indian Removal Act of 1830 forced tribes west of the Mississippi River. In 1887, the Dawes Act split reservation lands into small family holdings which were then swindled away.[131]

131 Bigelow Bill, and Bob Paterson, *Rethinking Columbus: The Next 500 Years*, 1998 Milwaukee, Wisconsin, p. 155.

In Canada, the government to this day is in conflict with First Nations bands throughout the country, over issues of **treaty rights**, right to **self governance**, clear-cutting and hydro-dam impact on the land, logging and fishing rights, and the legacy of sexual and physical abuse in forced Anglican and Catholic residential boarding schools for native children.[132]

In Canada, "more than 80 church-run, government funded schools operated for nearly a century, beginning in the 1880s."[133] The last residential school closed in 1986. What impact do you imagine these schools had on **First Nations'** culture?

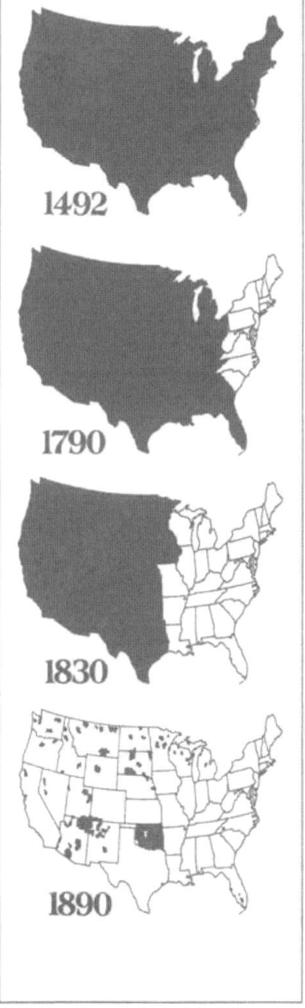

People say that a picture is worth a thousand words. This map by George Russell shows the proportion of land used by hundreds of different First Nations tribes at different points in history. Some numbers also convey information better than others. Fill in the chart below using estimation. Estimate the value for the row "Present day...".

First Nations Land: 1492 to 1890			
Year	Percent	Decimal	Fraction
1492			
1790			
1830			
1890			
Present day...			

1. Which format of number do you find most compelling? Explain your answer.

2. The population of the Americas was about 80 million people in 1492.[134] What is this as a percentage of Canada's current population?

3. In the year 1650, the population of First Nations people in the Americas was 95% less than in 1492, due to massacre, slavery and disease.[135]

   a. How many Native Americans remained by 1650?

   b. How many deaths per day does that amount to?

132 Ibid, p. 142-143.

133 Bigelow Bill, and Bob Paterson, *Rethinking Columbus: The Next 500 Years*, 1998 Milwaukee, Wisconsin, p. 136.

134 *Perspectives*, Spring 1992, p.4.

135 *Perspectives*, Spring 1992, p.4.

4. The following map shows the geographical region involved in a fictional boundary dispute. The provincial government and the Dene First Nations are in conflict over the northern boundary line of the **reserve**, as well as a proposal from Extenda Gas Corporation to drill for oil in land near the reserve.

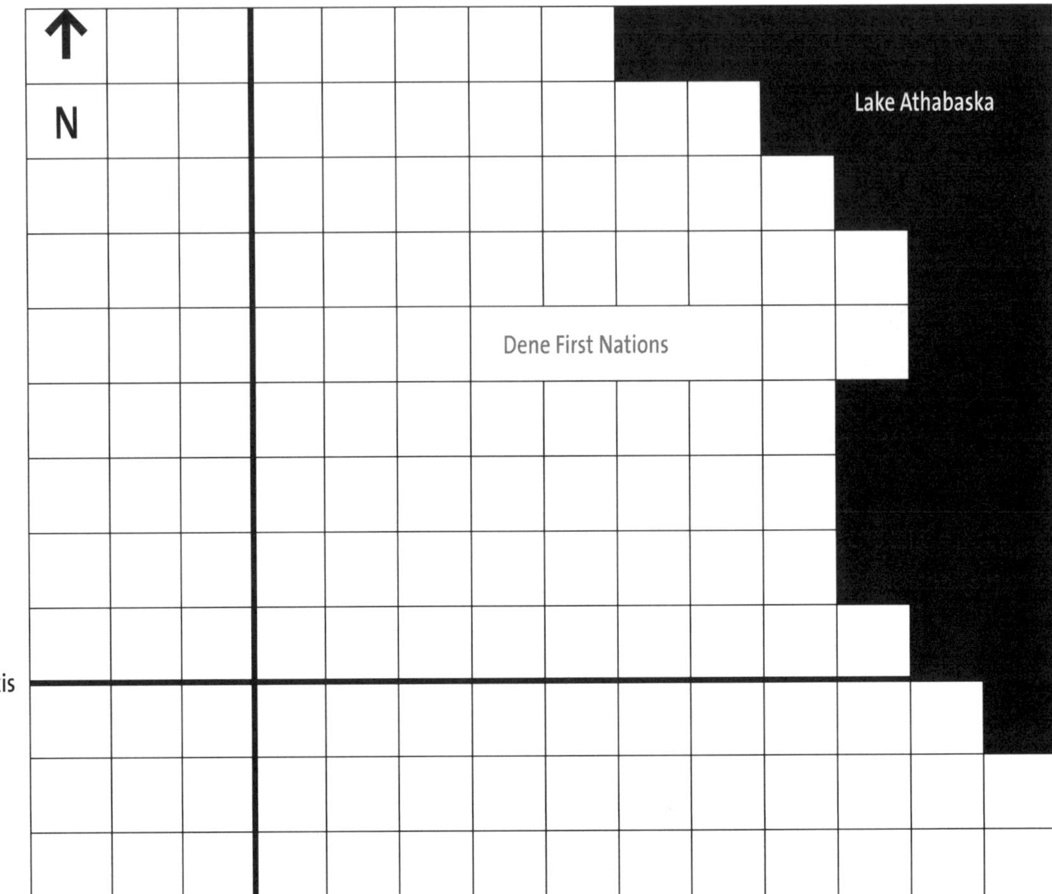

Mark the boundary lines for the Dene First Nations reserve:

a. Government claim: A(10, -1), B (-2,-1), C(-1, 5), D(8, 6) and the shoreline of Lake Athabaska.

b. First Nations claim: A(10, -1), B(-2,-1), C(-1, 5), E(6, 8) and the shoreline of Lake Athabaska.

The government claims that in the year 1879, the land surveyor who marked the land boundary wrote in his logbook that point D on the map was (N 76° E) from point C. The bar that would be in the ground at point D cannot be found.

5. Use your protractor. Is point D (N 76° E) from point C? If not, what point on the Cartesian plane seems likely as the north-eastern boundary?

6. The Dene First Nations claim that the surveyor did not measure and record correctly and point to a surveyor's bar that has been located in the ground at point E. By what angle would the surveyor have to be off, if he made this error?

7. Calculate the following areas, given that each square centimetre represents 1 square kilometre:

    a. The original reserve area proposed by the government.

    b. The reserve area based on the land surveyor's log book.

    c. The reserve area based on the bar in the ground.

8. Which boundary line do you think is the most fair? Explain your answer, and justify why you did not choose each of the other options.

9. A proposed oil well is planned by Extenda Gas at point (5,6). The following **toxicity** report is submitted by research scientists:

Toxicity Report Findings	
Distance from oil well	Toxicity Level
0 km	1.97
1 km	1.94
2 km	1.91
3 km	1.88
4 km	1.85

    a. Create an algebraic equation to describe the toxicity level (t) at any distance (d).

    b. Use a compass and draw **concentric** circles around the oil well site with radii of 1 km, 2 km, 3 km, 4 km, and 5 km.

    c. Use your algebraic equation to figure out the toxicity levels at each distance in (b). Show your work and label your map with the toxicity levels.

10. The safety levels for toxicity produced by the oil well are researched by the following three groups. Each group finds a different acceptable level:

Safety Standards	
Source	Acceptable Toxicity Level
Extenda Gas	1.96
Third party research lab	1.86
Research lab hired by Dene First Nations	1.80

    a. Use your algebraic equation to figure out the distances from the oil well that would be associated with each of the toxicity levels in the above chart. Show your work.

    b. Draw the three concentric circles on the map to show your distances in (a).

    c. Extenda Gas producing acceptable toxicity levels is referred to as a **conflict of interest**. Find out what this term means and explain it in the context of this situation.

    d. What motivation might the government have for suggesting the north eastern boundary point as (8, 6)?

11. A river runs through the territory. Mark out the river based on the following coordinates: (-3,9), (-2,8), (-1,8), (0,7), (1,5), (6,5), (7,2) and (8,2). Does this river change the assessment of risk in your opinion? Explain.

12. What would your recommendations be to solve this conflict? Justify your answer.

Food for thought...

In 1992, approximately $7 billion was spent to celebrate the 500th anniversary of the "discovery" of America. Canada's contribution was $40 million.

First Nations Canadians were allowed to vote beginning in 1961.

The average personal incomes of Canadian First Nations people living on a reserve are approximately half of the Canadian average.

- Learn more about First Nations' struggles in Canada, by researching the Lubicon Cree, the shooting of Dudley George at Ipperwash, the conflict at Oka or Caledonia, the struggle at the Grassy Narrows Reserve, or any number of others.
- Watch the movie *Kanesetake: 270 Years of Resistance*, a documentary about the conflict at Oka in 1990.
- Explore some of the following websites, listed in Rethinking Columbus:
- www.dickshovel.com for information about the American Indian Movement
- www.planet-peace.org for information on current First Nations' struggles
- www.cradleboard.org for links to many First Nations' sites
- Invite a speaker to your classroom from a local First Nations' advocacy organization.

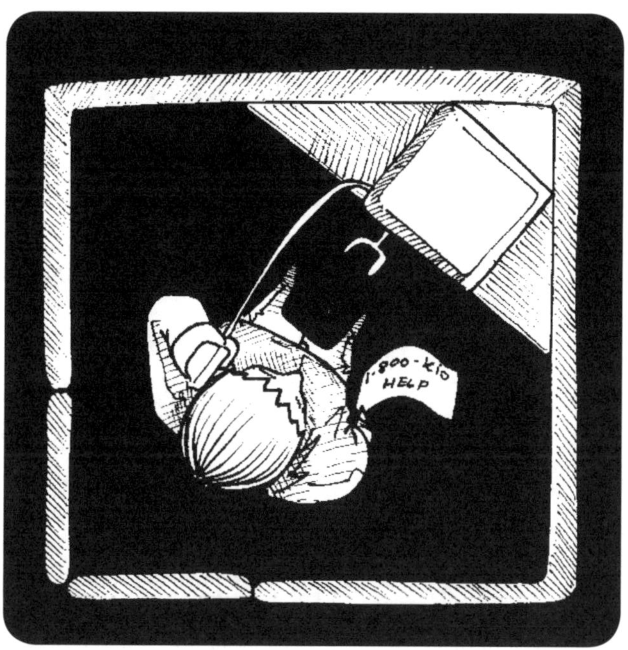

Larger Than Life

"All the world is full of suffering. It is also full of overcoming."
– Helen Keller

In the 1950s, the suicide rate for adults and elderly people were four and eight times, respectively, the suicide rate for youth. But in the past half century the rate for youth aged 15 to 24 has tripled, while adult and elderly rates have dropped. Suicide is now the second or third leading cause of death for youth in the United States, Canada, Australia, New Zealand and many countries of Western Europe.[136]

Good quality studies of thousands of people tell us that more often than not, suicide attempts are a signal for help rather than an effort to end one's life. We know that girls attempt suicide more often, while boys complete suicide more often, and that the contagion effect (where one incident leads to other incidents) is more evident in youth. We also know that divorce rates are highly **correlated** with youth suicide rates.[137]

Level of wealth, drug use, experience of victimization, **delinquency**, sexual activity, race, access to guns and quality of relationships within the family are all other factors. Figuring out which are the real roots of the problem and which are other expressions of the underlying problem is crucial to providing and increasing the support that people need.

---

136 Cutler, David and Edward Glaeser, Karen Norberg. *Harvard Institute of Economic Research*, Discussion Paper #1917 "Explaining the Rise in Youth Suicide" March 2001, abstract.
137 Ibid, p.5-9.

Why do you think that suicide is something that isn't often talked about, especially with youth?

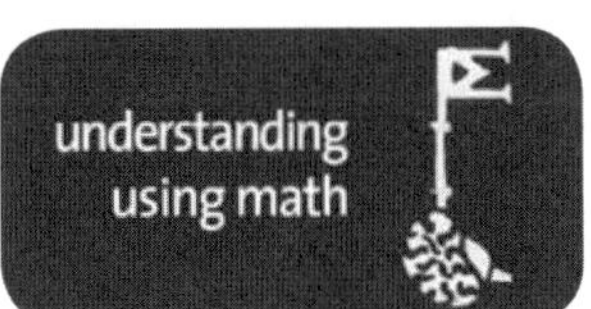

1. The overall rate of suicide in Canada is approximately 14 people per 100,000 per year.

    a. Approximately how many people does that amount to each year?

    b. Why do you think this number is typically given as a rate, rather than the absolute number that you calculated in part (a).

    c. The rate of 14 per 100,000 is an **average** of all Canadians. What this number hides is that some groups of Canadians will have higher rates and some will have lower rates. Name two groups that you think will have higher rates and explain your reasoning.

    d. Why might it be useful to break down the average rate into subcategories?

2. If you know that the ratio between the rate of **First Nations** young men between the ages of 15 and 24 who commit suicide and the overall Canadian rate is 6.4:1, what is the actual rate of suicide for First Nations young men between the ages of 15 and 24? What factors do you think contribute to this difference?

3. In the United States, the number of teens who complete suicide is one hundredth of one percent of the population. The number who attempt suicide is 4%.[138] How many times greater than the number of completions is the number of attempts, and why might this suggest that people are more often looking for help rather than attempting to end their lives?

4. The following statistics come from some years ago in the United States.[139] Some people suggest that the accidents rate might be lower while the suicide rate might be higher. Explain how that might be so.

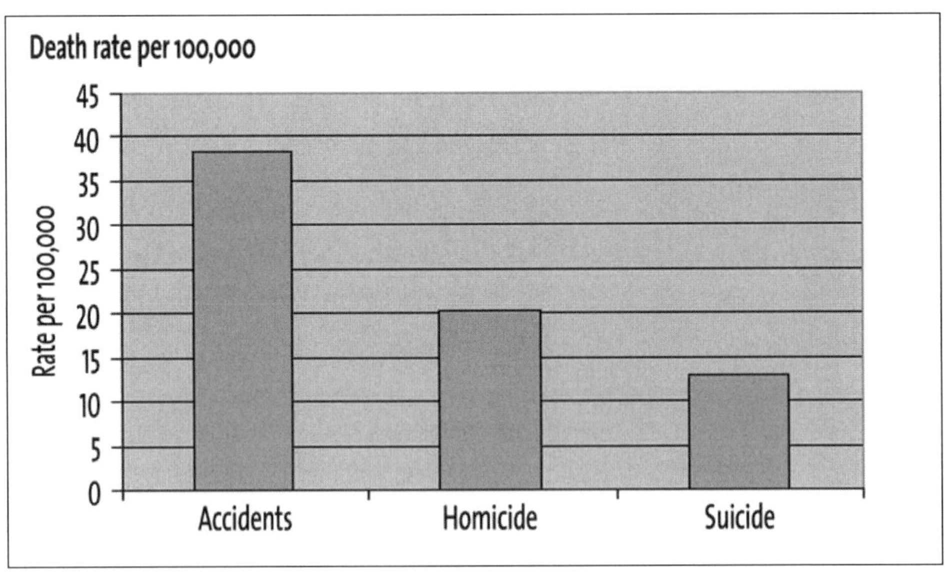

138 David Cutler, Edward Glaeser, Karen Norberg. *Harvard Institute of Economic Research*, Discussion Paper #1917 "Explaining the Rise in Youth Suicide" March 2001, p. 1.

139 David Cutler, Edward Glaeser, Karen Norberg. *Harvard Institute of Economic Research*, Discussion Paper #1917 "Explaining the Rise in Youth Suicide" March 2001, p. 8.

5. A pro-traditional families (i.e. marriage between man and woman) group uses the following two graphs and says that there is a definite correlation between divorce rates and suicide rates: as the divorce rate goes up, so too does the suicide rate. Use the Divorce Act dates from this graph and circle the same dates in the graph in question 6.

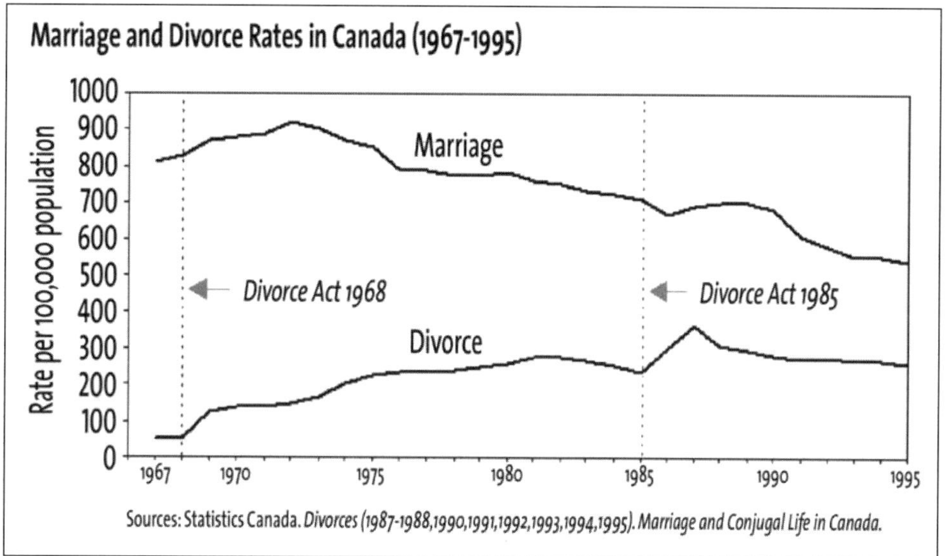

140

6. Review the following graph.

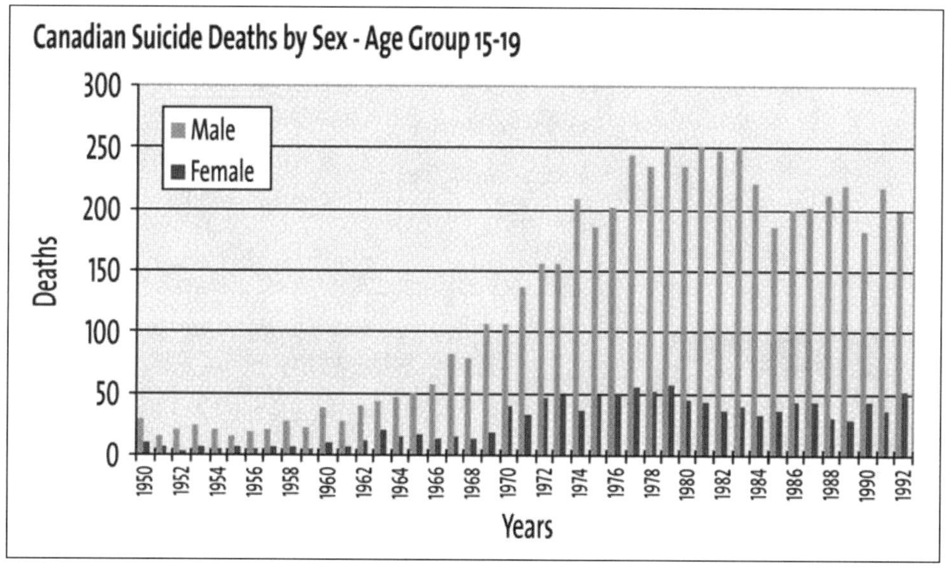

141

a. What do you notice about the difference between male and female suicide deaths? Why do you think this might be so?

b. Although there is a correlation between increased divorce rates and increased suicide rates, it does not mean that the relationship is **causal** (i.e. that one causes the other). Use the empty circles in the graphic on the following page to suggest reasons why the divorce rate has increased and why those may be better explanations for the increased suicide rate.

c. Why would it make a difference knowing the root causes of the problem - how might the solutions be different if you focused only on the increased divorce rate?

---

140 Selected Statistics on Canadian Families and Family Law — November 1997, Department of Justice
141 *Suicide in Canada* (1994), Mental Health Division, Health Services Directorate, Health Canada

d. Why do you think that a pro-traditional family group might have been making this point about increased divorce rates and suicide?

7. A group that wants fewer restrictions on guns presents the following table and claims that it proves that higher restrictions on guns lead to higher suicide rates. Analyze the table below and comment on the validity of the claim. Look for contradictions.

GUN CONTROL AND SUICIDE

Country — Level of restriction on civilian ownership of firearms	Suicide Rate
Denmark — high	31.6
Sweden — high	20.5
Norway — high	13.3
Scotland — high	10.1
England /Wales — high	6.7
Ireland — high	6.6
Japan — severe	14.3
Canada — moderate	12.3
Australia — moderate	12.2
USA — low	12.0
Israel — low	6.0

- Invite a public health nurse in to your classroom to talk about suicide
- Visit a local walk in clinic or crisis centre with the class, meet with the support people there, and get a tour.
- Look at the following support line numbers for Toronto and try to locate similar support groups and numbers for your region.
- The following numbers are Toronto support lines that are staffed by people who are trained to listen and to help. Calls can be made anonymously if you want information but don't want to give your name. Other adults who you trust are also good people to tell.

Kids Help Phone	1 800 668 6868
Rape Crisis	416 597 8808
Children's Aid Society	416 924 4646
Sexual Assault Care Centre	416 323 6040
Youth Link Support	416 922 3335
Gay Lesbian Bisexual Youth Line	416 962 9688 (4- 9:30 Sun-Fri.)

For local crisis and support lines in your community, please look in the front section of your phone book.

Do You Have Confidence In Those Results?

"Mud sometimes gives the illusion of depth."

– Marshall McLuhan

Two crucial factors surround the processes of taking **polls** and **surveys**: **validity** and **reliability**. Validity means that the data you collect is actually relevant to what you're trying to measure. For example, unless it's damaged, a thermometer is an accurate indicator of air temperature: the data you collect from it about temperature is valid. On the other hand, a common assertion is that there are more babies born and more crime during a full moon, but from careful research, we know that using the moon to measure number of births and the amount of crime is not valid.

Reliability asks, even if your measurement tool measures what you say it measures, does it do so in a consistent way, all of the time? A radar gun used by the police gives a valid measurement of car speed, but if it is damaged it could return unreliable data.

Confidence intervals are oftentimes mentioned in newspaper stories that cite research statistics. When you read, "The number of voters who prefer Candidate X is 35%, plus or minus 3%, and the results are accurate 19 times in 20", the author is saying that 95% of the time, results will fall between 32% and 38%. We can be more confident with a survey of more people, but it costs money to increase sample sizes.[142] A rough guide would suggest that a random sample of 100 people or less creates a confidence interval too wide to be reliable, while a sample of 1,000 people or more is reliable for most purposes.

142 Paulos, John Allen, *Innumeracy*. Hill and Wang, New York. 1988 p.111.

During election time, a newspaper article's title says "Conservative Party takes the lead: 33% support, versus the Liberal's 32%". The results, plus or minus 2%, are accurate 19 times out of 20. Explain why the title of the article is meaningless.

1. A student fills in a multiple choice test in science. When the mark is returned, the student receives a 35%. What are some of the reasons that the test mark might not be a valid indicator of this student's understanding of the science material? (These reasons are called **intervening and confounding variables.**[143])

2. You design a questionnaire to determine how people feel about skateboard parks. You then take the survey to 300 businesses in an area where the park is being considered for construction. 82% of the businesses respond that they think the park is a bad idea. If you wrote a news article for the local paper, what would be inaccurate about the title "Resistance inevitable: survey says 82% of people are opposed to skateboard park"?

3. Explain how it would be possible for 85% of the community to think a skateboard park would be a great idea, and how you could still get the results in question #2 above. Is this a problem of validity or reliability?

4. A survey in the paper says that 75% of people polled say that in the next election they will vote for the Green Party. Assuming that the survey was indeed random (for example, you weren't at a Green Party convention), what other question would you need to ask in order to verify reliability?

5. One of your favorite singers is promoting a particular food product, saying that it's the best product around. Is this a problem of validity or reliability or both? Explain.

6. A newspaper reports that a survey done on unemployment shows that it has dropped from 8.2% last year to 8.0% this year. The survey is accurate plus or minus 0.8%, 19 times out of 20. Explain why unemployment may have in fact increased from last year.

7. Someone trying to find out the answer to the question "If you had your choice, would you keep the **World Trade Organization** as it is, modify it, or scrap it altogether?" decides to do a random phone survey. What confounding variables could call into question the reliability of the data that is collected?

8. A magazine article about youth violence ends with a tear out survey about the story. In next month's issue the results of the survey are published. What confounding variables could call into question the reliability of the survey results?

---

143 Sagor, Richard, www.ascd.org/publications/books/100047/chapter9.html

9. A study is done on 4,644 patients to test the **efficacy** of a particular drug for treating cardiovascular disease. Half of the group gets the **placebo** and the other half gets the trial drug. The results are summarized as follows. Fill in the empty cells.

	Group taking drug	Group taking placebo
Cardiovascular event occurs, including death	651	826
Percentage of study group (half the total group):		

a. What is the relative risk? The relative risk is the event rate of the group taking the drug (event/number in group) divided by the event rate of the people taking the placebo (event/number in group).

b. For a 95% confidence interval, the range is your answer in part (a) plus or minus 8%. What is the range of relative risk?

c. Does your range include the value of 100%? If it did, what could that possibly mean?

d. Even given your range in part (b), is it possible that there is no difference between taking the drug and using the placebo? Explain.

In response to statistical results, always ask the following questions:

- How can I tell if the test or survey is valid?
- How can I tell if the test or survey is reliable?
- What is the confidence interval for the data?

The Weekend's Here

"They say that time changes things, but actually you have to change them yourself."

– Andy Warhol

Unions are organizations that started forming in Canada in the early 1800s as a response to bad working conditions.[144] Workers began to come together and **collectively bargain** with their employers for a better state of affairs: safety on the job, fair wages and a humane number of work hours each week. If the **employer** refused to negotiate, the workers could shut down the business by going on **strike**.

In 1794, printers in New York became the first American strikers. A growing number of unions were active by the 1820s, pushing to reduce the workday from 12 to 10 hours. Keep in mind that the work week was six days long at that time.[145] In 1872 the "**Nine Hours Movement**" in Hamilton and Toronto went on strike, an attempt to reduce the workweek to 58 hours[146] and unions became legal that year as a result of the conflict. The Fair Labor Standards Act which reduced the workweek to 40 hours has been in place in the US since 1938.

Although the present workweek is far shorter than it was 150 years ago, a rise in the workload- related stress has caused people to ask: what is going on? Are we returning to longer hours of work?

---

144 http://www.gciu.org/histcan.shtml Education Department of the Canadian Labour Congress "The Canadian labour movement."

145 http://www.socialstudieshelp.com/Eco_Unionization.htm Feb. 20, 2004

146 Hess, Suzanne. *The History of Labour Day.* http://www.historytelevision.ca/archives/labourDay/history/ Feb 20, 2004.

What benefits can you think of for reducing the number of hours in a workweek? Can you think of any drawbacks?

understanding using math

1. Based on the stem-and-leaf graph, answer the following questions:

Number Of Hours Worked Each Week (1999 Data)

Stem	Leaf
5	1, 2, 4, 9
4	0, 1, 6, 8, 9
3	7, 7, 7, 8, 9, 9
2	1, 7, 8, 8, 9

a. How many workers are in this sample?

b. What is the **mean**, **median** and **mode** for this data?

2. Based on this second stem-and-leaf graph from the same workplace five years later answer the following questions:

Number Of Hours Worked Each Week (2007 Data)

Stem	Leaf
5	4, 5, 6, 6, 7, 7, 9
4	1, 9, 9
3	7, 7, 7
2	1, 1, 2, 2, 3, 3, 4

a. How many workers are in this sample?

b. What is the **mean**, **median** and **mode** for this data?

3. Some **employees** are starting to report feelings of stress and exhaustion. The employer claims that by any average, nothing has changed. Is this true? How would you respond?

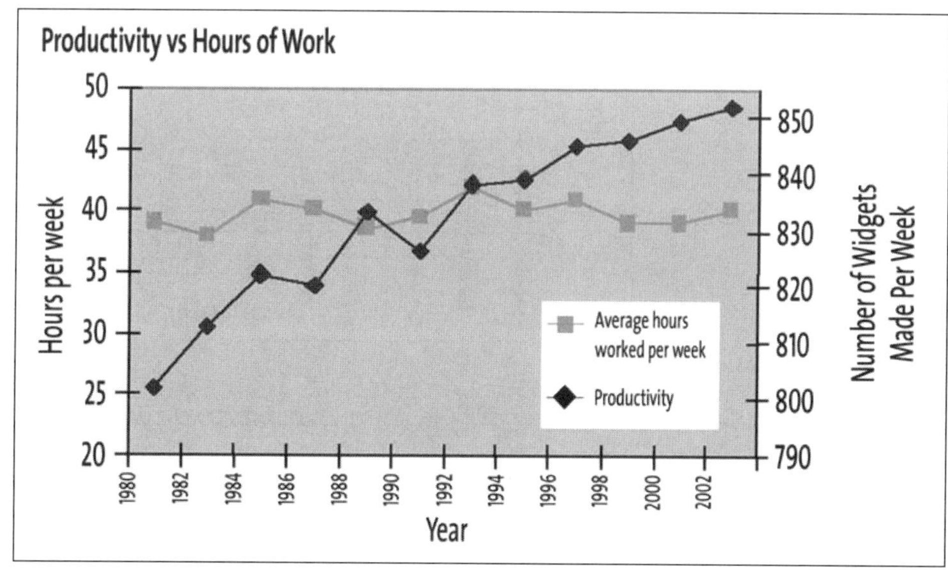

4. **Productivity** means the amount of work done in a certain amount of time. In the graph above, it means how many **widgets** a worker made per week.

   a. What is happening to the average hours that these employees work every week?

   b. What is happening to the number of widgets that each employee is making each week?

   c. Tick off all of the boxes below that you think could explain the observations you made in 4.a. and 4.b.

   - ❑ Better technology was introduced to make more widgets.
   - ❑ Better division of labour increased the number of widgets produced.
   - ❑ The complexity of the widget design was increased.
   - ❑ The employees were encouraged or threatened to speed up their work.
   - ❑ The complexity of the widget design was decreased.
   - ❑ Employees were working fewer hours per week.
   - ❑ Employees were working overtime hours and not reporting them.
   - ❑ Your own idea: ______________________________

5. Which options from the above list would cost the employer the most money? Which options would cost the employer the least money?

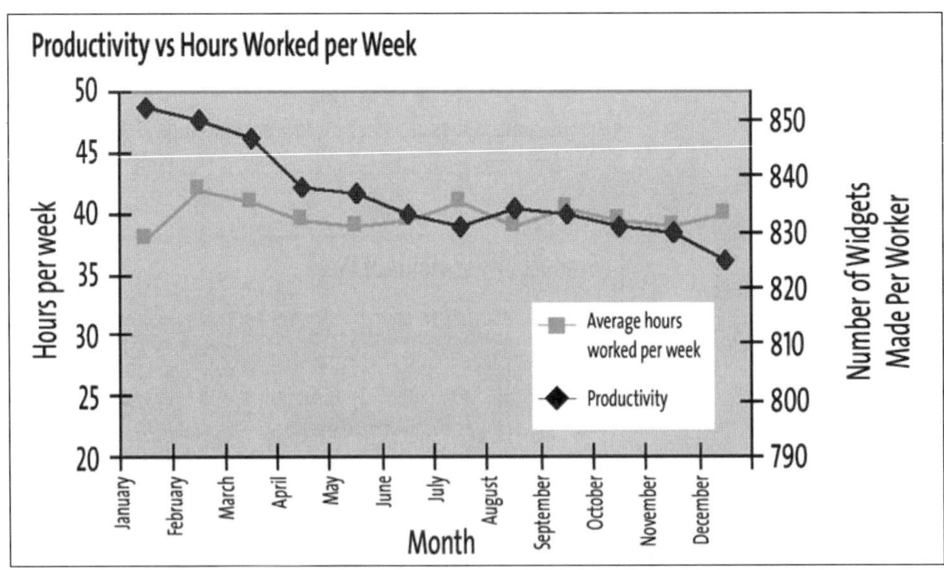

6. The above graph is a continuation of the next twelve months at the same workplace as the previous graph.

   a. What is happening with the number of hours worked each week?

   b. What is happening to the productivity?

   c. How might you explain what is happening in this workplace in these twelve months, given that productivity had been rising steadily for the past 22 years?

7. The employer argues that the cost of the products will need to go up in a unionized environment.

	Cost Product A	Cost Product B	Cost Product C	Cost Product D
Before unionization	$4.25	$12.99	$7.89	$24.99
After unionization	$5.02	$15.33	$9.31	$29.49

a. In this imaginary scenario, what is the relationship between the cost of products before the workplace is unionized and the cost of products after the workplace is unionized?

b. Write an algebraic equation to show the relationship between the two costs.

c. If a different product costs $67.35 before a union exists, how much will it cost after the union exists, according to the above chart.

d. Why might the cost of products increase in a unionized environment?

e. In this scenario, who pays for the increased demands of a unionized environment and why might this become a problem for the *employer?*

f. Can you think of a business today that markets itself on low prices? What is it, and do you think that they have unions?

8. In the 1980s, Ford, GM and Chrysler found that their workers worked an average of 45 seconds for every minute on the job. By changing the way the production was organized they got their workers to average 57 seconds for every minute on the job.[147]

a. In a forty hour work week, what is the difference in work time between the two rates of work speed?

b. How might the change in work speed affect the workers?

9. In Jonquière Quebec a group of employees were fighting to make their Walmart the first unionized Walmart. The chain employs 1.3 million workers in over 4,300 stores world wide and has more than 244.5 billion dollars in annual global revenues. The following graph compares the low and high end wages in unionized and non unionized grocery chains in Jonquière.[148]

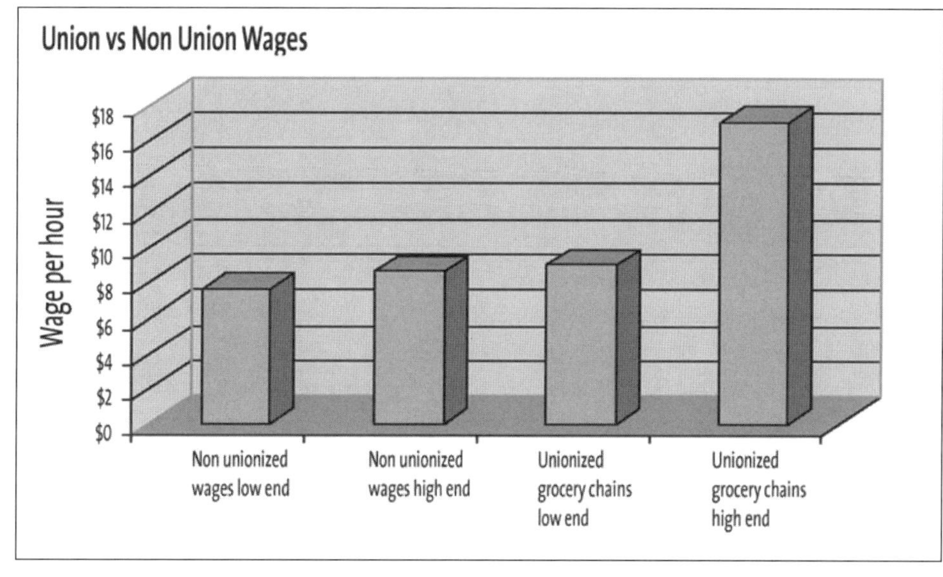

147 Gindin, Sam. Lecture notes. Social Justice course. Winter 2004.
148 *Toronto Star*, Jan. 31, 2004, D16.

a. What do you notice about the wages between unionized and non unionized workplaces?

b. Why do you think Walmart is so opposed to unions?

c. What do you think happened to the store in Jonquière? Find out...

- Have a union representative visit your classroom to talk about current issues and ways that workers can benefit from unions.
- Have a conversation with a person on a strike's picket line. What are the issues?

Is Justice Blind?

"It took me more than thirty years to learn that, unlike being male or being black, being nigger wasn't coded into my DNA."
– Carl Upchurch

Capital punishment, also known as the "death penalty", has not occurred in Canada since 1962, but does occur in 38 states in the USA. For the following reasons, there are a growing number of **critics** of capital punishment:[149]

1. According to a study of death penalty judgments over 23 years, the rate of error nationally was 68%. In other words, more than two thirds of those sentenced to be executed were later determined to be innocent.

2. States having the death penalty do not have lower crime rates or lower murder rates than states without the death penalty. In other words, the theory that the death penalty stops people from committing crime is highly doubtful.

3. Most people who are put to death are poor, and as such must rely on court-appointed lawyers who are notoriously under-paid, and in many cases incompetent or not motivated or able to properly defend their clients because of large caseloads.

4. The percentage of "black" people who are executed is grossly disproportionate to the percentage of people who are black in the United States. One of many studies showed that prosecutors tried to get the death penalty for 70% of black defendants with white victims, but only 15% of white defendants with black victims.

149 American Civil Liberties Union *Briefing Paper #14*, Spring 1999 www.aclu.org

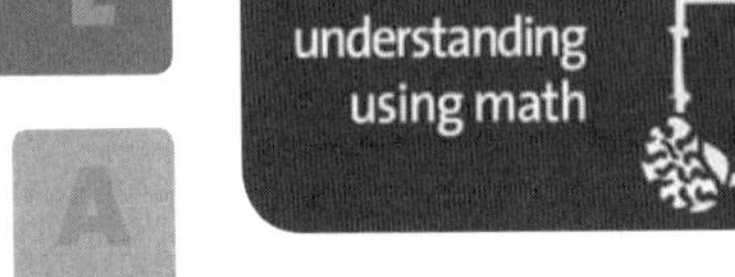

The total number of people executed since 1976 in the United States is 921 (as of July 23, 2004). In the south region of the U.S., 757 people have been executed since 1976. What percentage is that of the total and why do you think that it is so high? (Texas and Virginia alone account for 414 of the 757).

1. Open a **spreadsheet** program and create the following chart:

"Race"**	Percentage of Population	Percentage of Executions
White	80	56
Black	12	35
Other	8	9

**The idea of "race" is a complicated one: for an overview, see: "Does Race Exist?" by Michael Bamshad and Steve Olson in *Scientific American* December 2003, pp. 80-85

2. Choose a chart that best represents the data. Make sure to enter titles and labels. Print out your graph and hand it in with the assignment.

3. What do you notice about the comparison between the percentage of people who are "white" and executed and the percentage of people who are "white" in the United States.

4. What do you notice about the comparison between the percentage of people who are "black" and executed and the percentage of people who are "black" in the United States.

5. Upper and Lower Canada had the death penalty for murder, treason and rape in 1865. Executions in Canada continued until the last two hangings took place at the Don Jail in Toronto in 1962. Capital punishment was finally removed from the **Canadian Criminal Code** in 1976.[150] Find out how old your parents were in 1962 and if they remember that incident.

6. The **incarceration** rate in the United States is 725 per 100,000 people (the highest in the world).[151] What percentage of the people in the States is incarcerated? Why do you think the wealthiest country in the world imprisons the most number of its people?

7. The incarceration rate for African American males in America is 4,834 per 100,000. Compare this rate to the average rate in question 6 and explain how the average hides the reality for African Americans.

8. The overall chance that you will serve time in prison at some point in your life in the United States is 1 in 130: unless you're an African American man, in which case the chance that you'll serve time is one chance in three.[152] How many times greater is a one in three chance over a 1 in 130 chance?

---

150 http://canadaonline.about.com/library/weekly/aa072702a.htm
151 www.prisonactivist.org "10 Things You Should Know About Prisons in the U.S".
152 lwww.prisonactivist.org "10 Things You Should Know About Prisons in the U.S".

9. Of the more than 2 million prisoners in the States, more than 111,000 are in prisons run by private **corporations** for **profit** (like Wackenhut and CCA).[153] Explain why a for-profit prison system may not be in the interests of prisoners.

10. Find out from someone you know what the expression "justice is blind" means. Explain it in your own words.

Fast facts:

Number of youth executed in the United States in the past 25 years: **18**.

As of mid 2003, the number of youth on death row in the United States: **78**. Of those, 28 are in Texas alone.[154]

Other countries that execute youth: Iran, Pakistan, Yemen, Nigeria, Saudi Arabia.[155]

Spending on K-12 education in the U.S. in the past 20 years increased 33.4%. Spending on incarceration rose 571.4% in that same time.[156]

- Take a look at resources at www.prisonactivist.org (they have a youth section too: www.prisonactivist.org/youth) and Sister Helen Prejean's website www.moratoriumcampaign.org.
- Each year, Prisoners' Justice Day is on August 10th, in memory of Eddie Nalon who died in Millhaven prison in 1974. Prisoners refuse work and do not eat, while supporters raise public awareness about the conditions inside prisons, psychiatric institutions, immigration detention centres and youth prisons. See if anything is happening in your neighbourhood. Is it mentioned in the papers? Why or why not?
- Up to date information on execution figures can be found at www.deathpenaltyinfo.org.

---

153 www.prisonactivist.org "What is the Prison Industrial Complex?"
154 Prejean, Helen. *The Death of Innocents*. Random House. New York, 2004, p.210.
155 *The Globe and Mail*, "Digging a grave for capital punishment?", May 11, 2002, A3.
156 www.prisonactivist.org "Education vs. Incarceration: a stacked deck".

Driving While Black

"Pre conceived notions are the locks on the door to wisdom."

– Merry Browne

Racial profiling –vb. "any action undertaken for reasons of safety, security or public protection that relies on stereotypes about race, colour, ethnicity, ancestry, religion, or place of origin rather than on reasonable suspicion, to single out an individual for greater scrutiny or different treatment."[157]

In October of 2002, the *Toronto Star* newspaper published a series on racial profiling, using a police **database** of all Toronto arrests and charges from 1996 to 2002. Confirmed by a statistician at York University, the analysis found first, that people who are black and charged with simple drug possession are taken into custody more often than people who are white, and second, that black motorists are ticketed more often than white motorists for offences discovered after their cars were stopped.[158]

The Toronto Police Association brought a $2.7 billion **libel suit** against *The Star*, arguing that the series implied that all police officers are racists and **bigots** but the judge dismissed the suit, saying that no claim for libel can be made unless individuals are singled out. He also found a direct quote in the articles, clearly stating that to suggest that all officers were racists was **untenable**.

157 http://english2.globetrotter.net/news/cbc/canada/fs.cfm?source_id=CBC&id=1478466 Dec 9, 2003.
158 Tyler, Tracey, www.thestar.ca "Judge dismisses suit against Star" *Toronto Star*, June 25, 2003.

Both sides used the same raw data from the same database to make their arguments and came to different conclusions. Knowing how they approached the data should help you to decide which conclusion is **credible** and which is **smokescreen**. For some portions of our society, the answer may already be obvious.

Why is the fact that *The Star* used an independent statistician rather than its own staff crucial to the credibility of its analysis?

1. One area that *The Star* survey looked at was simple drug possession charges. In these cases, a police officer has some choice as to how to proceed. The officer can hand out a ticket and the offender later appears in court, or the offender can be taken into custody.

   Although the following actual numbers are **fabricated**, the pattern is accurate based on the survey.[159] What can you tell about the rate at which people who are black and people who are white are brought into custody on simple drug possession charges? Express your answer as an algebraic expression and as a ratio.

	Number brought into custody
Black offender	3004
White offender	1502

2. One criticism of the survey was that other factors ("variables") like previous criminal record, employment status, age, citizenship or country of birth might have accounted for the difference. *The Star* responded by explaining that those variables were taken into account. How could you design your analysis to eliminate the possibility that other factors were to blame? Pick one of the above variables and describe your strategy.

3. The professor that the Police Association hired to dispute the statistics removed eight of the 16 police divisions from his analysis. He argued that because the black population in those divisions was less than 6% the number was too small to be a valid sample.[160] Can you think of some reasons why removing the figures from small black populations in largely white neighbourhoods could have a big impact on the study? Explain.

4. The numbers that the Police Association analyzed used impaired driving data. In these situations, police have no choice and have to bring offenders into custody. Why might a situation where police officers have no choice be less useful than analysis of situations where police officers have choice?

159 Ibid.
160 "The Star's response **S**to the critics." *Toronto Star*, March 1, 2003.

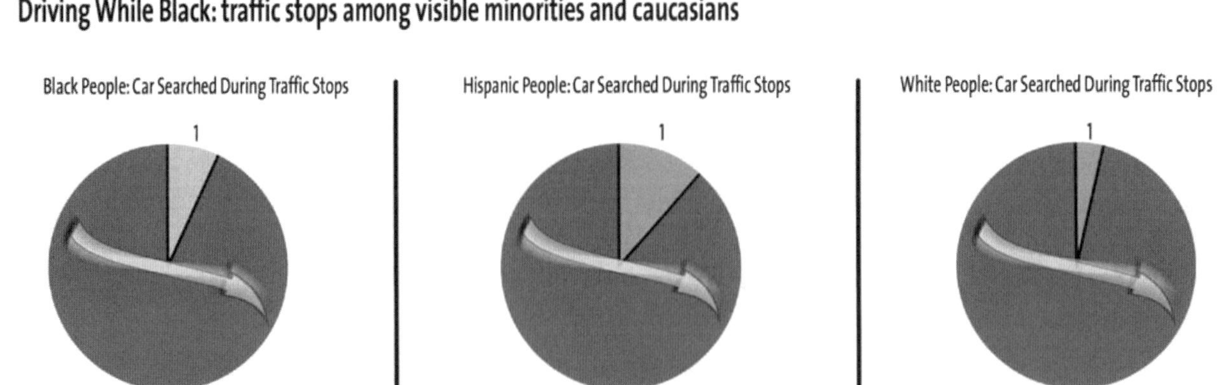

5. Beginning in January of 2002, police in Texas were required to track data on traffic stops resulting in **traffic citations** or arrests, and produce an annual report. The report produced the following results from Dallas[161] – represented as probability spinners:

    a. What is the probability that, if you are a person who is black and your car is stopped by the police in Dallas it will be searched?

    b. What is the probability that, if you are a person who is Hispanic and your car is stopped by the police in Dallas it will be searched?

    c. What is the probability that, if you are a person who is white and your car is stopped by the police in Dallas it will be searched?

6. For ten days in February of 2003, the Ontario Human Rights Commission asked people to call, write or email reports detailing experiences where they felt **discriminated** against based on their race. Six hundred reports flooded in.

    a. What is the average number of reports they received per day?

    b. Do you think that they received the average each day? What factors might the Commission want to consider so that they reach the broadest number of people?

161 "Blacks targets of police searches in Texas" *Toronto Star*, March 5, 2003

7. Adult **Aboriginal** persons are put in jail more than six times the national rate. Discuss the implications of the following chart.[162]

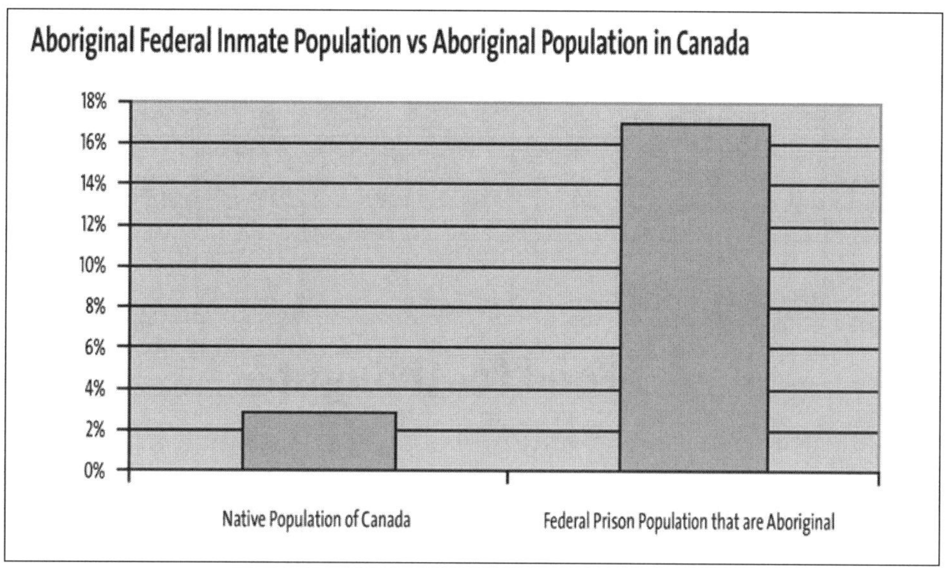

8. The following statistics have been collected on the make-up of the Toronto police force (the first two categories are for 2004 and the third category is for 2001).[163]

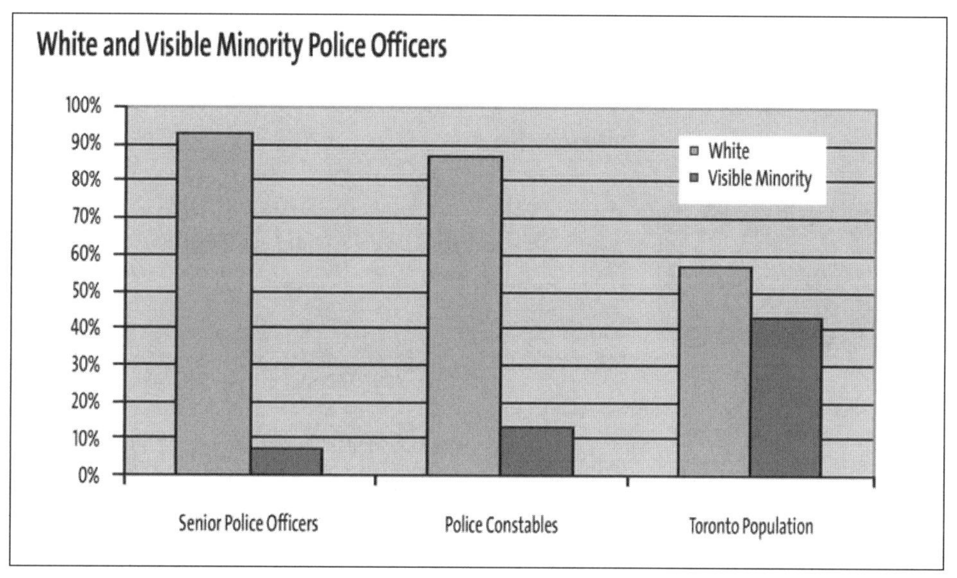

a. What do think these findings add to the discussion on racial profiling?

b. The solved murder rate for Toronto used to be almost 100%, and now has fallen to 52.3%. Although more of the victims today are young and black, the overall murder rate has not changed in decades.[164] Discuss, with the graph in mind.

---

162 Ontario Human Rights Commission. *The Impact of Racial Profiling on the Aboriginal Community*. www.ohrc.on.ca p.6.
163 Ruby, Clayton. "Fix the racial disconnect." *The Globe and Mail*. March 10,2004.
164 Ibid.

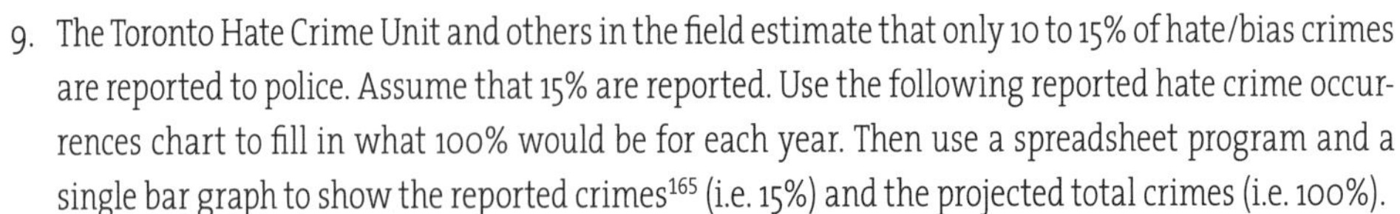

9. The Toronto Hate Crime Unit and others in the field estimate that only 10 to 15% of hate/bias crimes are reported to police. Assume that 15% are reported. Use the following reported hate crime occurrences chart to fill in what 100% would be for each year. Then use a spreadsheet program and a single bar graph to show the reported crimes[165] (i.e. 15%) and the projected total crimes (i.e. 100%).

Year	1993	1994	1995	1996	1997	1998	1999	2000	2001	2002	2003
Reported total	155	249	302	175	187	228	292	204	338	219	149
Projected total											

Food for thought...

Early European settlers in Canada had slaves of both Aboriginal and African descent. Canadian **Immigration policy** officially excluded people from China and gave preference to white Europeans for decades. African Canadians were **segregated** from whites in the Ontario school system until the 1960s.[166]

"That we have come as far as we have in forty years is hopeful though I believe it is more through the fact that Hitler's excesses made racism poisonous to any human individual than through our own virtue. That we have much further to go is incontestable."
– Isaac Asimov

- Listen to friends who are **visible minorities** about the difficulties that they face living in Canadian society.
- Visit a cultural center in your city or town and learn about a culture different than your own. Make connections with the people working there.
- Invite a police officer into the class room and ask him or her what they are doing to improve community relations. How are they recruiting new police officers that are representative of the community?

165 Toronto Police Service. 2003 *Annual Hate/Bias Crime Statistical Report*
166 *Canada's Creeping Economic Apartheid*. Centre for Social Justice, 2001. P. 43.

Making A Killing

"Children not yet born will have to pay the price of debt for wars they did not fight, for ideas they do not hold, for a regional and global system that no longer exists and for decisions made by regional and world leaders that are no longer in power."[167]

For 45 years, Russia and the United States were locked in an **arms race**, creating enough nuclear weapons to destroy the entire world many times over. In the past 20 years the United Nations has pushed for the dismantling and disposal of nuclear, chemical and biological weapons through a number of **international treaties**.[168]

There are people opposed to **disarmament**. Entire communities that depend on jobs from the **military-industrial complex** face unemployment and **poverty**. Multi-billion dollar defence **corporations** don't want to see their contracts disappear. And some government officials say that implementing the treaties will cost too much.

But there are high costs of conflict as well as failure to disarm. Aside from the money required to build weapons, there remains the environmental damage from aging arms, the reduction of human development from diverted funds, medical costs associated with conflict itself, and the millions of **refugees** created by war.[169] Although some will tell you that nuclear weapons prevent wars, the five declared nuclear countries have been in almost eight times as many wars since 1945 than have non-nuclear countries.[170]

---

167 Susan Willett, *Costs of Disarmament-Rethinking the Price Tag* United Nations Institute for Disarmament Research Geneva, Switzerland 2002 p. 59.
168 Ibid. p. 45.
169 Ibid. p. 50-57.
170 Ibid. p. 40.

Assume disarmament goes ahead. How might you lessen the impact of the short term costs to people who make their living from the military industrial complex?

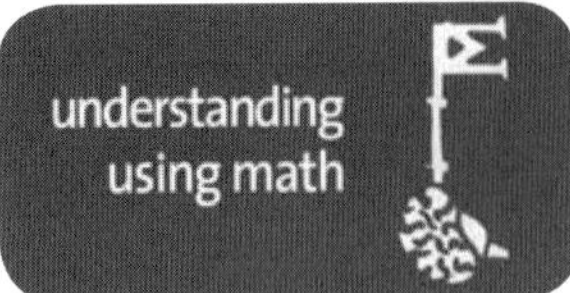

1. Stephen Swartz did extensive research on the costs of the United States nuclear arms program between 1940 and 1996.[171] What do you notice?

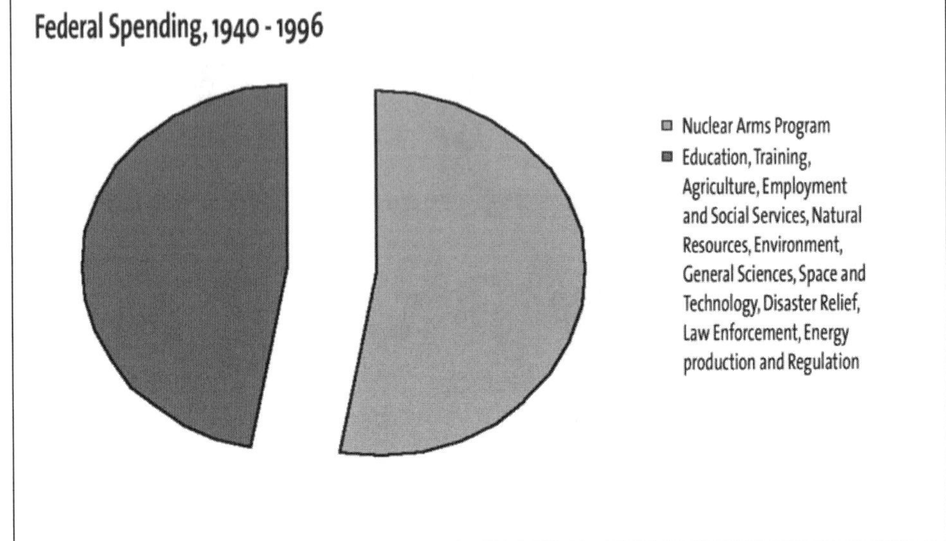

2. 87 countries in the world have landmines, which kill or maim an average of 26,000 people a year.[172] A study of landmine clean-up operations finds the following data.[173]

	Clean-up #1	Clean-up #2	Clean-up #3	Clean-up #4
Number of landmines	450	235	147	312
Cost of clean-up	$292,500	$152,750	$95,550	$202,800

a. What is the algebraic equation that represents the cost to clean up landmines?

b. The actual costs range between $300 and $1,000 per landmine.[174] How would you have to change your equation to account for the low end figure? How about the high end figure?

c. An initial **survey** found that the world had 110 million landmines. How much would that cost to remove, according to your equation in part (a)?

d. The estimate of 110 million landmines is now considered high and has been revised to 60-80 million. What would the new removal costs be, according to your equation in part (a).

e. The cost to make a landmine is $3-$30. What is the ratio of the cost to create landmines to the cost to dispose of landmines?

---

171 Willett, Susan. *Costs of Disarmament-Rethinking the Price Tag* United Nations Institute for Disarmament Research Geneva, Switzerland 2002 p. 51.
172 Ibid. p. 57.
173 Ibid, p.12 (based on real costs but not actual results).
174 Ibid p. 12.

3. In 1987, at the height of the confrontation between the United States and Russia, global military **expenditures** were $1.5 trillion a year. By 1998 that amount had decreased by 50.6%. But at the turn of the millennium expenditures rose by 5%.[175] What are the actual dollar figures for 1998 and 2000?

4. People acted with alarm when long time rivals Pakistan and India developed and tested nuclear bombs. A study was produced to explain to people what a nuclear bomb would do to a city like Bombay (Mumbai).

   The initial blast from a 15 kt bomb would have a projected radius of 1.1 km. There are approximately 23,000 people per square kilometre in Mumbai.[176] How many people would be affected instantly?

5. In 1997 a Chemical Weapons **Convention** stated that all chemical weapons plants and munitions had to be destroyed by 2007. By 2000, the Russian Federation was already asking for a deadline extension for destroying 1% of its chemical weapons **stocks**. One percent of its chemical weapons stocks amounts to 406,400 kg.[177] What is its total stock? Relate this number to something you can understand.

6. Suggest one reason that the destruction of chemical weapons was proceeding so slowly in the Russian Federation.

7. Pascal, a famous mathematician, once argued that if the outcome of some event is particularly large, it is worth considering carefully even if the probability of that event happening is very, very small. Apply his reasoning to the accidental launch of a nuclear missile. (There have been four near launches since 1962- three of them based on accidents in 1979, 1983 and 1995.)[178]

8. Maintaining the US nuclear complex costs $25 billion a year.[179] The clean up of nuclear weapons in the United States alone will cost 300 billion to 1 trillion dollars.[180] Pick one of these amounts and compare it to the cost for a **humanitarian** effort of your choice.

9. Graph the following. Worldwide, one trillion dollars is spent every year on wars while only 80 billion is spent on peace efforts.[181] Imagine what we could do if the numbers were reversed...

10. Using the following graphs,

    a. Calculate the total spending on military worldwide.

    b. Make one comparison of your choice.

---

175 Ibid, pp. 43-46.
176 Ibid, p. 54.
177 Willett, Susan. *Costs of Disarmament-Rethinking the Price Tag* United Nations Institute for Disarmament Research Geneva Switzerland. 2002, p. 9,10.
178 Ibid, p. 55.
179 Ibid. p. 31.
180 Ibid, p. 9.
181 *Toronto Star*, May 9, 2004, A10.

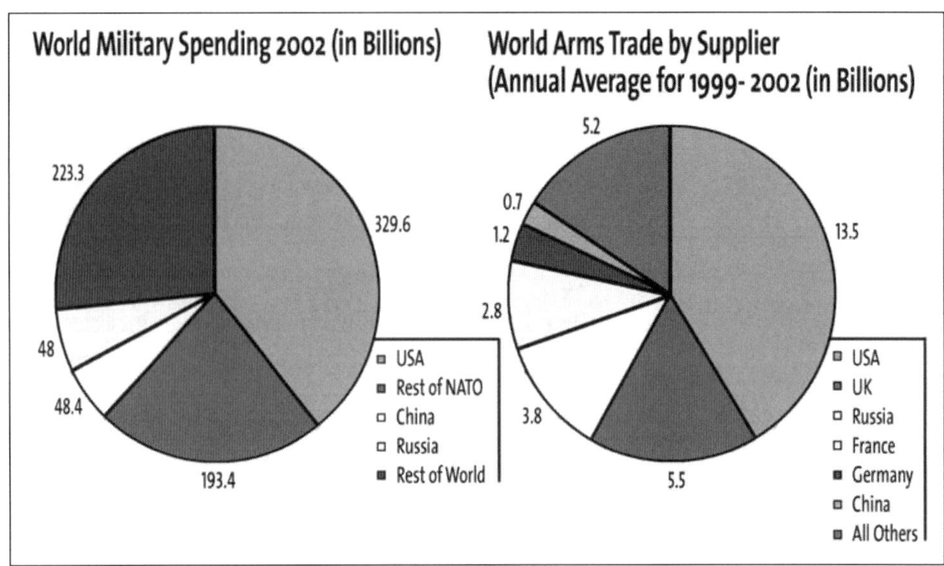

182

11. In today's wars, an estimated 10 civilians die for every soldier or fighter killed.[183] Write the algebraic equation for the number of civilian deaths. If the newspaper says that the number of soldiers killed in the most recent conflict is 1,254 approximately how many civilians do you think have died?

Food for thought...

Between 1945 and 2000 there were 280 major wars that killed 24 million people.[184]

Your teacher, when he or she retires, will collect a Canada Pension. This is money that the government collects from your pay check while you are working, invests, and then gives back to you when you retire.

The Canadian government invests that money in companies that sell weapons, tobacco, alcohol and oil. It invests $2.5 billion in more than 100 foreign and Canadian weapons makers, and $100 million in tobacco stocks (tobacco causes 45,000 deaths a year and costs the health care system $3.5 billion annually).[185]

- How does your teacher feel about his or her money being invested in these things? What could your class do about it?
- Find out your government's position on missile defence systems. Invite a politician in to your class to talk about defence spending. How much does it cost to put a new basketball court in a park in your community?
- Information about current armed conflicts can be found at www.ploughshares.ca.

182 Project Plowshares. "Armed Conflicts Report 2004 Poster".
183 www.redcross.ca
184 www.redcross.ca
185 Belliveau, Warren. "Banking on War." *NOW magazine*. August 12-18, 2004, pp. 22-23.

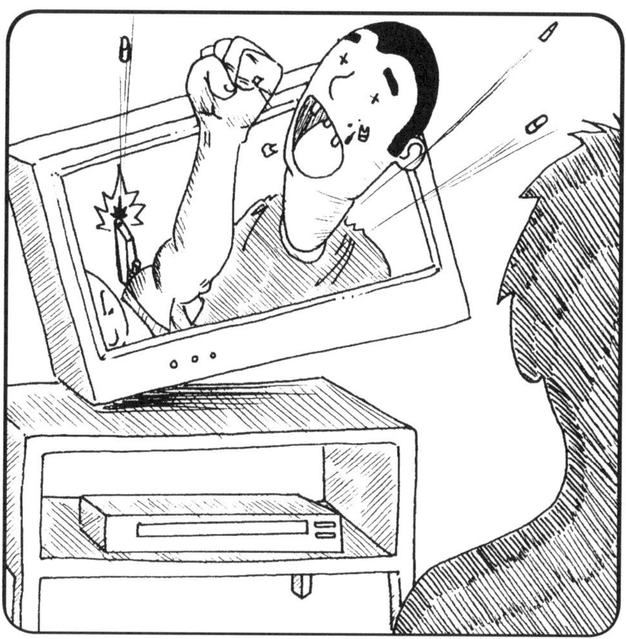

Correlated Or Causal?

"The pure and simple truth is rarely pure and never simple."
– Oscar Wilde

When trying to understand the relationship between two things, an important question that needs to be asked is, "Is it a **correlative** relationship, or is it a **causative** relationship?" A *causative* relationship means that one thing *causes* the other thing. After decades of battling the tobacco industry and their public relations firms, we are now able to use scientific studies to say that yes, indeed, smoking *causes* cancer.

If two things *occur at the same time*, but we are *unsure* whether one thing causes the other, we say that they are **correlated**. If you always do well on tests after having a chocolate bar, we start by saying the relationship is correlative. Some might say that the chocolate makes you happy and hence it is being happy rather than chocolate specifically that improves your test scores. Cause and effect has not been established. You might do further tests on chocolate and find that it has a chemical that stimulates brain cells. Now you are beginning to establish a causative relationship: chemicals in chocolate may cause better brain functioning, which may cause you to do well on your tests.

The greater the correlation, the more we investigate whether it has a causative relationship. To tell the degree to which two things are correlated we use a number called a "**coefficient**". If two things ("**variables**") always occur together, every single time, the coefficient is a perfect 1.0. If there is no relationship between the two variables, the coefficient is a perfect 0. And if the relationship is such that the presence of one variable always means the absence of the other we say that they have a perfect negative correla-

tion, with a coefficient of –1.0. An example of this last situation could be the use of a condom (variable one) and sexually transmitted HIV (variable two), which have a negative correlation, although it's not a perfect –1.0.

opening question

Why do you think that, although we know that smoking causes cancer, the coefficient for those two variables is 0.39? How do you explain that it's not a perfect 1.0?

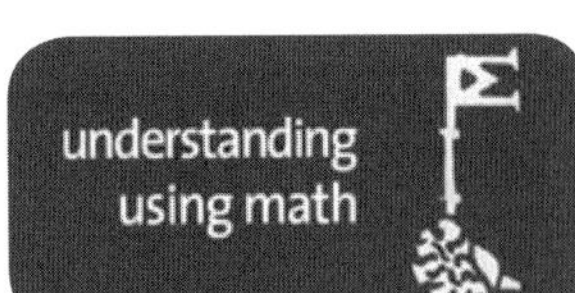

understanding using math

The following chart[186] shows two variables in column A, and their coefficient in column B.

Two Variables	Coefficient
Smoking and Lung Cancer	0.39
Media Violence and Aggression	0.31
Condom Use and Sexually Transmitted HIV	-0.20
Passive Smoking and Lung Cancer at Work	0.14
Exposure to Lead and IQ Scores in Children	-0.14
Nicotine Patch and Smoking Cessation	0.13
Calcium Intake and Bone Mass	0.11
Homework and Academic Achievement	0.10
Exposure to Asbestos and Laryngeal Cancer	0.09
Self-examination and Extent of Breast Cancer	-0.07

1. Enter this chart in a **spreadsheet** program. Create a bar graph. Follow the instructions, and include a title "Comparison of Coefficients", the x-axis label "Correlation" and the y-axis label "Variables". Print this graph and hand it in with your work.

2. In the above set of data, what is the second highest correlation between two variables, and what is the coefficient?

3. A small correlation is considered to be plus or minus 0.1, a medium correlation plus or minus 0.3 and a large correlation plus or minus 0.5. There are almost no perfect correlations.[187] Based on the coefficients in your chart, what could you argue about the value of homework?

4. Six professional groups in the United States (the American Psychological Association, American Academy of Pediatrics, American Academy of Child and Adolescent Psychiatry, American Medical Association, American Academy of Family Physicians, and the American Psychiatric Association) issued the following statement:

   "At this time, well over 1,000 studies...point overwhelmingly to a causal connection between media violence and aggressive behaviour in some children."[188]

186 *American Psychologist*, "Media Violence and the American Public". June/July 2001, p.481.
187 Ibid, p.480.
188 Ibid., p. 481.

Why might the entertainment industry claim that violent **media** simply reflects the violence that already exists in our society, rather than causes it?

5. Businesses spend millions of dollars to advertise using commercials on television, indicating that they believe that they can affect people's (buying) behaviour. Actually, business hopes for a success rate of only 1% of viewers.[189] Let's say five million Canadians watch a violent movie on television. What is 1% of five million viewers (the amount that we might expect based on the business **projections**, to show increased aggression)?

6. Surely, though, all of those people will not show levels of increased aggression that would be significant enough to provoke physically assaulting someone else. What if only 1% of that number was affected in that way? What is 1% of your last answer? Not surprisingly, the levels of **domestic violence** actually do increase after a football game is aired on television.[190]

7. A new study by U.S. researchers looked at the amount of time preschoolers spend in front of the television versus their ability to focus when they reach school age.[191]

# of hours per day watching TV in preschool years	1	2	3	4
Increase in chance of attention problem in school	10%	20%	30%	40%

   a. What algebraic equation describes the pattern in this table?

   b. Of 1,350 young children, the researcher found that one-year-olds watched an average of 2.2 hours of television per day.[192] Use your algebraic equation to show their average increase in attention problems by school age.

   c. By age three, the researcher found that the children watched an average of 3.6 hours of television per day.[193] Use your algebraic equation to show their average increase in attention problems by school age.

   d. Speculate as to why watching television when you are very young could have significant impacts on your ability to focus in school in later years.

8. A study of more than 700 people over the age of 17 compared their rate of violence and the amount of time they watched television daily as a 14 year old. The results held true for those who had had previous violent incidents and those who had not.

   The following table shows the average percentage of people involved in aggressive acts by age 16 to 22. Fill in what you think the girls and boys averages were (remember- they will have to average the average!).[194] Your teacher will put the actual answers on the board so that you can compare.

---

189 Madved, 1995, in *American Psychologist*, "Media Violence and the American Public". June/July 2001, p.482.

190 "Indiana University Bloomington Researchers Examine Relationship Between Football, Domestic Violence." *Ascribe Higher Education News Service*, May 25, 2003 pNA

191 Alphonso, Caroline. "TV Linked to attention problems." *Globe and Mail* A17, April 6, 2004

192 Ibid. p. A17.

193 Ibid. p. A17.

194 Shmid, Randolph. "Study Probes TVs Effect on Violence"..Associated Press, March 28, 2002.

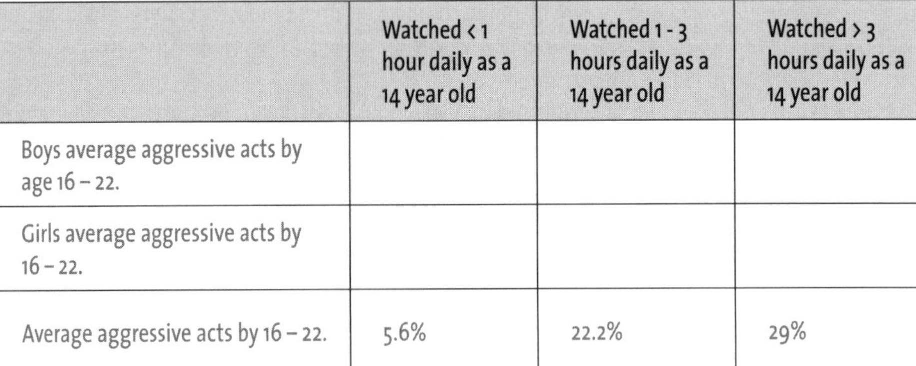

	Watched < 1 hour daily as a 14 year old	Watched 1 - 3 hours daily as a 14 year old	Watched > 3 hours daily as a 14 year old
Boys average aggressive acts by age 16 – 22.			
Girls average aggressive acts by 16 – 22.			
Average aggressive acts by 16 – 22.	5.6%	22.2%	29%

What does this mean to you?

- Find out what TV Turnoff Week is at www.adbusters.ca and organize one at your school.
- Sit with a younger brother or sister as they watch TV and ask them questions about what they're watching. Then take them out to play basketball.
- Watch the movie *Bowling for Columbine* or *Elephant* with family or friends and talk about it.

Rule Of Thumb

"To be free is not merely to cast off one's chains, but to live in a way that respects and enhances the freedom of others"

– Nelson Mandela

Violence in our society can be watched everywhere: television programs, movies, video games, advertising, and the nightly news. It may then come as no surprise that people also act out violence on each other, in a continuum of behaviour ranging from verbal put-downs, to **financial abuse**, physical and sexual assault, and sometimes to murder.

There are **statistically significant** differences in the experience of violence depending on **gender**. Because violence is connected with inequalities and power imbalances[195] it is important that "individual experiences of violence against women [are] assessed against the backdrop of historical, social, political, cultural and economic inequality of women."[196]

It used to be the law that a husband could beat his wife with a stick no greater than the thickness of his thumb. Today we have **civil domestic violence legislation**, along with sexual assault care centres, counselling assistance, crisis lines, shelters for abused women and **sensitivity training** for police.[197]

Mathematics is helpful in preventing violence. If social policies to support people are to be effective, they must originate from careful **surveys** and studies that accurately pinpoint the problems and track changes over time. Violence against anyone, of any gender, is unacceptable.

---

195 *Assessing Violence Against Women: A Statistical Profile.* Federal-Provincial-Territorial Ministers Responsible for the Status of Women, 2002. p. 2.
196 Ibid. p. 2.
197 Ibid. p. 4.

There are societies in the world where the women and children experience very little domestic violence. What do you imagine are the biggest differences between those societies and ours?

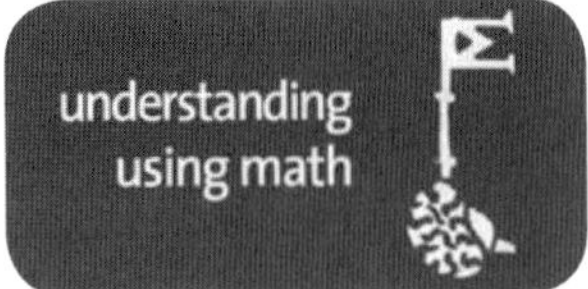

1. A woman's ability to leave an abusive relationship often depends on having the money to do so. **The Low Income Cutoff** is one measure of how many people are living in poverty. Based on Statistics Canada's Women in Canada, 2000-2001 report[198] answer the following questions:

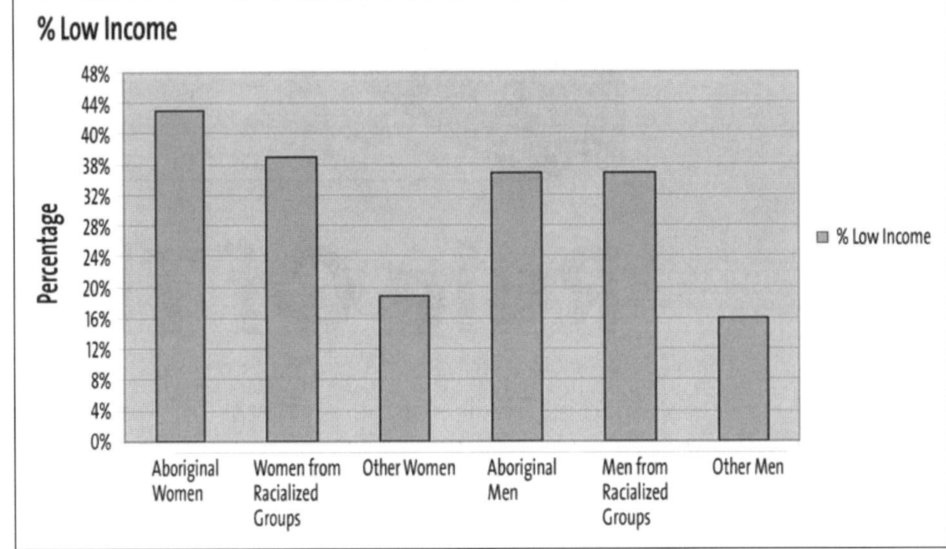

   a. Which groups are most at risk? Which are least at risk?

   b. What intervention could be made to address this particular issue of income **disparity**?

2. Statistics can be misleading because they under-represent the problem. Why do you think that "only a minority of sexual assaults and **spousal violence** cases are reported to the police"?[199]

---

198 Hadley, Karen. *And We Still Ain't Satisfied: Gender Inequality In Canada* A Status Report for 2001 National Action Committee on the Status of Women and Centre for Social Justice. P. 2.

199 *Assessing Violence Against Women: A Statistical Profile.* Federal-Provincial-Territorial Ministers Responsible for the Status of Women. P. 6.

3. What surprises you about the following graph?[200] Discuss with the class.

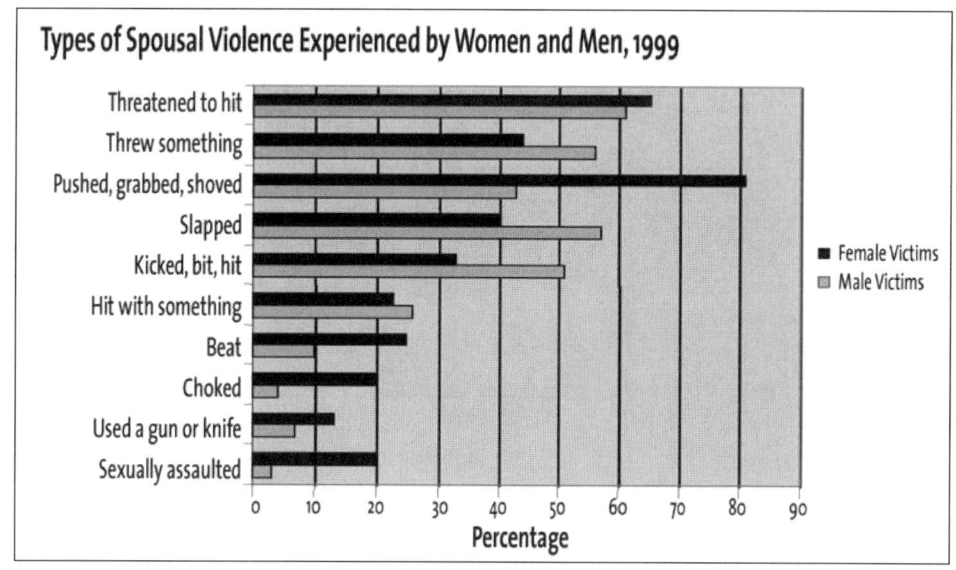

4. After reading the previous graph, could the **following** statement be true? If so, how could it change the viewer's understanding of the data?

   Nine hundred and ten women experienced violence from their male spouse and of the 910 women, 182 experienced sexual assault. One hundred men experienced violence from their female spouse and of the 100 men, 3 experienced sexual assault.

5. The graph in question three doesn't tell the viewer how many times the victim experienced each type of violence. How might that **distort** what is happening?

6. What does the following graph[201] add to your understanding when considered alongside the graph in question #3?

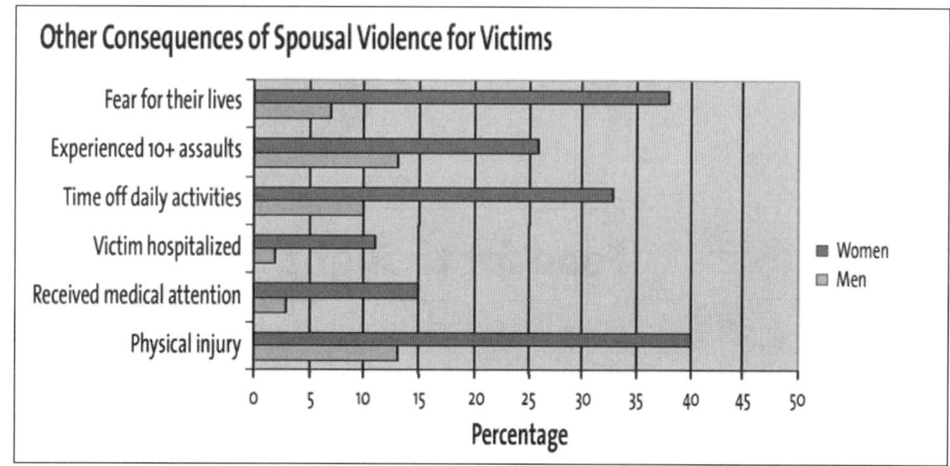

7. Look at the following graph and then circle the conclusions that you can make based on the graph from the list on the next page.[202]

200 *Assessing Violence Against Women: A Statistical Profile.* Federal-Provincial-Territorial Ministers Responsible for the Status of Women. P. 10.
201 Ibid, pg 30
202 Ibid, pg 30

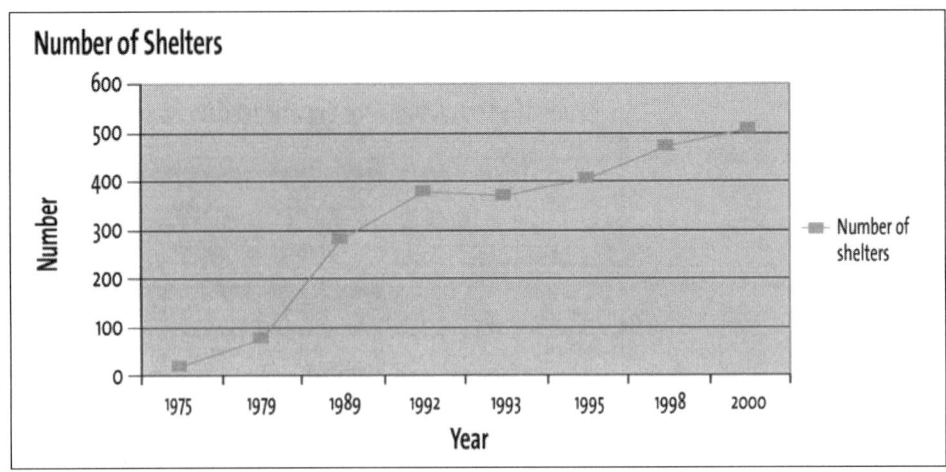

a. The number of shelters for abused women has been rising steadily since 1975.

b. The number of shelters grew a great deal between 1979 and 1989 because of increased funds from government.

c. The number of shelters grew a great deal between 1979 and 1989 because the **feminist movement** was very active during that time.

d. The number of abused women has been rising steadily since 1975.

e. The rise in shelters means that all women trying to escape abusive relationships will benefit equally.

8. Discuss the findings of Statistics Canada's Canadian Crime Statistics Report, 2000 (p. 60, Table 4.13):

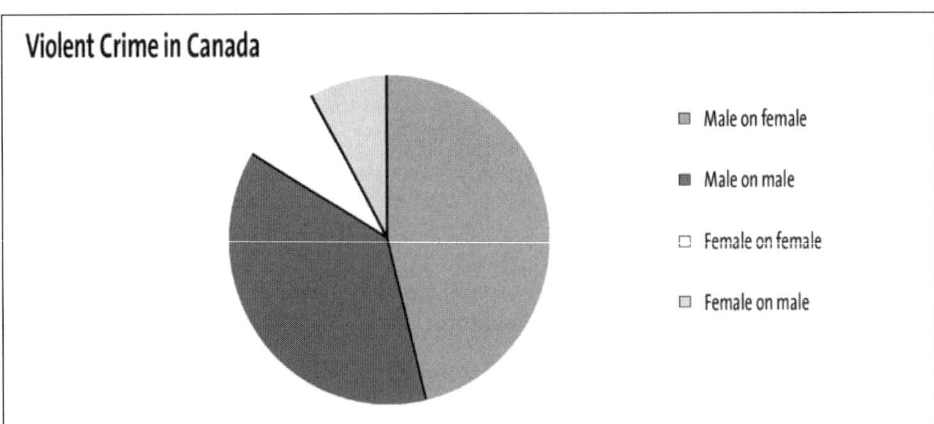

Food for thought...

Women own about 1% of the world's land.[203]

The United Nations estimates that women will have to wait until the year 2490 to achieve equal representation with men in the higher echelons of economic power.[204]

- Have a worker from a shelter visit the class to talk about the **shelter system** where you live.
- Find the **crisis hotline** numbers for your region and post them in your classroom.
- Post the Canadian Criminal Code in your classroom.

203 Seager, Joni. *The State of Women in the World Atlas*. Penguin, London. 1997. P. 76.
204 Ibid, p. 70.

Kidfluence

"Teens are more likely to be influenced to smoke by cigarette advertising than they are by peer pressure."

– "Influence of Tobacco Marketing and Exposure to Smokers on Adolescent Susceptibility to Smoking", *Journal of the National Cancer Institute*, October 1995.

People in the **marketing industry** will tell you. Kids start to develop brand loyalty at age two.[205] Twenty percent of American children are asking for specific products by age three.[206] The nag factor, whereby children pester their parents for products, takes centre stage between ages three and seven. 96% of American school children can recognize Ronald McDonald- beaten only by Santa Claus.[207]

While children under eight are at a disadvantage because their brain functioning makes it difficult to tell truth from "sort-of-truth",[208] 'tweens, age nine to twelve are a different story. A clever advertising strategy will try to appeal to "individuality" and "being smarter" about advertising.[209]

The tricky ones are youth. Playing off of the increased need to "fit in" with friends,[210] advertisers will move heaven and earth to associate their product with being "cool". Slightly older youth and the product must equate with "rebellion" and "controversy".

---

205 Moser, Ronald and Linda Horton. "The Marketing and Ethical Implications of Advertising to Children". www.olemiss.edu/courses/mktg351/Publication.htm

206 "Just the Facts about Advertising and Marketing to Children". The Centre for a New American Dream. www.newdream.org/campaign/kids/facts/html

207 "Unhealthy marketing to kids". Strategic Alliance Action Brief. www.eatbettermovemore.org

208 Moser, Ronald and Linda Horton. "The Marketing and Ethical Implications of Advertising to Children". www.olemiss.edu/courses/mktg351/Publication.htm

209 Sonya Felix, "Kid Stuff", www.childrenscreativemkt.com/articles/fullstory335.html Sept 1, 2001

210 Moser, Ronald and Linda Horton. "The Marketing and Ethical Implications of Advertising to Children". www.olemiss.edu/courses/mktg351/Publication.htm

Erika Shaker points out that the way marketers try to relate to youth is by sending the message "We know that you know that we want you to buy our product. Let's have a knowing giggle about this. You're past that. You're smarter than that. So buy our product because we acknowledge your superior market **savvy**."[211] The bottom line remains: sell product, make money, however you can.

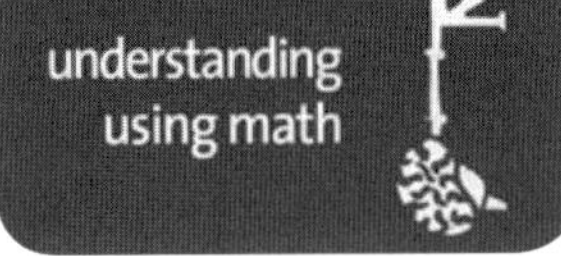

What people or personalities do you think children age three to seven should be able to recognize (besides friends and relatives)?

understanding using math

1. For one whole day, carry a small notebook and pen around with you. Every single time you see or hear an ad, make a **tally**. Ads may be everywhere: use the following tally chart so that comparisons can be made with your class.

Advertisement location	Tally	Total
Television commercials		
Radio ads		
Billboards		
Store awnings		
Posters/signs		
On products themselves (for example, at home or in a store)		
Internet		
Movies		
On clothing		
Other:		
	Total:	

   a. Total the ads that you saw in each section, and as a whole.

   b. With your class, determine the **mean, median, mode** and **range** for the classroom data.

2. Spending on advertising in the United States was more than $230 billion in the year 2001. There are about 105 million households in the States.[212] How much money was spent on advertising per household in 2001? Who pays for that advertising?

3. Canadian children and youth have their own money to spend, and also influence their parents'/guardians' spending. The following chart shows the relationship between these two categories.[213]

	Family A	Family B	Family C	Family D
Child/Youth Spending	$45	$37	$84	$74
Child Influenced Family Spending	$445	$366	$806	$718

---

211 Shaker, Erika. "Individuality.com: Empowering youth through consumption?" 2001, www.policyalternatives.ca/eduproj/ososconsumption.html

212 "Just the Facts about Advertising and Marketing to Children". The Centre for a New American Dream. www.newdream.org/campaign/kids/facts/html

213 Shaker, Erika. "Individuality.com: Empowering youth through consumption?" 2001, www.policyalternatives.ca/eduproj/ososconsumption.html

a. Although the relationship isn't exact, what is the algebraic equation that describes the pattern?
b. Businesses have determined that Canadian children and youth represent a $1.8 billion **market**.[214] Use your algebraic equation to find out how much money children and youth in Canada influence through their family.

4. Compare the amount of family spending Canadian children and youth influence to the amount American children under age 12 influence.

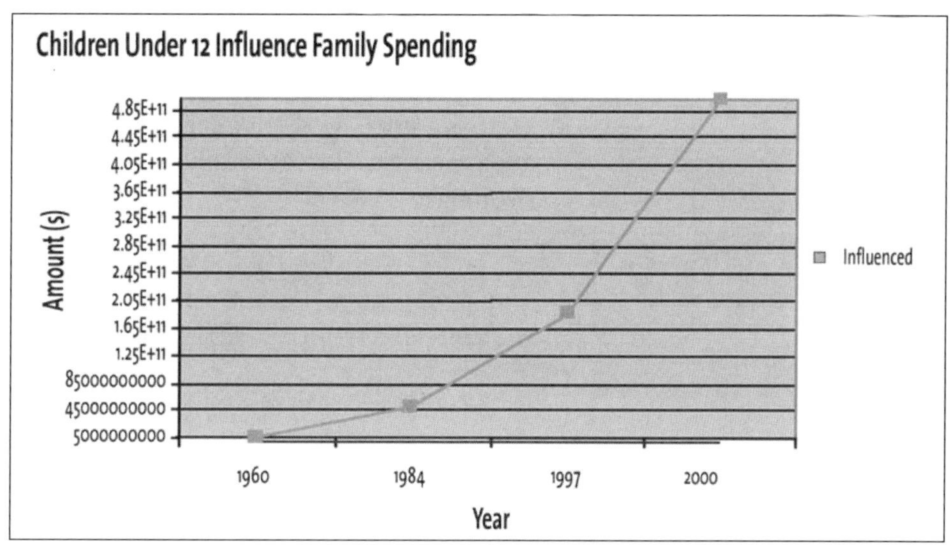

215

a. Explain what the **notation** on the y-axis means.
b. What kind of growth pattern does this pattern represent?
c. How might the labels on the x-axis mislead the viewer?
d. Draw a sketch of how the graph would look if the labels on the x-axis were corrected. Is the trend better or worse than originally presented?

5. A business in the United States called Channel One offers televisions to schools for free, in return for broadcasting time in the classrooms. The following pie graph shows the relationship between news and commercials in this broadcasting.[216]

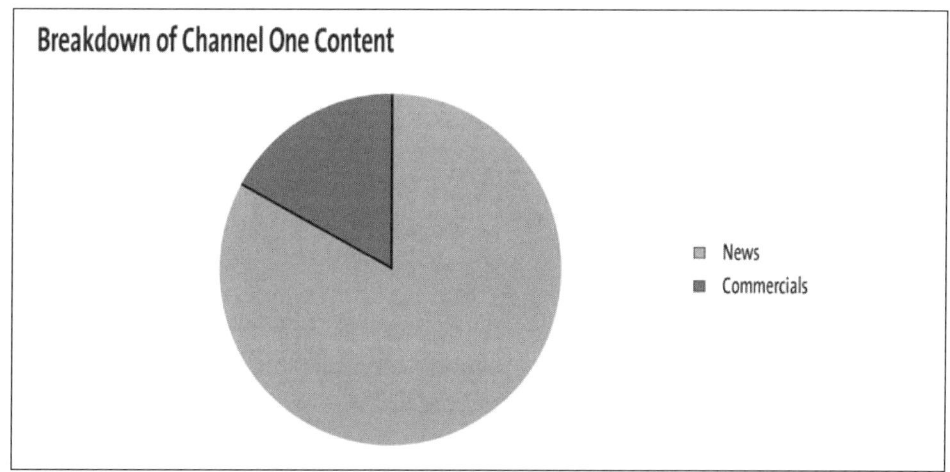

a. Use a protractor to calculate the percentage of commercial content in the broadcasting time.

214 Ibid.
215 "Just the Facts about Advertising and Marketing to Children". The Centre for a New American Dream. www.newdream.org/campaign/kids/facts/html
216 Ibid.

b. If the broadcast happens on 180 school days per year, and each day is a 12 minute broadcast,[217] how much commercial time to students watch per year at school?

c. Some people claim that advertising doesn't really influence buying behaviour, and yet some companies pay up to $195,000 for a 30 second ad on Channel One.[218] Discuss this with the class.

6. There are rules about how many minutes of commercials can be broadcast during children's programming. In one area, it's 10.5 minutes for every hour. Sometimes television stations will show more than 10.5 minutes per hour. If they are caught, they can be fined.

   a. Let's pick a (very) low advertising rate of $3,000 per 30 second commercial. What is the algebraic equation that describes the total revenue of a TV station based on commercial advertising?

   b. Let's say the average fine is $15,000 for showing more than 10.5 minutes of advertising per hour. If the TV station broadcasts only 12 minutes per hour, what is the number of hours it will take to break even if the station is fined?

   c. Using a **cost benefit analysis**, what is a TV station likely to do in your opinion?

7. The average child sees about 20,000 commercials per year.[219]

   a. What is the algebraic equation that describes the total number of commercials a person watches (assuming the rate remains constant)?

   b. If the average commercial length is 20 seconds, what is the algebraic equation describing the total time a person has spent watching commercials?

   c. Use your equation to find out how long it will take the average television viewer to have seen one full (school) week (about 30 hours)of advertising. How about a full summer vacation worth of advertising?

- Take a look at the list of 115 suggestions posted at www.newdream.org/ campaign/ kids/115tips.html. Why do you think some of the suggestions contradict each other?
- Take part in TV Turn Off Week in April where people from around the planet turn off their TVs and find other activities to do.
- Research what Sweden has been doing: in 1991 it banned advertising to children younger than 12. Has it been successful at lobbying the European Union as a whole to agree to this rule?
- The Quebec Consumer Protection Act makes it illegal to advertise to children 12 and under. Research what other Canadian provinces and territories have done to limit childrens' exposure to advertising.

217 Ibid.l
218 Ibid.
219 Ibid.l

Linked, Organized, Informed

"It is the framework which changes with each new technology and not just the picture within the frame."
– Marshall McLuhan

Tony Juniper describes the Internet as the most potent weapon in the toolbox of resistance, and for good reason.[220] Information technology now provides **activists** with a wealth of information and the means to share it high speed with like-minded people and organizations worldwide. In contrast to the **corporate**-owned and centrally managed **media**, the Internet is more **decentralized** and far less **hierarchical**.

Massive campaigns have been waged using a single computer, a modem, a telephone line and a fax machine. Case in point was the McLibel Trial, in which two London **grassroots** activists were sued because they set out to highlight what McDonald's was doing around the globe. The trial lasted 313 days, the longest in England's history and **spawned** the McSpotlight website, a "global **cyberplatform**" otherwise known as a public relations nightmare that was visited by millions of people.[221]

---

220 Klein, Naomi. *No Logo*. Alfred Knopf, 2000. p. 396.
221 Ibid, p. 389, 394-396.

When the **World Trade Organization** tried to meet in Seattle and Quebec City to design **free trade** rules for all of North, Central and South America, thousands of **protestors** were able to coordinate resistance, and in the case of Seattle, actually shut down the meetings. Their message: "this trade deal is not good for the vast majority of people- and we're organized and informed enough to stop it."

What is it about hierarchical organization that can be so limiting?

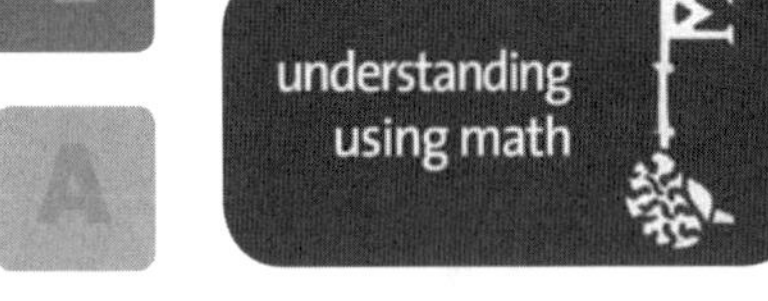

1. **Databases** are computer systems that can store huge amounts of information and allow people to retrieve it easily and selectively based on criteria that they decide. Information is important to effective **resistance**- it can justify and give vision to action.

    a. As a class, learn the skills required for the creation of a database. Create an "activist resource database" with the following "fields":

    Resource title

    Resource type (book, website, magazine, newspaper, organization)

    Resource author(s) or contact person

    Resource description

    Website address

    Phone number

    Resource Rating (one to ten, ten being the best)

    Key words

    Student reviewer

    b. Over the course of the school term, enter four resources into the database.

    c. At the end of the term, pull a report based on one of the following:

    Resources rated eight or higher

    All entries from three of your peers

    All websites

2. Imagine that information needs to be distributed quickly about an upcoming resistance demonstration or **boycott**. Imagine that each person who receives the information by email has an average of eight people in their in-box to whom they can send the information. What is the algebraic equation that describes the number of recipients per round of sending?

3. How long will it take to reach 30,000 people (assuming no overlap in people's in-box names)?

4. Plot the number of people reached in each round of e-mails. What kind of growth model did you graph? How many rounds did it take to reach a million people?

"Every time Shell sneezes, a report goes out on the hyperactive Shell-Nigeria-action **listserve**."[222]

5. The amount of memory space in a computer has developed rapidly over the past four decades. One byte of hard drive space holds a single number or letter. Each category below is one thousand times greater than the category above it.

   a. Fill in the following table:

Memory space	Byte equivalent	Name	Scientific Notation
1 byte	1 byte	One	1×10^0
1 kilobyte	1000 bytes	One thousand	1×10^3
1 megabyte	1,000,000 bytes	One million	
1 gigabyte			
1 terabyte			
1 petabyte			
1 exabyte			
1 zettabyte			
1 yottabyte			

   b. The Commodore C64 introduced in 1982 used 64 kilobytes of memory. How many bytes is that?

   c. Modern computers use as much as 512 megabytes of memory. How many bytes is that equivalent to? How many gigabytes is that equivalent to? How many terabytes is that equivalent to?

Some perspective: two petabytes of memory would hold the entire contents of all US academic research libraries and one zettabyte is equivalent to the number of grains of sand on all of the world's beaches![223]

6. Access to technology is an issue of equity. Who has restricted access to technology and how can this affect their educational progress?

7. While the social justice movement can use computers to make the world a better place, the same technology can be used by business to sell products to more and more people. In consumer-obsessed North American culture, this leads to the destruction of the environment. Graph the following data showing how quickly it took each technology to reach 50 million users and discuss with your class.

---

222 Klein, Naomi. *No Logo*. Alfred Knopf, 2000. p. 394.

223 Monroe, Parker. "A Yottabyte-Who Needs It?" *Bay Bytes Newsletter*. June 2004. P. 9.

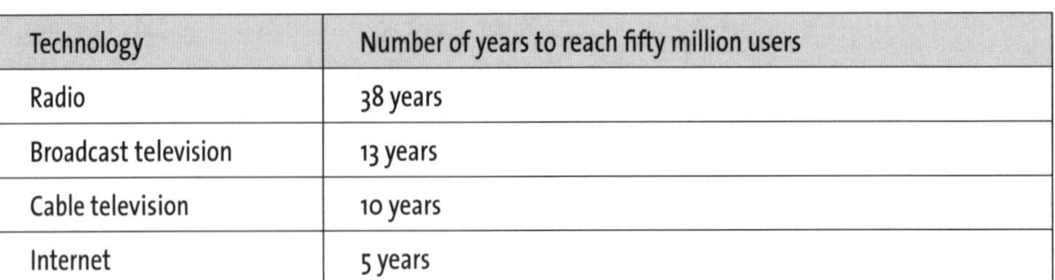

Technology	Number of years to reach fifty million users
Radio	38 years
Broadcast television	13 years
Cable television	10 years
Internet	5 years

make it better

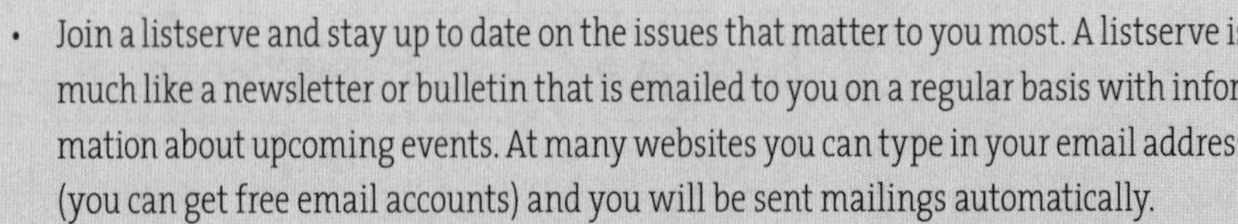

- Join a listserve and stay up to date on the issues that matter to you most. A listserve is much like a newsletter or bulletin that is emailed to you on a regular basis with information about upcoming events. At many websites you can type in your email address (you can get free email accounts) and you will be sent mailings automatically.
- Print the bulletins that you receive and post them in your classroom so that everyone has access to the information.
- Don't have access? Take a trip to your local public library and get on line...

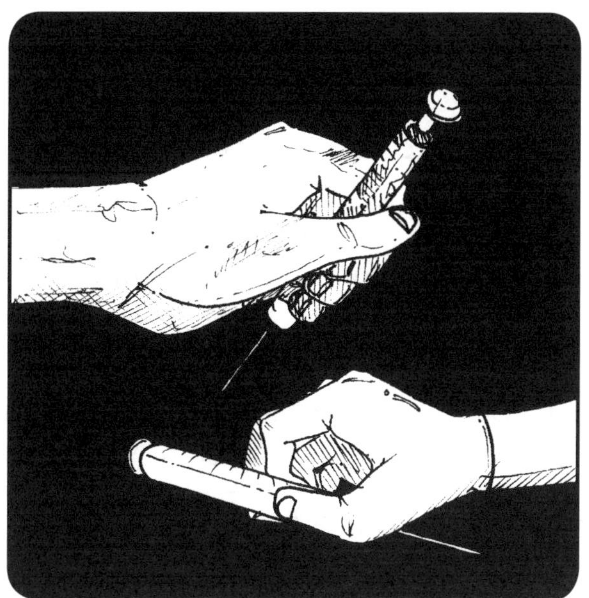

Going For Probable Silver

"Harm reduction requires an approach of pragmatism rather than purism-an acceptance that it may sometimes be better to go for a probable silver than a possible gold."
– John Strang

Harm reduction is a philosophical approach to drug problems and interventions, with an emphasis on reducing harms associated with drug use "rather than the prevention of drugs *per se*." Although it stands in direct contradiction to the '**war on drugs**' approach and **zero tolerance** enforcement, harm reduction does not preclude the idea that **abstinence** from drugs can be desirable.[224]

Needle exchange programs are one type of harm reduction. When HIV/AIDS erupted on the scene in the 1980s it quickly became apparent that sharing dirty needles helped to spread the virus. Offering drug users clean needles not only helped to slow the spread of the epidemic but it also created an opportunity to connect and build trust with addicted populations. Presenting a variety of treatment options then became possible.[225]

In the fall of 2003, Vancouver opened a supervised, safe injection site. Vancouver police and professionals worldwide see that treating drug addiction as a medical issue and not a criminal problem has

224 Hunt, Neil. "A review of the evidence-base for harm reduction approaches to drug use". www.forward-thinking-on-drugs.org/review2-print.html, pp.1-2.
225 Ibid, p.5.

humanitarian health benefits, but also economic and social benefits to the community as a whole.[226] Vancouver's safe injection site, Insite, is the only one of its kind in North America.

opening question

People are unlikely to give up driving a car, even given the number of fatal accidents, and the harmful environmental impact of driving. What harm reduction strategies do we as a society put in place to reduce the risks of driving?

understanding using math

1. The Netherlands are noted for their harm reduction approach to drug use while the United States is typically noted for its war on drugs approach. What implications does this graph[227] have?

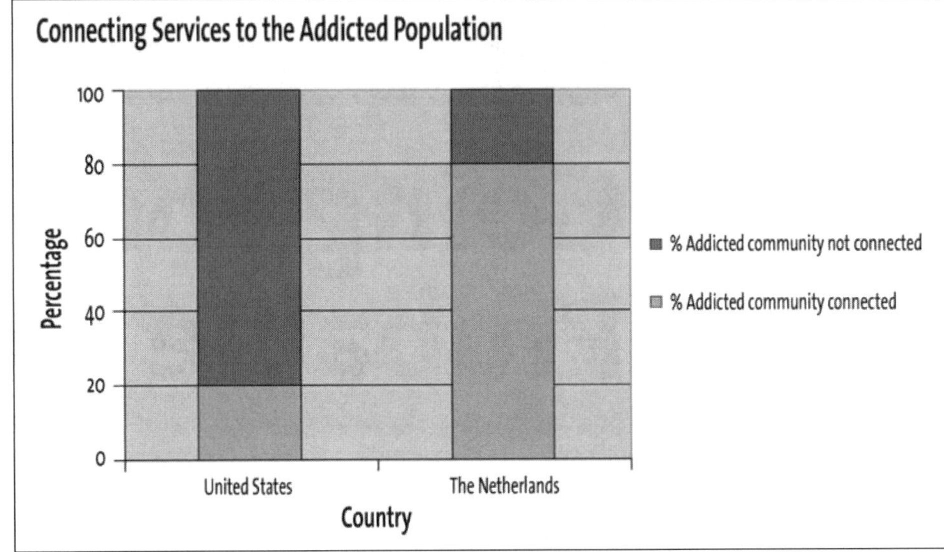

2. The question that immediately arises with needle and **syringe** exchange programs is "are they effective at lowering HIV risk behaviours and infection among drug users?" The following is a summary of 42 studies.[228]

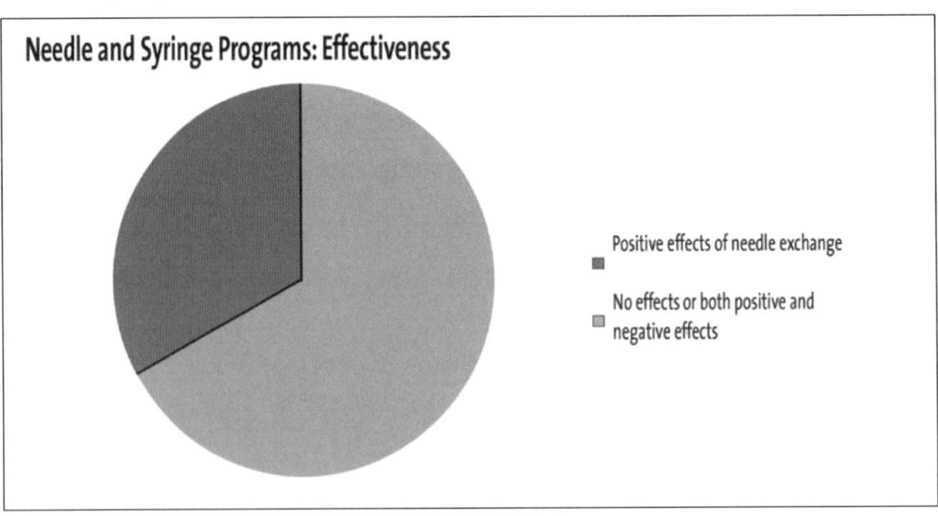

226 http://canadianharmreduction.com/readmore/newsbc_noproblem.html CBC March 3, 2004

227 Westermeyer, Robert. "Reducing Harm: A Very Good Idea". http://www.cts.com/crash/habtsmrt/harm.html

228 Hunt, Neil. "A review of the evidence-base for harm reduction approaches to drug use". www.forward-thinking-on-drugs.org/review2-print.html P. 10.

a. Approximately how many of the 42 studies showed positive effects?

b. The two negative associations were in studies comparing the needle exchange program clients with drug users who were not attending the program. Can you think of a reason why these two populations are different enough to warrant caution when interpreting the data?

3. Community based **outreach programs** may not distribute needles and syringes but do distribute bleach to disinfect needles, hand out risk reduction literature and condoms, and provide **referral** to services. A review of 36 publications found the following:[229]

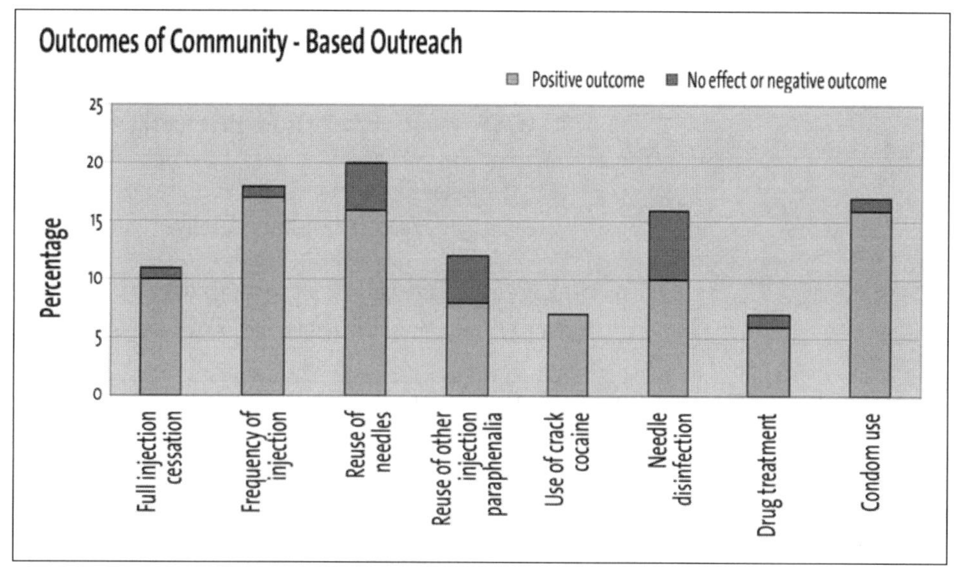

a. What surprises you most about the data?

b. What questions do you have that would need follow up study to find out?

4. Another question that is commonly raised is "are needle and syringe programs **cost effective**?" In other words, does the money that is put into the program pay off in the long run? A national review in New Zealand found the following pattern:[230]

Dollars put into the program	$5	$10	$20	$100
Dollars saved	$100	$200	$400	$2000

a. What is the algebraic equation that describes the savings per dollar of the needle and syringe program in New Zealand?

b. What do you think accounts for the money saved?

c. If the New Zealand government spent $50,000 on a needle and syringe program, how much would they expect to save over the long run?

229 Ibid. p. 11

230 Ibid. p. 11.

5. Methadone has been used for about 40 years to give to heroin and other opiate users as a substitute, to create a more controllable form of addiction. Methadone prevents withdrawal symptoms and the "highs" of heroin, enabling users to participate in **rehabilitation** programs. The immediate benefits of reduction in crime and criminal justice system costs are summarized by the following data from the United Kingdom.[231]

Money put into the program	£5	£10	£20	£100
Money saved	£15	£30	£60	£300

   a. What is the algebraic equation that describes the savings of the methadone treatment program in the United Kingdom?

   b. Why do you think that it is less than the savings found in New Zealand?

   c. If the United Kingdom spent $50,000 on a methadone treatment program, how much money could they expect to save immediately?

6. A study of methadone harm reduction programs with three different levels of support was conducted to compare the costs and benefits. The following graph details the findings.[232]

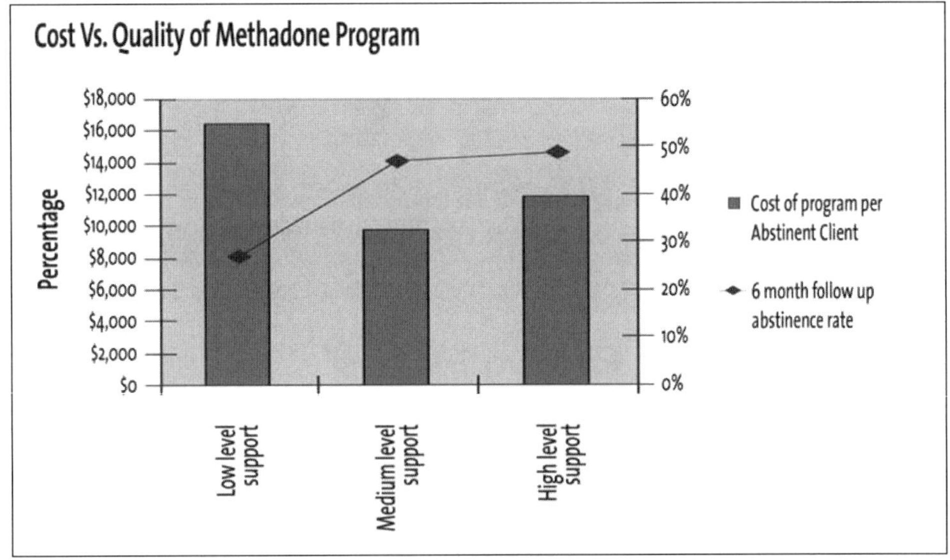

   a. Which program could you eliminate immediately, and for what reasons?

   b. How could you decide which of the other two programs is the most cost-effective?

- Have your teacher order the 68 minute "To Do No Harm" documentary for your classroom and discuss the film as a group. (212-213-6376 x 10)

231 Ibid, p. 14-16.

232 Hunt, Neil. "A review of the evidence-base for harm reduction approaches to drug use". www.forward-thinking-on-drugs.org/review2-print.html p. 17.

Welcome To The Club

"You can tell whether a man is clever by his answers. You can tell whether a man is wise by his questions."
– Naguib Mahfouz

In the 1990s in Canada, a social experiment was happening. The Canadian government reduced its role in providing help to people in the form of **social assistance** like **welfare** and **unemployment insurance** payments. It also began to turn some of the services that it provided over to the **private sector (privatization)**.

There are people who believe that the **market** will bring greater wealth to everyone if it is left to run its course. According to this political philosophy, government should not get involved in problems of inequality, poverty and employment. As the market does well, people will do well. A rising tide lifts all ships, so to speak.

What is interesting to note, however, is that even in years of greater prosperity, when the **GDP** was growing, the number of people who were poor *increased*, and employment *decreased*.[233] Also, contrary to the free market **pundits**, when Canada was in a recession period, the gap between rich and poor actually *narrowed*.

233 Yalnizyan, Armine. "Canada's Great Divide: The Politics of the growing gap between rich and poor in the 1990s". Centre for Social Justice, Jan. 2000, p.11.

The following lesson has to do with two particular **deciles**. A decile means one tenth of something. The poorest 10% of the population (or the poorest decile) raising children has been called "Club Poor". Club Rich is the wealthiest 10% raising children. Understanding what happened to Club Poor and Club Rich in the 1990s can give us clues about the market.

opening question

Can you think of any example in your life that challenges the idea that "a rising tide lifts all ships?"

understanding using math

1. Select two volunteers from your class. One will represent the bottom decile in Canada, and one will represent the top decile. The year is 1989 and the richest families are 39 times as wealthy as the poorest.[234] (This activity works better with a good set of walkie-talkies.)

    a. Have the student representing the bottom decile take 39 steps away from the person representing the top decile. They may have to step into the hall. If they are carrying a walkie-talkie have them describe how far they are from the class.

    b. How easy would it be for these two groups to talk to each other, given their current distance? What problem does that create?

    c. It's now 1993, at the height of the recession. The richest 10 % of Canadians are 257 times as wealthy as the poorest 10%.[235] Have the student in the hall take another 218 steps away and describe how far they are to the class. What impact does this have on communication between groups? Why do you think the top decile has no problem making its views known to the country?

    d. It's now 1997 and the country has recovered from the recession. The two groups are now 109 steps apart.[236] How many steps must the student in the hall take toward the classroom? Even though the country has recovered from the recession, what is the difference between 1989 and 1997 in terms of the gap between deciles?

2. Take a look at the two graphs on the next page.

    a. Describe what is happening in each of them in general terms. Draw in the **best fit line** for each graph.

    b. What makes the two graphs difficult to compare? What might you conclude if you looked at only the *general shape* of the graphs?

---

234 Ibid..
235 Ibid, p. 53.
236 Ibid, p. 53.

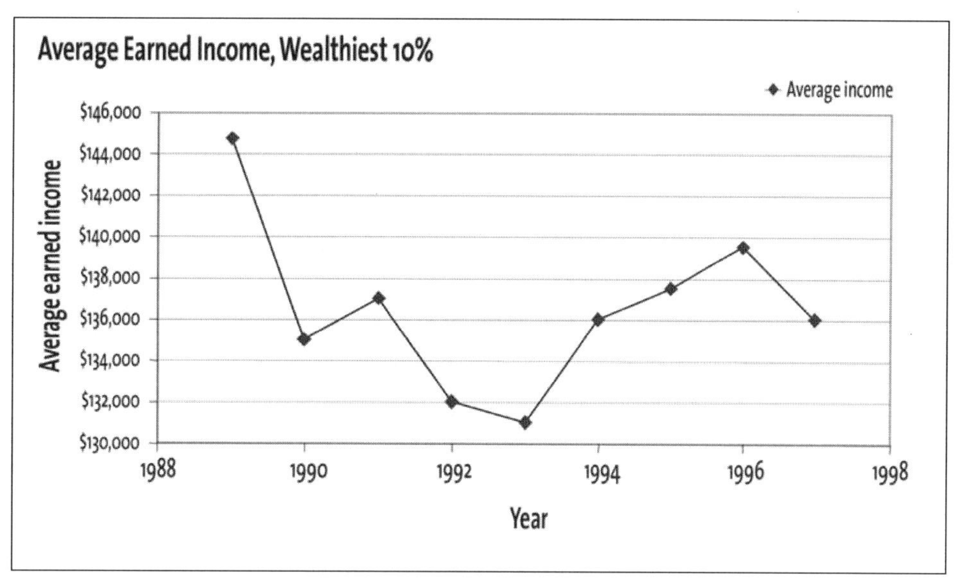

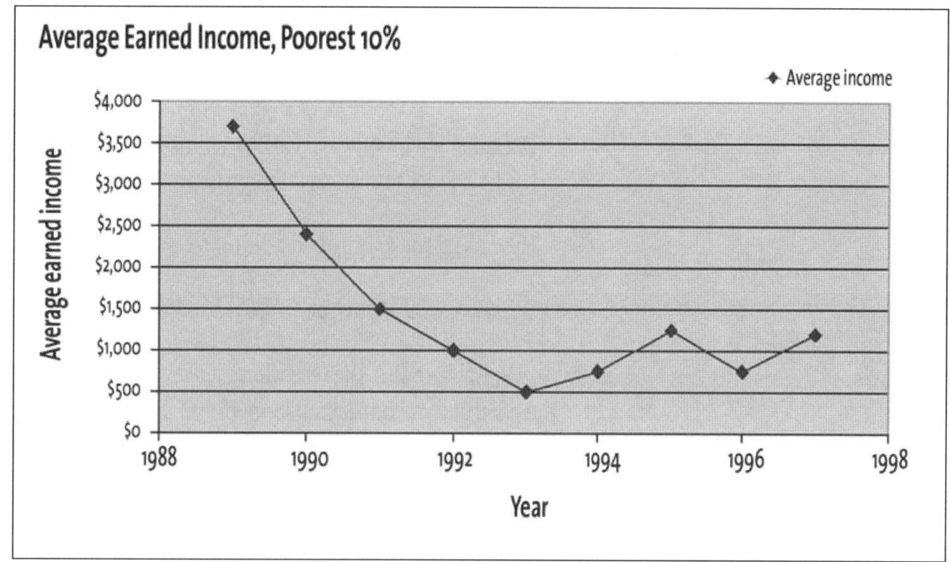

c. Open a spread sheet and create two tables, one for the poorest 10% of the population and one for the richest 10%, based on the following model, (which is calculated in 1997 constant dollars)[237]. Fill in the final column of each chart.

Year	Bottom Decile Average Yearly Earnings	Percentage of 1989 Earnings
1989	3,700	100
1990	2,300	
1991	1,500	
1992	1,000	
1993	500	
1994	750	
1995	1250	
1996	800	
1997	1250	

237 Ibid, p.2.

Year	Top Decile Average Yearly Earnings	Percentage of 1989 Earnings
1989	144,500	100
1990	135,000	
1991	137,000	
1992	132,000	
1993	131,000	
1994	136,000	
1995	137,500	
1996	139,000	
1997	136,000	

d. Bar graph the "Year" versus the "Percentage of 1989 Earnings" for both charts, setting the y-axis values to register from 0 (minimum) to 100 (maximum), with intervals of 10. Attach your graphs to this report.

e. Describe what happened to the shape of the new graphs. What does this tell you about how the richest 10 % of the population experienced these years as opposed to the poorest 10%.

f. How could the axis lines on the above graphs be changed to show the same idea?

3. Use the chart below to prove or disprove the following statement:

"It was inevitable that as the **recession** hit between 1989 and 1993, the gap between the wealthiest and the poorest Canadians would grow."

After tax income gap: ratio of average incomes, comparing top and bottom deciles of families raising children under 18.[238]

(Hint: the bigger the ratio, the bigger the gap.)

	BC	ALTA	SASK	MB	ONT	QUE	NB	NS	NFLD
1989	6.76	6.68	6.57	6.03	7.25	6.03	6.14	5.75	6.75
1990	8.68	6.67	6.95	6.43	7.28	5.99	6.39	6.58	5.76
1991	6.97	7.13	7.20	6.12	6.81	6.03	6.69	5.83	6.29
1992	6.67	6.88	7.66	6.82	6.60	5.67	6.93	6.32	6.40
1993	7.70	6.53	5.91	6.14	6.20	5.32	5.78	6.41	5.05

238 Ibid, p.32.

4. Use the chart below to prove or disprove the following statement:

"Most of the provinces closed the gap between the top and bottom deciles during the economic recovery period between 1994 and 1997."

After tax income gap: ratio of average incomes, comparing top and bottom deciles of families raising children under 18.[239]

	BC	ALTA	SASK	MB	ONT	QUE	NB	NS	NFLD
1994	6.83	6.72	6.28	6.14	6.15	5.66	6.09	6.79	5.62
1995	6.64	6.92	6.78	5.31	6.45	6.13	6.86	6.52	5.59
1996	8.48	8.19	6.37	6.20	7.22	6.30	6.44	5.67	4.94
1997	7.59	6.96	6.04	6.20	7.61	6.20	6.35	6.41	4.65

Food for thought...

The change in the average earned income for the poorest decile raising children between 1996 and 1997 "raised the earned incomes...from a level roughly comparable to the GDP per capita in the Democratic Republic of the Congo up to the average standard of living in Bangladesh."[240]

- Search out the poverty **advocacy groups** in your city or town and pay them a visit. What kinds of projects are they working on? Can you help in any way?
- Visit www.growinggap.ca to see where your family income fits into the rich-poor spectrum. What percentage of Canadians fall above / below your family? Are you surprised? Discuss your findings with your family.

---

239 Ibid, p. 32.
240 Ibid, p.16.

What Big Feet You Have...

"It wasn't the Exxon Valdez captain's driving that caused the Alaskan oil spill. It was yours."

– Greenpeace advertisement, New York Times, February 25, 1990

How much biologically productive land and water do you think it takes to support your lifestyle? Consider a piece of land big enough to supply the raw materials needed to make everything in your living space, and to reabsorb the wastes that you create each day. This is called your **ecological footprint**.[241]

Canadians have very big feet: we don't tread lightly on the planet. In fact, only Australians and Americans have bigger feet than we do. The average Canadian ecological footprint is 7.8 hectares, or about 15 football fields! And the problem is, if we shared the productive land equally amongst the planet's population, we're using about four times as much as our fair share.

Some things that we do obviously increase our foot size, like driving a car or taking long showers. Others may be less obvious, like eating meat, or buying food grown in far away places. Sometimes we also need to ask what choices are hidden from us, not offered in the first place and why they aren't offered to us.

---

241 http://www.rco.on.ca/wrw/ecofootprintFAQ.html

Who has a **vested interest** in limiting your choices of renewable energy such as solar and wind power?

1. One hectare (ha) is equivalent to 10,000 m^2. Imagine your hectare as a perfect square of land and fill in the length each side must be to make 10,000 m^2. Show the side length as kilometres, meters, centimetres, and millimetres.

Side length:

km:

m:

cm:

mm:

One hectare

or

10,000 m^2

2. Two hectares would be equivalent to 20,000 m^2. If your two hectares were in the shape of a perfect square, how long would each side be, in meters? What is this distance comparable to in your own life? (Remember that two hectares is a fair ecological footprint.)
3. How many full hectares would you need before you could make a perfect square of land again with a whole number as the side length? What will that side length be in metres?
4. Predict the next three perfect squares of land with a whole number as the side length.
5. Of course, your plot of land that supports your **consumption** doesn't need to be a square. For example, one hectare, or 10,000 m^2, can be created using different shapes. Draw two different rectangles, one triangle, and one polygon that each have an area of 10,000 m^2.
6. Find the perimeters of your polygon, rectangles, triangle and the original square: which plot of land would cost most to put a fence around?
7. The following table lists the average ecological footprint for five countries and the fair eco-footprint. Transfer hectares into square meters, and fill in the second column. Then calculate the side length of a perfect square of land for each case and put that in the third column.

	Hectares	Square meters (m2)	Side length of perfect square of land
United States	10.3		
Australia	9		
Canada	7.8		
Germany	5.3		
India	0.8		
Fair eco-footprint	2		

8. Create a comparative box graph like the model below (the model is not proportionate, and not complete). Choose a scale for your graph and make the boxes proportional to the side lengths in question #7.

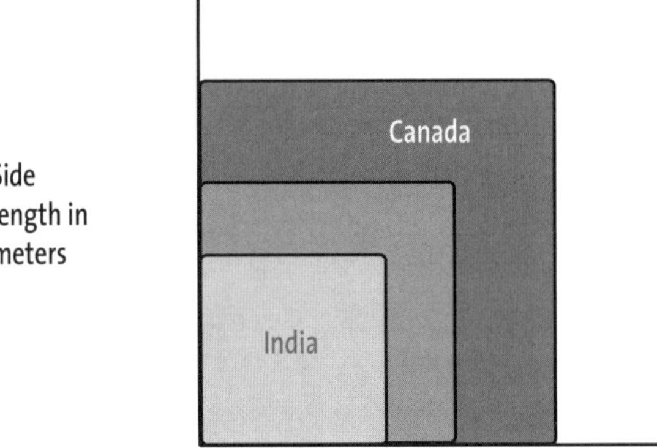

9. Pretend that all of the people on the earth consumed at a rate comparable to the Canadian ecological footprint of 7.8 hectares. If there are about six billion people on the planet, and the planet has about 11.7 billion hectares of productive land, how many planets of equal size and productive land would be required to support this consumption?

10. The *Worldwatch 2004 Report* lists the amount of water required to create 10 grams of protein, and 500 calories of different foods[242] (see below).

    a. How many times more water is required to produce 10 grams of protein from beef than from potatoes?

    b. If you used 301.5 litres of water to get 45 grams of protein from potatoes how much water would you need to get 45 grams of beef?

    c. How many times more water is required to produce 500 calories from corn than from poultry? Than from beef?

Food	Water Consumed to supply 10 grams of protein (L)	Water consumed to supply 500 calories (L)
Potatoes	67	89
Onions	118	221
Maize-corn	130	130
Pulses-beans	132	421
Wheat	135	219
Rice	204	251
Eggs	244	963
Milk	250	758
Poultry	303	1,515
Pork	476	1,225
Beef	1,000	4,902

242 *Worldwatch Report 2004* p. 54.

Food for thought...

The high meat content of the average U.S. diet costs 5.4 cubic meters of water per person per day. An equally nutritious vegetarian diet uses half that amount of water.[243] To produce a single two gram microchip for a computer requires materials 630 times its own mass, including water, elemental gasses, chemicals and fossil fuels.[244]

"To be a vegetarian is to disagree – to disagree with the course of things today: starvation, world hunger, cruelty, waste, wars..."

– J.B. Singer

- Go to the **Recycling Council of Ontario's** website to find out your own eco-footprint at www.rco.on.ca/ecofootprint.html. Choose one thing from the questionnaire to improve on a consistent basis for the next six months.
- Buy locally produced fresh food.
- Walk or bike as often as possible. Take public transport for further distances.
- Reduce, before reusing and recycling. Buy recycled products.

243 *Worldwatch Report 2004*, p. 54.
244 *Worldwatch Report 2004*, p. 44.

Blunt Force Trauma

"Standardized tests tend to measure what matters least."
– Alfie Kohn

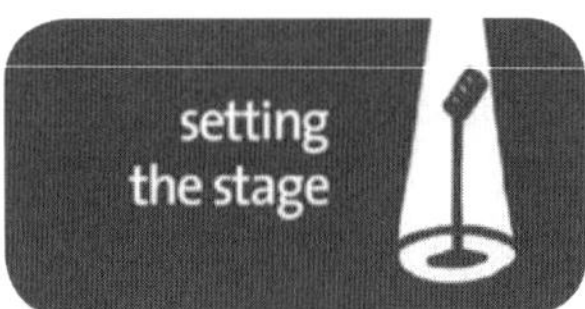

If you go to school in Ontario, you have probably experienced the province-wide tests in grades three and six, called EQAO. These are called "**standardized**" **tests**, because everyone in the province takes the same one. **Proponents** of these tests say that we need "**accountability**"- in other words, we need to know if teachers and schools are doing a good job of educating students.

Recently, there have been some outspoken **critics** of standardized tests. Some of their objections are as follows:

1. They test for low-level facts and skills: how well students memorize facts, words or formulas, rather than complex problem solving and understanding.[245]
2. To be cost effective they have to be marked efficiently, which again means more simple questions are required.[246]
3. Test anxiety prevents some students from doing their best, so the scores are unreliable.[247]

---

245 Kohn, Alfie. *The Schools Our Children Deserve.* Houghton Mifflin Company, New York. 2000. P. 20.
246 Ibid, p. 75.
247 Ibid, p. 76..

4. Testing benefits students of higher **socio-economic status**. In other words, those with more money do better.[248]

Why might students who come from families with more money tend to do better on these tests? Try to think of two reasons.

1. Open a **spreadsheet** program. Complete a chart following the example below:

College Admission Test Scores by Family Income, 1998	
Family Income ($)	**Average Score**
10000	873
20000	918
30000	972
40000	993
50000	1015
60000	1033
70000	1048
80000	1062
100000	1084
105000	1130

This data was collected on a standardized test in the United States called the SAT College Admission Test. Students' scores are used to determine entry into colleges.[249]

2. Use your chart to create a scatter graph ("XY"). Make sure that the graph connects the data with smoothed lines. Don't forget titles and labels.

3. How would you characterize the trend in your graph in one clear sentence?

4. Select the whole graph and copy it. Paste a copy of it below your first graph. Put your cursor over the y-axis and right click the mouse: select "Format Axis". Choose "Scale" and set the minimum to 850, the maximum to 1150, the major unit to 25, the minor unit to 25, and change the value that the x-axis crosses the y-axis to 850. You have just changed the **range** of data that the y-axis considers. Have you made the range smaller or larger than your original graph, and what impact did that have on the graph?

5. Copy your second graph and paste the copy slightly below your second graph. Right click on the x-axis, and choose scale. Put the minimum at zero, the maximum at 450,000, the major unit at 150,000, the minor unit at 30,000, and the crossing of the y-axis at 850. Have you made the range of the x-axis smaller or larger than your first two graphs? What impact did that have on the graph?

248 Ibid, p.77.
249 Kohn, Alfie. *The Schools Our Children Deserve*. Houghton Mifflin Company, New York. 2000. P. 262.

6. You have now displayed the **same data** in three different ways. Explain which graph you would use and why, if you wanted to make the point about standardized tests being "**classist**". Then explain which graph you would use and why, if you were trying to defend standardized tests.

7. Are any of the graphs you made **biased**? Explain.

8. Print out your spreadsheet and the three graphs and submit them with this assignment.

9. The idea of publishing schools' test scores in newspapers has been suggested. Do you think that this is **ethical** given what you now know? Explain your answer.

- Explore the website www.fairtest.org and write down one thing that you learned while you were there. Alternately, find your own website that deals with standardized testing. Write down the website you visited and one thing that you learned while at that site.

- Write a letter to the Minister of Education and ask how much money is spent each year to administer standardized tests (including the marking of standardized tests). Ask your teachers how they would spend that money within the school system. How would you spend that money?

Totally SAP-ped

In the world of international finance...one player can always be made to pay: the poor.

– 50 Years Is Enough

The **World Bank** is an institution that loans money to its 184 member countries, at interest rates lower than market rates. The money is meant to build infrastructure like roads and power plants. But the money is also meant to change the way a country's economic system works, by funding what are called **structural adjustment programs**, or **SAPs**.

SAPs are designed by another global institution, the International Monetary Fund, or **IMF**. The IMF also gives loans to developing countries, which usually need money to pay back large amounts of debt and the interest on that debt. The IMF gives out these loans as long as the country receiving the loan agrees to restructure its economy with a SAP. The IMF says that with a SAP, the developing country will earn enough hard cash to be financially balanced.

SAPs do the following things: they **devalue the currency** of the country, they cut or stop government **subsidies** for basic foods and fuels, they remove taxes on **imports**, they cut basic services like education, housing, environmental protection and health and sell those services into the private sector, they cut government budgets, and they encourage the people to grow and **export "cash crops"** for the world **market**.[250] All of these are things that devastate the country and benefit the rich countries and foreign **investors**.

250 50 Years is Enough, Frequently Asked Questions About IMF/World Bank, March 2004, pp.1-3.

SAPs are applied to many countries at the same time. If all of these countries are making cash crops (flowers, coffee, sugar, tea, tobacco, cocoa) to sell on the world market, what will happen to the world market prices for these crops?

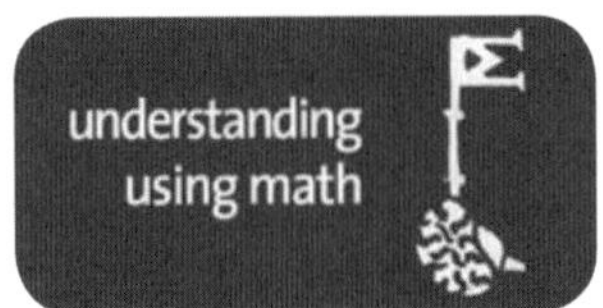

1. In some institutions, each member gets a single vote for when decisions need to be made. But in the World Bank and the IMF each nation's vote depends on how much that nation gives to the bank. Big changes in **policy** direction require 85% of the vote.[251]

   a. If the World Bank and the IMF ran on one vote per country, how many of the 184 member countries would need to agree to make a big policy change?

   b. Under the current voting system, the United States has between 15.5% and 18% of the vote in these institutions. How many of the 183 other countries would need to agree to make a policy change that the US didn't agree with?

2. Under the directives of a structural adjustment program, the government sells its hospitals to a foreign company for millions of dollars, and uses that money to pay back a part of its debt. The foreign company now runs the hospitals as a business, and in order to make money, charges user fees. Indicate what you think the consequences of this will be (circle):

Number of people visiting the hospital	Increase or	Decrease
Number of people dying	Increase or	Decrease
Number of hospital worker layoffs	Increase or	Decrease
Amount of labour advancements/unions	Increase or	Decrease
Number of hospital closures	Increase or	Decrease

3. A study is done to examine the extraction of natural materials from a country that is undergoing structural readjustment. It seems that in emphasizing cash crop export, the natural environment is suffering. Based on the following chart:

	Lumber Industry (kg)	Oil Industry (barrels)	Sugar Industry (kg)	Copper Industry (kg)
Total Exports Before Structural Adjustment	4,026	10,643	7,890	4,512
Total Output During Structural Adjustment	4,912	12,984	9,626	5,505

251 "50 Years is Enough, Frequently Asked Questions About IMF/World Bank", March 2004, p.2.

a. Find the relationship between the amount of exports before and during the SAP, and express that relationship in an algebraic equation.

b. Predict what the output of phosphorus is during structural adjustment if its output before the SAP was 16,431 kg/week.

c. How likely is it that this increased output of natural resources is environmentally **sustainable**? Justify your answer.

4. The following graph is based on data from four countries that implemented user fees in their hospitals and schools as a part of their structural adjustment programs.[252]

a. A new user fee of 33 cents for a health centre visit in Kenya led to what percentage loss of patients?

b. What percentage increase occurred after user fees were scrapped in Kenya? Why do you think it didn't return to 100%?

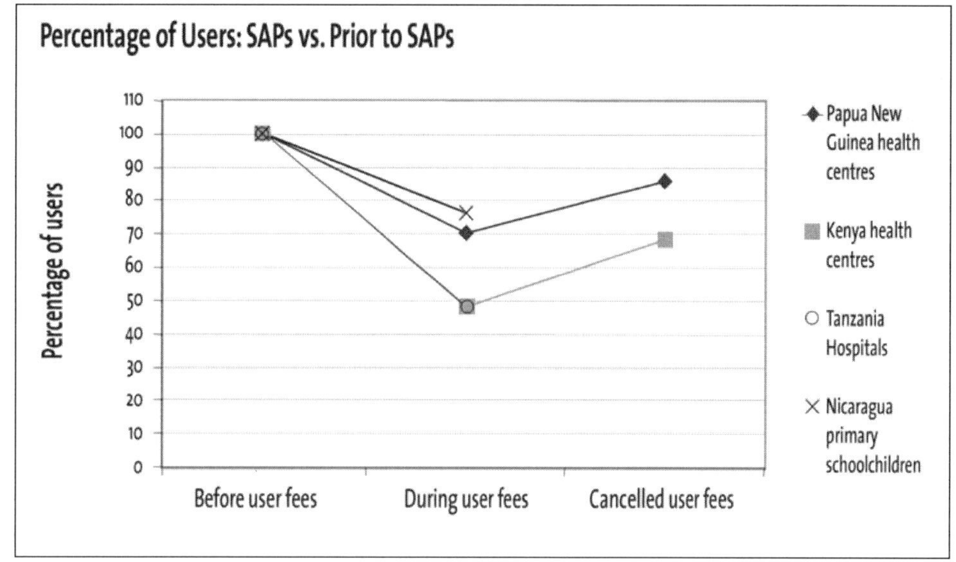

c. If the number of children attending school in Nicaragua was 22,109 prior to the introduction of user fees, how many attended after the user fees were imposed?

d. When school fees were eliminated and uniforms were not required in Malawi, the enrolment in primary school went from 1.9 million to 2.9 million students almost instantaneously (including a majority of girls).[253] What percentage increase was this? Why do you think it was girls who were the main **beneficiaries**?

---

251 www.50years.org

253 www.50years.org

5. Look at the following statistics from Uganda in Africa,[254] and find the algebraic equation that describes the pattern.

Money spent on health	Money spent on debt repayment
$1	$5.67
$2	$11.34
$3	$17.01
$4	$22.68

6. If the government of Uganda spent $5,000,000 in healthcare in 2004, how much would they be spending in **debt repayment** that same year?

7. The external debt for Africa, with the exception of South Africa, was $203 billion in 1996. That figure was 313% of the value of its exports.[255] What was the value of Africa's exports? (In 2006 the external debt for Africa is approximately 300 billion.[256])

- Explore the resources at the 50 Years Is Enough website: www.50years.org.

254 www.50years.org/factsheets/debt.html Fact Sheets DEBT March 25, 2004
255 Ibid.
256 http://www.africaaction.org/campaign_new/debt.php

What's A Gerrymander?

"A lie would have no sense unless the truth were felt dangerous."
– Alfred Adler

setting the stage

Just over two and a half centuries ago in the year 1744, a man by the name of Elbridge Gerry was born in the State of Massachusetts. He would become the Governor in 1810 and soon afterwards introduce a law that allowed him to re-draw (re-district) the boundaries of his voting region. Voting regions should have an appropriate population mixture and unfair tampering with the borders that benefit a particular **political party** is not allowed. Gerry's political opponents said that he had redistricted his area unfairly, using a very peculiar shape that seemed to reach out and encompass areas where most people voted for him. The peculiar shape looked like a salamander. The term "**gerrymandering**" was coined soon after.[257]

There are three ways to gerrymander, all of them illegal. The first method, called the "excess vote", is creating voting regions that enclose most of the opposition within just a few regions (that they will win), while outside of those regions there will be very few opposition votes. The "wasted vote" method creates a few regions that dilute the opposition votes in a large number of other regions. And finally the "stacked" method involves creating a region that has irregular borders to link up the majority party's power.[258]

L

257 http://geography.about.com/library/weekly/aa030199.htm
258 Ibid.

Name one issue that the people in a region might use to elect or reject a particular political party. Pick a very specific issue and explain it using a few sentences.

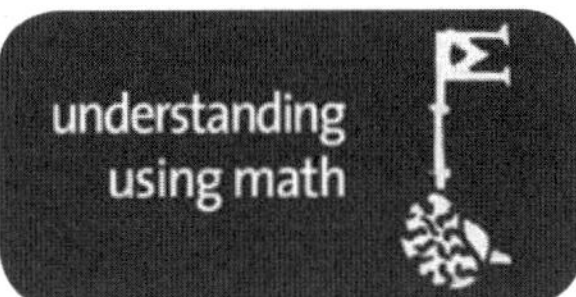

1. The scenario: you are the leader of Party A, elected to power three years ago by a large majority. However, a recent poll conducted throughout the province shows that you are currently lagging behind Party B. Your task is to modify the voting regions so that you can win the next election.

   You will need to know how to find the area of irregular shapes, which means that you will also need to know how find the area of squares, rectangles and triangles. To fill in this chart, use the "Provincial Polling Results" map and the questions on the next page.

Region	Area (km²)	Party A Support Before/After		Party B Support Before/After		Party C Support Before/After		Region currently won by Party...	Newly formed region can be Party...
1									
2									
3									
4									
5									
6									
7									
8									
9									
10									
11									
12									
13									
	Overall Area:	Totals Before/After		Totals Before/After		Totals Before/After		Current Overall Party Winner:	New Overall Winner:

a. Calculate the area of each region. Each square is a square km (km²).

b. Count up the total support for each party in each region. Fill these totals in on the **left** side of each Party column (the shaded side). Do not fill in the right side yet.

c. Based on the three party totals, decide what party would currently win each region. The party who has the most votes in the region wins. Fill in your answer in the "Region currently won by party..." column.

d. Decide the current overall party winner. The overall winner is the one that has the most regions.

REGION 1
REGION 2
REGION 3
REGION 7
REGION 4
REGION 5
REGION 6
REGION 11
REGION 8
REGION 9
REGION 13
REGION 10
REGION 12

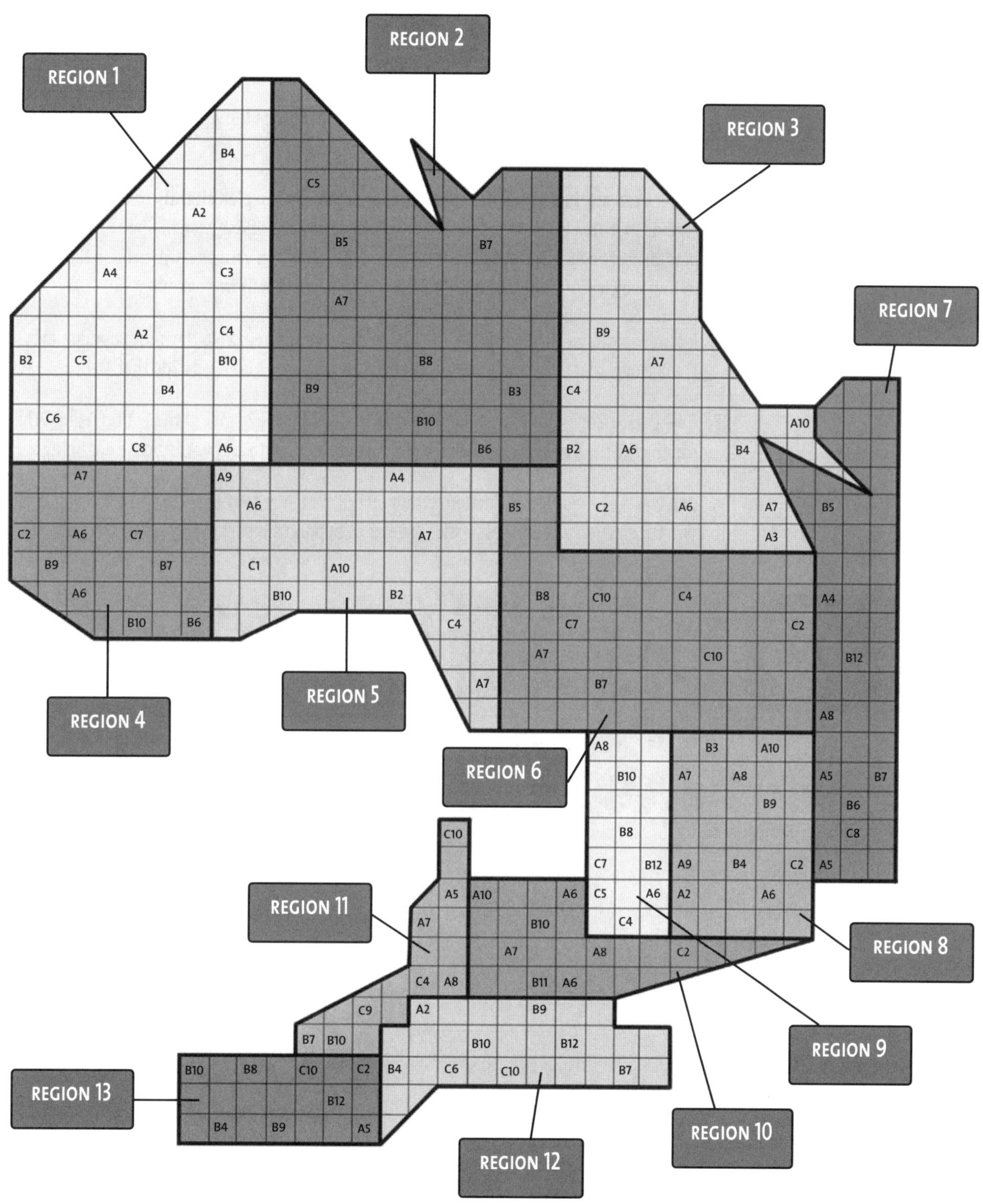

L

2. Who would win if you didn't change the boundaries of the voting regions, and the results of the pre-election poll were accurate on polling day?
3. As the regions are currently, how many people are in each region?
4. Why do regions 1, 2, 3, and 6 have more area than the other regions?
5. List the regions which are controlled solidly by one party. List the regions where two or more parties are close in levels of support.
6. Using a **red marker**, adjust the boundaries of each polling region **slightly** so that you can turn the regions that are close into a win for Party A. Once you have done that, fill in the new levels of support for each region in the **right** side of each party column in your chart. Also fill in the last column, telling which party will win the region and which party will win overall.
7. Is it possible to go from being the least popular party in a region to the most popular party with a change of borders? Give an example from your map if you managed to do that.
8. Give two reasons that you could use to justify moving the border of the voting region. The more convincing the better, because the public is going to want to know why you're changing a border.
9. Can you win a provincial election without having a majority of support? (In other words, can you win the election while other parties have more popular support than you do?) Explain.

- Invite members of the different political parties into your classroom to talk about the ways the voting process could be made more democratic.
- Before you do, research the different between "**first past the post**" voting and "**proportional representation**" voting. You might try the following website for your research: www.electoral-reform.org.uk.

Coming Clean...?

"When we talk about equal pay for equal work, women in the workplace are beginning to catch up. If we keep going at this current rate, we will achieve full equality in about 475 years. I don't know about you, but I can't wait that long."

– Lya Sorano

An image of children racing in the front door after school flashes on the T.V. They grab messy snacks from the refrigerator and turn the kitchen counter into a sloppy mess, before running out the back door to play in the park. Mom sweeps in and in an instant wipes the counter clean with a sponge and the latest in chemical cleaning products.

Later, images of dad making dinner- a special occasion, clearly. And he's forgotten that spaghetti sauce spills harden like cement to the table tops. As the kids dump dishes into the sink and dad saunters off for a nap, in sweeps mom, smiling, to wipe up the mess with a sponge and the latest chemical cleaning products.

Pan to a shot of the downstairs laundry room. All of those dirty clothes that look like their owners have been through army combat training. No worries, TV viewers at home. Mom will show you that what goes in grimy comes out sparkling clean with the latest in chemical cleaning products.

Everything you see is purposeful and carefully planned. Market surveys and focus groups are very expensive- not to mention the money involved in making and broadcasting commercials, people's salaries, and the cost of the product itself. If everything's so carefully thought out, why does it look like we're living in the 1950s with mom doing all the cleaning? Aren't we past those **stereotypes**?

What do you think? Do stereotypes sell product? Why or why not?

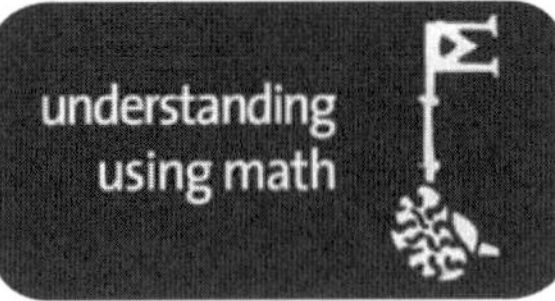

1. Collect and bring into class at least one of the following:
   a. A print ad or ads for cleaning products that have a person in them, or
   b. A videotape of a commercial for a cleaning product
2. Take some time to share the ads and commercials with classmates. Do you see any common themes?
3. Use the chart below to classify the ads, or create your own classification chart.

Number of women doing the cleaning	Number of men doing the cleaning	Number of children/youth doing the cleaning	Total number of cleaning ads

4. Calculate each of the categories in question #3 as a percentage. What do you notice? Why do you think that this is the case?
5. There are ways to increase your market share without advertising. Let's look at laundry detergent. The original scoop design for your laundry detergent is shaped in the following way:

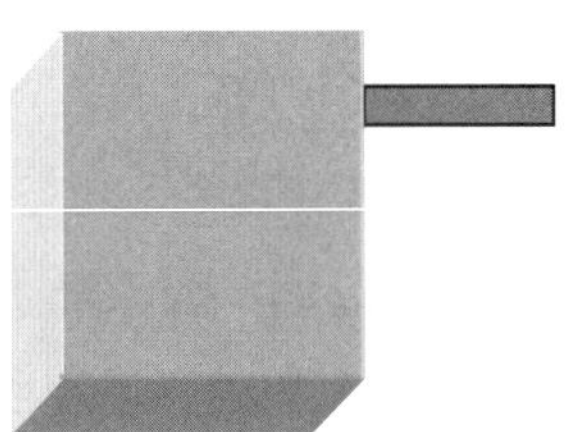

The dimensions of the base are 5 cm. by 5 cm. The height of the scoop is 7 cm. Assume that the market research is correct and that the majority of consumers use 85% of the full scoop. Calculate the volume of laundry detergent used with each scoop. Show all of your work.

6. A new scoop design is proposed. The designer says it will increase market share because it looks about the same size but holds more product. It is shaped in the following way:

To prevent consumers from thinking that the new scoop is a different volume (and by extension, that they should modify how much detergent they pick up with the scoop) the designer says the diameter of the base should be 5 cm. and the height of the scoop should remain the same as the first scoop. Assume that consumers still fill this scoop 85%. Calculate the volume of detergent used with each scoop. Show all of your work, and use 3.1416 as the value of pi. Is the designer correct?

7. Each full box of detergent is 2,500 cm^3. Calculate how many scoops it would take to finish the full box for each of the two designs (show your work). Is the new design more or less **profitable** than the original design? Explain.

8. Calculate the percentage that the smaller scoop is compared to the bigger scoop. If one box of detergent is $5.99, of which $1.78 is profit, use the percentage that you calculated for the scoop size to figure out the gain or loss of profit per box using the new design. Show your work.

9. A third design is proposed. It looks like the following:

The designer argues that the diameter of the base should actually be equal to the distance from one corner of the square base (on the original design) to the opposite corner. Calculate the new diameter using the **Pythagorean theorem**. The height remains 7 cm. What is the volume of the new scoop? Show your work.

10. If consumers don't notice the difference in the size of this new design, and still fill the scoop 85% full each time, how many cubic centimetres will the new scoop use? Show your work.

11. Calculate how many scoops it would take to finish the full box for the new design (show your work). Is the new design more or less profitable than the original design and the second design? Explain.

12. How **ethical** do you think this particular way of increasing product sales is? Explain.

Food for thought...

Product placement is a form of advertising where businesses pay to put their products in television shows and movies. Sometimes they can be used or mentioned by the actors. A seven second close up shot of Sunlight laundry detergent on the show *Everybody Loves Raymond* cost $22,980.

- Write a letter to the head of the company and ask why stereotypes persist in its advertising material.

A Little Goes A Long Way

"Only when the last tree has been cut down,

Only when the last river has been poisoned,

Only when the last fish has been caught,

Only then you will find that money cannot be eaten."

– Cree Prophesy

It's late at night. 2 am. You wake up wanting a drink. Something's not right- call it **premonition** or paranoia, you wake your partner and the kids and scramble into your run-down truck. Relatives live on the far side of town, which may or may not be far enough. Tonight passes quietly, but two days from now, a gas leak at the local pesticide plant will kill 8,000 people almost immediately, and the toxic wastes contaminating the soil and the groundwater will make the region one in which you wouldn't grow a garden, let alone raise a family.

More than half a million people in Bhopal, India were exposed to lethal gasses from the Union Carbide pesticide factory in December of 1984. To this day, 30 people a month continue to die as a result of the incident, and survivors have been plagued with **chronic illnesses**, aborted pregnancies and a host of genetic defects.[259]

In Canada, more than 100 companies **vie** for **profit** in British Columbia's sour gas industry. Sour gas is rich in sulphur and is extracted from the ground in the form of hydrogen sulphide, a deadly poison. It doesn't take much: at 100 parts per million, hydrogen sulphide is lethal in seconds. Lower levels of exposure can cause neurological and reproductive problems- some suggest cancer as well.[260]

In B.C.'s sour gas industry, wells used to be drilled back in the mostly unpopulated bush. That's begun to change: companies are now drilling closer to residential homes.[261] Can you think of an economic reason why this might be the case?

1. Your pencil probably has a mass of 5 grams. What would 100 parts per million be if your 5 gram pencil was equivalent to a million? Answer in both grams and milligrams. Could you use a triple beam balance to find that amount?
2. Suppose a student has a mass of 50 kg (about 110 pounds). What would 100 parts per million be if 50 kg was equivalent to a million? Answer in kilograms, grams, and milligrams.
3. A sample was taken of 865 pregnant women living one km from the Bhopal plant. Of the 486 live births, 68 babies did not survive their first month.[262] How does this rate compare with the 2.6 to 3% rate of **infant mortality** before the accident?
4. A study is released on the **toxicity levels** at different distances from a chemical spill. Based on the following table, find an algebraic equation that describes the pattern.

Distance from spill	Toxicity level (mg/L)
0 metres	5.34
100 metres	5.27
200 metres	5.20
300 metres	5.13

5. This particular chemical is highly toxic at 4.5 mg/L or more. How far is that from the spill site?
6. If the density of the population in this region is 25,000 per square kilometre, how many people fall within the highly toxic zone? What shape will that zone be?

259 International Campaign for Justice in Bhopal "Bhopal Survivors Protest Dow's Presence at the World Summit on Sustainable Development", http://www.corpwatch.org/bulletins/PBD.jsp?article=3708 April 5, 2004

260 Siegel, Shefa.l *The Smell of Money: British Columbia's Gas Rush* www.corpwatch.org/issues/PRT.jsp?articleid=10328 March 13, 2004

261 Ibid.

262 www.bhopal.net Arpil 5, 2004

Chemico Profit Statements

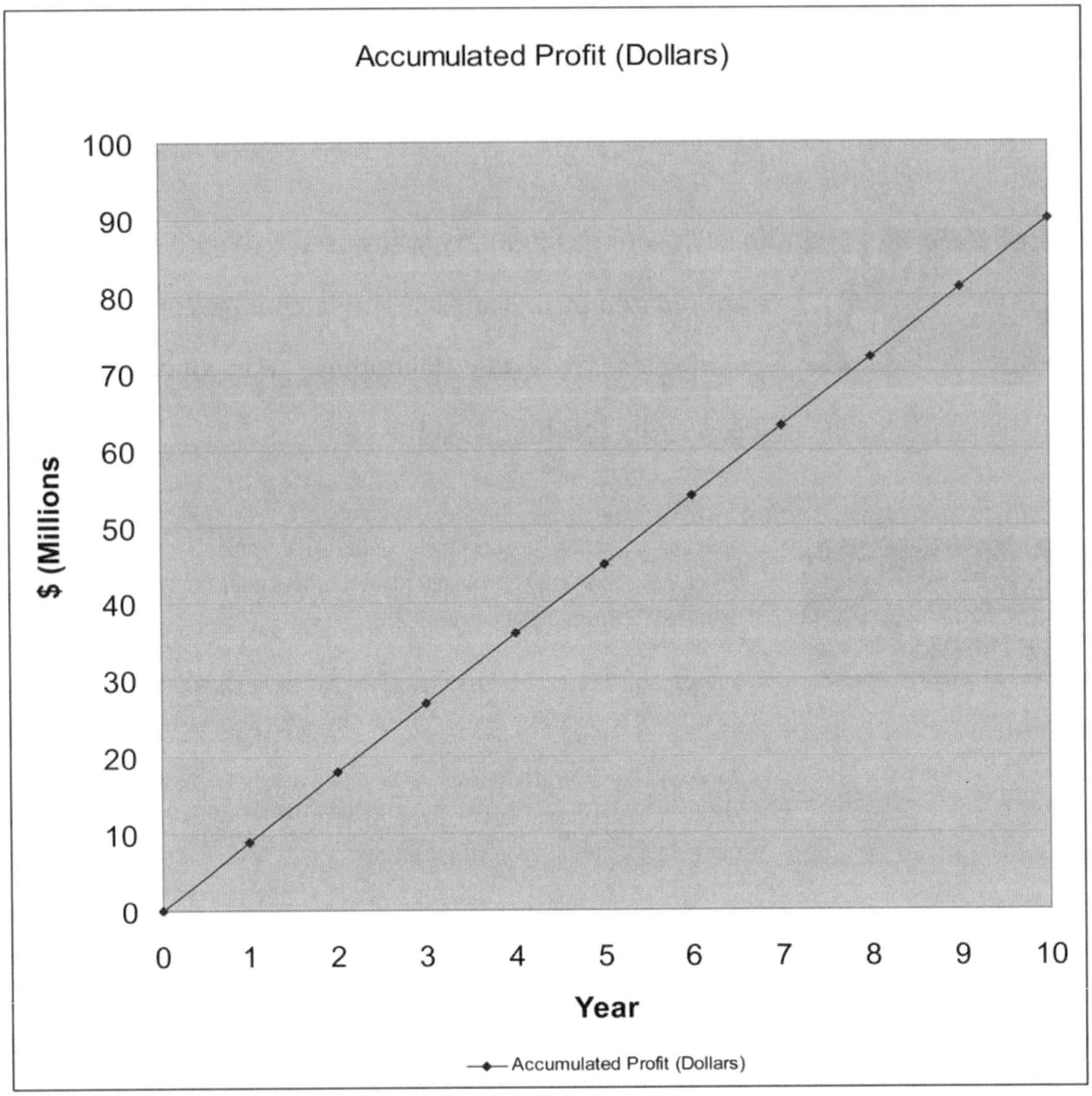

Accumulated Profit (Dollars)

$ (Millions)

0 10 20 30 40 50 60 70 80 90 100

0 1 2 3 4 5 6 7 8 9 10

Year

Accumulated Profit (Dollars)

7. From the graph, determine the algebraic equation that defines Chemico's accumulated profits (Chemico is a fictitious company).

8. Assuming the pattern continues in the same way, what will this company's **accumulated** profits be in year 25?

9. This fictitious company is successfully taken to court and prosecuted on average once every year, for environmental damage caused by toxins leaked from the plant, spills in transport of materials, illegal dumping, and use of prohibited substances. The algebraic equation that describes the accumulated cost of the fines is as follows:

$F = 1{,}000{,}000Y$ where F is the amount of accumulated fines in dollars and Y is the number of years.

a. Draw in the line that shows the accumulated fines over the ten year period.

b. Assuming that the company pays the fines, what is the algebraic equation that defines the company's net accumulated profits (the accumulated profits subtract the accumulated fines)?

10. The company could pay to replace its ageing machinery with newer, more environmentally friendly systems. They could increase the number and quality of filters on their smoke stacks and improve emergency warning technology. Staff could be trained on a regular basis. The company could put money into research and development in order to find less toxic materials for production.

    A study is done to determine the annual cost of these measures. The algebraic equation that describes the pattern is as follows:

    $C = 4{,}000{,}000Y$ where C is the accumulated cost to implement the above improvements, and Y is the number of years.

    a. Draw in the line that shows the accumulated costs over the ten year period.

    b. Explain why it's better for the company to continue to destroy the environment and take its chance in court rather than implement the improvements to the system. (This is called cost-benefit analysis.)

11. An environmental **lobby group** pushes the government to change the laws to allow for stiffer fines. They suggest that the way fines should be handed out is more effective if it follows this pattern:

    $E = 1{,}000{,}000Y^2 + 1{,}000{,}000Y$ where E is the accumulated costs of these stricter environmental fines and Y is the number of years.

    Use the algebraic equation to draw in the line that it describes over the ten year period.

    a. How is this line different than the original accumulated fines line? Which line is **linear**, and which is **non linear**? Why does it matter?

    b. By visual inspection, in which year do the accumulated fines equal the accumulated profits? Bonus: solve this using algebra only, by making the accumulated profits equation equal to the accumulated fines equation, and solve for Y.

    c. Based on the new system of fines, how long do you think it would take the company to implement new environmental designs and systems? Explain your answer.

- Buying organic foods means that you aren't supporting the pesticide industry.
- Riding your bike means that you aren't supporting the oil and gas industry.

The Return Of Tobin Hood

"I believe that the unarmed truth and unconditional love will have the final word in reality. This is why right, temporarily defeated, is stronger than evil triumphant."

– Martin Luther King

Who would've thought it? Twenty odd years ago a Nobel prize winning economist named James Tobin suggested that we raise some money for global **social causes** by **taxing currency exchange transactions**.[263] Dubbed the "Tobin Tax", it's gaining favour around the world as we sit here and do math.

Over $1.5 trillion a day changes hands on **foreign exchange markets**[264] but 80% of that figure is "**speculative**". In other words, most of the trading has very little to do with products (like lumber, or pork bellies, or steel) and a lot to do with currency gambling.[265] A currency speculator bets on whether a currency will rise or fall in the short term future. If they guess right, they make money.

Unfortunately, this casino-like gambling process pulls huge sums of money out of national economies very quickly and other speculators quickly pull out of the burning ship as well, in a domino effect. The country is left in financial crisis and money that normally goes into **social programs** is frantically used by the government to prop up their currency. The most vulnerable people suffer, as witnessed in the recent currency crises in Latin America, Asia and Africa.

263 www.waronwant.org *The Tobin Tax: Win-Win for the World's Poor.* p. 1.
264 *Costing the Casino Report Introduction* www.waronwant.org
265 www.waronwant.org *The Tobin Tax: Win-Win for the World's Poor.* p. 1.

Putting a small tax on each currency transaction would make it less **profitable** to speculate and would raise money for global causes. A tax of 0.1% (or 10 cents for every $100) could raise between $50-300 billion each year.[266] Compare this to the United Nations' estimate for universal social services to end poverty: $40 billion per year.[267]

Who would be opposed to the Tobin tax and for what reasons?

1. The Foreign Exchange Market (FOREX) is the richest **market** in the world. More than $1.2 trillion worth of currency is traded each day.[268]

   a. A stack of $100 bills amounting to one million dollars is about 1.83 metres (or 6 feet) high. How high a stack of $100 bills would be equivalent to the $1.2 trillion worth of currency traded each day?

   b. Compare this height to the height of Mount Everest.

   c. Remember: that's each day.

2. There are 250 trading days in the year.

   a. How high would that stack of $100 bills be in one year?

   b. Compare that with the distance from the Earth to the moon.

3. The relationship between the amount of money we spend on **goods and services** everywhere in the world each year (G) and the amount of money that is traded in the currency exchange market (C) is as follows:

   C = 50 G

   a. How much is the annual amount of money we spend on goods and services compared to the amount we spend on speculative gambling?

   b. Why is spending on goods and services likely to be more healthy for a country than speculative gambling?

4. The purest form of speculation is called "**arbitrage**". Suppose that the exact same product, let's say pork bellies, are selling on two different stock exchanges for different prices. On market A, they are selling at $10 a share. On market B, they are selling at $10.25 a share. Arbitrage is where you buy the shares on market A and immediately turn around and sell them on market B.

   a. You have access to $500,000. Using the above example, how much profit can you generate by speculation on the pork bellies?

   b. Since the transaction is essentially instantaneous, how much risk to your money would you have experienced?

266 Ibid, p. 2.
267 Salmon, Blaise. "Tobin Tax Motion Passes in Canada's Parliament". March 24, 1999. www.ceedweb.org/iirp/canadanames.htm.
268 www.tobintax.org "Frequently Asked Questions About the Tobin Tax". P. 2

5. Here's how speculation in foreign currency works. Let's say you think that the Japanese currency, the Yen is going to go down in value. You borrow a lot of Yen, and then convert that Yen into another currency that you think will be stable. If the Yen then goes down in value, you pay back your loan and make a profit. Try it:

    a. Borrow 5,000,000 Yen. Convert your Yen into Canadian dollars ($1 CDN = 80 Yen). How many Canadian dollars do you have?

    b. Let's say the Yen devalues and now $1 CDN = 120 Yen. Pay back your 5,000,000 Yen. How much do you have left over in Yen? In Canadian dollars?

6. If you speculate to make profit, you're not always going to be correct. The following is a speculation game, where you may lose your **investment**.

    a. Create a table showing all of the possible sums if you roll two dice together.

    b. How many possible different rolls are there?

    c. Based on table #1 below, bet on a category (for example "the currency will jump slightly in value", and invest a certain amount of money (for example, $100,000). Roll the two dice.

    d. Refer to table #2 to see how you did. Calculate your profit or loss.

Table #1
Pick a Category...
"The currency will jump a great deal in value"
"The currency will jump slightly in value"
"The currency will fall slightly in value"
"The currency will fall a great deal in value"

Table #2	
If you roll...	The result is...
A sum of 2 or 3	You're really right- profit 10% of your investment
A sum of 4 or 5	You're pretty close- profit 5% of your investment
A sum of 8 or 9	You're off, but not too badly- lose 5% of your investment
A sum of 11 or 12	You're way off- lose 10% of your investment

    e. What is the probability that you are "really right"? In the real world, how might you increase your chances of being "really right"?

    f. Why don't you profit if the currency does not change in value?

7. Computers can now do much speculation without the aid of human intervention. Programs update prices at a rate of 200 times per second.[269] What fraction of a second does it take to update prices (numerically as a decimal number and in words)?

269 Davis, Jim. "Globalization and Social Justice Conference". Chicago, May 9-11, 2002. P. 9.

8. Let's pretend that you are in charge of a committee to distribute the money collected from a Tobin Tax ($50-300 billion per year). What would you spend the money on? The following chart shows the additional amount of money required each year to adequately address these social issues.[270]

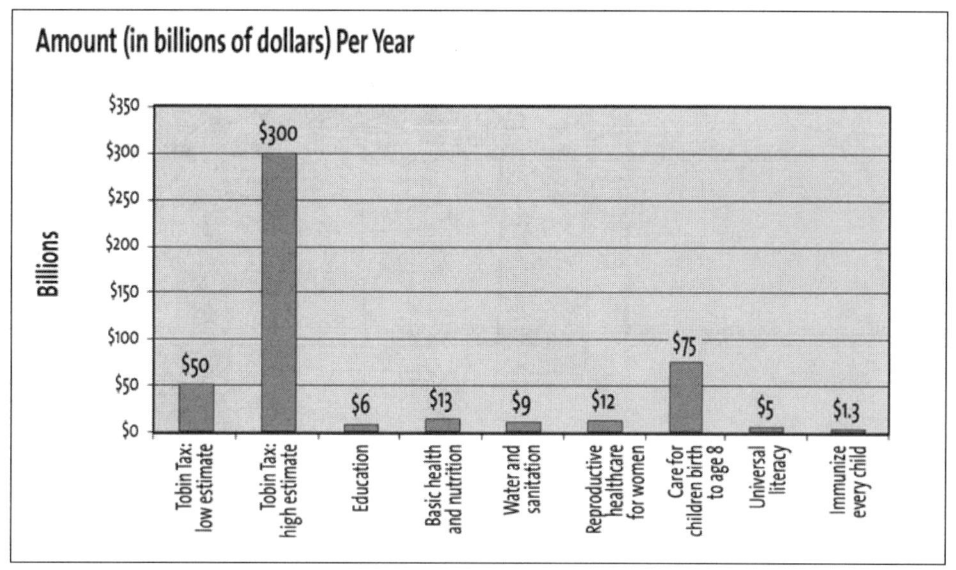

Food for thought...[271]

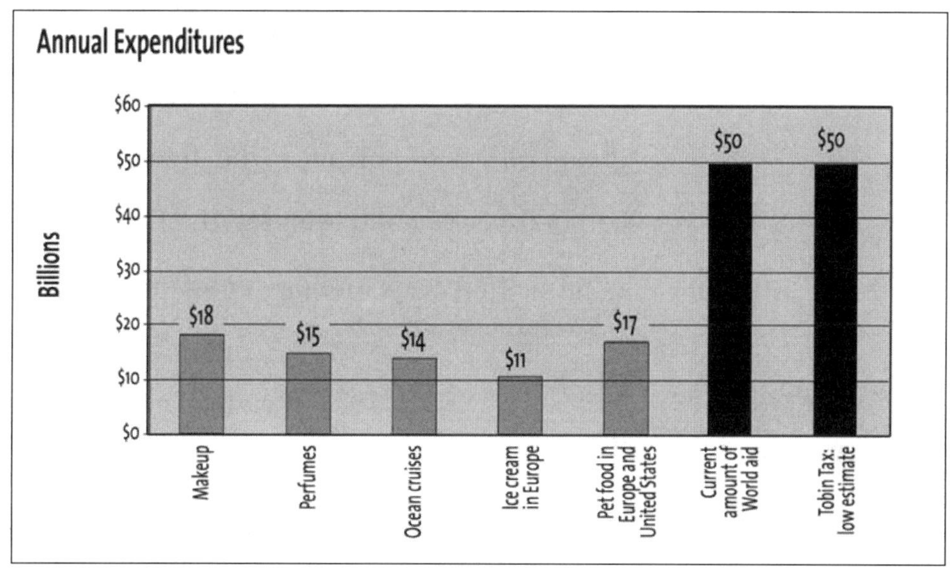

- Try currency speculation yourself to get a sense of how it works: there's an excellent game at www.waronwant.org/game/ .
- Call your **Member of Parliament** and ask them what they are doing, if anything, about the implementation of a **Tobin Tax**.

270 "The Robin Hood Tax, Introduction" www.waronwant.org
271 *Worldwatch Report 2004*. P. 10.

Buying Your Eyes

"The 20th century has been characterized by three developments of great political importance: the growth of democracy, the growth of corporate power and the growth of corporate propaganda as a means of protecting corporate power against democracy."

– Alex Carey as quoted by Noam Chomsky

Channel One Network in the United States advertises to business clients: "We have the undivided attention of millions of teenagers for 12 minutes a day." In return for installation of televisions and computers in 60% of American schools, Channel One is allowed to broadcast a 12-minute mix of **advertising** and news.

Given that Canadian youth "control 20 billion dollars of **discretionary spending**, and develop **brand loyalties** that are said to last a lifetime"[272] it was only a matter of time before a Canadian version of Channel One appeared. In 1992 and 1994 Youth News Network tried to gain access to schools in Alberta and Nova Scotia but strong parent outcry stopped the attempt. Backed by large **corporate** partners and a **public relations** firm, YNN made its move on Meadowvale High School in Ontario.

The contract with the school required a single 12 minute broadcast in year one, and then in the following five years a guarantee that 80% of the students would watch the daily broadcast 90% of the time. In return for student eyes, YNN would pay the school $150,000.[273]

---

272 Heather-Jane Robinson, "What are our children watching?" Canadian Association of Media Education Organizations
273 Michelle Landsberg, "This algebra class brought to you by Nike" *Toronto Star*, May 21, 1999.

Do you think that $150,000 is a lot of money to give to a school? Why or why not? What would it buy?

Television networks provide commercial time in their programming to businesses so that the network can make money. In their first year, CNN and ESPN collected $24 million and $10 million in advertising **revenue** respectively. In Channel One's first year, it collected $51 million.[274]

1. Using a **spreadsheet** program, create a graph to show the three advertising revenue figures. You choose the type of graph that best displays the data. Make sure to include a title and a legend.
2. Why do you think that Channel One was able to collect so much more advertising revenue it its first year?
3. In the 12 minutes of YNN programming, there are 2.5 minutes of commercials. A typical Canadian school year is approximately 200 school days. How many minutes of commercials would each student view per year?
4. To put a 30 second commercial on CNN during prime time it costs anywhere between $1,000 and $30,000. How many days would it take for YNN to break even with its $150,000 contribution to the school if it charged businesses only the lowest CNN rate ($1,000 per 30 seconds). Show your work.
5. When the show Star Trek Enterprise was City TV's top rated show (in other words, the show that most people tuning into this station watch), the rate to show a 30 second commercial was $9,000. How many days would it take YNN to break even with its $150,000 contribution to the school if it charged businesses the $9,000/30 second rate? Show your work.
6. The money that YNN would collect after it's break even date and to the end of the year might give us an indication of whether the $150,000 was generous enough (putting aside for the moment questions of **ethics**). Calculate the amount of money from the break even date to the end of the school year. Use an average cost for the 30 second segment this time.
7. Joseph Rotman (currently a director of the Bank of Montreal, Barrick Gold Corporation, Ovation Inc., Premdor Inc., and TrizecHahn Corporation) contributed $15 million dollars to the University of Toronto but it cost him only $6 million because of **tax write-offs**.[275] What percentage of the original donation is $6 million? (Do you think he made any demands of the university in return for his money?)

274 Heather-Jane Robertson "What are our children watching?" CAMCO.
275 Clarke,Tony and Sarah Dopp. *Challenging McWorld*. Canadian Centre for Policy Alternatives. 2001, p. 17.

8. A (fictitious) study of business leaders is conducted to find the number one reason that connections with schools are important to business. Their results are summarized below:

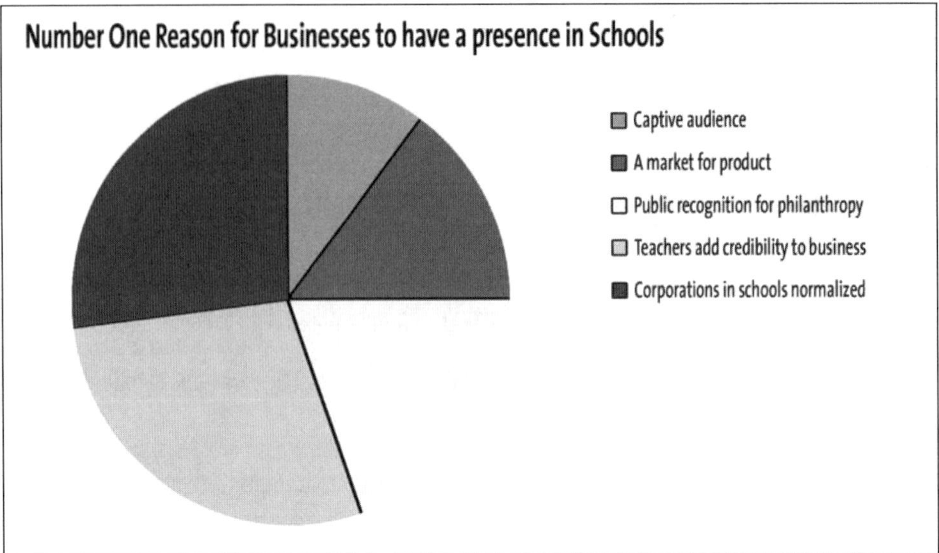

a. Figure out the percentages for each category using a protractor.

b. Do you think that these results would be realistic? Why or why not? What do you think would be different?

Food for thought...

AT&T, McDonald's and Chrysler have all **sponsored** curriculum materials for use in schools, published by Scholastic Inc.[276]

- Explore your school for corporate influence. Arrange a meeting with the teachers and the principal to discuss these business partnerships with the school. Who benefits? Who loses?

276 Ibid, p. 41.

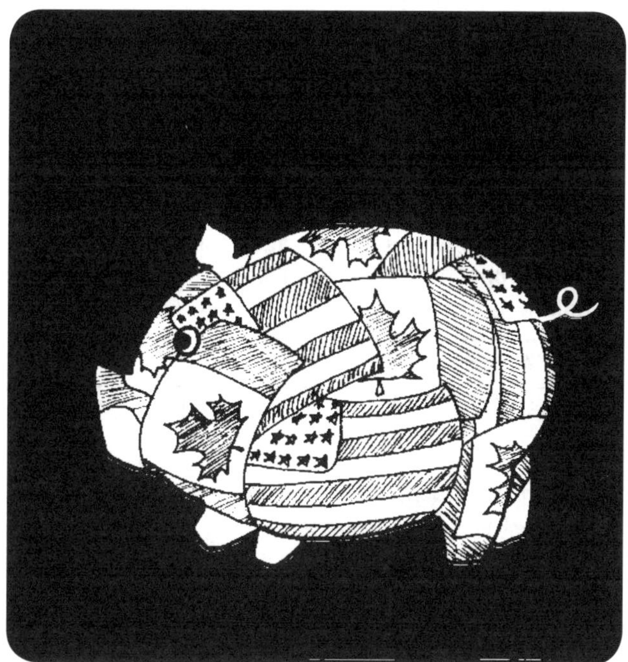

Oink Oink...

"The moment you live something, you are teaching it, whether you want to or not."
– Dadi Janki

It's true. We North Americans amount to a paltry 5 % of the five billion people on the planet Earth. Strangely enough, we consume 33% of the world's **resources** and produce half of its organic waste.[277]

Take lawns, for example. Americans use approximately 30 billion litres of water on their grass each day, and the average irrigated lawn uses 38,000 litres per summer.[278] That's like 19,000 two litre bottles of pop on one lawn! How many deaths worldwide result from lack of access to safe water?

How about paper? Americans use 300 kilograms of paper per year. People in **developing nations**, on average, use 18 kilograms per year. People in India use four kg per year and 20 African nations use one kg per person per year.[279]

What is your guess with electric power? Nigeria uses 81 kilowatt hours (kWh) per person. Egyptians use 217 kwh. Americans use 12,331 kwh on average.[280] Not surprising, since it's required to run televisions (835 per 1,000 people), clothes washers (owned by more than 77% of the country), and refrigerators (115 per 100 households). Brazilians have 349 TVs per 1,000 people. In India, only six percent of people have clothes washers and there are only 12 refrigerators per 100 households.[281]

---

277 *Adbusters*, "7 TV Uncommercials & the Culture Jammer's Video"
278 *Worldwatch 2004 Report*, p. 59.
279 Ibid, p. 9.
280 Ibid, p. 9.
281 Ibid, pp. 9, 34.

opening question

Why do you think that North Americans **consume** so much in comparison to the rest of the world's population (suggest two possibilities). If it's not fair, why do they get away with it?

understanding using math

Relationship between the average consumption of a person from North America and a person from Mexico (North America in this case refers to the United States and Canada):

North American	10	40	110	285
Mexican	2	8	22	57

1. Explain the relationship between the average **consumption** of a person from North America and one from Mexico. You might want to start by saying, "For each one kilogram of resources someone in Mexico uses, a person in North America uses (this many kilograms)."

2. Write an algebraic equation to describe the relationship. First select two **variables** (letters), one to represent each of the categories. Then use your last answer to create an algebraic equation to show the pattern.

3. If a person from Mexico used 23 kilograms of resources, how much would his or her North American counterpart be using?

Relationship between the average consumption of a person from North America and a person from China (North America in this case refers to the United States and Canada).

North American	20	80	140	200
Chinese	2	8	14	20

4. Explain the relationship between the average consumption of a person from North America and one from China. You might want to start by saying, "For each one kilogram of resources someone in China uses, a person in North America uses (this many kilograms)."

5. Write an algebraic equation to describe the relationship. First select two variables (letters), one to represent each of the categories. Then use your last answer to create an algebraic equation to show the pattern.

6. If a person from China used 23 kilograms of resources, how much would his or her North American counterpart be using?

Relationship between the average consumption of a person from North America and a person from India (North America in this case refers to the United States and Canada):

North American	90	150	300	600
Indian	3	5	10	20

7. Explain the relationship between the average consumption of a person from North America and one from India. You might want to start by saying, "For each one kilogram of resources someone in India uses, a person in North America uses (this many kilograms)."

8. Write an algebraic equation to describe the relationship. First select two variables (letters), one to represent each of the categories. Then use your last answer to create an algebraic equation to show the pattern.

9. If a person from India used 23 kilograms of resources, how much would his or her North American counterpart be using?

Open a **spreadsheet** program - create a table based on the following example:

Consumption Rates by Region

North American	Mexican	Chinese	Indian
60	12	6	2
90	18	9	3
120	24	12	4
150	30	15	5
180	36	18	6
210	42	21	7
240	48	24	8
270	54	27	9
300	60	30	10

10. Highlight the entire table and create a Scatter chart with points connected by smooth lines. The X-axis should be North American Consumption, the Y-axis Other Regions' Consumption. Print out your graph and hand it in with this assignment.

11. Why is the scale on the X-axis so large? Why is it not the same as the Y-axis scale?

12. What is the slope for each of the lines on the graph?

13. What would your graph look like if you used the same scale as your Y-axis for your X-axis?

14. The following chart shows how much gas was used to make four trips, comparing a Standard Utility Vehicle (SUV) with a compact car.[282]

	Trip One	Trip Two	Trip Three	Trip Four
SUV's Gas Use	12 L	21 L	39 L	69 L
Compact Car's Gas Use	4 L	7 L	13 L	23 L

282 *Worldwatch Report 2004*. p. 63.

a. In words, how much more gas does an SUV use compared to a compact car?

b. Write an algebraic equation to describe the relationship. If a SUV needed 144 L of gas to get somewhere, how much would a compact car require?

c. It takes 18 litres of water to produce 1 litre of gas.[283] If a compact car required 108 L of gas to get somewhere, how much water was used to make that gas? If an SUV was used for the same trip, how much water was used?

- Use your bike or walk whenever possible.
- Always reduce the amount of products you purchase before reusing and recycling.

283 *Worldwatch Report 2004*. p. 63.

The Winner Takes It All...?

"Fifty one percent of a nation can establish a totalitarian regime, suppress minorities and still remain democratic."

– Erik von Kuehnett-Leddihn

Imagine: your class takes a vote on how to spend a gift of several thousand dollars. 12 vote for new books for the library, 11 vote for a pool table in the student lounge, and 10 vote for basketball hoops on the blacktop behind the school. The new books win, right? But hold on...21 people, more than half of the class, wanted something other than books! How is that fair?

That's how provincial and federal voting works in Canada. It's called **first past the post** voting, or winner takes it all: in technical terms, the "single member plurality system" (SVP). In all 308 Federal ridings where political candidates face off, the winner gets the seat in **Parliament** and the other parties get $1.75 per vote. No wonder 49% of Canadians are unhappy with SVP, and only 23% are in favour.[284]

A different way to vote is called **proportional representation (PR)**. There are several types of PR, but what generally happens is that if a party gets 41% of the votes (for example), they get 41% of the seats. In other words, all votes count. Because PR is not an all-or-nothing high stakes competition like SVP, it

284 Pilon, Dennis. *Canada's Democratic Deficit: Is Proportional Representation the Answer?* The CSJ Foundation for Research and Education. 2000. P. 35

"tends to lead to better representation of women and minorities,"[285] who are underrepresented in our government. Proportional representation voting is common in many European countries, and even Manitoba and Alberta tried it out between 1920 and 1960.[286]

In first past the post voting, why do you think political parties will tend to be **conservative** and have more men running as candidates?

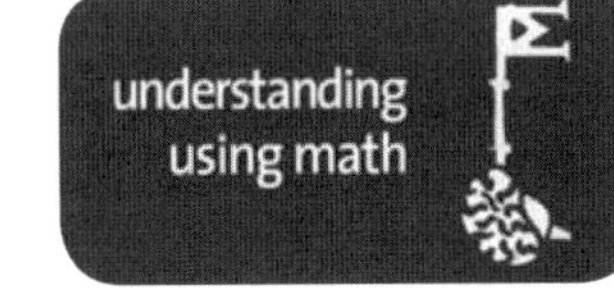

1. The following diagram is of a fictitious country that has five voting regions ("ridings"), and three political parties (A, B, and C). In a recent election the voting results were as follows:

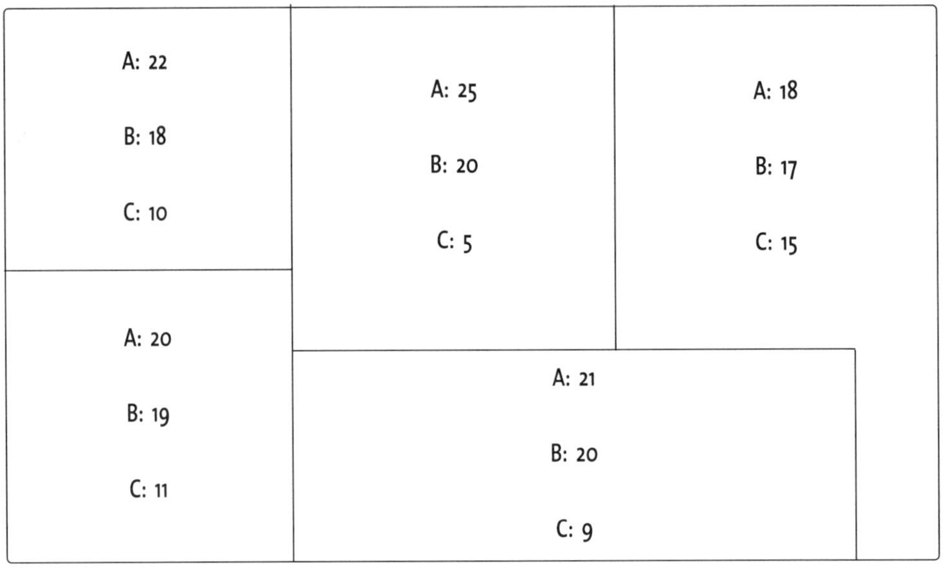

A: 22
B: 18
C: 10

A: 25
B: 20
C: 5

A: 18
B: 17
C: 15

A: 20
B: 19
C: 11

A: 21
B: 20
C: 9

   a. Fill in the following table. First fill in the number of ridings that each party wins if using the first past the post system (the party that has the highest votes in the riding wins). Then calculate how many seats each party would get under a PR system, by adding up all of the votes for each party and calculating them as a percentage of the total.

Party	First Past the Post System: Number of Wins	Proportional Representation System
A		
B		
C		

   b. Would Party A in a first past the post system rule with more than 50% of the popular vote? What percentage of the popular vote do they have?

   c. Under a first past the post system, Party B gets no seats in Parliament. What percentage of seats to they get under a PR system? Which is fairer? Explain.

285 Ibid. p. 20.
286 Ibid., p. 10.

d. Party A rules for four years and does a very poor job. People are really fed up and election time is around the corner. Party B has some similar policies as Party A, as well as some different ones. Party C has a bunch of different policies that seem fairly **progressive**. Explain the dilemma the voters have, and what might happen at voting time. Keep in mind the levels of support each party had at the last election.

2. Look at the following chart[287] and graph and answer these questions:

   a. Which parties got more seats than the votes they received? Which party benefited most, as a percentage of the votes that they received?

   b. Which parties got fewer seats than the votes they received? Which party lost the most, as a percentage of the votes that they received?

Party	Percentage of votes	Percentage of seats
Bloc Quebecois	12.5	17.5
Liberal	36.8	43.8
New Democratic Party	15.6	7.1
Progressive Conservative	29.6	31.2
Other	5.5	0.3

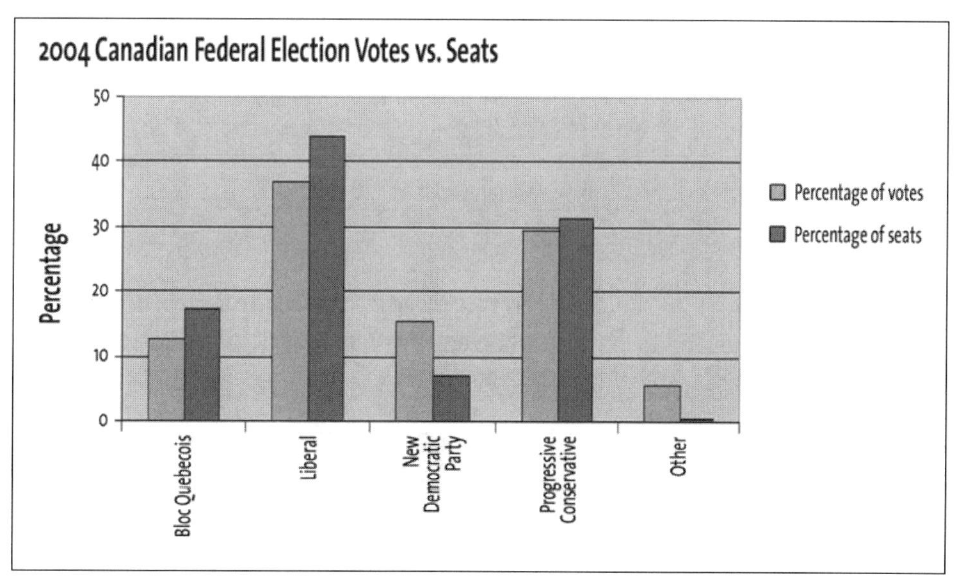

3. If a **riding** has only two candidates competing, and 600 people vote using first past the post, how many votes does the winner need to beat his or her opponent? What percentage is that?

287 *Toronto Star*, June 29, 2004, A1.

4. If you have three candidates in a riding, and 600 people vote using first past the post, what is theoretically the lowest number of votes that a candidate could get and still win? What percentage is that?

5. Let's pretend that there are 1,000 people in a country, but because of discouragement with the voting process, only 67% show up to vote. Let's also pretend that it's a first past the post race with three candidates. What is the lowest number of votes that a candidate needs to win to win the election? What percentage is that of the entire country? Why might some people believe that the winning party has no real right to lead?

6. The Federal Conservative Government that decided to promote free trade (which has been very good for many business people and very bad for many workers) was elected with 42% of the popular vote.[288] What percentage of the voters voted against the Conservatives?

7. Look at the following chart by Statistics Canada, entitled "**Federal general elections, by electors, ballots cast and voter participation**"[289] and make three observations for discussion with the class. (*In the 2004 Federal Election voter turnout was 60.5%)

Voter participation	1988	1993	1997	2000
Canada	75.3	69.6	67.0	61.2
Newfoundland and Labrador	67.1	55.1	55.2	57.1
Prince Edward Island	84.9	73.2	72.8	72.7
Nova Scotia	74.8	64.7	69.4	62.9
New Brunswick	75.9	69.6	73.4	67.7
Quebec	75.2	77.1	73.3	64.1
Ontario	74.6	67.7	65.6	58.0
Manitoba	74.7	68.7	63.2	62.3
Saskatchewan	77.8	69.4	65.3	62.3
Alberta	75.0	65.2	58.5	60.2
British Columbia	78.7	67.8	65.6	63.0
Yukon	78.4	70.4	69.8	63.5
Northwest Territories	70.8	62.9	58.9	52.2
Nunavut	x	x	x	54.1

8. As of May 2004 the number of women in lower or single houses of Parliament can be put in rank order. The country that is ranked first has the most women in their Parliament as a percentage. Try your hand at this mix and match:

Country	Rank options (not in order)	Rank (your guess)
Cuba	1	
Sweden	2	
USA	3	
Canada	7	
Argentina	10	
Rwanda	36	
Denmark	58	

288 Pilon, Dennis. *Canada's Democratic Deficit: Is Proportional Representation the Answer?* The CSJ Foundation for Research and Education. 2000. pp. 17,19.

289 http://www.statcan.ca/english/Pgdb/govt09c.htm April 15, 2004.

In perspective:

Seventy of the world's 211 democracies use a first past the post system, while 74 use some form of proportional representation.[290]

In the 2004 Federal Election, the average number of votes per party to gain one seat in Parliament was: 31,000 (Bloc), 37,000 (Liberal), 40,000 (Conservative), 111,000 (NDP) and the 580,000 votes that the Green Party got amounted to no seat at all.[291]

- Visit the Fair Vote Canada website for up to date information and things you can do to support electoral reform (www.fairvote.ca).

---

290 Dauncey, Guy. http://www.gowebtide.com/freeyourvote1/media/commonGroundMag/commGroundArticles.html
291 "Make Every Vote Count", Fair Vote Canada, www.fairvote.ca p.2

"GATS Terrible!!"

"The most effective way to restrict democracy is to transfer decision making from the public arena to unaccountable institutions: kings and princes, priestly castes, military juntas, party dictatorships or modern corporations."

Noam Chomsky

The **World Trade Organization (WTO)** is a group that overseas the rules of international trade. It originally began after World War II as the **General Agreement on Tariffs and Trade (GATT)**, and is based on the idea that free trade between countries leads to increased economic growth which is supposedly good for everyone. **Free trade** means that barriers to corporate profits, like **taxes** and **government subsidies**, are eliminated.

One of the WTO's programs is called GATS, which stands for the General Agreement on Trade in Services. GATS is highly controversial because it has to do with the transfer of public services into private for-profit services. The big public services involved are water, education, postal, healthcare, energy and social services.

Public services currently represent a lot of value. Each and every year the money spent globally on water services is about $1 trillion. Education services account for $2 trillion. Social services: $2.5 trillion. Healthcare totals $3.5 trillion dollars. And energy services are worth a stunning $4 trillion!

In the hands of elected governments, these services can be provided to people fairly well. In the hands of large **transnational corporations**, these services tend to be provided to people who can afford to pay for them.

How does a service that is run to make a profit tend to discriminate in favour of those people who are economically more stable?

1. If the following line segment is equivalent to "one million", what line length would be required to represent 400 billion (world wide postal services are worth $400 billion a year)?

2. What unit of measurement would be most appropriate for your answer in question one? Give the length using the new unit of measurement.

3. What line length would be required to represent $3.5 trillion (global healthcare services are worth $3.5 trillion a year)? Give your answer in centimetres, meters and kilometres and suggest which units are most appropriate.

4. Name a place that you could go from your classroom that represents the distance you calculated in question #3.

   The **Free Trade Area of the Americas (FTAA)** is the largest trade agreement in history- linking 34 of the 35 countries in North, Central and South America together (which country do you think is excluded?). It is currently being negotiated, and it expands the GATS agreement. Meetings of trade ministers from these countries as well as representatives from the top corporations have taken place every few years. Two of the most recent meetings were in Quebec City in 2001 and in Miami, Florida in 2003.

5. The ratio of **protestors** to police at the Quebec Summit was roughly 11:2. There were approximately 8,000 police. How many protestors were there? Equate that number to some number that you know.

6. A four kilometre long, 10 foot high fence was erected to keep protestors out of the meeting zone. The budget for the police and the fence was $46 million. A "**People's Summit**" was organized outside the fence by **NGOs** and **trade unions** and they were given $287,000 by the federal government.[292] Compare the two budgets- how much bigger is one than the other? What implication do these numbers have?

7. The Brazilian government allowed a **plebiscite** in which the people could vote on whether or not they wanted the FTAA agreement. About 10 million people voted and 98% of them voted against the FTAA. What is 98% of 10 million? Do you think that the Brazilian government will listen to what the people said in the vote? Why or why not?

---

292 Chossudovsky, Michael. "The Quebec Wall: What lies behind Free Trade Area of the Americas (FTAA)?" www.nadir.org/nadir/initiativ/agp/free/chossudovsky/quebec.htm April, 2001.

8. In the year 2000, a London company took charge of Cochabamba's (a city in Bolivia) water system.[293] Water costs in households increased based on the following chart.

	Household A	Household B	Household C	Household D
Water costs before privatization	$35.00	$43.00	$26.00	$31.00
Water costs after privatization	$122.50	$150.50	$91.00	$108.50

a. What is the algebraic equation that describes the pattern of increased costs for water?

b. What do you imagine happened when these price increases took place?

10. Privatized healthcare can lead doctors to over-prescribe and engage in costlier and unnecessary treatments. Explain how, when profit is the motivating factor, the following situations are likely to happen:

a. In Brazil, **caesarean sections** are more common with private patients.[294]

b. In India, private providers ask for more tests to be taken on patients.[295]

c. In **developing countries**, private pharmacies over-prescribe expensive drugs.[296]

d. In privatized healthcare markets, a focus on **curative** services using drugs has increased and preventative services have decreased.[297]

- Subscribe to the organization 50 Years Is Enough, which keeps tabs on the **World Bank**, the **IMF**, and the **World Trade Organization**, at www.50years.org.
- Find out the organizations that are fighting **privatization** in your community and see what local **initiatives** are being undertaken. How can you help out?
- Check out the CCPA's Trade and Investment Research Project at www.policyalternatives.ca

293 United Nations Development Programme. *Human Development Report 2003*. New York. Oxford University Press. 2003. p. 117.
294 Ibid, p. 113.
295 Ibid, p. 113.
296 Ibid, p. 113.
297 Ibid, p. 114.

Breaking The Silence

"Staying quiet is as political an act as speaking out."

– Arundhati Roy

When children and youth are abused, a culture of silence exists that can prevent or prolong **disclosure** of the abuse. The pain of secrecy particularly affects survivors of sexual abuse. The person who is abusing may be a trusted friend, relative or authority figure and may use physical threats, promises of rewards or warnings that people will get in trouble if the secret is revealed.[298]

I am almost 17 years old and have been sexually abused when I was four or five years old. I have never told anyone about it all these years. I've kept it inside myself. I've sometimes felt it was my fault but now I know it's not. This experience is something I want to forget, but I know I will always remember the unpleasant things I was forced to do.

– Grade 12 female student

I don't really like talking about it. I get upset. I was sexually abused when I was five and never told anyone. I never told anyone because I thought it was my fault and if I wasn't alive it wouldn't have happened.

–Grade 8 male student[299]

---

298 Canadian Red Cross, Prevention in Motion 2nd Edition, 2000, p. 28.
299 Ibid., p. 28.

Males are less likely to disclose abuse for a number of reasons, some of which include: the (mistaken) belief in our society that males cannot be victims, the (mistaken) belief that abuse is a sexual act (rather than an act of power) and the (mistaken) belief that if a boy's body responds sexually, he is gay or somehow responsible for the abuse.[300] **Homophobia** plays into the reluctance to tell, as most **victimisers** are male.

Although there are many ways that people show their grief, "21 to 36% of sexually abused children will show little or no symptoms."[301]

Why would sexually abused children show "few or no symptoms"? Does this mean that the impact is less for those who show no symptoms?

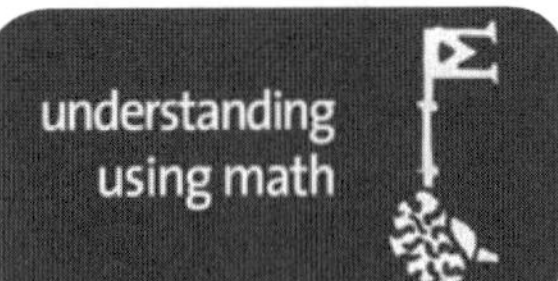

Reasons Why Abuse Was Not Disclosed	%
I was scared.	74%
I was embarrassed.	60%
I didn't want to get in trouble.	55%
I didn't want to get anyone else in trouble.	47%
No one would believe me.	46%
I still love the other person.	29%
It was my fault as much as the other person.	29%

1. Open a **spreadsheet** program. Complete a chart following the example above. Create a bar graph and make sure to enter the x and y-axis labels and your title. Hand in the graph with this assignment.

2. Which response surprises you the most, and why?

3. Why do all of the responses add up to more than 100%? How is that possible?

4. On the same spreadsheet page, make a second chart that looks like the following example. Hand in the graph with this assignment. Don't forget a title and labels for the x and y axis.

Reasons for Disclosing Unwanted Sexual Experiences	%
I couldn't hold it in any longer	76%
I wanted it to stop so my life could go on	56%
I wanted him/her to be punished	56%
I finally felt comfortable enough to tell	53%
I was afraid someone else would get hurt if I didn't tell	50%
I was afraid I'd get hurt if I didn't tell	48%
I couldn't eat/sleep/think anymore	41%
I got tired of the unwanted sexual experiences	41%
Someone else convinced me to tell	40%
Someone else told me of their unwanted experiences	35%
I was pregnant or afraid that I might be pregnant	31%
There was a school program about unwanted sexual experiences	28%
I told because I didn't want to go home	22%

300 Ibid., p. 34.

301 Oates, O'Toole, Lynch, Stem & Clooney. "Stability and change in outcomes for sexually abused children". *Journal of the American Academy of Child and Adolescent Psychiatry*, 33 (7), 1994, pp. 945-953.

5. Which response surprises you the most, and why?

6. Using the spreadsheet program, display one of your graphs in a different way, and make an argument for whether or not it makes understanding the data easier. Hand in this graph with your assignment.

Food for thought...

The two countries in the world that have not ratified the UN Convention on the Rights of the Child are the United States and Somalia.

- Invite a public health nurse in to your classroom to talk about abuse prevention and intervention.

- Visit a local walk in clinic or **crisis centre** with the class, meet with the support people there, and get a tour.

- Look at the following support line numbers for Toronto and try to locate similar support groups and numbers for your region. For local crisis and support lines in your community, please look in the front section of your phone book.

- The following numbers are Toronto support lines that are staffed by people who are trained to listen and to help. Calls can be made anonymously if you want information but don't want to give your name. Other adults who you trust are also good people to tell.

Kids Help Phone	1 800 668 6868
Rape Crisis	416 597 8808
Children's Aid Society	416 924 4646
Sexual Assault Care Centre	416 323 6040
Youth Link Support	416 922 3335
Gay Lesbian Bisexual Youth Line	416 962 9688 (4- 9:30 Sun-Fri.)

Mad

"That's one of the frailties of the human condition – people fear that which is not familiar."

– Spike Lee

Mental illness refers to a difference in thinking, mood or behaviour that leads to serious distress and difficulty functioning in the world. Mental illnesses range from mild to severe and can affect all ages, cultures, and income levels. One in five Canadians will personally experience some form of mental illness at some point in their lifetime but because of the **stigma** attached, people may not come forward for help.[302]

Mental illnesses include mood disorders like depression and bipolar disorder, schizophrenia, anxiety, personality and eating disorders.

The causes of mental illness are very complex and are usually an interplay of genetic, biological, personality and environmental factors. Many people experience the onset of symptoms in adolescence or young adulthood, but when addressed, many of these illnesses can be effectively treated.

A lot of work is being done to understand the relationships between the different mental illnesses, the risk and **protective factors** and the best way to provide services for those who need them.

302 "A Report on Mental Illness in Canada", http://www.hc-sc.gc.ca/pphb-dgspsp/publicat/miic-mmac/chap_1_e.html

Why do you think that the stigma associated with mental illnesses creates a huge barrier to diagnosis and treatment?

understanding using math

1. Which of the following conclusions can you draw from the following graph?

   In almost all age groups, females are hospitalized in general hospitals for anxiety disorders at a greater rate than males.

   Females experience more anxiety disorders than males.

   The number of hospitalizations is generally increasing as people get older.

   In the age 15 to 19 category those rates translate into roughly 5,100 young women and 2,400 young men.

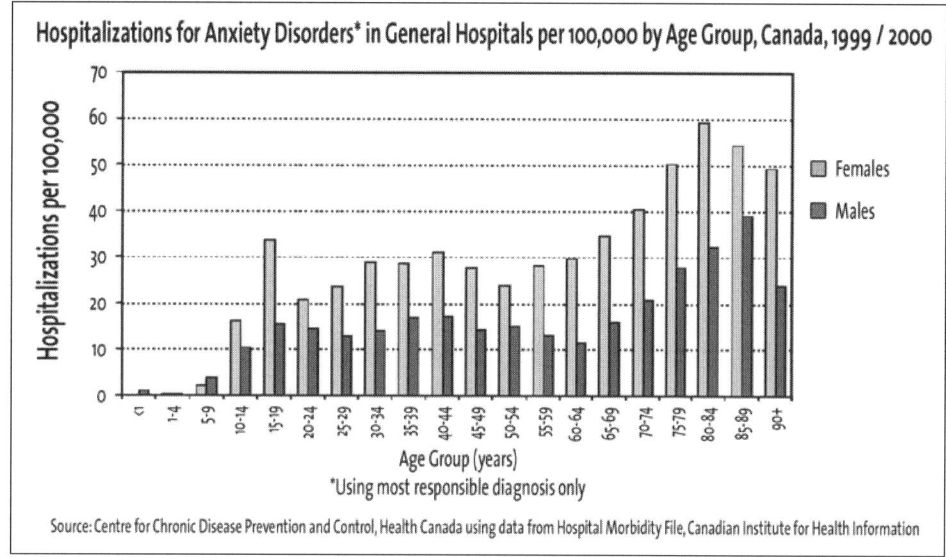

2. 86% of hospitalizations for mental illnesses occur in general hospitals. Can you think of any drawbacks to this trend?

3. The following are estimates of one year **prevalence rates**, which measure the approximate percentage of the population that has the disorder during any one year period.

Eating Disorders	Male	Female
Anorexia	0.2%	0.7%
Bulimia	0.1%	1.5%

   If you assume that the male and female populations are approximately equal, and the one year prevalence for females with anorexia was 100,000 people, how many males would have anorexia? What do you think accounts for the **disparity**? Which disparity between males and females is greater, anorexia or bulimia?

4. Using data on physician billing, hospitalization, and activity restriction, Health Canada roughly estimated the cost of mental illnesses as $244 per Canadian.[303] Write an algebraic equation for the total cost of mental illnesses in Canada and solve it using 30 million as a rough population estimate.

303 "A Report on Mental Illness in Canada", http://www.hc-sc.gc.ca/pphb-dgspsp/publicat/miic-mmac/chap_1_e.html

5. A later study found that the costs approximated $480 per Canadian, and that this figure was probably an underestimate.[304] Write the algebraic equation for the total cost of mental illnesses in Canada and solve it. Can you think of a reason why addressing the stigma associated with mental illness would be crucial to lowering these costs?

6. If you research the top ten causes of disability in Canada, you would find that four in ten are due to mental illness.[305] Express this finding as a probability.

7. Two competing theories for the causes of mental illness are social causation (in which social factors lead to anxiety and distress) and social selection (in which biological inheritance plays a key role).

   Suicidal behaviour is often linked with discussions about mental illness. A study of youth aged 11 to 15 found that experiencing five or more stressful life events (divorce, serious illness) led youth to harm themselves at a rate of 9.5%, while youth whose childhood was categorized as carefree harmed themselves at a rate of 1.2%.[306] What is the ratio between these two groups and what theory of mental illness does this tend to support?

8. A study published in 2003 by the *Journal of the American Medical Association* followed 1,420 youth aged nine to 13 years for eight years. The researchers found that youth who moved out of **poverty** saw a decrease (within four years) in the frequency of psychiatric symptoms to the levels experienced by children who had never been poor.[307] What theory of mental illness does this tend to support?

   Conduct and oppositional disorders were most affected by the move out of poverty, while anxiety and depression saw little effect. What do you think that finding suggests?

9. One in five Americans also experience a diagnosable mental illness in a given year, but only one third of those individuals seek treatment.[308] What fraction of Americans both experience a mental illness and seek treatment?

10. In Toronto on any given night, up to 4,500 people stay in 66 shelters. It is estimated that 30% of the people living on the street live with mental illnesses. Approximately how many of the 4,500 people have a mental illness? Why is this important to know?

---

304 Ibid.
305 Ibid.
306 Frith, Maxine. "The Poverty and Misery Behind Child Suicides" http://www.psychiatry24x7.com/ news/avscontent.jhtml?topic=child&id=28503089&itemname=e0824028.1iwo 2001
307 "Relief of poverty associated with improvement in some psychiatric disorders" - *Pediatric Mental Health* http://www.psychiatry24x7.com/news/avscontent.jhtml?topic=depression&id=30700004&itemname=c1023265.9who 2003.
308 "Myths About Mental Illness Abound" http://www.psychiatry24x7.com/news/ avscontent.jhtml?topic=depression&id=28503259&itemname=p1005052.6000 2001.

- An excellent page of resource links on the internet is posted at www.mooddisorders-canada.ca/report/english/chapter1/resources.htm.
- "Educating the public and the media about mental illness is a first step toward reducing the stigma and encouraging greater acceptance and understanding of mental illness." Create a display board of information and resources to educate students in your class and your school.
- The top 10 myths about mental illness, found at http://www.psychiatry24x7.com/news/avscontent.jhtml?topic=depression&id=28503259&itemname=p1005052.6000, may be helpful.

Media Monopoly

"The more hegemonic the system, the more the imagination is struck by the smallest of its reversals"

– Jean Baudrillard

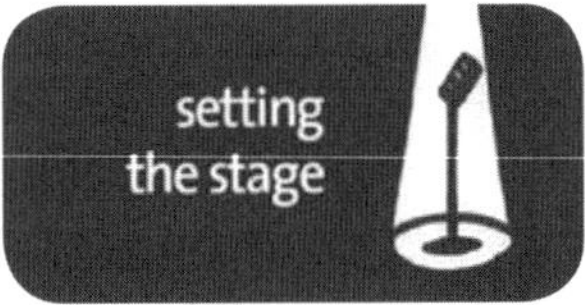

Malcolm X once said, "If you're not careful the **media** will have you hating the people who are being **oppressed**, and loving the people who are doing the oppressing." When many different points of view are available for the public to read in the papers and on the internet, listen to on the radio, and watch on the television it's more difficult to deceive people. Hidden though, is the fact that many of the different sources of news and information in Canada and the United States are actually owned by very few companies.

When a handful of businesses own most or all of their part of the market (for example, the book market, or the telecommunications market) it's called a "**monopoly**". In 1983, 50 **corporations** controlled the U.S. media. Now only six control the market.[309] In Canada, it's down to five. In addition to limiting **freedom of expression**, the focus of the news can be managed to favour some groups and oppose others.

A study of 41 mainstream papers in Canada found that of their 2,620 staff only four were **Aboriginal** people, in spite of the fact that people of **First Nations** amount to 3% of the population.[310] Likewise, reporting on race, class, gender, and sexuality is distorted in a system largely run by wealthy, white men, who are by law required to "put the profits of their investors ahead of all other considerations."[311]

---

309 www.mediachannel.org/ownership/
310 www.media-awareness.ca May 17, 2004
311 http://www.fair.org/media-woes/corporate.html

Aren't four First Nations staff members out of 2,620 about equal to 3%? What's the issue?

1. During the Canadian Oka crisis in 1990, in which First Nations people protested the destruction of their property for the expansion of a golf course, the media tended to portray the resistors as fierce and violent warriors. The people who emerged after the crisis are described as follows:

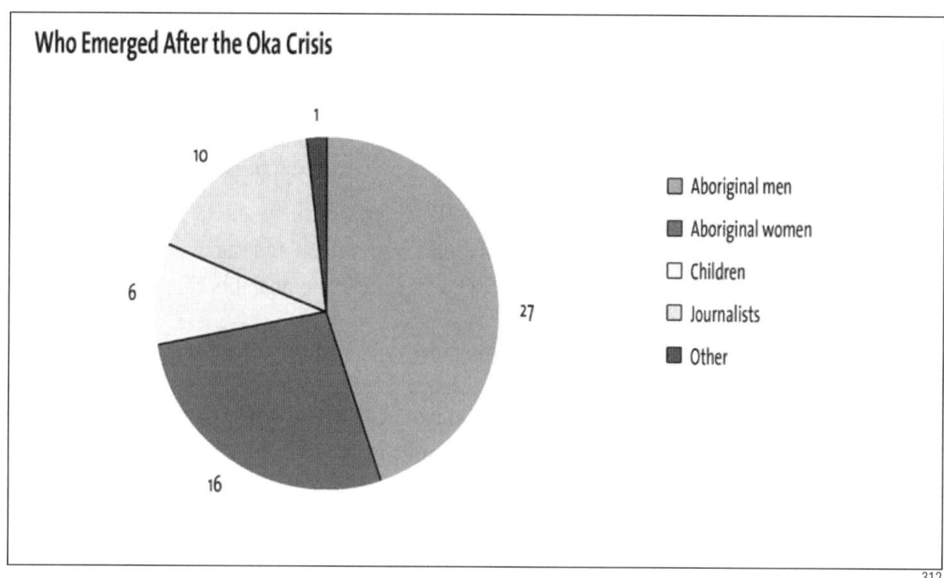

312

Of course, this selection of numbers misrepresents the people who were present during the conflict. Re-create the pie graph using a spreadsheet, including one more category of people. The number of soldiers and police present during the crisis was 4,000. How does that change the nature of the graph?

2. Who we see on television influences who we believe are experts and qualified professionals. Far more often than not, men are represented as the experts in business, politics and economics, while women are highlighted in stories about accidents, natural disasters and **domestic violence**.[313]

A survey by the Association of Women Journalists looked at news coverage of women's issues in 70 different countries in the year 2000.

	Percentage
Stories quoting women	18
Stories quoting men	72

	Percentage
Women-related stories	10
Men-related stories	90

a. What is the probability that you would hear the perspective of a woman in these 70 countries?

b. What is the probability that you would read a story about women's issues in these 70 countries?

c. How might these things be damaging to men?

312 www.media-awareness.ca May 17, 2004
313 Ibid.

3. The City University of New York did an analysis of two years of PBS prime time programs, looking specifically at the stories about working class lives and concerns and stories about the **upper classes**. They found that 27 hours had been devoted to **working class** issues and 253 hours had focused on the wealthy. Create a visual comparison to highlight these differences. Why is this important?

4. In his book *Innumeracy: Mathematical Illiteracy and Its Consequences* John Allen Paulos reminds us that "**rarity** leads to publicity". The profit-driven need to use shocking violence gives us the impression that terrorist kidnappings and cyanide poisonings are our biggest threats, while in fact more than 300,000 Americans die annually due to smoking.[314]

   a. A jumbo jet seats about 270 people. How many jumbo jets a day would have to crash for a full year to amount to the number of people who die due to smoking each year?

   b. There were about 3,325 casualties due to terrorism in the United States between 1996 and 2001, well over 99% of them due to the September 11th tragedy.[315] Assume the American population is 300 million and calculate the probability that you would be a casualty from terrorist action and the probability that you died from smoking during those five years.

   c. Why is knowing this information useful in designing public policy?

5. During times of war, which tend to be frequent, media control of content can significantly reduce the flow of **legitimate** material for debate and discussion. For example, in the United States during January and February of 2003, less than 1% of the guests on network talk shows were anti-war advocates, while on February 15, 2003 hundreds of thousands of Americans marched in protest to the war, with millions worldwide taking part.[316]

   Find one statistic about the war in Iraq that surprises you. Where did you find it? Is your source **credible**? How can you tell?

6. The Tyndall Report monitors how much time is spent by the big three television networks in the United States: ABC, NBC and CBS. In all of 2004, the number of minutes spent on the nightly newscasts reporting on the genocide happening in Darfur was 18 minutes, five minutes and three minutes for each of the networks respectively. The total for the three networks spent reporting on Martha Stewart in 2004 was 130 minutes.[317] Plot this as a pie graph and discuss its implications.

Food for thought...

The Canadian Association for the Advancement of Women, Sports and Physical Activity found that of all sports coverage in major Canadian daily papers, women athletes account for a mere 3%.[318]

- A list of **activist** material for action can be accessed at http://www.media-awareness.ca/english/resources/taking_action/take_action_index.cfm.

314 Paulos, John Allen. *Innumeracy: Mathematical Illiteracy and Its Consequence*. Hill and Wang, New York, 1988, p. 82.
315 Barker, Jonathan. "The no-nonsense guide to terrorism." *New Internationalist Publications*, p. 29.
316 Jensen, Robert. "The Failure of US Journalism" Al Jazeera, Nov. 2004..
317 Kristof, N. "All Ears for Tom Cruise, All Eyes for Brad Pitt." www.media-alliance.org/medianews/ July 26, 2005.
318 www.media-awareness.ca May 17, 2004.

Sick And Tired

"Law and justice are not always the same. When they aren't, destroying the law may be the first step toward changing it."
– Gloria Steinem

Large companies spend millions of dollars to research new types of drugs and chemicals. For example, in **agribusiness** it takes ten million dollars to develop one new active ingredient to improve crops, followed by eight years of **field trials**.[319] The process of making new drugs for human beings takes many years and must involve **clinical trials** in which animals and then humans are tested to ensure that the drug has no, or few, harmful side-effects. When a new drug is created, the company wants to **recoup** the money that it has spent (and presumably, to then make **profit**).

In order to secure profits by being the only producer of a new drug, the companies depend on **patent laws**, which allow them 20 years as the sole provider, meaning that other companies are not allowed to make and distribute significantly cheaper non-brand name versions (**generic drugs**).

The HIV/AIDS epidemic in Africa is a situation where patented drugs could help to alleviate suffering, but the costs to buy these name-brand drugs are **prohibitive** for people who are poor. Cheaper HIV/AIDS drugs can be made, but it is illegal under the current patent laws.

What do you think drug companies will set as priorities for new drug development (in other words, what types of drugs will they focus on) and most importantly, why do you think that?

319 George, Susan. *How the Other Half Dies*. Pelican Books, 1976.

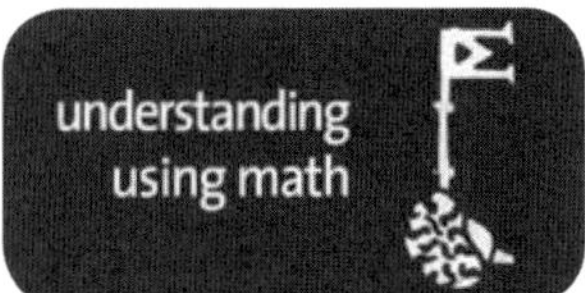

1. "Every year, 14 million people die worldwide from **communicable diseases** such as AIDS, tuberculosis and malaria- 97% of these people live in **developing countries**."[320]
   a. What is 97% written as a fraction (hint: what does "%" mean?)
   b. What is 97% of 14 million people?
   c. What is 3% of 14 million people?
   d. Write your two fraction components as decimals.
2. Display the previous two numbers in a circle graph done by hand (hint: a circle is 360°, so what is 97% of 360?). Make sure that you include a title that describes to your audience what you are showing, and a key. Hand your circle graph in with your work.
3. What factors do you think contribute to this phenomenon? Why do most people who die from these diseases come from developing countries?
4. Think of one or more *underlying* causes to the factors that you listed in the last answer. In other words, is there something that creates those factors?
5. There were 1,223 new drugs created between the years 1975 and 1996. Eleven of those new drugs were to treat tropical diseases,[321] which would be **predominantly** found in developing countries. What is 11 as a percentage of 1,223?
6. Using a **spreadsheet**, create a pie graph to show the comparison between the number of drugs created to treat tropical diseases and the drugs created for other diseases or reasons. Don't forget your descriptive title and key. Hand this in with your work.
7. Why do you think that there are currently no new research projects being launched for cures to tuberculosis and sleeping sickness, but research projects are being launched to "cure" baldness?
8. One of the **ethical** debates of today has to do with the millions of people in Africa who will die from AIDS if they don't get treatment, and who cannot afford the high price of the drugs. Cheaper **generic** versions of anti-viral drugs do exist, but cannot be produced because of the patent laws. What would you do to solve the problem?
9. Although drug companies say they need 20 years to recoup their research and development costs, one drug company made $589 million with one AIDS drug in 1999 alone: which was *more than double* its R & D costs. Can you guess what these pharmaceutical companies spend so much money on, if it's not R&D?
10. Stephen Lewis, the United Nations Special Envoy for HIV/AIDS in Africa has been working to provide cheaper generic drugs to people in need. A typical name-brand drug cocktail can cost more than $10,000 per person per year. Under a new plan, **UNICEF** will buy generic drugs using funds from the World Bank and the Global Fund to fight AIDS, Tuberculosis and Malaria, for as low as $140 per person per year.[322] What percentage is $140 of the brand-name price?

- **Medecins San Frontieres** (Doctors Without Borders) is involved with the above issues. Go to their website www.msf.ca (or find one of your own that has to do with this topic) and write one thing that you learned while at that site.

---

320 WHO/MSF. *International Journal of Infectious Diseases*. No. 2, 1999.
321 Ibid.
322 Fox, Maggie. "Deal reached for cheaper AIDS drugs". *Globe and Mail* April 6, 2004. A14.

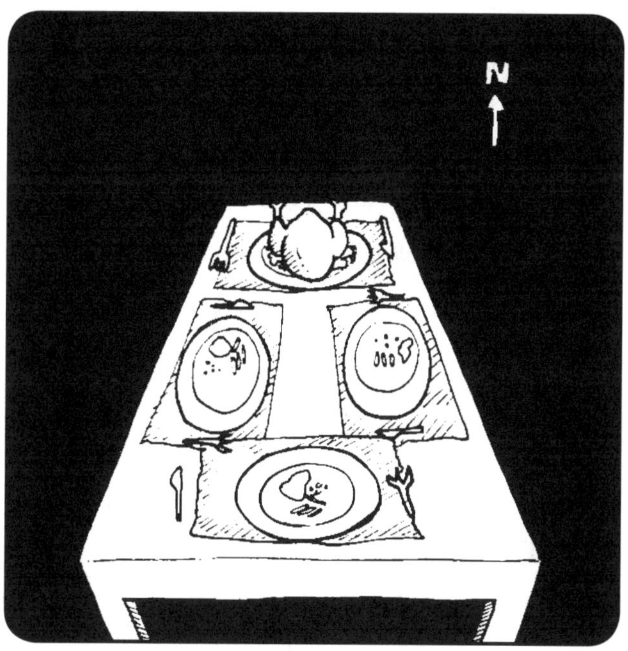

The Poverty Of Distribution

"Where justice is denied, where poverty is enforced, where ignorance prevails and where any one class is made to feel that society is an organized conspiracy to oppress, rob and degrade them, neither persons nor property will be safe."
– Frederick Douglass

Susan George, in her book "How the Other Half Dies- the Real Reasons for World Hunger", argues that world hunger is not a matter of having too little food to feed everyone, but is rather the consequence of unequal distribution of the world's food. She suggests that the business of agriculture, called **agribusiness**, is focused on maximizing **profit**, which in many cases is a barrier to sharing food more equally.

Agribusiness is carefully controlled by a small number of companies in the United States. Wealthy businesses spend money to develop new technology and chemicals to improve **crop output** (things like herbicides, pesticides, and insecticides). If developing countries want to compete in global **markets**, they need the new technology. But the multinationals control the process: they decide the amount of help that they give out, the direction of the projects and the methods used, in ways that will be first and foremost beneficial to the multinational.[323]

323 George, Susan. *How the Other Half Dies- the Real Reasons for World Hunger.* Pelican Books.

The States is also known for its destruction of hundreds of tons of food. This is called "**intervention buying**", where the government steps in and buys up large quantities of food so that it doesn't go onto the world markets. If too much food goes onto the world markets, it will drive the prices down and mean less profit. Maximizing profit ends up causing world hunger.[324]

Sometimes when expensive new technology is introduced into developing countries it doesn't provide lasting benefits. Can you think of any reasons why this could be the case?

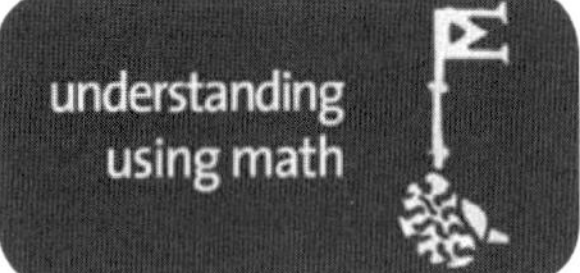

Relationship between time and the number of people who die from hunger:

# of hours	6	18	12	24
# of people who die from hunger	2400	7200	4800	9600

1. Explain the relationship between the number of hours and the number of people who die from hunger. You might want to start by saying "For each one hour, (this many people) die from hunger."
2. Write an algebraic equation to describe the relationship. First select two **variables** (letters), one to represent each of the categories. Then use your last answer to create an algebraic equation to show the pattern.
3. How many people die worldwide from hunger each month? Use your equation and show your work. Make a comparison of your answer to something similar For example, the number is like the Sky Dome (now called the Rogers Centre – Why do you think the name Sky Dome – which was chosen by the public – got changed to the name of a corporation?) in Toronto being filled with spectators three full times.
4. The **World Food Programme** has done more current research and suggests that the number of **kids** who die each year from hunger-related diseases is 14 million.[325] Calculate how many kids that means per day, per hour and per minute. Show your work.

---

324 Ibid.
325 From the "World Food Programme Hunger Map Guide".

5. Create a picture of one of those three answers in question four as a comparison to something that you can understand. For example, perhaps the number per hour is the same as the number of people who can fit in a five-story apartment building. If this was the case, draw the apartment building. (Find your own visual comparison...)

6. Why do you think that there isn't huge global outcry at the number of people dying of hunger? Think of the number who died on September 11th and the outrage that it caused.

Number of children who die each day of hunger:	**35,615**
Minutes of silence:	None
Plans for international response:	None
Plans for saturated network coverage:	None
Stock exchanges:	No effect
Alarm level:	Low
Primetime news reports on possible perpetrators of the crime:	None[326]

7. Sometimes people argue that the problem is overpopulation of developing countries: "if they didn't have so many babies, they wouldn't have poverty and hunger."

a. If you and your family live in abject poverty, why is it possibly in your interest to have larger families? Isn't this counterintuitive?

b. Use the following table[327] to make a convincing counter argument to the idea that poverty and hunger is a problem caused by having too many babies.

	Birthrate per thousand Prior to social reforms*	Birthrate per thousand after social reforms*
Taiwan	41	26
Korea	45	30

(*social reforms including better healthcare, better education, higher wages and fairer distribution of land)

Food for thought...

"In the 1980s hunger declined in general throughout the entire world, with two exceptions: sub-Saharan Africa and the United States– the poorest part of the world and the richest part of the world– there hunger increased."[328]

- Organize a hunger strike at your school where students pledge not to eat for 24 hours (juice and water is encouraged). Have people sponsor the students and send the money that you raise to the World Food Programme (www.wfp.org). The hunger site (www.thehungersite.com) has useful resources and facts to help with the strike.

326 *Adbusters*, Jan/Feb 2002 #39
327 George, Susan. *How the Other Half Dies- the Real Reasons for World Hunger.* Pelican Books, 1976.
328 Chomsky, Noam. *Understanding Power.* Random House, 2006p. 365.

Just Desserts?

"If the misery of the poor be caused not by the laws of nature, but by our institutions, great is our sin."

– Charles Darwin

The Centre for Social Justice produces a poster of the top one hundred Canadian **corporations** in **finance**, **manufacturing**, resources and services. Some names you might know, like Canadian Tire and Air Canada. Others you may never have heard of, such as Domtar and Onex. Common to the entire group is that they have huge influence over the economy and their workers.

The **salaries** and **compensation** of the top hundred **Chief Executive Officers** are also listed. A salary is the amount a person makes on their pay check- the CEOs with listed salaries range anywhere from a low of $85,449 (if you can call that low) to a high of about $2 million dollars a year.

Compensation, however, is salary plus all benefits including bonuses, stock options and other perks that have monetary value. Compensation can take the form of straight cash, homes, cars, health club and golf club memberships, free financial advising and millions of dollars worth of **shares** and **stock options**.[329] Of the top 68 publicly traded companies where compensation is known, Canadian CEOs received an average of $7.2 million dollars in compensation in 2002.[330]

By contrast, the average Canadian worker earned $35,417 in the year 2002, and **minimum wage** workers earned $14,102.[331] A free company car alone could easily be three times a minimum wage earner's yearly salary.

---

329 MacDermid, Robert and Hugh MacDermid. Exposing the Face of Corporate Power. Centre for Social Justice. Nov. 14, 2003, pp 5-7.
330 "Exposing the Face of Corporate Rule and the CEOs who pull the strings" (poster). Centre for Social Justice.
331 Ibid.

Why do people in the world make huge sums of money while others struggle by on a couple of dollars a day?

understanding using math

1. Of the top 100 Canadian CEOs,
    a. How many do you think are women?
    b. How many do you think are from a **racialized group**?
2. If you took the average compensation of a Canadian CEO for the year 2002 ($7.2 million), how many years ago would a minimum wage ($14,102) earner need to start in order to match a single year of the CEO's salary? What was happening at this time in history?
3. When you have a lot of money, you can contribute that money to **political parties** that will hopefully pass laws in your favour ("I scratch your back, you scratch mine"). The following information is based on contributions to the Paul Martin Liberal Party Campaign between July 1, 2002 and October 31, 2003.[332]

Type of Contributor	Number of Contributors	% of Contributors	Contributions	% of Total Contributions
Corporation	1,978	60.8	$8,741,533	72.9
Individual	1,243	38.2	$3,102,617	25.9
Trade Union	33	1	$146,200	1.2
Total	3,254	100	$11,990,370	100

    a. Who contributed the most money to the Liberal election campaign? Why would they do that?
    b. Who contributed the least money to the Liberal campaign? Why would they contribute so little (where might they contribute more money?).
    c. The top twenty four of the 1,243 individual contributions were $25,000 or more, and amounted to $1,183,500. Almost all of these individual contributors can be linked to corporations.[333] Re-create the table above with these 24 individuals and their contributions inserted in the corporation category. What difference does this make to the percentages?
4. The Federal Large Corporation Tax (LCT) was just reduced from 0.225% to 0.2%.[334] If a large corporation had revenue of $16.9 billion (like Imperial Oil did in 2002), what savings does this cut in the LCT amount to? Who loses out when the tax drops?
5. In the United States, Phillip Knight was the CEO of Nike Inc. for the year 2003, and his total compensation was $2,879,035.[335]
    a. Figure out what Phil makes in one hour. For this calculation, assume 52 weeks in a year, five work days in a week, and eight hours in a work day. (For yourself, compare this to what your parent makes in one hour.) Show your work.
    b. If a minimum wage earner in the United States makes $5.15 an hour, how many minimum wage earners could be paid with Phil's salary?

332 MacDermid, Robert. "Summary Tables of Contributors to the Paul Martin Leadership Campaign", p.1.
333 Ibid, pp.1, 8.
334 www.pwcglobal.com April 15, 2004, p. 26.
335 www.aflcio.org/corporateamerica/paywatch/ April 15, 2004

c. Presidents of the United States earn about $411,290 per year on average. How many U.S. Presidents could be paid with Phil's wage?

d. Two billion people on the planet live on $2 a day or less. If you took Phil's annual salary, how many people could he support for one year? Show your work.

6. H. Scott is the President and CEO of Wal-Mart stores. For the year 2003, his annual compensation was worth $28,963,872.[336]

   a. How much does he make per hour? Per minute? (Does H. Scott make more in one minute than your parent does in one day?) Show your work.

   b. How many years ago would a minimum wage earner ($5.15/hour) need to start in order to earn what H. Scott earned in 2003? What was happening in the world that long ago?

7. A house in Toronto can sell for $200,000. How long would it take H. Scott to totally pay off a house at this price? How many houses could he buy at this price in one year? Show your work.

8. S. Sanger is the Chairman and CEO of General Mills and earned $17,255,951 in 2003.[337]

   a. How much does Sanger make per hour and per minute? Show your work.

   b. It costs $28.48 to pay for a teacher's set of materials to run a classroom in a poor country.[338] How many sets of materials could one buy with Sanger's yearly salary? Show your work.

   c. Measles causes death 300 times more often in poor countries than in **industrialized countries**. Because it depresses the appetite and causes diarrhoea and vomiting, the body loses essential nutrients like vitamin A. A lack of vitamin A can cause blindness: in Africa, measles is responsible for half of the children who are blind.[339] The cost to immunise a person against the measles is 26 cents. How many people could get immunised on Sanger's annual salary? Show your work.

   d. Polio is a horrific disease that affects the central nervous system, causing paralysis and death. To pay for a vaccination, it costs eight cents per dose and requires four doses. How many people could have their four doses of polio vaccination if we used Sanger's annual salary? Show your work.

9. There are approximately 2,000 businesses that market themselves as "socially responsible". They have an annual turnover of approximately $2 billion together. The other 80-100 million other businesses have a turnover of about $20 trillion.[340] What percentage of sales is from socially responsible businesses?

- Have your teacher purchase the "Exposing the Face of Corporate Power" poster from the Centre for Social Justice at www.socialjustice.org ($8). Post it in your classroom. Talk about what it means.

- For an eye opening experience, compare your parent or guardian's salary to that of a CEO at the website www.aflcio.org/corporateamerica/paywatch/. Or compare the salary of a Canadian minimum wage worker (about $15,000 per year).

336 Ibid.
337 www.aflcio.org/corporateamerica/paywatch/ April 15, 2004.
338 www.unicef.org
339 www.unicef.org
340 Ransom, David. "Fair Trade- small change, big difference". *New Internationalist*. 2000

If Syrup Costs 2 Cents A Cup...

"Corporations cannot commit treason, or be outlawed or excommunicated, for they have no souls."
– Harold Coffin

The multiplex theatre looms in front of you like Mount Everest, except snow peaks are replaced with neon and the listings of 20 movies currently playing. Step inside. A massive lobby made of glass and steel encloses the video game arcade to your right, the **concessions** ahead and the ticket booths to the left. Step right up. That'll be $12 for your ticket. Ah well, you only live once, right?

Anyone hungry? The popcorn smells good- the small and medium bags look about the size of change purses, so you go for the large. Cost: $5.50. You'll be thirsty, so hand over another $4.50 for pop. A nagging thought enters your head...doesn't the syrup to make the pop cost about two cents a cup? And how much could the popcorn kernels be? five cents? But you just handed over ten dollars...?!!

There are all kinds of hidden costs in the products that we buy. Property rent, maintenance, wages, materials, **taxes**, **marketing**, packaging, transportation and legal costs are just a few, not to mention CEO salaries and perks. We as consumers pay for all of these things in the price of the product, but rarely know how the business divides up the money. And sometimes we probably wouldn't agree.

If you had your choice between a $12 ticket in a massive movie theatre, or an $8 ticket in a regular sized building, which would you prefer? Would you prefer that the theatres cut spending on **advertising** in half and reduced your ticket price by $2?

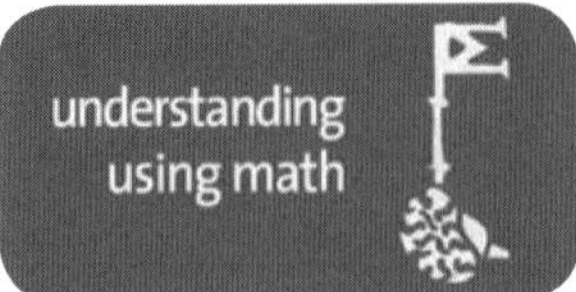

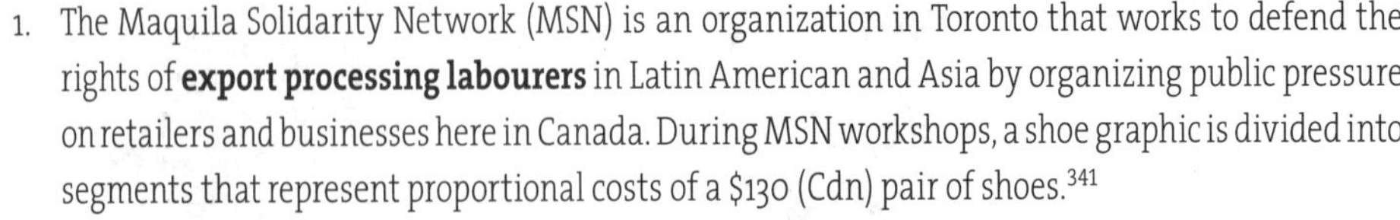

1. The Maquila Solidarity Network (MSN) is an organization in Toronto that works to defend the rights of **export processing labourers** in Latin American and Asia by organizing public pressure on retailers and businesses here in Canada. During MSN workshops, a shoe graphic is divided into segments that represent proportional costs of a $130 (Cdn) pair of shoes.[341]

   a. Complete the chart, based on a $130 pair of shoes.

   b. Use the shoe image and as best you can, divide it up proportionally, based on each cost associated with the shoe. Explain how you were able to do this task accurately, when the shoe is an irregular shape.

   c. Make two comparisons between numbers in the chart.

Paid to:	Percentage Breakdown:	Actual cost:
Factory	Wages: 0.4%	
	Materials: 8 %	
	Profit: 2%	
	Other: 1.6%	
Transport and Tax	5%	
Shoe Company	Research: 11%	
	Publicity: 8.5%	
	Profit: 13.5%	
Retail Store	50%	
	Total: 100%	Total: $130

341 "Stop Sweatshops Educator's Handbook". Maquila Solidarity Network, 2000. p 23.

2. There are all sorts of costs associated with running a movie theatre. Rent, repairs, ushers, cleaning staff, projectionists, equipment, heating, water, marketing, the cost of the movies...you get the picture. In order to make a profit, theatres turn to the concessions stand. Find and write the algebraic equation that describes the profit from popcorn sales[342] from the following chart.

	Family A	Family B	Family C	Family D
Money Spent on Popcorn	$5	$15	$22	$26.50
Amount of Profit to Theatre	$4.50	$13.50	$19.80	$23.85

If the theatre sells $9,780 on popcorn one night, how much profit did they make? Use your algebraic equation. Why does it make sense to put extra butter and salt on the popcorn?

3. A study is done to find the relationship between the amount of money spent in grocery stores in North America and the amount of money spent on packaging.[343]

	Store A	Store B	Store C	Store D
Money Spent In the Store	$33	$55	$198	$275
Proportion Used to Pay For Packaging	$3	$5	$18	$25

   a. Explain in words the relationship between the amount of money a person from North America spends in the store and the portion of that amount that goes to pay for packaging of the goods that are purchased.

   b. Write an algebraic equation to show the relationship between the two **variables**.

   c. Let's say that in a year, a family spends $5870 on food and $4631 on other consumer goods. What is the total amount spent on packaged goods and the portion of that total that was spent on packaging.

4. It is not uncommon to see a trend for marketing costs as outlined in the following table.[344]

	Store A	Store B	Store C	Store D
Money Spent In the Store	$7.55	$54	$72	$102
Proportion Used to Pay For Marketing	$3.02	$21.60	$28.80	$40.80

   a. Explain in words the relationship between the amount of money a person from North America spends in the store and the portion of that amount that goes to pay for marketing of the goods that are purchased.

   b. Write an algebraic equation to show the relationship between the two variables.

   c. If you spent $10,500 in the store, how much went to advertising?

---

342 Epstein, Edward. "The Popcorn Palace Economy", Jan 2, 2006, www.slate.com/id/2133612/

343 Mclnychuk, Mary. *Go Global with Kids.* YMCA Canada. 1995.

344 Atlantic Canada Food Marketing Guide: "Marketing costs, even without including advertising, represent a very large part, up to 40% of the typical wholesale price for a grocery product." www.gnb.ca

5. Let's go back to the family that spent $5,870 on food and $4,631 on other consumer goods. What is the proportion of that money that will have been spent to pay for marketing those goods?

   Create a pie graph to show the amount of money this family spent in total (the whole circle will represent the total) and the proportion of that total that was spent on packaging and marketing. Make sure to include a title and a legend.

6. If we could remove the cost of marketing from our purchases, it would seem that the **consumer** would save a lot of money. Why do you think that businesses are **reluctant** to stop marketing?

make it better

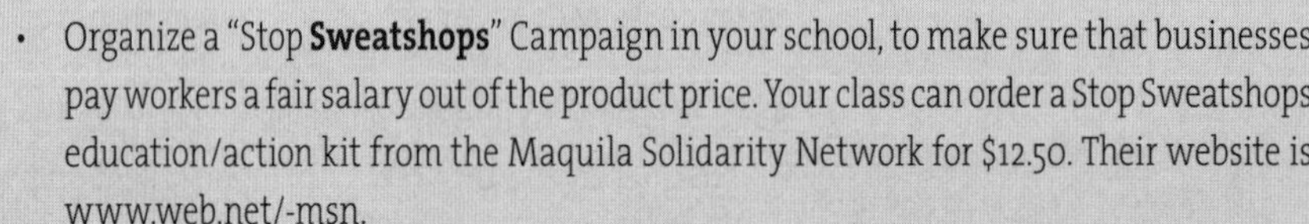

- Organize a "Stop **Sweatshops**" Campaign in your school, to make sure that businesses pay workers a fair salary out of the product price. Your class can order a Stop Sweatshops education/action kit from the Maquila Solidarity Network for $12.50. Their website is www.web.net/-msn.
- Buy products with as little packaging as possible. Some food stores allow you to package bulk product in your own reusable containers.

Healthcare For The Masses

"Of all the forms of inequality, injustice in health care is the most shocking and inhumane."

– Martin Luther King

Look around you. People who are **destitute**, ill, homeless, struggling with mental illness, even criminals, all packed into this **poorhouse**. Not a soul here has access to hospitals and doctors. After all, this is the year 1900 in Canada: only the wealthy can pay for these services.

The Depression years of the 1930s are devastating: people working for two cents an hour, 100 hour weeks, and still with no **insurance** for unemployment or hospital care. But then the war comes and people watch as the Canadian government has more than enough money to send Canadians off to fight, and to die, overseas.[345] People get angry.

After much public pressure, the first programs begin to appear: **family allowance money** for people with children, **old age pensions**, and finally- despite resistance from the business community, the private drug companies and medical and dental associations- comprehensive, universal, accessible health-care paid for by the government.[346] It was 1966. **Life expectancy** would rise four years in the next 15 years.[347]

345 Barlow, Maude. "Profit is Not the Cure A Call to Citizens' Action to Save Medicare". March 2002, pp. 6-7.
346 Ibid, pp 8-11.
347 Ibid, p. 15.

Times are changing. At every turn, businesses associated with health care push to open Canada's health services to the for-profit system, like the United States has. They produce reports telling of increased efficiency and better care. But do the numbers add up...?

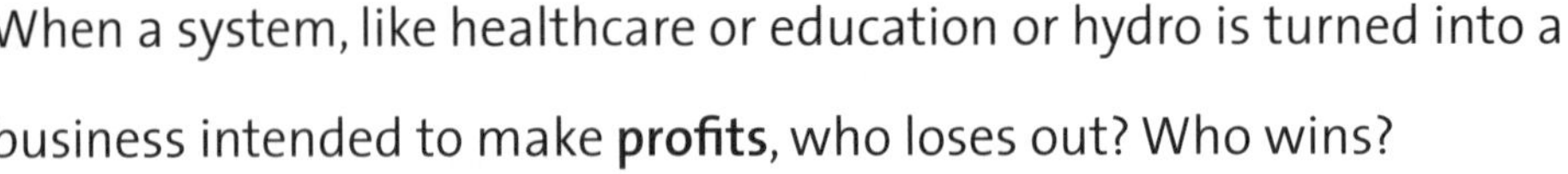

When a system, like healthcare or education or hydro is turned into a business intended to make **profits**, who loses out? Who wins?

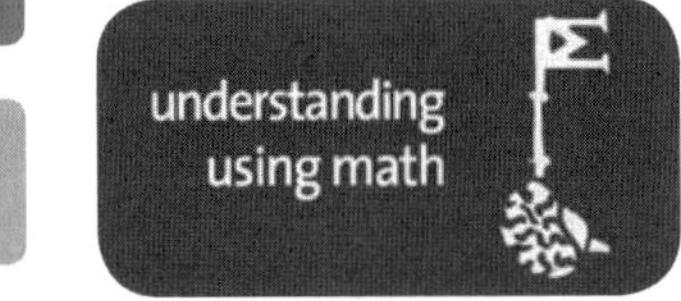

1. The following chart is an imaginary scenario where different approaches to healthcare are examined. For the same illness, there are six treatment options a doctor can suggest (A-F), or no treatment. The cost associated with each treatment is listed in column two.

    a. Roll a single die. The number you roll will be the number of people who opt for no treatment. Fill in all four cells in the first row with the number you rolled.

    b. Roll the die again. This is the number of people who opt for treatment A. Fill in all four cells in the second row with the number you rolled.

    c. Continue the process for all treatment options- if a cell is not available, it means no treatment is offered.

    d. In the Scenario 3 column, cross out each number and put beside it half of the value that you originally rolled. Do the same for the Scenario 4 column.

Cost to Insurance Company

Treatment Option	Cost per Treatment	Number of Treatments: Scenario 1	Number of Treatments: Scenario 2	Number of Treatments: Scenario 3	Number of Treatments: Scenario 4
No treatment	$0				
A	$2,000				
B	$3,000				
C	$4,000				
D	$5,000				
E	$15,000				
F	$22,000				

Scenario 1: All treatment options are offered by the doctor.
Scenario 2: The doctor does not suggest treatment options E and F, because they are pressured by the insurance companies not to.
Scenario 3: Only healthy patients are insured, so fewer treatments are claimed.
Scenario 4: Only healthy patients are insured and the doctor does not suggest treatment options E and F when claims do come up.

2. Based on your rolls of the die, fill in the following chart, by multiplying the treatment cost by the number of treatments for A to F and adding them together:

	Total Cost: Scenario 1	Total Cost: Scenario 2	Total Cost: Scenario 3	Total Cost: Scenario 4
Cost of all treatments				

3. When healthcare is run as a for-profit business, as it is in the United States, people's health is not always the primary concern: often the cost of treatment is most important.

   In your own words, based on your work above, explain why only one of your four scenarios is ideal in a for-profit system. Use your numbers to make your point.

4. A **privatized** healthcare system is often promoted (with millions of **advertising** dollars) as the most **cost-efficient** system. But by three important measures, it isn't at all:

	United States	Canada
Administrative Costs to run the system*	24 cents for every health care dollar spent	10 cents for every health care dollar spent
Amount employer pays in premiums	8.2% of gross pay	1% of gross pay
Average costs for care per person* per year	$7000	$3,298

(*in Canadian funds[348])

   a. What is the algebraic equation describing the difference in health care administrative costs between Canada and the United States? Use your equation find out how much the States would pay if Canada spent $28 million in **administration**.

   b. What is the algebraic equation that describes the difference in average health care costs per person per year between Canada and the United States? Use your equation to find out how much more money we'd need to spend on our 30,000,000 people if we had a system like the States does.

   c. Based on the above chart, how could you argue to **employers** that it is in their economic interests to fight for a public health care system?

348 Barlow, Maude. "Profit is Not the Cure A Call to Citizens' Action to Save Medicare". March 2002, p. 20.

Food for thought...

The **World Health Organization (WHO)** is a **United Nations** organization devoted to the promotion of health worldwide. WHO has meetings where standards are made to protect people's health. Nestle sends more **delegates** to these meetings than most governments do. And Pfizer, a **pharmaceutical** company, has more staff in its **marketing** department than all of the staff of the WHO.[349]

make it better

- Visit the Council of Canadians at www.canadians.org to get involved.
- Visit the Canadian Health Coalition at www.healthcoalition.ca to get involved.
- Visit Save Medicare at www.savemedicare.com to get involved.

---

349 Ibid, p. 45.

Sheltered From The Storm?

"It is organized violence on the top which creates individual violence at the bottom."

– Emma Goldman

It used to be that the Canadian **Federal government** contributed money to build **social housing**: affordable homes for people who could not afford soaring **market** rents. In fact, between 1964 and 1993, the government built an average of 20,000 affordable housing units each year. In 1993, they stopped.[350]

In the next few years the provinces and territories, which also created affordable housing, lowered their spending. Only 940 units were built across Canada in the year 2000. All of these cuts were made despite the research that shows a negative **correlation** between the rate of homelessness and the amount of low cost housing (in other words, low cost housing is associated with less homelessness). When you consider the cuts to **employment insurance, welfare** and **disability benefits** that were made at the same time, some problems emerge.[351]

First and foremost, the Canadians who need support the most find themselves on massive waiting lists (some longer than 60,000 families) for affordable places to live. The number of people using **food banks** and **homeless shelters** has soared (including the number of children who use these services). And the short term financial savings from not building housing have social and economic costs that are significant and long term.

---

350 Falvo, Nick. *Gimme Shelter! Homelessness and Canada's Social Housing Crisis.* Centre for Social Justice. The CSJ Foundation for Research and Education (my numbers are fabricated- the ratio is from the study). May, 2003.
351 Ibid.

The two most important factors in getting people out of shelters and into stable housing are **income support** and **subsidized housing**. We need to look at why Canada only exceeds the USA and Spain in social renting as a percentage of total households- behind Japan, Finland, France, UK, Sweden, Germany, Ireland, the Netherlands, Australia- and of course, the average.

What costs do you think are associated with having people living on the streets and in shelters?

understanding using math

1. The following graph depicts the drop in social housing units created by the Federal and Provincial governments between 1980 and 2001.

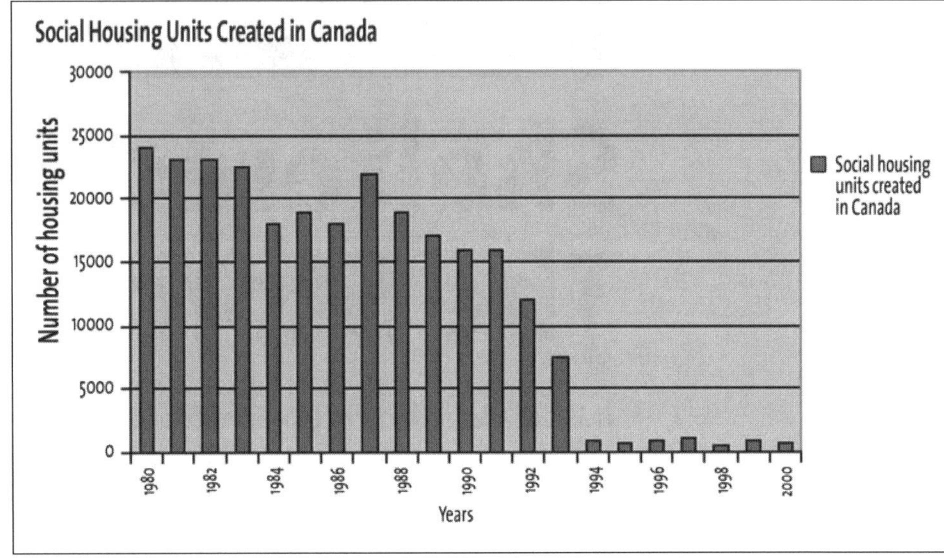

Source: Campaign 2000, "Honouring our Promises Meeting the Challenge to End Child and Family Poverty, 2003 Report Card on Child Poverty in Canada", p. 10.

2. If you used the average number of social housing units created per year over the period between 1964 and 1993 (20,000), how many more units would've existed today if the Federal Government hadn't stopped support in 1993?
   a. Why is that calculation misleading, based on the graph?
   b. Find the average number of units created per year using data from 1992 to 1994. Based on that average, how many more units would've existed today with Federal support?
   c. Speculate as to what the people who needed these housing supports have done to survive.
3. The number of households in Canada that are substandard (called **core housing need**) increased 38% in five years, to 18% in 1996. What percentage of Canadian households lived in core housing need in 1991?

4. A study is done to compare **Aboriginal** families and non-Aboriginal families with respect to the use of **substandard housing**.[352] Use the table below to figure out the ratio between the two groups.

	City A	City B	City C	City D
Number of Aboriginal people in substandard housing	1,533	3,323	3,989	6,786
Number of Non-Aboriginal people in substandard housing	786	1,687	2,035	3,410

5. In Calgary, church congregations have come together to provide emergency shelter. Looking at the graph between 1999 and 2003-2004, how would you characterize the change in the number of beds?[353]

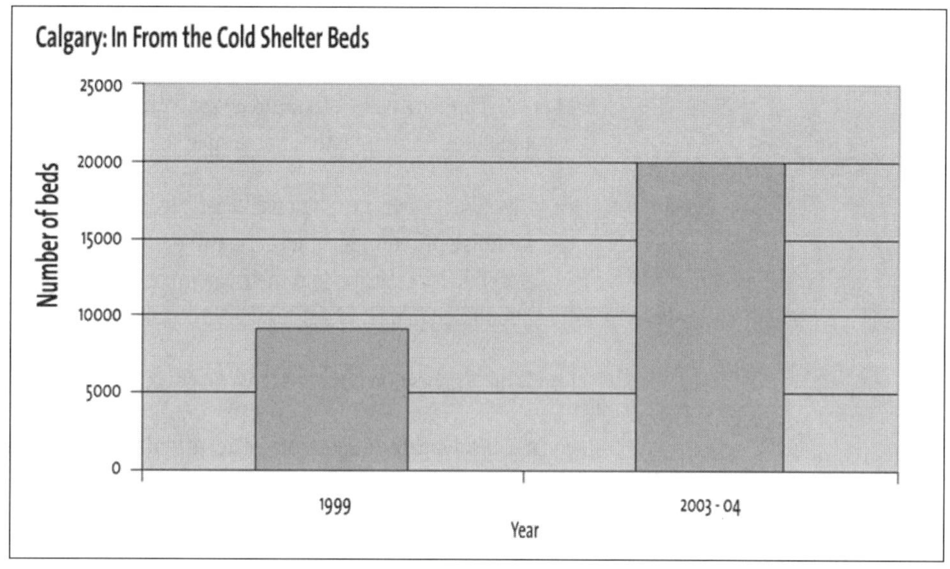

352 Ibid (The numbers are fabricated - the ratio is from the study.)
353 Axworthy, Thomas. "Enough talk: Homeless must become priority..." *Toronto Star*, 2004.

6. While the governments may be saving money by not financing affordable housing, there are significant costs associated with having people live on the streets and in shelters.

Health measure	Instances of Illness in the Homeless Population	Instances of Illness in the General Population
Arthritis/ rheumatism	46	22
Emphysema/ chronic bronchitis	58	12
Asthma	75	26
Epilepsy	92	15
Mortality rate per 100,000, age 18-24	2.6	0.4
Tuberculosis	170	18
HIV infection	241	5

The table above shows a comparison of different health problems in the **homeless** population and the general population. Being a sample, what is important is the **relative** relationship between the two populations.[354] Assume that the sample sizes were the same.

a. Describe the relative relationship between each population for each measure. Exact measurement is not required: you can use approximations. For example, the homeless population experiences arthritis and rheumatism at a rate approximately double that of the general population (a ratio of 2:1).

b. What implication does this have for government spending?

7. If you are an **advocate** for more and better affordable housing **and** you want to argue that it makes economic sense, how would you use the table below? (Assume that it costs about $3,000 per day per person to be in a hospital.)

Cost per person	Homeless	Housed
Shelter Costs per night	$36.50	$26.00
Rate of hospital admittance	10	2
Average length of stay in hospital	6 days	2 days

8. For every person who is homeless and admitted to the hospital, what amount of expenditure is required in comparison to a person who is housed? Why do you think this is so?

354 Falvo, Nick. *Gimme Shelter! Homelessness and Canada's Social Housing Crisis.* Centre for Social Justice.The CSJ Foundation for Research and Education. May, 2003.

9. The following is a diagram of a floor plan, with the average floor space of an American home in 1975. The entire number of square metres has been encapsulated in this single floor. Each square represents four square metres.

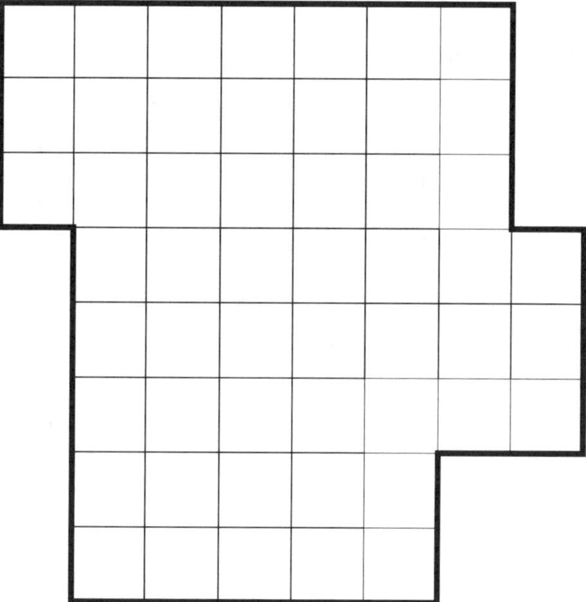

a. How many square metres was the average American home in 1975?

b. By the year 2000, the average American home was 38% larger. Use a black marker and increase the floor design by 38%.

c. The average American home in the year 2000 was 26 times the living space of the average person in Africa.[355] Use a red marker and indicate the living space of the average African within the American floor layout for the year 2000.

Food for thought...

Canada is the only industrialized country that has no national housing policy.

- Learn about the Toronto Disaster Relief Committee's 1% solution, which asks the Federal, Provincial and Territorial Governments to increase their spending on affordable housing by 1%. (It is projected that an increase by 1% would generate an additional 80,000 construction jobs.)[356]
- Canada is one of the few industrialized countries that does not have a housing bill of rights entrenched in law, providing affordable housing to all people. Call your **Member of Parliament** to see what they are doing to promote a housing bill of rights.

355 *Worldwatch 2004 Report*. P. 32.
356 Falvo, Nick. *Gimme Shelter! Homelessness and Canada's Social Housing Crisis*. Centre for Social Justice. The CSJ Foundation for Research and Education. May, 2003.

Clear Sight

"Marketing is what you do when your product is no good."

– Edwin Land

Seeing clearly- that's what it's all about when trying to **decipher marketing claims**. And that's what makes a lawsuit against Johnson and Johnson over contact lenses so ironic.

The **plaintiffs** in the case complained that the exact same contact lenses were being marketed as both two week lenses and one-day, single-use lenses. In effect, **consumers** ended up buying more product than they actually needed. For two small pieces of rubber, an estimated six million people spent $1.1 billion dollars on unneeded product before Johnson and Johnson settled for about $860 million.[357]

Statistics and numbers are used often in marketing claims, but usually without enough meaningful context for consumers to judge the quality or desirability of the product. John Allen Paulos, in his book Innumeracy says, "When statistics are presented so nakedly, without any information about sample size and composition, methodological protocols and definitions, **confidence intervals**" and so on, it is very difficult to draw any sort of meaningful conclusions. What are we to understand from claims like "100% Chance of Great Taste!" and "Up to 70% off"? At the very least, we should understand that clear sight requires asking the right questions.

---

357 http://www.globalethics.org/newsline/members/issue.tmpl?articleid=08050113160587

Linguist Noam Chomsky says that measurement is **ideological**: one must always decide what is to be measured and how and these are choices that will necessarily influence the outcome. How might this relate to measurement in marketing? Can you think of an example where this is the case in the marketing of a product?

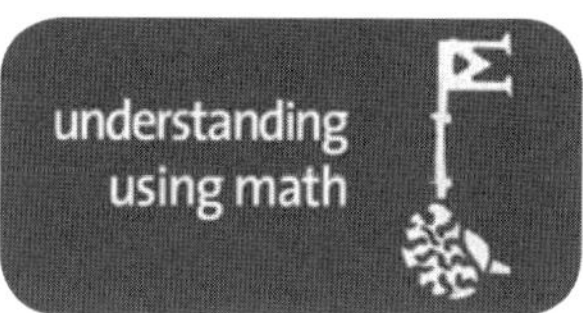

1. A product in a store is originally marked at $15.25. The price has been crossed off and someone has marked "20% off". Clearly, the item is having difficulty being sold, because the storeowner approaches you and says, "I'll take another 20% off of the sale price. That's 40% off of the total! What a deal!" Explain the store owner's mistake and correct the statement.

2. Company Z advertises a survey that it has **commissioned** on whether or not its product is better than its competitor, Company W. The survey finds that indeed, Company Z's product is superior. Explain two ways in which this finding could be misleading, and assume that the study is not a lie.

3. A number of studies point to a general relationship between drinking milk and the incidence of cancer: the more a society tends to drink milk, the more likely it is that their cancer rate is higher. Explain why the statement "Drinking milk causes cancer" may be inaccurate.

4. Heart disease and cancer are the two leading causes of death in the United States. Explain why considering the potential number of years of life lost might cause you to focus your attention on accidental deaths, like car accidents, falls, gun mishaps and drownings.

5. Use the following chart to prove why students have no time for school. Then explain the **fallacy** involved in the way the activity is structured.

Activity	Proportion of the year	Actual Time (Days)
Sleeping	1/3	
Eating	1/8	
Summer vacation and holidays	1/4	
Weekends	2/7	
		Total:

6. Sometimes, the absolute number of some event happening is given, with no regard for the number of people in the whole population being considered. A study argued that the game Dungeons and Dragons was causing the young people playing it to commit suicide, and said that 28 teenagers who regularly played the game had taken their lives.[358]

   For teens, the general suicide rate is about 12 per 100,000 per year, and at the time, as many as three million teenagers were playing Dungeons and Dragons. Put the above argument into perspective using these figures. Does that mean that the game was not a **causal** factor in the 28 deaths?

358 Paulos, John Allen. *Innumeracy.* Hill and Wang. New York. 1988. P. 126.

7. A company advertises that their product reduces acne 98% of the time. What other significant question should you ask before deciding whether to pay the $10 per tube?

8. **Loss leaders** are products that are put on sale at very low prices, sometimes at cost or lower, in order to lure people into the store. Complete the chart below to argue why it makes sense for a storeowner to sell a product at a price below what he or she paid for it.

	With no loss leader	With a loss leader
Average number of customers per day	152	196
Average profit per customer	$3.24	$2.95
Average daily profit		

9. If a store owner buys a particular shirt for $12.95 and the regular mark-up price (the store price) is 30% higher, how much does it sell for?

   How much would the store owner have to mark up the price to make the same amount of profit and be able to claim that the shirt is 20% off?

10. An advertisement encourages people to come into a particular store this weekend and enjoy savings: "Up to 80% off everything in the store." Explain how this statement could be technically accurate, but absolutely misleading.

Food for thought...

"The truth will set you free. But first, it will piss you off"

– Gloria Steinem

- Create a parody ad that spoofs the information in a regular ad. Post your creation in the classroom or in the school halls. You may get some ideas at Adbusters, on the web at www.adbusters.org.

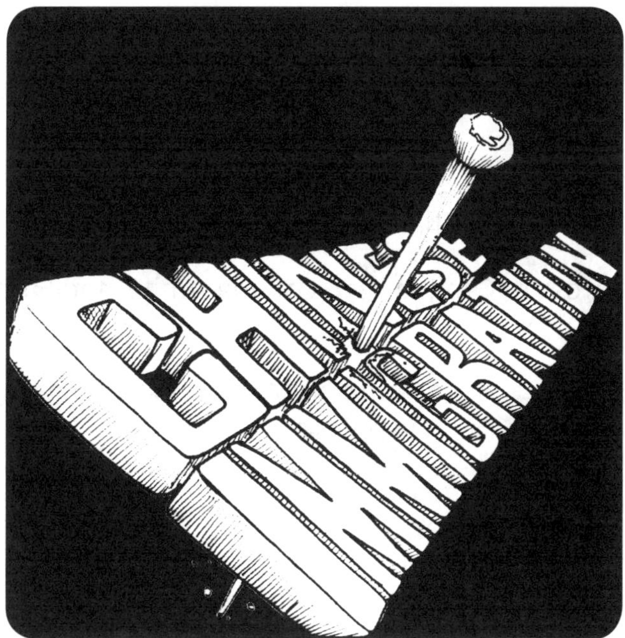

The Last Spike

"Fair play with others is primarily the practice of not blaming them for anything that is wrong with us. We tend to rub our guilty conscience against others the way we wipe dirty fingers on a rag."
– Eric Hoffer

Just as the last spike was being driven into the Canadian Pacific Railway in 1885 the Canadian government passed the **Chinese Immigration Act**, establishing a $50 head tax for **immigrants** coming from China. Seventeen thousand Chinese had been working since 1881 to build the railway[359] but now Canada wanted them out.

By 1903 the **tax** increased to $500 per person. And on July 1st, 1923, having extracted $18 million in taxes over the past twenty years, the Canadian government moved to block Chinese immigrants altogether by passing the **Chinese Exclusionary Act**. Thousands of men were unable to reunite with their families. For the next 24 years the Chinese community marked July 1st as Humiliation Day, closing their stores in protest.

Originally, the Immigration Act served to maintain a white, **Eurocentric** Canada. "Preferred" countries were European, while the people from Asia, Africa, the Caribbean and Latin America were seen as undesirable. By 1967, an immigration policy based on a points system was introduced to emphasize labour

359 Haggart, Kelly. www.cbc.ca/news/indepth/chinese/index.html May 19, 2004.

market requirements, family reunification, **humanitarian** issues and skills.[360] All Canadians except for our **First Nations** communities are immigrants and yet the Canadian government has always set priorities- resulting in different life chances for immigrants and particularly immigrants of **racialised groups**.

How would Chinese rail workers unable to afford to bring their wives across to Canada keep Canada 'white' and Eurocentric?

1. How much is $50, the original **head tax** in 1880, worth in today's terms? Use an annual inflation rate of 3% (that's a rough Canadian average).

2. How much is the $500 head tax in 1903 worth in today's terms? Use the inflation rate of 3% per year.

3. What is $18,000,000 in 1923 worth today? Use the 3% inflation rate.

4. Of the 17,000 Chinese rail workers 700 died because they were given the most dangerous jobs. Of the total number of students at your school, how many would not survive if they were working as a Chinese rail worker in the early 1900s?

5. Human Resources Development Canada keeps **employment equity** data that among other things, tracks the status of people who are **visible minorities**. In the following table, racialised group refers to Chinese, South Asian, Black, Arab/West Asian, South East Asian, Filipino, Latin American, Japanese, Korean, and Pacific Islanders.[361]

	Racialised Group	Percentage of Total	Total Workers
Fire fighters	335	1.50%	
Police Officers	1,850	3%	
Judges	90	3.66%	
Elementary/Kindergarten Teachers	9465	4%	
Secondary School Teachers	8,385	5%	
Lawyers	2,885	5%	
University Professors	6,500	14%	
Food Service Counter Attendants and Food Preparers	22,995	17%	
Light Duty Cleaners	26,505	19%	
Kitchen and Food Service Helpers	26,945	24%	
University Educated		34%	
Harvesting Labourers	4,410	40%	

   a. Fill in the final column, using the figures in the first two columns.

---

360 Galabuzi , Grace Edward. *Canada's Creeping Economic Apartheid*. CSJ Foundation for Research and Education. August, 2001. P. 35.
361 Ibid, pp. 7, 73-74.

b. The year this data was collected, racialised groups accounted for 11% of the population of Canada.[362] What do you notice about the types of professions where racialised groups are underrepresented?

c. What do you notice about the types of professions where racialised groups are overrepresented?

d. Some people suggest that racialised groups are not qualified to do particular jobs. The percentage of Canadians who have a university degree is 19%. Using the chart, how could you **problematize** the "under-qualified" argument?

6. Some people suggest that immigrants need time to adjust to the country and that the longer they have been here, the more economically stable they will be. Use the following table[363] to dispute, support or complicate that argument.

	Visible minority immigrants	Other immigrants
	Average earnings	
Pre-1956	$28,378	$34,350
1956-1965	$36,910	$34,011
1966-1975	$32,852	$33,399
1976-1985	$24,279	$29,286
1986-1990	$19,960	$24,533
1991-1995	$15,042	$20,809

7. The following data was compiled by Statistics Canada in 1995.

Racialised population born in Canada: Average employment income	All other Canadian born workers: Average employment income
$18,565	$26,521

a. Statistics Canada suggests that the reason that the racialised population made less than the non racialised population is that they were younger (the **median** age was lower by more than 11 years).[364] Is this a possible explanation? Explain.

b. Statistics Canada also suggested that another reason was that one third of racialised Canadians were employed full time for the full year, while a full half of non-racialised Canadian workers had full time for the full year.[365] How could **systemic racism** play a role in these figures?

8. A study was conducted on the experiences of Muslim women applying for work in the manufacturing, sales and service sectors in Toronto. While applying, half of the women wore the traditional **hijab** while the other half did not. Resumes were forged and women were selected so that race, age, accent, country of birth and experience in Canada were all the same. The women were all trained how to present themselves and ask for job applications. Here are some of the findings:[366]

362 Ibid, p. 75.
363 Ibid, p. 64.
364 Ibid, p 66.
365 Ibid..
366 Persad, Judy Vasht and Salome Lukas. *No Hijab is Permitted Here. Women Working With Immigrant Women*. December, 2002.

Applicant was immediately asked/was not immediately asked to fill out an application form and/or leave a resume

	Total Sites	Fast Food	Retail Stores	Garment Factories	General Factories
Applicant without hijab immediately asked and applicant with hijab not immediately asked	62.5%	33.3%	40%	100%	75%
Applicant without hijab not immediately asked and applicant with hijab immediately asked	12.5%	33.3%	20%	0%	0%
Both applicants immediately asked or both not immediately asked	25%	33.3%	40%	0%	25%

a. Why is it critical that the only difference in the women applying is the hijab?

b. Why was it important to train all of the women to approach the employer for job applications in the same way?

c. In this study, which job sector is the most discriminatory toward women who wear the hijab? The least **discriminatory**? How would that help in the **allocation** of resources to solve this problem?

d. The study was conducted on three fast food outlets, five retail stores, four garment factories and four general factories. Fill in the chart above to show the absolute numbers of workplaces as opposed to the percentages. What caution should we immediately mention, given the absolute numbers of workplaces that were examined?

Food for thought...

More than one half (52%) of recent immigrants with a university degree worked in a job requiring only high school education at some point during a six year period. This was almost twice the proportion of 28% amongst their Canadian born counterparts.[367]

The Head Tax was reintroduced in 1995 for all immigrants to Canada. It's called the "Right of Landing Fee."

- Locate a community support group where you live that **advocates** on behalf of racialised groups. Invite someone from the group to come in and speak to the class about barriers that racialised groups face in our country. What are these people doing to make it better? How can you help?

367 Statistics Canada, *The Dynamics of Over-qualification: Canada's underemployed university graduates.*, 11-621-MIE 2006039, April 2006, p. 8.

Your Title Goes Here

Stories help us learn, and here's your chance to tell one about a **social justice** issue important to you. Why begin with a two or three paragraph tale? Kieren Egan writes:

> Recent research has confirmed what myth-users knew long ago- that we remember a set of vivid events plotted into a story much better than we can remember lists or sets of explicit directions...The great power of the story is that it engages us as well as requiring our cognitive attention; we learn the content of the story while we are emotionally engaged with its characters and events.

Stories that are connected to our worlds- that we can see in our daily lives- are easier to understand. Often, justice issues that at first seem to be taking place on the other side of the world are actually linked to our immediate lives. One **maththatmatters** lesson started with sweatshops in Asia and ended up with the home workers in Toronto (and the clothes on our own backs!)

In a few paragraphs you won't be able to tell the whole tale. But you can introduce your topic and prepare your audience to ask some questions. It may be easier for you write this first section last, after having done the research for the lesson.

This opening question is intended to spark discussion, so it should be open-ended. Open-ended means that nobody can answer in a single word, like "yes" or "no". "What do you think about...", "How might ..... be connected to ....?", and "What reasons can you think of for....." are just a few examples of open ended questions.

Math can help people understand social justice by looking at patterns and relationships, quantities, probabilities, different ways of measuring the world, and statistical analysis.

In fact, there are so many myths tossed around by people who have their own interests at heart that it can be very powerful to pull out a set of numbers or a comparison that directly contradicts the myth. Math gives credibility to a social justice **advocate**.

Finding numbers is often not difficult. Most books on justice issues are filled with statistics, and the internet can be a treasure chest of numbers as well. Organizations in your community that advocate on behalf of people with less power often have their own publications or can direct you to resources. Whatever you do, always reference your work so that people can find the data themselves and if necessary, verify that it is credible. This is very important.

You may find that you have too many numbers, in which case build your lesson with variety in mind. Nobody wants to do 10 questions on scientific notation. Or analyze 8 pie graphs in the same lesson. Look to some of the lessons in **maththatmatters** and use some of the different types of questions.

Also keep in mind that your questions are best if they teach you something. The math should be necessary for the learner to understand the concept. If it feels like the math is tacked on, your audience may feel like you don't really need the math. If that's truly the case, it's better to find another question.

- If you can't do anything meaningful about the problem then why learn about it? You may not be able to shut down an unjust organization on your own, or single handedly put an end to sweatshops, but remember what Margaret Mead once said:

  "**Never doubt that a small group of thoughtful committed citizens can change the world; indeed it's the only thing that ever has.**"

maththatmatters

Answers

Super Size-It? Really? - Answers

Suggested Activity...

The U.S. Department of Agriculture recommends no more than 40 grams of refined sugar per day, equivalent to about one can of fizzy pop. One can of pop contains up to 11 teaspoons of sugar.[368]

Have the students take sugar cubes and a triple beam balance, and calculate how many sugar cubes amount to 40 grams. Ask if that looks like about 11 teaspoons worth. Have the students look at the information on a number of different pop cans to see if they can tell how much sugar is inside.

Using the sugar cubes, have the students develop an algebraic equation to describe the amount of sugar in any number of pop cans (they could demonstrate the pattern with the sugar cubes). Ask them to use their algebraic equation to figure out how many cans of pop you'd need to drink to intake one kilogram of sugar (you might have a one kilogram bag of refined sugar on hand).

Answers

Opening question:

The fast food industry is adamantly opposed to unions because unions provide a voice for employees that allow them to negotiate for better working conditions. Better working conditions, like wages and benefits, cost the employer money and thus cut into profits.

Understanding using math:

1. The relationship between the number of adult workers and the number of teenage workers injured in these fast food chains is one to two. In other words, teenagers are twice as likely to be injured. Algebraically this is expressed by:

   $T = 2A$

   where T is the number of injured teenagers and A is the number of injured adults.

2. Possible reasons that teenagers experience more injury: not enough training provided, safety standards not high enough for new workers, young workers less likely to speak up if unsafe conditions exist.

3. The table shows an exact two to one ratio between teenage and adult injuries: in real life the numbers would be only approximately two to one.

4. $A = 100{,}000$ $T = 2A$ $T = 2 \times 100{,}000$

   Therefore, $T = 200{,}000$. 200,000 teenagers are injured each year.

368 Lofthouse, Catherine. "Are Fizzy Drinks Doing This To Our Children?" *Guardian Weekly*, Jan. 23-29, 2003, p. 22.

5. Reasons include large amounts of available cash, security measures used in banks and gas stations are not feasible in fast food restaurants, fewer workers are on duty late at night, workers (who represent 2/3 of the robbers) don't get paid well and see an easy opportunity.) Hundreds of fast food restaurants are robbed each week.

6. Annual sales are one hundred seven billion, seven hundred seventy eight million, seventy two thousand dollars, or $\$1.07 \times 10^{11}$. This number is about 18 times the number of people on the planet. \$1.65 billion is 1.65×10^{9}. or \$1,650,000,000.

7. Although minimum wages are higher than in the 1960s, they are worth less in real terms because things cost proportionately more. In other words, the cost to live has gone up faster than the minimum wage.

8. \$15,000 x 1.20 = \$18,000 The employer would have to pay \$18,000.

9. In order to avoid paying the additional 20%, an employer could ensure that his or her workers worked less than 40 hours a week, and then just hire more workers to cover the work.

10a. \$599x = \$760 x = 760/599 x = 1.27

Therefore, a unionized worker has a 27% advantage over a non-unionized peer.

10b.

Men:	\$667x = \$805	x = 805/667	x = 1.21
Women:	\$523x = \$696	x = 696/523	x = 1.33
African American:	\$491x = \$665	x = 665/491	x = 1.35
Latino:	\$419x = \$632	x = 632/419	x = 1.51
Asian:	\$681x = \$759	x = 759/681	x = 1.11

Therefore, the group that benefits most from a unionized environment is Latino workers, with an advantage of 51% over their non-unionized counterparts.

10c. Many answers are possible. Notice that unionized women make just slightly more than non unionized men and that unionized Latinos make less than non unionized men.

10d.

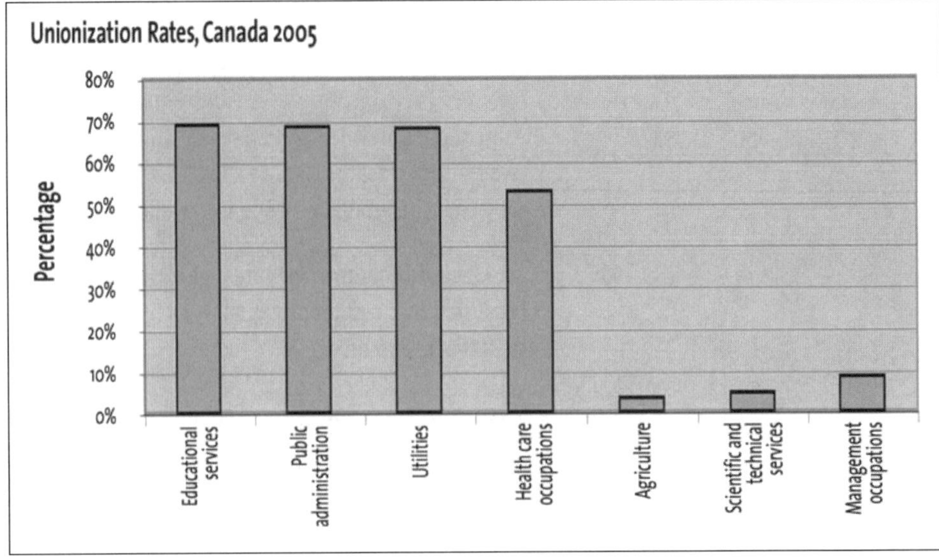

10e. The private sector fights to prevent unions because unions lower profit margins.

11. 240 billion

Standard notation: \$240,000,000,000

Scientific notation: 2.4×10^{11}

33 billion

Standard notation: \$33,000,000,000

Scientific notation: 3.3×10^{10}

12. Standard notation might impress upon the reader a greater sense of the problem.

13. $G = 1.2 \times 10^6 d$ where G is the amount of garbage in kilograms and d is the number of days. A year's worth of garbage would have a mass of 438 million kilograms. Divide an elephant's mass into this number to see the equivalent number of elephants to 438 million kilograms.

Get Tough On Youth? - Answers

Suggested Activity...

The five question quiz on page two is something that students could take to poll other classrooms and other grades. The answers from a sample of adults, either teachers or parents, would make an interesting comparison to the answers provided by students.

Alternatively you could hand out the following in a mix and match scenario: match the municipal service to the amount that your parents or guardians taxes go toward (the following is based on the 2003 Toronto property tax[369] – you may wish to find the budget for your city or town). The conversation about how money should be spent could be interesting (specifically, you may want to tailor the talk to crime prevention versus addressing crime- which budget lines do you think amount to crime prevention?).

369 "2004 City Budget Community Workbook", p. 9.

(Mix these up)

Police	$431.20
Fire	$186.48
Shelter, Housing & Support	$185.77
Debt Charges	$165.16
TTC	$154.53
Social services	$150.47
Transportation	$120.47
Parks and Recreation	$101.85
Library	$82.56
Solid Waste Management	$74.81
Public Health	$47.20
Children's Services	$42.36
Emergency Medical Services	$31.20
Information and Technology	$26.51
Finance	$24.47
Grants	$23.72
Facilities and Real Estate	$21.38
Homes for the Aged	$19.11
Human Resources	$17.06
Council	$11.94
Urban Development Services	$10.80
Other	$6.93

Answers

Opening question:

Newspapers are big businesses, and must generate profits. The most sensational stories are the ones most likely to draw readership and sell papers. Stories about petty theft and property crime or the complexities of court trials and sentencing are likely to generate less press than murders and other violent crimes.

Understanding using math:

The answers for the quiz, questions one through five, are listed on page three of the assignment sheet.

2. The number of youth charged (Y) with homicide per number of days (D) can be expressed in a couple of ways, depending on which part of "every week to ten days" you use.

   $Y = 1/7D$ or $D = 7Y$

   $Y = 1/10D$ or $D = 10Y$

   If $D = 365$, then $Y = 1/7 \times 365$. $Y = 52$ or

   $Y = 1/10 \times 365$. $Y = 37$

   Between 37 and 52 youth are charged each year with homicide in Canada. This is far less than the number of adults charged with homicide in Canada each year.

3. Assuming that all of the youth charged are actually guilty, which is an inaccurate assumption, the youth responsible for homicide as a percentage of all homicides can be found as follows:

   Adults (590) + Youth (about 45) = 635 total number of homicides.

   $45/635 = 0.07$. Youth are responsible for about 7% of all homicides in Canada.

4. $Y = 2.9A$ or $A = 0.34Y$

   where Y is the rate of incarceration for youth, and A is the rate of incarceration for adults.

   If A = 46 per 100,000 $Y = 2.9A$ $Y = 2.9 \times 46$ $Y = 133$

   The rate of incarceration for youth in 1997 was 208 per 100,000.

5. Aboriginal youth are remanded at five times their representation in the population. They are sentenced to custody at approximately 4.5 times their representation in the population. And they are put on probation at more than three times their representation in the population. These numbers would suggest that Aboriginal youth are coming into contact with the justice system far more than we would expect, and could lead us to examine systemic biases that would lead to this.

6. Individuals band together into lobby groups: more.

   Police intervention: increases.

   Media stories about youth crime: increase.

   Judges become more punitive.

   Politicians make more changes in youth crime laws.

   Public believes that youth crime is serious enough to change the law.

   Public intolerance to youth increases.

7. As soon as you can divert three youth from prison you've matched your $300,000 grant.

Who Runs The Show? - Answers

Suggested Activity...

(A background paper for teachers is available at the Canadian Centre for Policy Alternatives. It is entitled "The Share of Income Tax Paid by the Rich" by Neil Brooks.)

Select two or three students to represent transnational corporations.

Set up your classroom into three regions, to represent three countries. Ask a group at each region to (a) set the minimum wage for its citizens, (b) set the corporate tax rate, and (c) give the percentage of successful prosecutions of corporations for environmental degradation. Put these three figures on a placard. For example:

Minimum wage: $5.50

Corporate tax rate: 10%

Successful prosecution rate: 20%

Have each region display their placards and the students representing the transnationals decide which country to move their business to. Discuss (the lowest numbers in all three categories are best for business). Explore how this leads to what some call the "race to the bottom" where countries compete against one another to lower wages and environmental standards.

Answers

Opening question:

Environmental standards tend to set out the expectation that business will protect the environment: this oftentimes costs money. Likewise, new and safer equipment and modification of the work environment to protect workers costs money. Spending on these issues means less profit, which means a business is less competitive with other businesses.

Some people argue that increasing environmental standards and worker safety will increase competitiveness (and in some cases this has been demonstrated). Economic benefits come from re-using waste or selling it to another business that can use it. Worker retention reduces costs, as does a healthy workforce (fewer sick days).

Understanding using math:

1.a. This trend is great for business: between 1966 and 1996 the tax rate dropped from 18% to 10% (that's a 44% drop!).

1.b. To make up for the loss in revenue from corporate tax, the individual tax increase during the same period went from 20% to 43%. That's an increase of 215%!

1.c. If the government doesn't collect the same amount of tax, it becomes more difficult to pay for social programs.

1.d. Whether or not a corporation will actually integrate into the community, creating long term jobs and attracting further investment is questionable. Certainly in developing countries this has not usually been the case: as better opportunities open up in other countries, the business packs up and leaves.

2. Many comparisons are possible. For example, the number of youth alcohol and drug prevention programs that could be funded using the deferred taxes owed by Imperial Oil would be 7,266. That would service more than 4.7 million youth.

3.a.

Canada:	5.43×10^{11}
China:	5.22×10^{11}
Mexico:	3.77×10^{11}
India:	2.94×10^{11}
Mitsubishi:	1.85×10^{11}
General Motors:	1.69×10^{11}
Denmark:	1.46×10^{11}
Ford Motor:	1.37×10^{11}
Turkey:	1.31×10^{11}
Saudi Arabia:	1.17×10^{11}
Norway:	1.10×10^{11}
Israel:	7.78×10^{10}

3.b. Many comparisons are possible. For example, the company sales for General Motors are more than two times Israel's GDP.

4. It's hard to disagree that tax dollars should be spent wisely with the greatest possible impact. It's also hard to argue against accountability. But when you consider that Canada's debt has been created in large part due to tax breaks for the wealthy and for corporations, our attention might better be focused on making these groups accountable.

5.a. Employees net change:

Stelco:	-1983
CNR:	-1967
Bank of Montreal:	-6515

5.b. No. All three of the examples made profits in the millions (the Bank of Montreal made $1.4 billion in profit in 2002) while laying off thousands of employees.

In The Zone - Answers

Suggested Activity...

Understanding how long a twelve hour or sixteen hour work shift feels can be a little abstract. Try setting up an assembly line in the classroom, where each student adds a single connecting centicube to a centicube widget. (When the completed widget reaches the end of the line, a student can disconnect it and another student can return the centicubes to the assembly line so that nobody runs out.) After an hour of doing the exact same (boring) thing, discuss how sixteen hours of the same work must feel, six days a week. How would it affect other areas of your life: family, community participation, ability to look for better work or to organize the workplace?

Alternatively, the package from the Maquila Solidarity Network has a sweatshop bingo card that you could begin the class with.

Answers

Opening question:

Multinationals can distance themselves from responsibility for the working conditions within the factories when they don't own them. They can produce workplace codes that sound ethical, and if the factory owner doesn't post the code, doesn't post it in the language that the workers can read, or doesn't follow the code, the factory owner can become the scapegoat for the problem.

Understanding using math:

1. $9,783 ÷ 0.28 (cents per hour) = 34,939 hours

   34,939 hours ÷ 70 hours/week = 499 weeks

   499 weeks ÷ 52 weeks/year = 9.6 years, or 9 years 7 months

   Subtract nine years and seven months from today to figure out when a Haitian worker making Disney products would have to start to make what the CEO earns in an hour.

2.a. If it takes 50,000 workers 19 years to make what Nike spends on advertising in one year, it would take one worker 19 x 50,000 years, or 950,000 years.

2.b. 950,000 years ago is a long time ago. The rise of agriculture was 10,000 – 500 BC. The Ice Age was in its coldest phase 18,000 – 15,000 BC. Modern humans migrated out of Africa about 100,000 years ago. Homo erectus reached Europe and Asia about a million years ago.

3.

Canadian workers:	$11.42 per hour	x	800 workers	=$9,136/hour
American workers:	$10.56 per hour	x	1,450 workers	=$15,312/hour
German workers:	$12.56 per hour	x	760 workers	=$9,546/hour

Added together:	$33,994 per hour for the current labour force.	
New scenario:	800 + 1,450 + 760	=3010 workers (same as before)
3010 workers x	0.30 per hour	=$903 per hour (a savings of $33,091 per hour).

For a 70 hour week (amounting to 90,300 extra person hours, since your workers in Canada, the United States and Germany were working 40 hours a week) your costs are $903 x 70 hours, or $63,210. Your last workforce, working 90,300 fewer hours, cost you $1,359,760 per week. So you save $1,296,550 per week and get 90,300 extra hours as well.

Multiplied by a 52 week year, that amounts to a savings of $67,420,600, and an added bonus of 4,695,600 extra work hours.

4. In order to pay for fixed costs, the following trends are likely.

Amount of products produced increases.

Speed that employees work increases.

Wages decrease.

Employee benefits decrease.

Push to open new markets increases.

Amount of advertising increases.

5. 236,000,000 x 0.75 = 177,000,000 women working in the garment industry.

6.a. If the rate of pay is $5.50 per hour, the total pay is represented by P, and the number of hours is represented by H:

P = $5.50(H)

6.b. When H = 70 hours,

P = $5.50 (70)

P = $385.00

6.c. If the rate of pay is $0.14 per piece of clothing, the total pay is represented by P, and the number of pieces produced is represented by C:

P = $0.14(C)

6.d. If the homeworker makes 42 pieces of clothing per hour,

P = $0.14 (42)

P = $5.88 in one hour. In this case, it's better to be paid by the piece (an extra 38 cents an hour).

6.e. Pay per hour is now calculated at:

P = $0.12 (C) where P is the pay per hour and C is the number of pieces of clothing made per hour.

P = $0.12 (42)

P = $5.04 per hour, or multiply by 70 to get $352.80 per week. This is $32.20 less than when she was paid by the hour rather than by the pieces of clothing she produced.

6.f. The worker must make up $5.50 - $5.04, or 46 cents each hour. She can do this by producing 0.46 ÷ 0.12, or 3.83 more pieces of clothing per hour. That amounts to about 268 more pieces of clothing per week, just to match her original weekly salary.

6.g. Not only do you have to work faster, but you have to maintain the pace consistently. In other words, you have to be working just as fast Friday, after 65 hours of work, as you were working Monday morning when you started the week. If you have a headache, or you hurt yourself while producing the clothing, you still have to maintain the pace.

7.a. The average shoe price is ($100 + $180) ÷ 2, or $140.

The difference in shoe price and the cost to make the shoe (D) per pair sold (S) is:

D = $135 (S)

Not all of the $135 is profit- money has to be paid to transport the product, to pay the workers, to pay rent for the store, and so on.

7.b. If (S) = 30,

D = $135 (30)

D = $4,050

8. $10.97 ÷ $0.20 = 54.85

The worker would have to work about 55 hours to make enough to buy the shirt.

None Is Too Many...? - Answers

Suggested Activity...

Have students use an atlas to note the population and area of the following countries. Then have them calculate the number of Jewish refugees that each country took as a) a percentage of their population and b) a percentage of their land area. Compare these countries to Canada.

United States	(200,000+ Jewish refugees)
Palestine	(125,000 Jewish refugees)
Britain	(70,000 Jewish refugees)
Argentina	(50,000 Jewish refugees)
Brazil	(27,000 Jewish refugees)
China	(25,000 Jewish refugees)
Chile	(14,000 Jewish refugees)
Bolivia	(14,000 Jewish refugees)
Canada	(<5,000 Jewish refugees)

Answers

Opening question:

King's policies regarding immigration are notably absent, as is the St. Louis situation. His achievements, including mediating between the United States and Britain during the Second World War are listed. Who chooses what goes into history books is an important discussion to have with the students.

Understanding using math:

1. The students will create a spreadsheet that mimics the Reference Chart in the assignment.
2. The range for this set of data is 248,000.
3. The range is quite high- when the students graph the data it is clear that a consistent number of immigrants were not let into the country. There was a lot of variability.
4. Immigration plummets after 1930, which may be in part due to the Depression, as well as Kings' immigration policies. Large spikes may indicate a crisis in another part of the world where Canada stepped in a took a larger number of refugees.
5. The mean is 100,851.
6. The median is 89,000.
7.

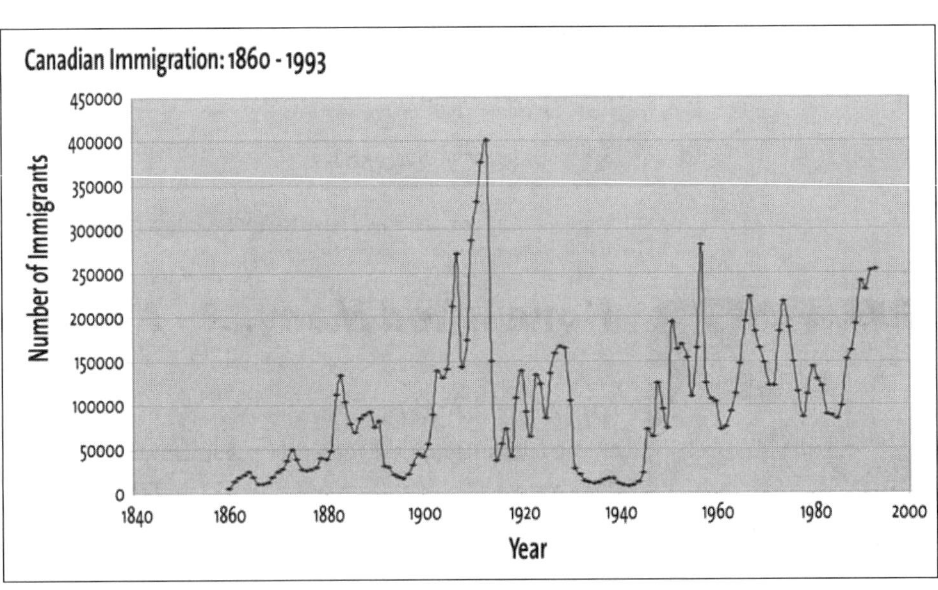

8. Between 1933 and 1944 refugees were let in at a rate of 17,000 a year or less (to a low of about 8,000 in 1942).

9. 1860: 6,000

1941: 9,000

1942: 8,000

1943: 9,000

(There is a filter function on spreadsheets that can be taught to find this answer easily.)

Pride And Progress - Answers

Suggested Activity...

Put a photocopied picture at each workspace, one per group of students. Ask them to black out 10% of the picture (How did they do it? Discuss...). Does the picture make sense when it's modified? If students who are gay, lesbian, bisexual, and transgendered/transsexual make up about 10% of the population, what can be learned from this activity. (This activity supplements the quotation).

Answers

Opening question:

There may be many answers to this question, or very few. The word leaders is used intentionally in the question to encompass possible political, religious, or other community leaders.

Understanding using math:

1.

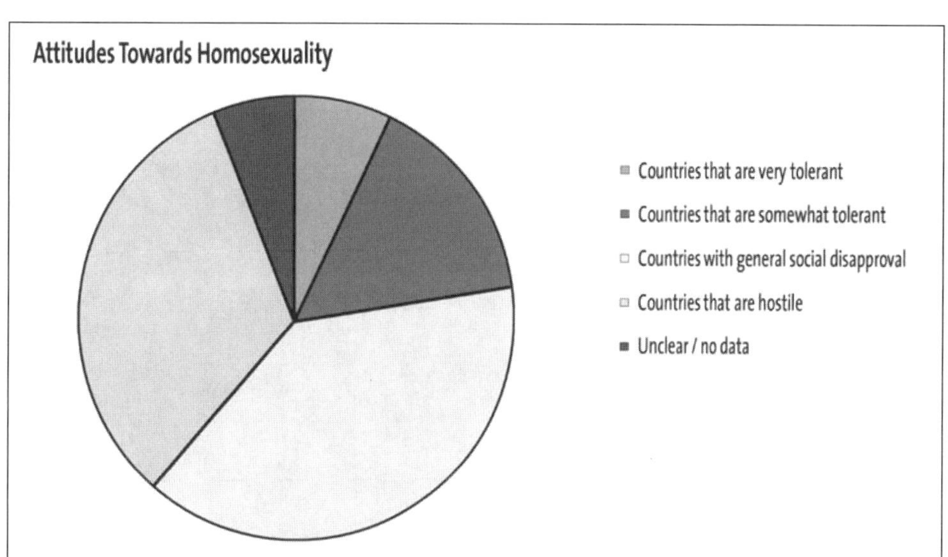

a. Many observations are possible. One is that about a quarter of the countries are somewhat to very tolerant towards homosexuality.

b. Field peoples thoughts about changes in the past ten years. If they feel things have changed, what do they attribute these changes to? How could they find out?

2. a. Speculations will vary. One idea is the power of mass media, and the growing number of television celebrities who play openly gay characters. Political leaders and organized activism around sexuality may also come up in the class discussion.

2.b. The category "Feel the Same" doesn't tell you what proportion feel tolerant or intolerant!

3.a. Between 15 and 20% increase.

3.b. More support comes from women, francophones, younger people, Liberals/Bloc/NDP, and people with more education.[370]

4. Younger people are far more open to the idea of same-sex marriage. This will probably lead to more acceptance in the future as these younger people pass on these values to their children.

5. Approximately 33,425 (actually 34,200).

6. People may speculate that the difference is a number of things. One suggestion is that religious fundamentalist groups in the United States that oppose homosexuality are greater in number than in Canada. You could do further research by finding the leading groups advocating against same sex marriage and that would give you a sense of the reasons (economic, political, religious).

7.a. Nothing on the graph proves that people who are gay have more money. Just having a credit card and a debit card doesn't necessarily mean that you use them more or have more money.

7.b. One idea is to market holidays to people who are gay, or use nightclubs as important venues for marketing material.

7.c. Businesses may promote diversity over time, when it is in their financial interests to do so.

---

370 *Toronto Star*, February 12, 2005 A4.

Roasted - Answers

Suggested Activity...

The following tables and information comes from Anthony Wild's book "Coffee: A Dark History". Have your students look at the following information and discuss what they see.

Tea			
Top 10 Producers	'000 Tonnes	Top 10 Consumers	'000 Tonnes
1. India	806	1. India	655
2. China	676	2. China	478
3. Sri Lanka	284	3. Turkey	166
4. Kenya	249	4. Russia	153
5. Turkey	171	5. United Kingdom	137
6. Indonesia	165	6. Japan	137
7. Japan	89	7. Pakistan	108
8. Iran	60	8. United States	93
9. Argentina	50	9. Iran	91
10. Bangladesh	47	10. Egypt	73

Coffee			
Top 10 Producers	'000 Tonnes	Top 10 Consumers	'000 Tonnes
1. Brazil	1941	1. United States	1121
2. Vietnam	676	2. Brazil	765
3. Columbia	560	3. Germany	567
4. Mexico	387	4. Japan	404
5. Indonesia	361	5. France	319
6. Cote d'Ivoire	328	6. Italy	307
7. India	324	7. Spain	188
8. Guatemala	312	8. United Kingdom	138
9. Ethiopia	210	9. Ethiopia	98
10. Uganda	186	10. Netherlands	95

You'll notice that four of the top ten producers of tea are former British colonies and a full five of the top ten consuming countries are producers of tea themselves. But with coffee, "the flow between coffee production and consumption is primarily from developing countries to Western countries, and there is far less of an internal market for the major producers than there is with tea. Coffee thus continues to be a much more overt product of the historical colonial system."

A handful of multinational coffee buyers have, with the help of the World Bank, locked farmers into a trading system that has seen the farmers' revenue drop from 40% in 1991 to 13% in 2004.[371]

371 Wild, Anthony. *Coffee: A Dark History*. Fourth Estate, London. 2004, p. 226.

Answers

Opening question:

People who don't make a living wage will experience hunger and health consequences, and may be unable to afford education for their children, or respond to natural disasters. People in a community that lives in poverty find other ways to survive: sometimes in the lucrative drug trade, sometimes becoming involved in the army or militia, both which can lead to civil unrest and violence.

Understanding using math:

1.a. Notice that the Fair Trade levels out the prices that coffee farmers receive.

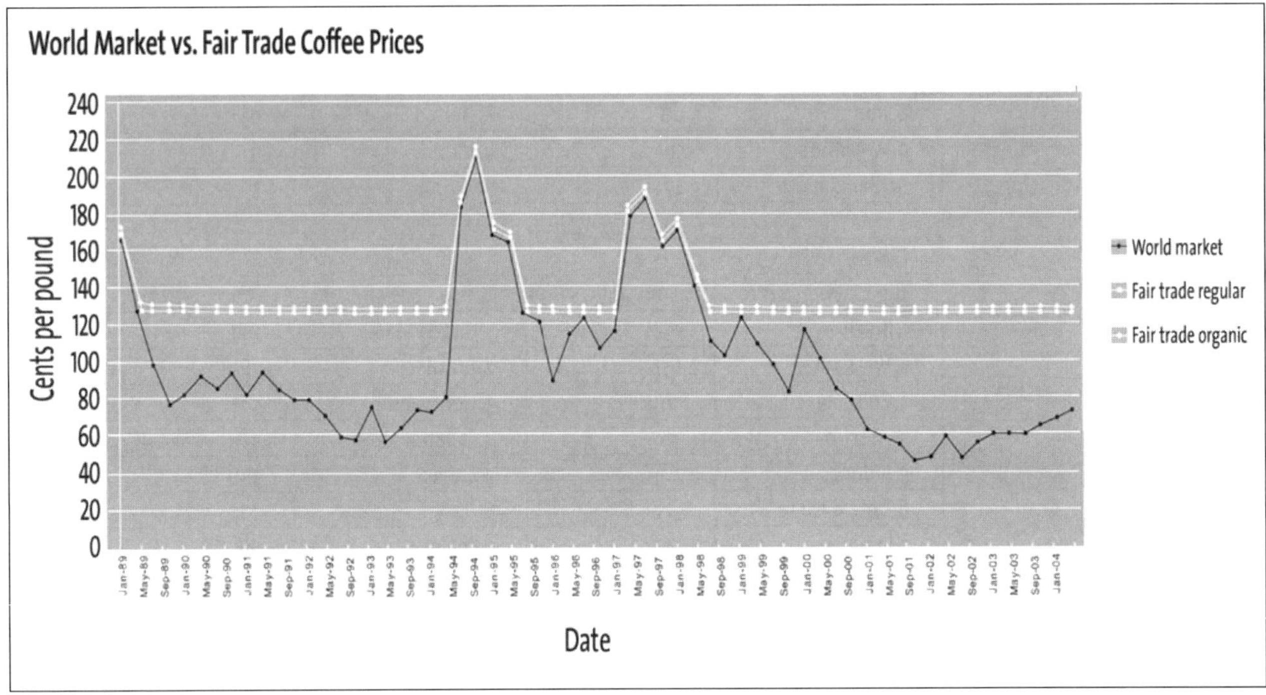

1.b. There were big changes in the first half of 1989, the last half of 1994, the first half of 1995, the first half of 1997 and the first half of 1998.

1.c. You notice that the price drops are prevented under Fair Trade, while maintaining the opportunity to make more profit when the market rises. Overall, this means the volatility is more limited.

1.d. Using a spreadsheet you can teach your students how to create trend lines. The following are the trend lines for the world market prices and the fair trade organic prices. The difference is that the best fit line for fair trade coffee is higher than the best fit line for the regular market prices.

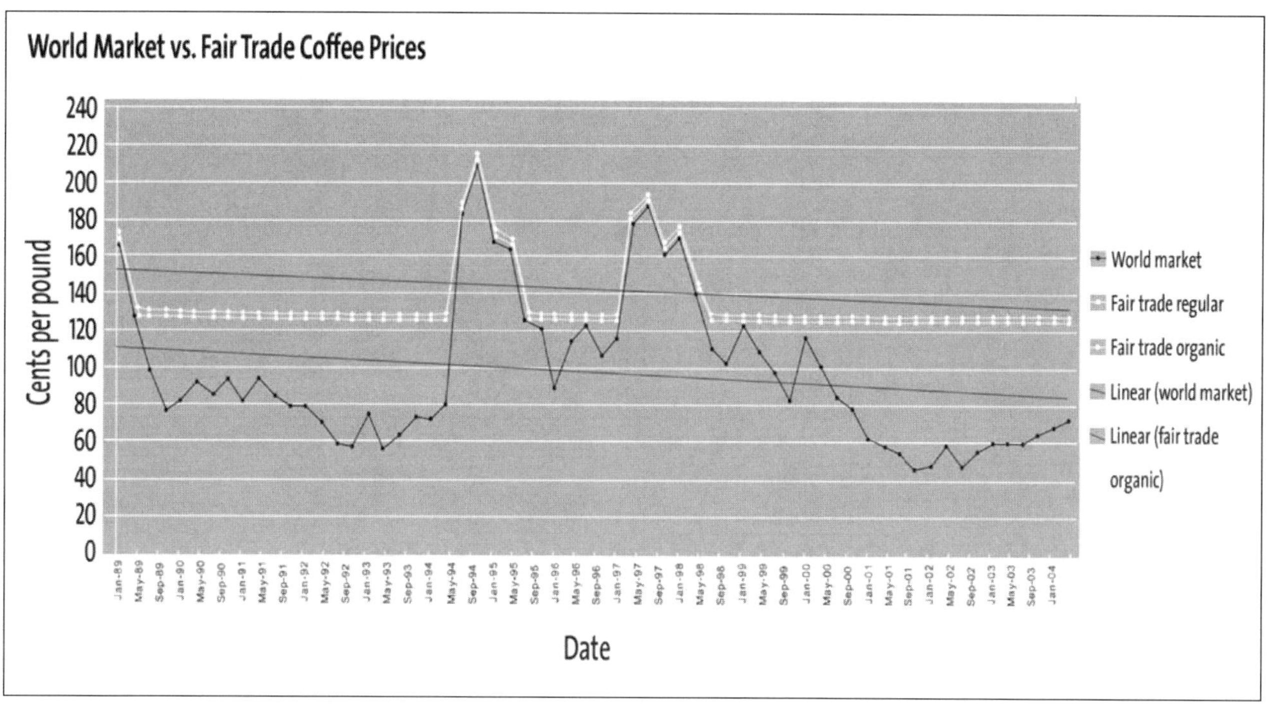

2.a. Shade grown plants:

P = 2000H where P is the number of shade grown plants and H is the number of hectares of land

Sun grown plants:

P = 7000H where P is the number of sun grown plants and H is the number of hectares of land

2.b. S = 3.5D where S is the number of plants grown in the sun and D is the number of plants that could grow in the same area but in the shade

What this means is that you can get 3.5 times the number of coffee plants if you grow them in the sun rather than in the shade. Short term profitability dictates that you should grow your plants in the sun. In the long term, the destruction of the soil may ruin the opportunity to grow the coffee plants.

2.c. If each plant in the sun has a higher yield of coffee than each plant in the shade, growing plants in the sun is more than 3.5 times as profitable in the short run.

3. There are approximately 2.2 pounds in a kilogram. Two kilograms would then be 4.4 pounds. 2500 coffee cherries per pound multiplied by 4.4 pounds is 11,000 coffee cherries!

4. 1/3 x 25,000,000 = 8,333,333.3

So about eight million three hundred thousand farmers run small operations.

5. A very tiny number of families own a very large number of the coffee production. If there are about 250 wealthy families and they amount to about half of a percent of the families, then the total number of families can be found as follows:

0.5/250 = 99.5/x x = 99.5 x 250 ÷ 0.5 x = 49,750

There are about 50,000 other families.

6.a.

Year	Millions of pounds of coffee	Percentage increase over the past year
1999	2	-
2000	3.69	184.5%
2001	7	189.7%
2002	9.8	140%
2003	18.7	190.8%

6.b. If you add up the four percentage increases and divide by four, the average increase works out to be 176.25%.

6.c. Using the average increase, 18.7 x 176.25% = 32.96.

Approximately 33 million pounds of fair trade coffee could be sold in 2004.

6.d. 100 – 0.35 = 99.65%.

0.35/7 million = 99.65/x x = 99.65 x 7 million ÷ 0.35 x = 1,993,000,000

In other words, there was close to two billion pounds of regularly traded coffee in 2001!

Side-Lined- Answers

Suggested Activity...

Have each table of students represent the elected representatives of different cities. They are to decide how to spend one million dollars in their city on poverty reduction.

For the purpose of simplicity, have each table decide what to do with the million dollars by allocating four quarter million dollar grants to programs for the following groups:

A. Those people who live in desperate poverty- far below the poverty line.

B. Those people who live deep in poverty.

C. Those people who live just below the poverty line.

Grants that go to programs for group A and B will not decrease the poverty line in the city, because those people are so far below the poverty line that they will move up towards it, but not past it. What are the political implications for this decision making?

Answers

Opening question:

The experience of being poor is relative to the community in which you live means that the amount of money you have doesn't determine whether you live in poverty as much as how much you have compared to others in your community. The Consumption Basket Measure is an absolute measure of poverty. Equity Based Measures are relative measures of poverty- they consider where everyone else is in the community.

Understanding using math:

1. The most restrictive consumption basket measure is the Fraser Institue measure, at $18,603. It contains the fewest items (or the cheapest). The most inclusive consumption basket measure is the Social Planning Council of Metro Toronto measure, at $44,668. It contains the most items (or more expensive items).

2. Poverty rate: Market Basket Measure 12%

   0.12 X 30,000,000 = 3,600,000 people

   Poverty rate: Low Income Cut Off 17%

   0.17 X 30,000,000 = 5,100,000 people

   So, depending on which measure you use you include or exclude one and a half million Canadians.

3. If you use the Fraser Institute measure of the poverty line, there will be fewer people considered to be living in poverty, because more people will be able to reach the poverty line of $18,603. This is compared to the Low Income Cut Off: fewer people will reach the $29,163, so more people will be considered to be living in poverty.

4. If the problem of people living in poverty is smaller, you can spend less on it. The money you would've spent on social housing or social assistance can then go into other things. Anyone who would benefit from that money could use a lower poverty line to their advantage.

5. Number of people using food banks in 1989: 378,000.

   96% increase in food bank users between 1989 and 2000.

   378,000 x 1.96 = 740,880 people using food banks in the year 2000.

   Number of people using food banks in 2005: 824,040

6. Number of people using food banks in 1989: 378,000.

   Number of people using food banks in 2003: 778,000.

   378,000 x X = 778,000 so 778,000 ÷ 378,000 = X

   X = 2.06, or a 206% increase over 1989 levels.

7.a. The increase is from about 14% to 25%: poverty has increased 178% between 1989 and 2003.

7.b. The overall average masks the fact that the number of Aboriginal children living in poverty is approximately 2.2 times the average rate, the number of children who are visible minorities and living in poverty is approximately 1.8 times the average rate, and the number of children with a disability living in poverty is approximately 1.6 times the average rate.

8. The number of children with health problems decreases as annual household income increases from about \$15,000 to about \$30,000. The number of children with health problems then remains fairly constant until the annual household income gets beyond \$70,000, at which point the number of health problems begins to drop again.

9. 13% of 25% of 30,000,000 Canadians = 0.13 x 0.25 x 30,000,000

= 975,000 children

9% of 25% of 30,000,000 Canadians = 0.09 x 0.25 x 30,000,000

= 675,000 children

10.

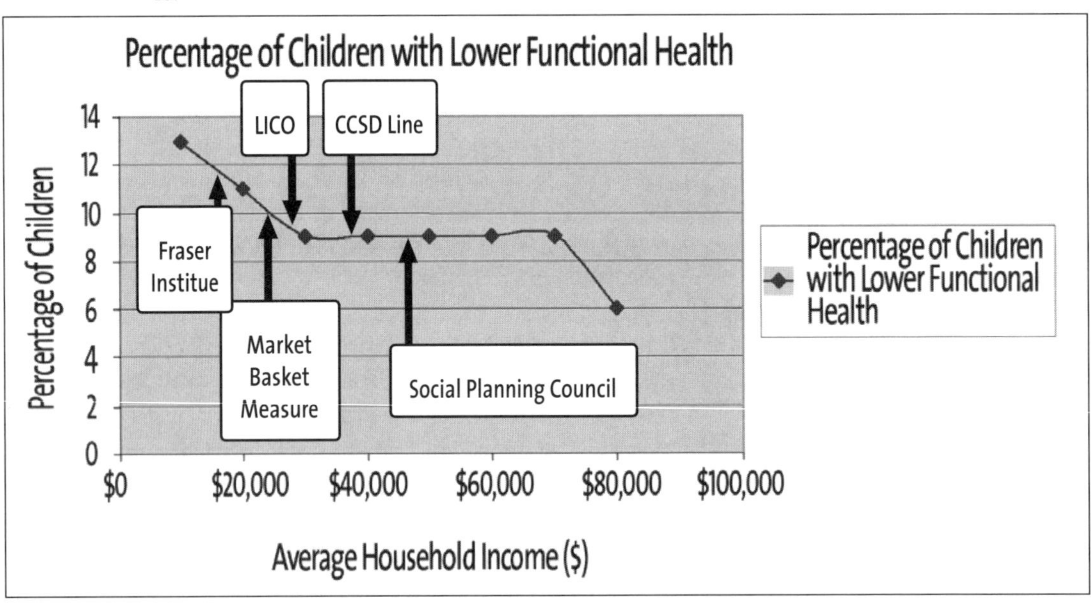

11. If you use the Fraser Institute poverty line, you're not going to consider the children above that line. If you use the LICO poverty line, you're going to address the health needs of about 300,000 more children (see answer to question #8: 975,000 - 675,000 = 300,000).

12. If there is a strong correlation between inequality and poor health, you must look at poverty in relative terms, because inequality has to do with relative terms.

13.a. For all cities, the area of the box combines the two issues of poverty rate and poverty gap. Therefore, City A has a poverty level of 0.3 x 14, or 4.2. City B has a poverty level of 0.4x 11. or 4.4. City C has a poverty level of 0.5x 8, or 4.0.

From worst poverty level to least worst: City B, City A, City C.

13.b. Finding the area of each box tells you the size of the problem. Visually, this is easier to understand for many people.

13.c. City B has a lower poverty rate than City A, but City B has the bigger problem, because its people, on average, live in greater depth of poverty than City A. City C has almost half the poverty rate of City A, so you might expect poverty not to be an issue. However, the people in City C are much deeper into poverty than City A, so the relative size of the problem in both cities is about equal (4.2 and 4.0).

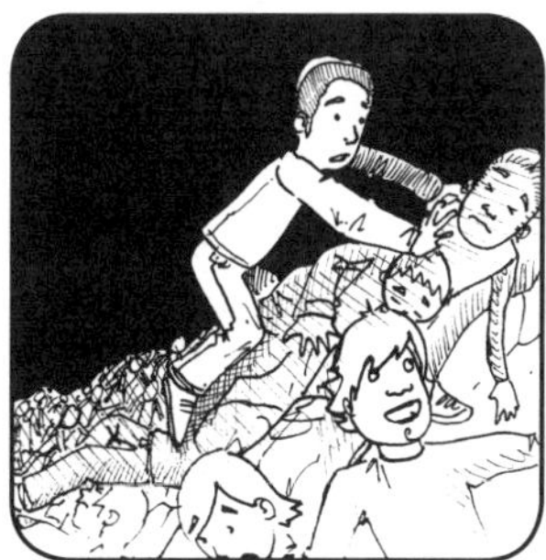

Poor Sport- Answers

Suggested Activity...

Play the Prisoner's Dilemma game outlined in the first question.

Answers

Opening question:

There may be several possible answers to this question. One is that when the goal is "winning", and the way to achieve that goal is by beating others, it's more difficult to develop empathy for those others. From the other perspective, working together cooperatively to achieve common goals is more likely to help people to understand and care for each other.

Understanding using math:

1.a. The maximum score possible for Player A, if Player B never turns in Player A, is 5 points multiplied by ten rounds, or 50 points. Player B could achieve 50 points if Player A never ratted out Player B. But if they both cooperate by not turning each other in, they can together get a sum of 60 points.

1.c. Quite possibly, when one player turns the other in, a climate of distrust begins and both players begin to turn each other in. Answers may vary.

2. Students share the results of their study on conversations between men and women.

3.a. Higher achievement through cooperation is likely because more people work toward a common goal: two (or more) heads are better than one. All ideas can be shared and developed- they don't have to be hidden from an opponent. Different people's strengths are maximized because everyone is on the same team. Two groups also don't spend time developing the same thing.

3.b. Simple tasks don't require a lot of complicated thinking where the benefit of group thinking can be maximized. Since most good learning in a classroom is complicated, the implication is that cooperation is the best way to maximize learning in schools.

4.a. B = Cooperative behaviour level before exposure to cooperative activities.

A = Cooperative behaviour level after exposure to cooperative activities.

$A = 3.5B$

4.b. The study suggests that cooperation can be taught.

5.a. The actual ratio between studies showing cooperation promoted self esteem compared to studies showing competition promoted self esteem is 81:1.

5.b. The study suggests that if we are interested in promoting the self esteem of our sport and recreation participants, we should be playing cooperative sport and recreation.

Darth Vader Has Arrived - Answers

Suggested Activity...

In December of 1987, the United Nations passed a series of resolutions having to do with disarmament. One of the resolutions put forth was to ban all weapons in outer space ("Star Wars"). One hundred fifty five countries voted: one hundred fifty four passed the resolution. The United States did not.[372]

A second resolution was to ban the development of new weapons of mass destruction. The resolution was passed by 135 countries, the United States being the only country that did not pass it.[373]

Ask the class to represent visually the ratios of 154:1 and 135:1. They might use coins, or drawings on the chalk board, or centicubes. What does this tell us about world opinion about disarmament?

Answers

Opening question:

Any business involved in the development of the missile defense system will benefit greatly. The estimated costs of development and maintenance of such a system have been over one trillion dollars. Based on Chomsky, the technology industry will also greatly benefit from the huge taxpayer subsidy to the development of the next generation of computer systems (required for the missile defense system).

Understanding using math:

1. 79 out of a total of 146 amounts to approximately 54%. Just over half of the countries voted to make the ABM Treaty stronger. Looking at how many are opposed may give you a better sense of how much international support there is for the ABM Treaty. 5 out of 146 countries opposed the resolution, amounting to about 3.4%.

2. 3 out of a total of 161 amounts to a probability of approximately 1.9%, or about 2 chances in 100.

3. One possibility may be that to effectively guarantee the security of so many nuclear weapons, the United States may be agreeing to quite substantial costs.

---

372 Chomsky, Noam. *Understanding Power.* Random House, p. 87.

373 Ibid. p. 87.

4. 156 countries voted in favour out of a total of 160, which amounts to a probability of 97.5%. Since there were no opposed votes, the probability of spinning an opposed vote is zero. Four abstentions amounts to a probability of 2.5%.

5. T = total number of warheads in a single missile

N = number of missiles

T = 5N so if N = 25, T = 125

and if N = 60, T = 300

6. T = total number of targets in a single missile including decoys

N = number of missiles

T = 25N so if N = 25, T = 625

and if N = 40, T = 1000

7. \$100,000,000 x 1.3 = \$130,000,000 (Canadian dollars).

\$130,000,000 ÷ \$40,000 = 3250 students who could have a free, 4 year university degree off of the costs of a single (failed) military experiment.

8. As one example, we could wipe out all of the items in the first column for 20 years with the \$1 trillion that are the anticipated costs on a missile defense system.

Item:	Additional \$ per year required8	# of years	Cost
Reproductive health care for all women	1.2×10^{10} or 12,000,000,000	20	\$240,000,000,000
Elimination of hunger and malnutrition	1.9×10^{10} or 19,000,000,000	20	\$380,000,000,000
Universal literacy	5×10^{9} or 5,000,000,000	20	\$100,000,000,000
Clean drinking water for everyone	1.0×10^{10} or 10,000,000,000	20	\$200,000,000,000
Immunize every child	1.3×10^{10} or 1,300,000,000	20	\$26,000,000,000
		Total Cost:	\$946,000,000,000

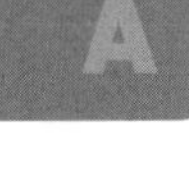

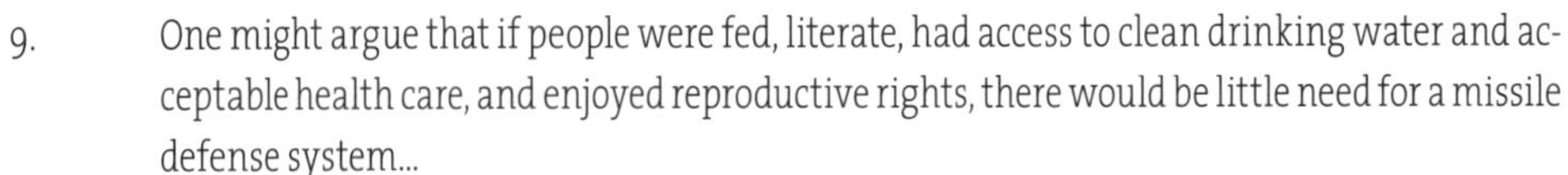

9. One might argue that if people were fed, literate, had access to clean drinking water and acceptable health care, and enjoyed reproductive rights, there would be little need for a missile defense system...

Some 'Fare' Better Than Others - Answers

Suggested Activity...

A one hundred million dollar subsidy from the Canadian government is planned for Ford's Oakville plant in Ontario. A single welfare recipient with a child can get $13,828 per year in welfare support. Ask the class to figure out how many people on welfare could be paid for the year with the single subsidy given to Ford. (Approximately 7232 people)

Answers

Opening question:

The logic is that corporations that aren't given favourable tax breaks will pick up and move their businesses to other places in the world where taxes are lower. Governments don't want businesses to do that because it means fewer jobs for its citizens, and a smaller tax base.

Understanding using math:

1. One possibility is that the government is getting more and more of its tax dollars from Canadian citizens, rather than corporations.

2.a. Prior to the tax reduction, a corporation earning $60 million a year would have paid $60,000,000 x 0.225% = $135,000.

After the tax reduction, a corporation earning $60 million a year would have paid $60,000,000 x 0.2% = $120,000 (so a saving of $15,000).

2.b. A corporation earning $36 million a year would have been paying

$36,000,000 x 0.225% = $81,000. Since it makes less than the new limit to pay this tax, it will be exempted from the $81,000 altogether.

3. A 25% tax rate on 100 million dollars a year amounts to $25 million in tax per year. Over a ten year period, that would amount to $250 million in tax.

4.a. For a person with a disability on welfare, the province from the four listed that would give the least financial support is Alberta ($7,596, or 40% of the poverty line).

4.b. For a single parent with one child, the province from the four listed that would give the least financial support is Alberta ($11,619, or 49% of the poverty line). The most support comes from Newfoundland ($14,670, or 73% of the poverty line).

5. Students may pretend they come from a particular category in question five and figure out how much money they have left at the end of the week on their welfare budget.

War Within - Answers

Suggested Activity...

Put a chart on the board, or create a handout similar to the following:

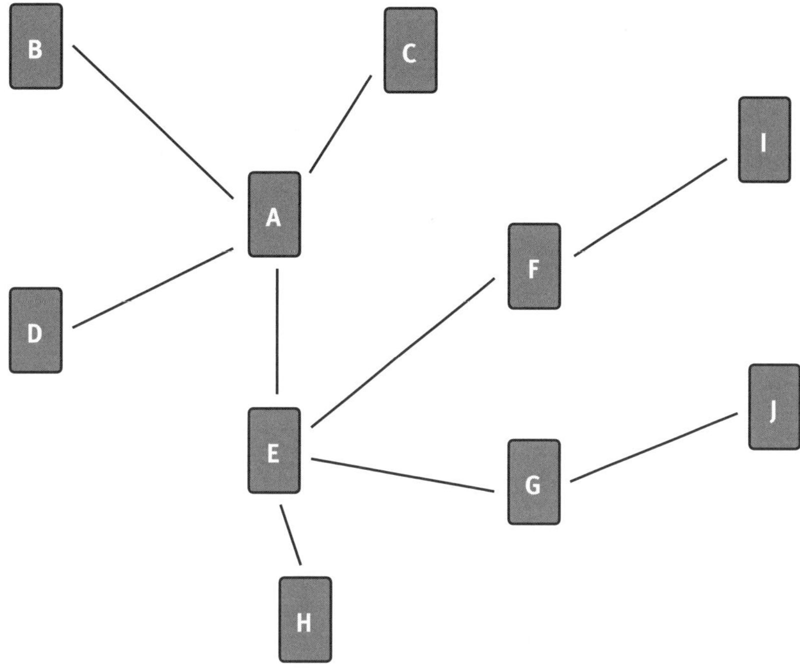

If the letters represent people, and the lines between them represent unprotected sexual contact in which the HIV virus may have been passed, then if B has HIV, who amongst the group is safe from HIV infection?

The only possibilities are C and D, if they had sexual relations with A prior to A's sexual contact with B. Use this to demonstrate that having unprotected sex is like having sex with every partner your partner ever had.

Answers

Opening question:

Public awareness of HIV and AIDS is aided in part by campaigns that require a basic level of literacy (although creative outreach that does not depend on literacy is happening). Poverty can lead to people selling their bodies for sex, or can encourage people to be involved in the lucrative drug trade, both which contribute to the spread of the disease.

Understanding using math:

1.a. I = youth infected with HIV

T = time in seconds

$I = \frac{1}{14}T$

1.b. The number of seconds in a day is 86,400. So using the equation, the number of youth infected with HIV in a day is 6,171.

1.c. 6,171 x 365 = 2,252,415 youth infected each year with HIV. That's approximately the population of Toronto.

2.a. C = increase in per capita income

D = decrease in infection rate as a percentage

C = 500 D

2.b. If the per capita increase was $3,000, 3,000 = 500D, and D is 6. The rate of infection would decrease by 6%.

2.c. The most likely answer is that having money allows more choice to people, and given more choice, they may avoid high risk behaviours that put themselves at risk of infection.

3.a. The ratio of infection rate for women compared to the rate for men is 3:1.

3.b. Women are more vulnerable to HIV infection for physiological reasons (reproductive tract infections make HIV infection more likely, and are more easily transmitted and harder to diagnose in women) and social reasons (for example in Mozambique, three out of five girls are married by 18, 40% to much older sexually experienced men who pass on the HIV, and abstinence or condom use is not a viable option). The fact that women have less power leaves them less able to refuse risky sexual practices.[374]

3.c. Not at all. Men need to be just as careful and not engage in unprotected sex.

4. Various comparisons are possible.

5. Many possible graphs can come out of the data from the chart.

Disabled By Prejudice - Answers

Suggested Activity...

Try playing 'The Card Party' to generate discussion about the way we treat each other in society. Give everyone a card from a deck of playing cards- make sure that they don't look at the face. Aces are low, Kings are high. Each person walks around the room with their card on their forehead so that others can see it. People are to interact with others as if they are at a party, and based on their social status, as indicated by the card. Subtle behaviour to indicate preferences and dislikes is the goal, and at the end everyone must guess what their own card was based on how people treated them.

The debrief may go in many directions. How did it feel to be an ace or a two? How did people treat you? What did you do as a result? How many people knew their status within two cards? Within one card? Exactly? How do people in the middle behave and why?

---

374 *State of the World Population 2002*, UNFPA, pp. 29-30.

Answers

Opening question:

It's important to see that groups of people are not monoliths: that within groups there are many other groups that have greater or lesser amounts of power and privilege. For example, within the group 'people with a disability', you might explore how an individual's sex, race or sexuality impacts their experience. Do justice advocates take into account the multi-layered barriers that people face?

Understanding using math:

1. The common reaching zone is between 90 and 140 centimetres.

2. The comfortable common reaching zone is between 90 and 120 centimetres.

3. You might do an exploration of your particular school, but possibilities include light switches, shelving units, coat hooks, bathroom mirrors and so on.

4. If ramp length is represented by 'L' and ramp height is represented by 'H', then the algebraic equation $L = 12\,H$ describes the pattern.

5. If the ramp is 9 metres in length, you might convert that to centimetres (900 cm). Because $L = 12\,H$, $900 \div 12$ is the height of the ramp at the 9 metre mark. The answer is 75 centimetres, or 0.75 metres.

6. As soon as the student has the height between street level and the top of the stairs, they can apply the algebraic equation to find the distance of the ramp. If a ramp already exists, they may want to see if the pattern holds true.

7. The picture of the ramp at the front of the school should be to scale, which may require a lesson on how exactly this is achieved.

8. A ramp length of 20 centimetres for every 1 centimetre rise is less steep than a length of 12 centimetres for every 1 centimetre rise, by approximately 1.7 times ($20 \div 12$).

9. Students should be able to apply the new algebraic formula $L = 20\,H$ to find the new length of the ramp at the front of the school.

12. The area of a circle with diameter 1.5 metres is found using the formula $A = \prod r^2$. The radius is half of the diameter. The area amounts to approximately 1.8 m^2.

14. It may be useful for this discussion to have an outside advocate who does work in the field to speak to specific questions about disability and prejudice.

Too Close For Comfort - Answers

Suggested Activity...

The Toronto Disaster Relief Committee's Shelter Inspection Report states that a sleeping area should be 3.5 square metres and the distance between mats should be 0.75 metres. How many beds can the students fit in the classroom?

Answers

Opening question:

There are several reasons that people who are homeless give for not wanting to sleep in shelters. In addition to overcrowding and the spread of disease, there is the worry of theft and violence, the difficulty getting uninterrupted sleep because of the noise of others, the schedules that shelters keep (getting everybody out particularly early in the mornings), and the fact that some shelters have very few bathroom facilities.[375]

Understanding using math:

1. Different sleeping arrangements will yield different numbers of sleeping spaces. Have the students compare their drawings to find the most efficient use of space within the parameters given. It is possible to fit 22 beds within the room.

2. The total floor space is given by length of the room multiplied by the width, or 8 metres by 12 metres. There are 96 square metres.

3. 96 square metres divided by 22 people is approximately 4.36 square metres per person. That's less than the amount that the United Nations sets for refugee camps.

4. If there are 22 people for two washrooms, that amounts to a rate of 11 people per washroom. How many students in the classroom share a washroom with ten others at home?

5. Students may or may not feel comfortable sharing the size of their living spaces. Answers will vary.

6. The answers will vary and teachers should let students decide what they will and won't share.

7. The rate of people per square metre in a wealthy area of town may be a real eye-opener and so as a teacher I bring at least one example with me to class for this question. A home in a wealthy area of Toronto could easily be 5 to 10 thousand square feet. Transferring that into square metres can be done by multiplying by 0.0929: 464.5 m^2 to 929 m^2.

8. a.

   If T is the time in days and N is the number of people infected, then N is equal to 2^T.

---

375 Toronto Disaster Relief Committee. The Shelter Inspection Report.

b.

Time, in days	Number of People Infected
0	1
1	2
2	4
3	8
4	16
5	32
6	64
7	128
8	256
9	512
10	1024

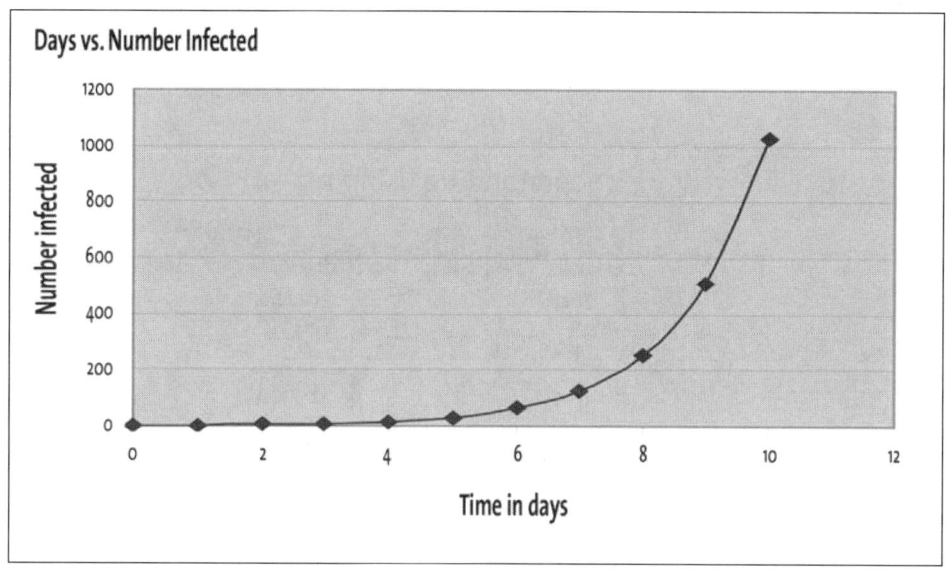

This is an example of exponential growth.

c. Unchecked and at the same rate of infection, you would reach 10,000 infected on day 14. ($2^{13} = 8{,}192$ and $2^{14} = 16{,}384$.)

d. Among other things, close contact with infected people can spread disease, as well as systems that can't easily identify and isolate the sources of the disease. A shelter system that produces transience of people who live in close quarters is a potential disaster waiting to happen.

Our Home and Native Land...? - Answers

Suggested Activity...

Re-enact the point in history where Europeans brought together First Nations chiefs from many different regions and gave them small boxes with cloth inside that had been covered in smallpox. When the chiefs returned to their communities with the 'gifts', it destroyed entire villages.

Answers

Opening question:

There are lasting social impacts of communities torn apart by the residential school system and the abuse that children suffered in these institutions. You may want to take a look at part of the movie *Where the Spirit Lives* (1989, directed by Bruce Pittman). It is the story of a young First Nations girl named Komi, who is kidnapped as per Canadian policy in 1937 and forced to live in a residential school.

Understanding using math:

First Nations Land: 1492 to 1890			
Year	Fraction	Decimal	Percent
1492	1/1	1.00	100%
1790	85/100	0.85	85%
1830	55/100	0.55	55%
1890	5/100	0.05	5%
Present day...			

These are approximations: you can ask your students to explain the reasoning behind their own estimations.

1. Answers will vary.

2. 80 million is approximately 2.7 times or 270% of Canada's population.

3.a. 5% of 80 million is 0.05 x 80,000,000, or 4,000,000 people remaining by 1650.

3.b. In 158 years (or 57,670 days) approximately 76,000,000 First Nations people died. That amounts to roughly 1318 people per day for 158 years.

4.

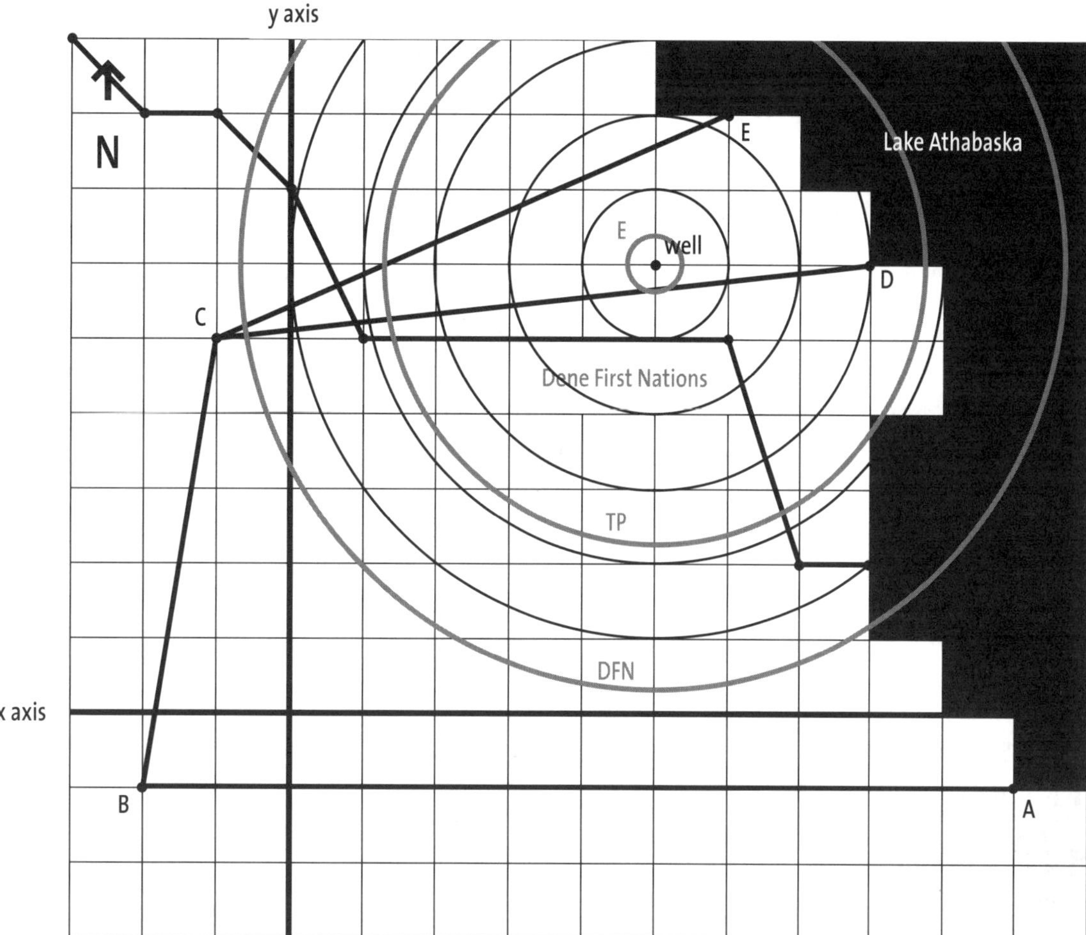

5. No. Point (7,7) is most likely based on the reading in the log book.

6. Approximately 6 degrees off.

7.a. Government reserve area: 66.5 square kilometres.

7.b. Surveyor's log reserve area: 72 square kilometres.

7.c. Bar in the ground area: 76 square kilometres.

8. It's probably going to be a choice between the survey's bar boundary at (6,8) or the surveyor's log book reading at (7,7).

9.a. $T = 1.97 - 0.03D$ where T = toxicity level and D is the distance from the oil well.

9.b. See map above.

9.c. When D = 1 km T = 1.94

When D = 2 km T = 1.91

When D = 3 km T = 1.88

When D = 4 km T = 1.85

When D = 5 km T = 1.82

10.a. $1.96 = 1.97 - 0.03D \quad D = 0.33$ km

$1.86 = 1.97 - 0.03D \quad D = 3.6$ km

$1.80 = 1.97 - 0.03D \quad D = 5.6$ km

10.b. See map above.

10.c. A conflict of interest is, as an example, a situation in which a group has financial interests at stake (Extenda has the potential future profits from the oil well at stake), and that group provides evidence that their project is safe to the community. An independent third party opinion is better because the independent party has no vested interest in the outcome of the toxicity report- they don't care what the results say, whereas Extenda clearly does.

10.d. If the boundary is (8,6) then the proposed oil well does not fall on the First Nations reserve. If it's (7,7) or (7,8) it does. If the government wants the project to go ahead (so that, for example, it can benefit from taxing Extenda, then it makes sense to argue that the boundary is (8,6).

11. The river runs past the more toxic region near the proposed oil well site. A river could carry toxins further than they might go ordinarily, as well as affecting the wildlife associated with the river ecosystem (and damage to Lake Athabaska where the river ends).

12. Various answers possible.

Larger Than Life - Answers

Suggested Activity...

The Red Tree, by Shaun Tan (Simply Read Books) is an excellent children's book appropriate for this age group that raises the issue of depression.

Answers

Opening question:

Suicide tends to be a taboo topic in our society- it usually isn't talked about. Some people may feel that young people don't have suicidal thoughts; some people may feel that talking about it may actually encourage people to take their lives. There may be other reasons as well. When it isn't talked about, the problem becomes one of isolation: when people don't feel that they can reach out and get help, the situation can become worse.

Understanding using math:

1.a. If there are approximately 30 million people in Canada, that amounts to approximately 4,200 people who take their lives annually.

1.b. A rate makes comparisons between different population sizes possible. For example, the United States has many more people than Canada, but if the number of people who committed suicide was 5,800 we wouldn't know if that was more or less comparably to Canada unless we turned it into a rate.

1.c. Two possibilities are men, and people from First Nations communities.

1.d. It's important to create subcategories so you can more accurately pinpoint the problem and be able to come up with interventions that help the groups most at risk.

2. Approximately 90 per 100,000 (89.6). There's a historical difference between the populations: First Nations groups have had their land and their rights stripped from them by European colonizers creating a legacy that continues today in the form of many different types of problems. High suicide rates is one of them.

3. The number who attempt suicide is 400 times greater than those who complete it, suggesting that many people are probably using suicide attempts as a way to get someone to care and help.

4. Some of the accidents may in fact be suicides. In some cases the cause of death may not be clear.

6.a. The number of suicides committed by boys is much greater than those committed by girls. Students may speculate about the different reasons why this is so. You may want to ask how the differences in the way boys and girls are socialized may play a part. Youth who are gay have very high suicide rates as well, most probably due to the intolerance they face.

6.b. Students might list: poverty, problems with health, parental stress from the workplace environment, divorce being less taboo, and so on. With all of these answers, you can ask again: 'what do you think the root cause of this is?' (i.e. what is the root cause of poverty?)

6.c. The root causes of the problem could be very different than the increased divorce rate leading you to address the problem in ways that didn't help. If the root problem is poverty, you might address the problem by raising the minimum wages or providing universal child care or increased subsidized housing.

6.d. There are some religious reasons why marriage is important: to see the marriage rate dropping and people doing things that go against church doctrine (couples living together out of wedlock for example) could be enough to try and get people to believe that suicide is causally linked to divorce.

7. A couple of contradictions exist within the table: England and Wales have high gun control and one of the lowest suicide rates; the same is true with Ireland. Also, the United States has low gun restriction and a suicide rate of 12 per 100,000 while Japan's gun control is severe and it's suicide rate is comparable, at 14.3 per 100,000.

Do You Have Confidence In Those Results? - Answers

Suggested Activity...

Tape a handful of television commercials that have claims about the product being sold. Have the students evaluate the claims thinking about the terms "validity" and "reliability".

A

Answers

Opening question:

If the results are accurate 19 times in 20, then 95% of the time the result for the Conservatives will fall between 31 and 35% of the support, and the Liberals will have 30 to 34% of the vote. What that means is that because of the overlap, the Liberals could actually be in the lead.

Understanding using math:

1. Validity asks "is this measuring what you say it does?" In this case, perhaps the student got inaccurate answers because they couldn't understand the English in the question, or understood the English but didn't understand what the question was asking. In both cases, the student could know the science material, making the test invalid.

2. The sample of people asked is a very specific type of sample: it's all businesses, who may have some reason that they don't want the skate park (perhaps they think it and the youth who use it will keep customers away).

3. Other community members who realize the value of the skate park may be overwhelmingly in favour of having it built and may make up the vast majority of people in the area. So if the survey is meant to figure out the entire community's feelings about the skate park and it's only given to a specific population of people, the results are not valid. (The survey itself may be valid though.)

4. You would have to ask if the voter's choice is likely to change.

5. It's likely that the singer is a) unqualified to know whether the product is the best on the market and b) being paid to say it is regardless, so the claim is not valid. While on payroll, the singer's response is likely to be reliable (reliably positive about the product), while after being on payroll his or her response may not be reliable.

6. The survey has a range, so the unemployment level listed at 8.0 may be anywhere between 7.2 and 8.8. Since it was 8.2 last year, unemployment may in fact be higher this year.

7. If the sample size of the random survey was too small (say for example 150 people were called), the results are probably unreliable.

8. The answers that are returned may be accurate measures of how the respondents feel about the story, but the group that responds is a self selected group: only those who have the time or interest are responding, which may not give you a sense of how the readers in general or the public at large feel about the story. The results are unreliable.

9.

	Group taking drug	Group taking placebo
Cardiovascular event occurs, including death	651	826
Percentage of study group	28%	35.6%

9.a. The relative risk is 78.7%.

9.b. The range of relative risk (for a 95% confidence interval) is 70.7% to 86.7%.

9.c. The range doesn't include 100% but if it did it could mean that there is absolutely no difference between the drug and the placebo's effectiveness.

9.d. Yes- remember that values fall within the range 95% of the time: 5% of the time they will fall outside of that range, so while it looks likely that the drug has a statistically significant effect, it's possible that it doesn't.

The Weekend's Here - Answers

Suggested Activity...

Employers will try to maximize the amount of time that their workers are performing effectively in order to maximize profit. Ask the students if they are aware of the ways in which the workplace has been modified to get workers to work faster (what do they think of these things?). Wikipedia, an online encyclopaedia lists ergonomic design changes, automation, computerization, and perfuming or deodorizing the air. A study from Cornell University found that workers typed more if the office temperature was higher (from 54% to 100% if the temperature was raised from 18.8 degrees Celsius to 25 degrees Celsius- and with fewer errors).

Answers

Opening question:

The benefits of moving to a shorter workweek include more work-family balance, where people can pursue other interests and personal growth, and where people are more likely to feel rested when they do come to work. Shorter workweeks with flexible scheduling, working from home or over the internet, can be useful for parents needing childcare.

Understanding using math:

1.a. There are 20 workers in this sample.

1.b. The mean is 40 hours, the median is 39 hours and the mode is 37 hours.

2.a. There are 20 workers in this sample.

2.b. The mean is 40 hours, the median is 39 hours and the mode is 37 hours.

3. It is true that all averages are exactly the same. However, a close look at the stem-and-leaf plots show that there are more people working fewer hours a week and more people working more hours a week in 2007. In other words, a polarization is happening.

4.a. The average number of hours that these employees are working each week has remained about the same over the past 22 years: 40.

4.b. The number of widgets produced by each worker each week has steadily increased, from about 800 in 1980 to about 850 in 2007.

4.c. The following reasons could explain the increased productivity:

- Better technology was continually introduced to make more widgets.
- Better division of labour increased the widgets produced (again, continually).
- The employees were encouraged or threatened to speed up work (again, continually).
- The complexity of the widget design was decreased (again, continually).
- Employees were working overtime hours and not reporting them.

5. The most expensive option from the list is probably the introduction of better technology. Getting workers to speed up or work overtime without pay is the cheapest option, although the following questions ask whether that really is the cheapest option.

6.a. The number of hours worked by each employee remains about the same, at 40 per week.

6.b. The productivity has fallen in the twelve months, from about 850 to 825 widgets per worker.

6.c. There are a number of possible explanations: if the workers are feeling stressed from overwork they can be less productive. Being tired reduces the quality of work. Resentment at being pushed unreasonably or at having little control over the workplace environment can lead to intentional slow downs. Absenteeism can increase, in the form of sick days and personal leaves.

7.a. The cost of the products after unionization are 18% more than before.

7.b. If 'A' represents the cost after unionization and 'B' represents the costs before, then A = 1.18B.

7.c. $79.47

7.d. Unions fight for higher wages and benefits which cost the employer money.

7.e. In this scenario, part or all of the costs are being passed along to the customer in the form of higher prices, which could mean that shoppers choose to shop elsewhere.

7.f. Many stores market themselves on low prices, so there are several possible answers.

8.a. It's the difference between 30 and 38 hours of work in a 40 hour week.

8.b. Working at higher rates of speed during your work day can lead to burnout and higher levels of stress.

9.a. The highest wage in non unionized is still lower than the lowest wage in the unionized workplace. The highest unionized wage is about double the highest non unionized wage.

9.b. Higher wages cut into Walmart's profits.

Is Justice Blind? - Answers

Suggested Activity...

Ask for a few volunteers at the front of the class. Explain that you're going to throw a single die, and if the number that comes up is a one, two, three, or four you'll give them each ten cents. Then pick someone out of the group whose clothing makes them distinct from the others- for example, she's the only one wearing green socks, and explain that in her case, because of the green socks, she'll only get the dime each time if you roll a one. You may want to ask about the probability for each scenario, and debrief around how it feels to be singled out for different treatment based on things that don't really matter (or in the case of racism, sexism, homophobia and so on, things you have no control over).

Answers

Opening question:

82.1% of the people executed in the United States since 1976 have come from the southern part of the country. In her book *The Death of Innocents*, Sister Helen Prejean notes that while African Americans make up 12% of the American population they amount for more than 40% of those condemned to death: "the legacy of slavery is evident not only in the imposition of a disproportionate number of death sentences on African Americans, but also in their mass incarceration in jails and prisons."(p. 217)

Understanding using math:

1. & 2.

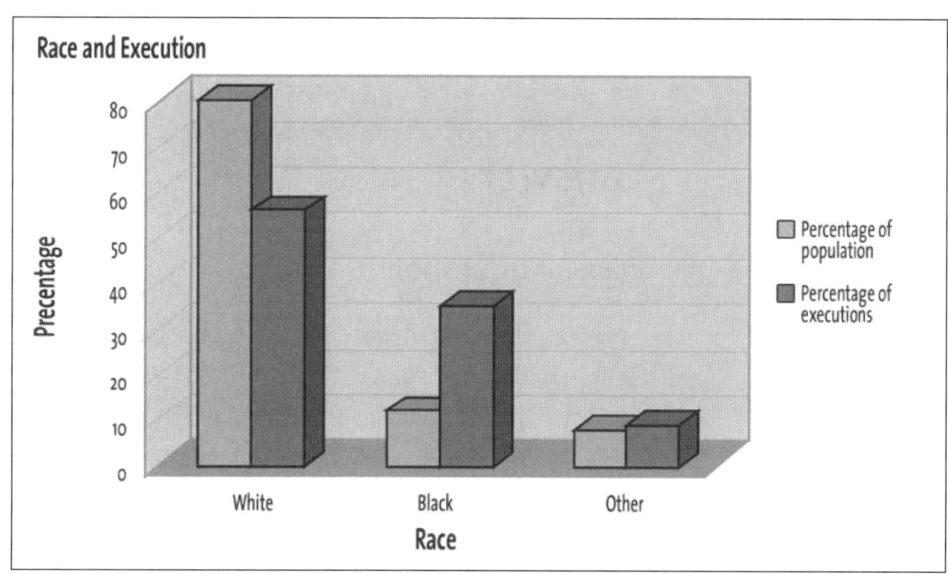

3. The percentage of people who are 'White' in the United States is 80% and yet the number of prisoners who are 'White' and executed is 56%. In other words, people who are White are underrepresented in the executions.

4. The percentage of people who are 'Black' in the United States is 12% and yet the number of prisoners who are 'Black' and executed is 35%! In other words, people who are Black are overrepresented in the executions.

5. Various answers are possible.

6. 725 per 100,000 people amounts to 0.725%. One could argue that with a society that has bigger gaps between the rich and poor, prisons play a bigger role in dealing with the resultant discontent. Also, a privatized prison system makes money by having people imprisoned.

7. The rate for African American males is 6.67 times greater than the average rate. For a point of comparison, South Africa incarcerated 'black' males at a rate of 851 per 100,000 at the height of apartheid.[376]

8. A one in three chance is just slightly more than 43 times greater than a one in 130 chance.

9. If a prison makes profit by being full of prisoners, it would be in its best interests to a) make sure that it has prisoners and b) make sure prisoners stay as long as possible. Of course, when profit becomes the priority, the rights of prisoners take a back seat.

10. The expression 'justice is blind' is meant to capture the idea that justice should be impartial– a decision making body not influenced by biases that are irrelevant.

Driving While Black - Answers

Suggested Activity...

Facilitate a discussion about how it feels to be a youth in our society- specifically; what's it like to go into a convenience store? How are they treated by adults? How does it feel to be treated a particular way based on qualities that they cannot control (age, skin colour, sex)? Are the forms of discrimination they experience overt or more subtle? Which feels worse and why?

Answers

Opening question:

Any research done on an organization by the organization itself should be subject to a high level of scrutiny- this is called a conflict of interest when the research is about something the organization could have done poorly or dangerously. For example, information distributed to the public by the tobacco industry about the subject 'nicotine' would be highly suspect. Independent researchers are people who have no ties to the people or group they are reporting on, and stand nothing to gain or lose from reporting a particular way- they are said to be more neutral.

---

376 Prejean, Helen. *The Death of Innocents*. Random House. New York, 2004, p. 217.

Understanding using math:

1. In this research people who are Black are twice as likely to be brought in on simple drug possession charges as people who are White. That's a ratio of 2:1, or in an algebraic equation where 'B' is the number of people who are black and brought in on drug possession charges and 'W' is the number of people who are white and brought in on the same charges $B = 2W$.

2. All of these variables need to be considered and "controlled for"- in other words, a researcher must make sure that their results are not due to some factor other than the one they are trying to study. One way of controlling for the factor 'age' might be to compare people of the same age, so that you know the outcome isn't influenced by that variable.

3. Although it is true that small sample sizes can skew data in ways that misrepresent the truth, one possible answer to this question is that the regions with a small number of people who are Black may be the very regions where there is a higher level of discrimination against them. Eliminating this data could make it seem as if there was no problem.

4. If you analyze situations where police officers have no choice in their protocol you can't tell whether they are discriminating: they have to (in theory) follow the guidelines that are laid out. If you look at situations where police officers have a choice in their behaviour, you can look to see if there is a pattern appearing in their choices. This is what the *Toronto Star* series attempted to do.

5.a. The probability in this study that your car will be searched if you are stopped and you are Black is P(0.071), or just over 7%.

5.b. The probability in this study that your car will be searched if you are stopped and you are Hispanic is P(0.125), or 12.5%.

5.c. The probability in this study that your car will be searched if you are stopped and you are White is P(0.037), or just under 4%.

6.a. 600 calls in 10 days amounts to an average of 60 calls per day.

6.b. Presumably there were different numbers of callers each day- possibly more at the outset as people were first given the opportunity, or perhaps more as time went on and more people became aware of the opportunity to call in. In order to maximize participation, the Commission could make sure to advertise the study in a wide variety of environments and in a wide variety of ways.

7. The graph shows that a disproportionate number of adult Aboriginal people are in Federal jails, in comparison to their number in the Canadian population in general. There are many problems with jailing people in general let alone in a way that is seemingly discriminatory. For example, the impact upon children within a family where a parent is jailed can have long term consequences. For more information on prison reform, see the website for the Prison Justice Action Committee (www.pjac.org).

8.a. Visible minority groups are underrepresented in the police force, which can lead to a lack of trust of the police within certain communities. Making a police force representative of the community could lead to better communication between police officers and community members.

8.b. If certain communities are more suspicious or fearful of police than they are of people within their communities committing crimes then people may not come forward with useful information, leading to fewer crimes solved.

9.

Year	1993	1994	1995	1996	1997	1998	1999	2000	2001	2002	2003
Reported total	155	249	302	175	187	228	292	204	338	219	149
Projected total	1033	1660	2013	1167	1247	1520	1947	1360	2253	1460	993

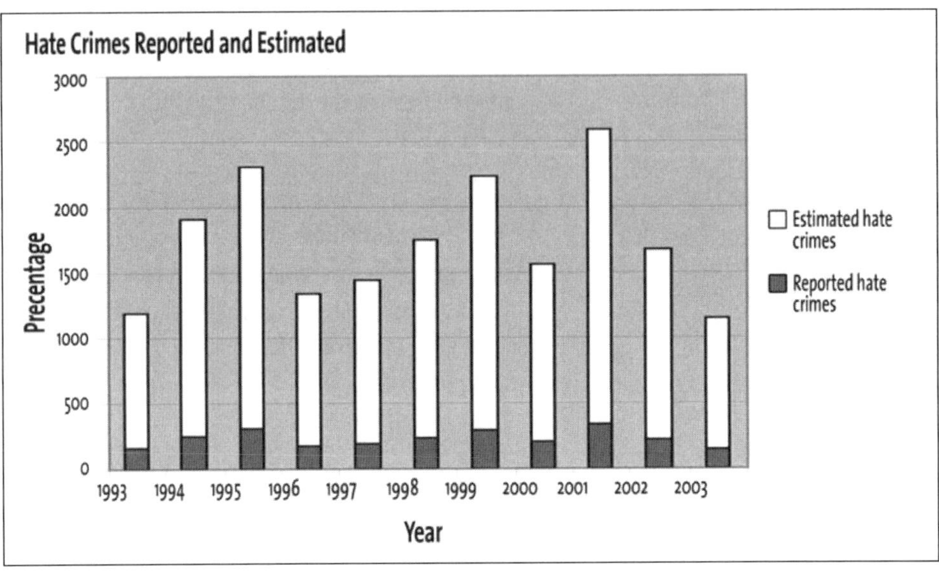

Making A Killing - Answers

Suggested Activity...

This activity is not my own, but one used by a Mines Action Canada (minesactioncanada.com), an organization that does work to educate about landmines throughout the world. Cut out circles on brightly coloured paper about the size of your fist. On one side write "Pick Me Up" and on the back write that the person who has just picked this up was seriously hurt or killed by a landmine. Then put five circles around your classroom before your students enter. See what happens when the circles are picked up and start a discussion about what happened.

Answers

Opening question:

People with jobs within the military industrial complex have skills in that area and could be used to dismantle and dispose of weapons and other armaments. Finding alternative uses for dismantled parts could be an initiative from within the weapons industry itself. Converting facilities into peaceful, community based spaces could provide jobs for people within the industry. Government support during the transition would lessen the impact of job loss as well.

Understanding using math:

1. Clearly, if the funds for the nuclear program alone had been diverted into other social services based programs, communities would be much better off. According to the graph, the programs other than the nuclear program could have been more than doubled by diverting the funds.

2.a. If C represents the total cost to clean up landmines, and L represents the number of landmines, then C = 650L.

2.b. For the low end figure, C = 300L and for the high end figure C = 1000L.

2.c. If L is 110,000,000 then C = 650 x 110,000,000. C = $71,500,000,000.

That amount is 71.5 billion dollars.

2.d. Using 60 million landmines, C = 650 x 60,000,000. C = $39,000,000,000.

Using 80 million landmines, C=650 x 80,000,000. C = $52,000,000,000.

2.e. It depends on which figure the student uses to create the ratio. If they use the average cost to make a landmine and the average cost to clean one up, the ratio is 16.5:650, or approximately 1:39. So an average landmine is about 39 times more costly to clean up than to make.

3. 1,500,000,000,000 x .506 = $759,000,000,000. Subtract this number from 1.5 trillion if you want 1.5 trillion decreased by 50.6%. That means that the 1998 amount spent on global military expenditures in 1998 was $741 billion. If that then increased by 5% by the year 2000, $741 billion multiplied by 1.05 is $778,050,000,000.

4. If the radius of the blast is 1.1 km, then the area of the circle created by the blast is found by $A=\prod r^2$. $A = 3.8\ km^2$. If there are approximately 23,000 people per square kilometre in Mumbai, then 87,400 people would be instantly affected by a single bomb. That's a lot of people.

5. Simply multiply 406,400 kg by 100 to get the total: 40,640,000 kg. A single whale can have a mass of up to 150 ,000 kilograms. So Russia's chemical weapons are equivalent to the mass of about 271 whales. That's a lot of waste!

6. The costs associated with the safe storage or destruction of chemical weapons are considerable. As the Russian Federation began to restructure it's economy in the 1990s it may not have had as its economic priority the destruction of chemical weapons.

7. Pascal might argue that because the consequence of even one missile launched by mistake would be so large, all missiles should be destroyed. Or perhaps he would have argued that we should spend trillions of dollars to develop a fail-safe missile defence shield. What do you think?

8. Many answers are possible. For a list of possible humanitarian expenditures, you may want to refer to the lesson Darth Vader Has Arrived.

9.

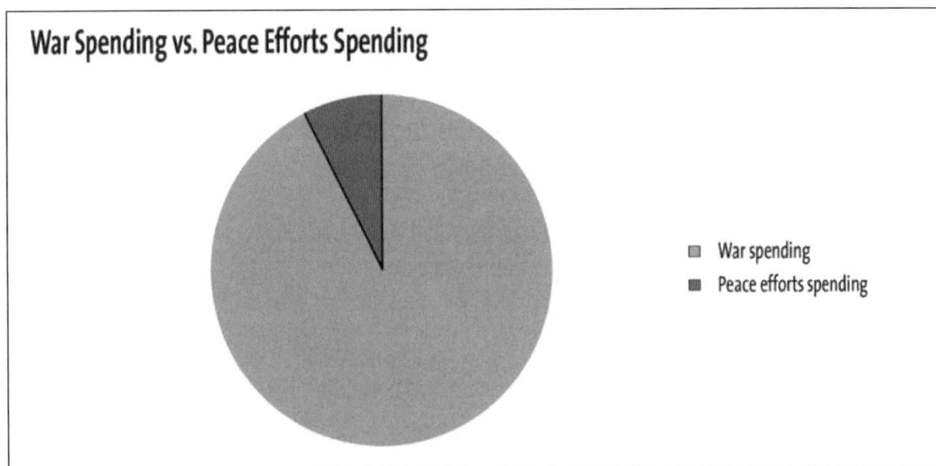

10.a. Total worldwide military expenditures in 2002 amounted to $842.7 billion.

11. If 'C' represents the number of civilians killed and 'S' represents the number of soldiers killed, then C = 10S. 12,540 civilian casualties.

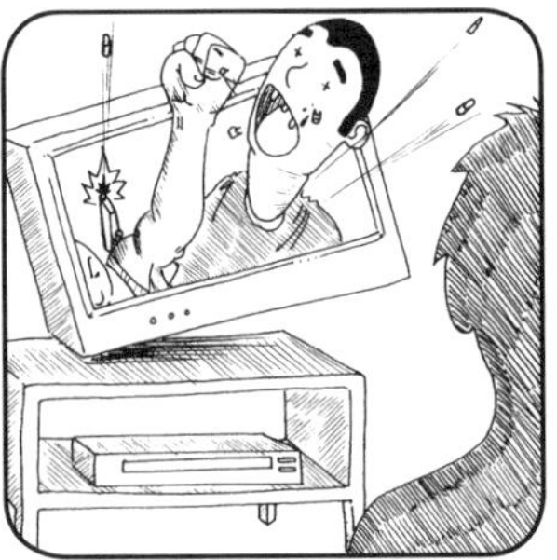

Correlated Or Causal? - Answers

Suggested Activity...

Michael Kesterton writing for the *Globe and Mail* notes that kids in the U.S. spend more time watching television by age six than they will spend talking to their fathers in their whole lives. Discuss. (Do you think it's any different in Canada?)

Answers

Opening question:

There are many factors that cause cancer and while smoking contributes to various types, it does not guarantee that every smoker will necessarily develop cancer.

Understanding using math:

1.

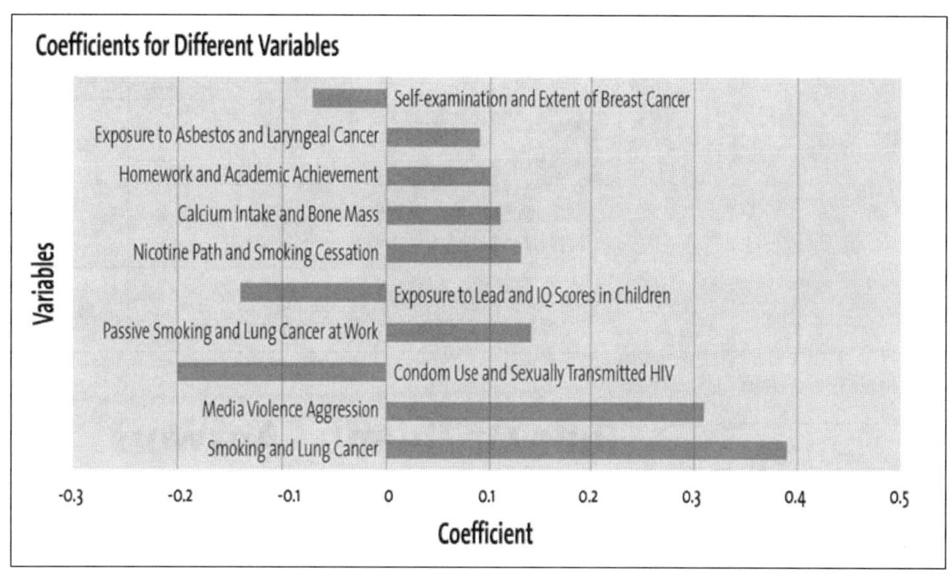

2. The second highest correlation in the data is between 'media violence' and 'aggression', at 0.31.

3. According to the research, the correlation between homework and academic success is only small, at 0.1. You could argue that the value of homework is negligible and need not be done.

4. If the entertainment industry admitted that its product caused violence then someone could attempt to make them (financially) responsible for that violence.

5. 1% of 5,000,000 viewers is 50,000 people. You could argue that influencing a person's buying behaviour and influencing their level of aggression are quite different. You could argue that it's easier to influence their level of aggression!

6. 1% of 50,000 is 500 people.

7.a. If 'T' represents the number of hours a child spends in front of a television each day during their preschool years and "C" represents the percentage increase in the chance that the child will have attention problems at school, then C = 10T.

7.b. If T = 2.2 hours then C = 22% increase.

7.c. If T = 3.6 hours then C = 36% increase.

7.d. Programming on television is full of very quickly changing images, ideas, sounds and colours. If concentration is a learned skill, you don't have much opportunity to learn it by watching television. As a simple experiment, ask the students to count how many times the camera shot changes within a 30 second commercial.

8.

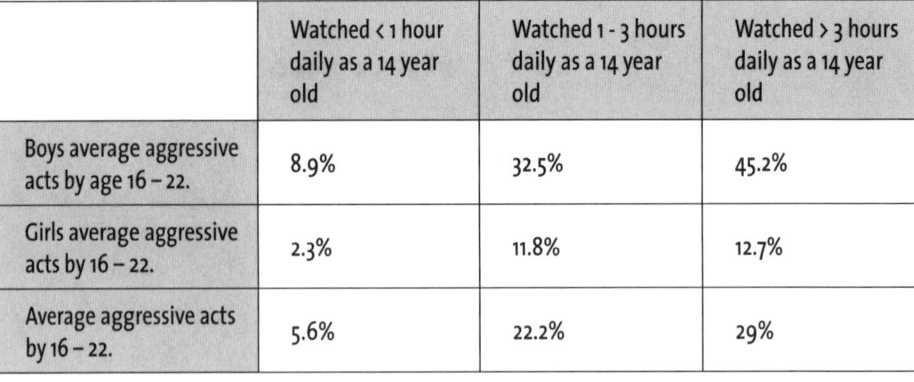

	Watched < 1 hour daily as a 14 year old	Watched 1 - 3 hours daily as a 14 year old	Watched > 3 hours daily as a 14 year old
Boys average aggressive acts by age 16 – 22.	8.9%	32.5%	45.2%
Girls average aggressive acts by 16 – 22.	2.3%	11.8%	12.7%
Average aggressive acts by 16 – 22.	5.6%	22.2%	29%

Rule Of Thumb - Answers

Suggested Activity...

It may be useful to have someone from a women's shelter or a crisis line worker come into the class to answer questions the students may have. Alternatively, there is a children's book called "Hear My Roar: A Story of Family Violence" by Dr. Ty Hochban and Vladyana Krykorka which is useful as a conversation starter.

Answers

Opening question:

Studies on some societies with less hierarchical structure where power is shared between men and women have shown that the level of violence is much reduced.

Understanding using math:

1.a. The two most at-risk groups based on low income are Aboriginal women and women from racialized groups.

1.b. Increasing the minimum wage would affect this situation because women from racialized groups are overrepresented in minimum wage jobs. Also universal child care and increased subsidized housing.

2. People may not report spousal violence to the police if they are too scared, either of their partner, the police, or both.

4. It depends on what is meant by the X-axis label 'Percentage'. If it means "Percentage of all victims, both male and female" then the statement in question four could not be true. But if it means "Percentage of female victims and Percentage of male victims" then the statement could be true and the graph would be visually misleading. Essentially you would be masking the total numbers of victims in each sex, which would mask any differences in magnitude between the sexes. In terms of finding solutions, that's an important distinction to understand.

5. If, for example, men on average experienced one of the types of abuse a single time and women on average experienced the same type of abuse eight times, both would register as the exact same thing in this graph: "yes- I have experienced the abuse". So what is masked is the amount the abuse is experienced.

6. The graph shows that the consequences for men and women experiencing spousal abuse are quite different.

7. Of all of the possible answers, only (a) is true- there has been a general steady increase in the number of shelters. The reasons why are not communicated in this graph.

8. One interesting thing to note is that the vast majority of violent crime in Canada, whether the victim is male or female, is committed by men. You might engage your class in a discussion of why they think that is so and how they think that affects men and women.

Kidfluence - Answers

Suggested Activity...

Cut out the logos of several businesses, using logos that don't have the name of the company in them. Have the students try to identify the businesses and calculate what percentage of the logos they knew. Ask them why they think they knew the logos and how early in life they remember being aware of marketing (you could graph the ages too).

Answers

Opening question:

Many different answers are possible, but perhaps discuss whether Ronald McDonald is a desirable option (and why or why not).

Understanding using math:

1. Answers will vary depending on class results.

2. About $2,190 per household.

3. The money that the consumer pays for when they purchase products at the store is used to pay for advertising.

4.a. The amount of parents' spending that children and youth influence is close to ten times their own direct spending. If 'P' represents the amount of money spent by parents and influenced by their children, and 'C' represents the amount of money spent by the children, then P = 10C.

4.b. P = $18,000,000,000

5.a. The higher numbers are represented by a form of scientific notation. The 'E' represents 'x 10' and the 11 refers to the exponent associated with the 10. For example, 4.85 E 11 means 4.85 x 10^{11}, or 485 billion.

5.b. The curve looks like exponential growth (not linear growth).

5.c. The dates are not listed at a constant rate- there are different amounts of time between each label, which distorts the look of the graph.

5.d. The sketch should make the first twenty four years look like very slow growth (low incline) and the last three years significantly more pronounced.

6.a. The protractor reads 60 degrees, which amounts to 16.7%.

6.b. 180 days x 12 minutes per day x .167 = 361 minutes of advertising per school year.

6.c. There's usually a disconnect between the many students who don't feel that they are influenced much (or at all) by advertising, and the amount of money that business spends on advertising.

7.a. If 'T' represents the total revenue of the TV station from advertising and 'N' represents the number of seconds of advertising, then T = 100N.

7.b. 12 minutes per hour is an additional 90 seconds per hour of advertising, which, using the formula is $9000 more revenue each hour. So within 1.7 hours, $15,000 would be generated.

7.c. If the fine is $15,000, the number of seconds it takes to break even is 150, or a mere two and a half minutes of commercials. Because the fine is so low in this case, it makes sense that the television station would break the rules because it could pay off the fine quite easily.

8.a. If 'T' represents the total number of commercials viewed, and 'N' represents the number of years, then T = 20,000N.

8.b. If 'T' now represents the total amount of time spent watching commercials in seconds, and 'N' represents the number of years, then T = 400,000N.

8.c. One full school week is about 30 hours, or 108,000 seconds. Using the formula 108,000 = 400,000N, N amounts to 0.27 years, or just over three months.

If we say that summer vacation is a full two months, or 62 days, and we ask how long it would take to see the equivalent number of 24 hour days of straight commercials, T becomes 5,356,800 seconds and N amounts to 13.39 years.

Linked, Organized, Informed - Answers

Suggested Activity...

For this lesson, basic database skills will need to be taught. There are a number of different types, each with their own way of entering, organizing and retrieving the data.

Answers

Opening question:

Hierarchical structures make it very difficult for people within the organization to communicate quickly and effectively with each other (top down orders can be quick but lack any dialogue)- the few people at the top are usually far removed from the mass of people at the bottom. People can join in wherever they're at on the Web and communicate within a community structure.

Understanding using math:

2. If 'N' represents the number of rounds of email and 'T' represents the total number of people contacted, then $T = 8^N$.

3. It would take five rounds of emails to amount to 32,768 people contacted. Four rounds would only amount to 4096 people contacted.

4. This is an exponential growth curve; it took 7 rounds (surpassing both one and two million people in the seventh round).

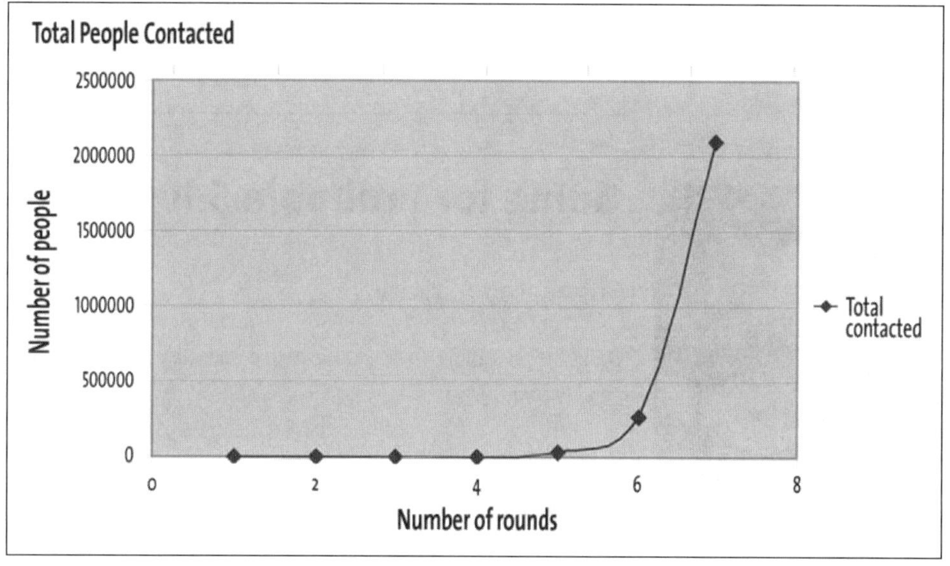

5.a.

Memory space	Byte equivalent	Name	Scientific Notation
1 byte	1 byte	One	$1X10^0$
1 kilobyte	1000 bytes	One thousand	$1X10^3$
1 megabyte	1,000,000 bytes	One million	$1X10^6$
1 gigabyte	1,000,000,000 bytes	One billion	$1X10^9$
1 terabyte	1,000,000,000,000 bytes	One trillion	$1X10^{12}$
1 petabyte	1,000,000,000,000,000 bytes	One quadrillion	$1X10^{15}$
1 exabyte	1,000,000,000,000,000,000 bytes	One quintillion	$1X10^{18}$
1 zettabyte	1,000,000,000,000,000,000,000 bytes	One sexillion	$1X10^{21}$
1 yottabyte	1,000,000,000,000,000,000,000,000 bytes	One septillion	$1X10^{24}$

5.b. 64,000 bytes

5.c. 512 megabytes is the same as 512,000,000 bytes, or 0.512 gigabytes, or 0.000512 terabytes.

6. Computers cost money, so those with less wealth may be less able to access computers. In schools this could lead to inequities as the students using home computers gain the associated skills faster.

7.

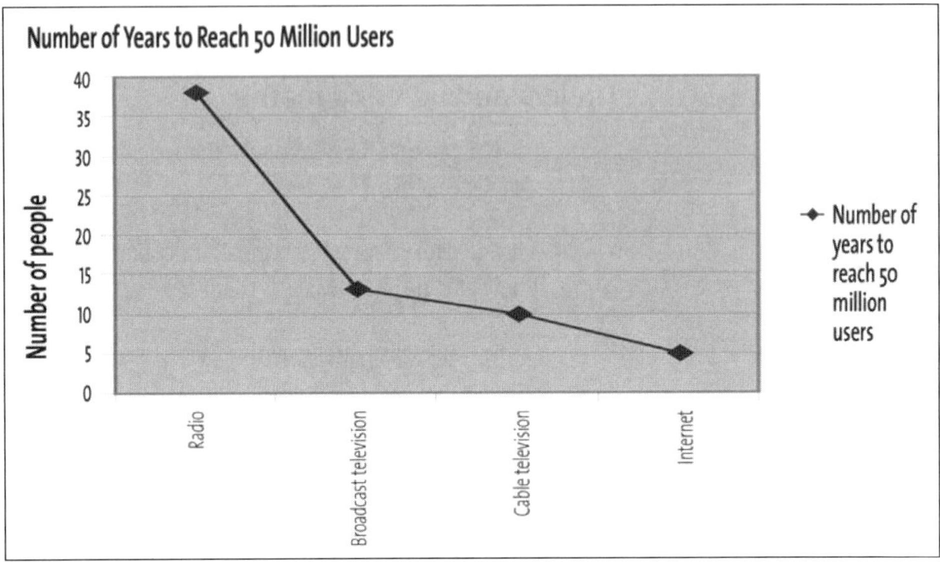

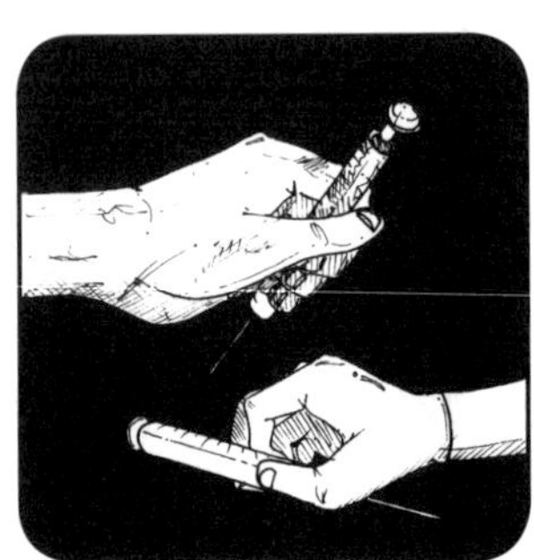

Going for Probable Silver - Answers

Suggested Activity...

Order the 68 minute *To Do No Harm* documentary for your classroom and discuss the film as a group. (212-213-6376 x 10)

Answers

Opening question:

We put many harm reduction strategies in place for car use. Seatbelts and airbags reduce the severity of injury in crashes, speed limits allow drivers more time to respond to possible obstacles, and laws put limits on what levels of alcohol drivers can have in their bloodstream and still safely drive. There are very strict laws for baby and child seats as well.

Understanding using math:

1. In the Netherlands, 80% of the addicted population is connected to support services, which means that they can get help if they need it. This has broader social implications as well, for example by limiting the spread of diseases, and reducing crime.

2.a. Two thirds of 42 is 28 studies showing positive effects.

2.b. At least two suggestions have been made. The first is called the selection effect, wherein the people who use the program are a group of people who tend to have higher rates of risk taking and infection and where higher risk attenders are less likely to drop out of the program. So for example, cocaine users tend to inject more and engage in more risky sexual behaviours than heroin users. The second suggestion is called the dilution effect, wherein the measurable impact of the program is diluted when the users of the program have access to clean needles and syringes from other sources. Both of these things are called confounding processes and may make the results look like a result of the harm reduction program when in actual fact that may not be true.[377]

4.a. If 'S' represents the amount of money saved, and 'M' represents the amount of money spent on the needle and syringe program in New Zealand, then S = 20M.

4.b. Savings are possibly from health care costs, costs associated with crime, and revenue generated when people are able to maintain employment.

4.c. S = 20 x 50,000 so S = $1,000,000.

5.a. If 'S' represents the amount of money saved, and 'M' represents the amount of money spent on the methadone program in the United Kingdom, then S = 3M.

5.b. The United Kingdom study was looking at immediate, direct benefits rather than the long term and indirect savings of having healthy community members.

5.c. S = 3 x 50,000 so S = $150,000 in direct savings.

6.a. The lowest level of support costs the most and leads to the lowest abstinence rate, so it should be eliminated as an option.

6.b. The middle level of support costs less than the highest level of support but leads to a lower abstinence rate, so you would need to figure out the abstinence rate per dollar at the middle and highest levels of support and decide which one makes the most sense.

Welcome To The Club - Answers

Suggested Activity...

This activity is from "Challenging Class Bias" put out by the Toronto District School Board.

Use ten chairs in a straight line next to each other to represent the ten deciles of wealth in Canada. Ask for ten volunteers from the class. The year is 1980. The top ten percent of Canadians own 57% of all private wealth. Have one student sit down and use 5.7 of the chairs. Have the next student take up another 1.6 chairs. The rest of the eight students can have a seat in the remainder of the chairs.

It's now Ontario in 1999. The person representing the bottom decile doesn't get a chair- they owe money (on average over $10,000 per family) . The second, third, fourth, fifth and sixth students can sit on the bottom 1.2 chairs. The last four students can have the remaining 8.8 chairs. Discuss what's happening and how it felt to be in different groups.

377 Hunt, Neil. "A review of the evidence-base for harm reduction approaches to drug use". www.forward-thinking-on-drugs.org/review2-print.html

Answers

Opening question:

For example, on talent elimination-based shows, the rising level of interest in the show benefits the top few performers disproportionately to the mass of the rest of the contestants.

Understanding using math:

1.b. When it's hard to communicate because there is a gulf between populations, it can lead one group to feel isolated and resentful of the other.

1.c. The people closest to the wealth have access to things like the media, which allow them to communicate their ideas often and effectively to everyone else.

1.d. The student should take 148 steps back toward the class. This position is close to 3 times the distance away from the class as the original 1989 levels.

2.a. The best fit line for both graphs is a curve downwards.

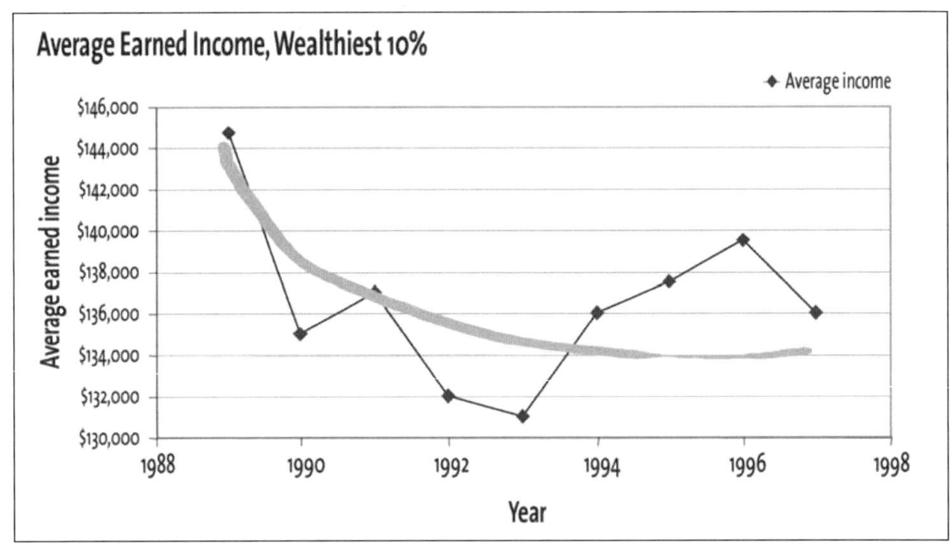

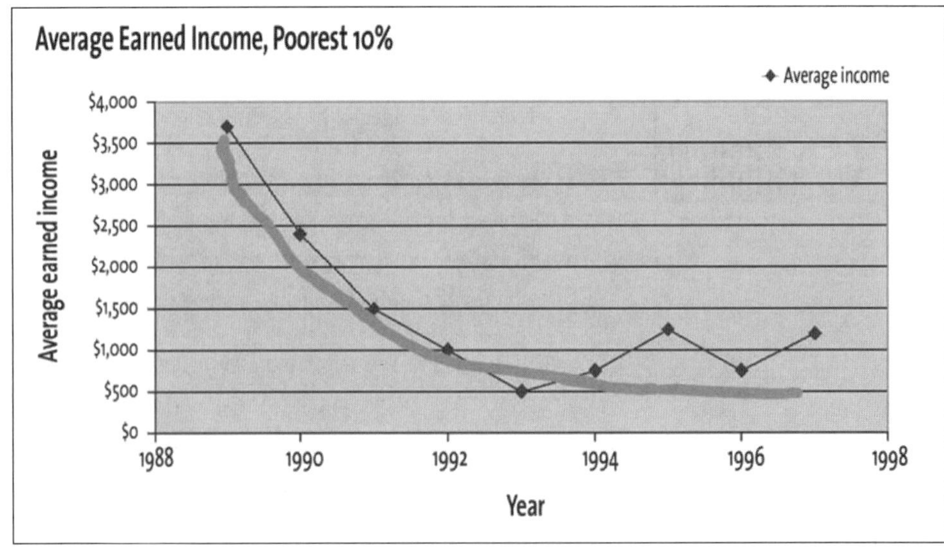

2.b. It's difficult to compare the two sets of data because the Y-axis in each graph has a different range. You might conclude just by looking at the above two graphs that both the richest and the poorest group sustained significant financial damage.

Year	Bottom Decile Average Yearly Earnings	Percentage of 1989 Earnings
1989	3,700	100
1990	2,300	62
1991	1,500	41
1992	1,000	27
1993	500	14
1994	750	20
1995	1250	34
1996	800	22
1997	1250	34

2.c.

Year	Top Decile Average Yearly Earnings	Percentage of 1989 Earnings
1989	144,500	100
1990	135,000	93
1991	137,000	95
1992	132,000	91
1993	131,000	91
1994	136,000	94
1995	137,500	95
1996	139,000	96
1997	136,000	94

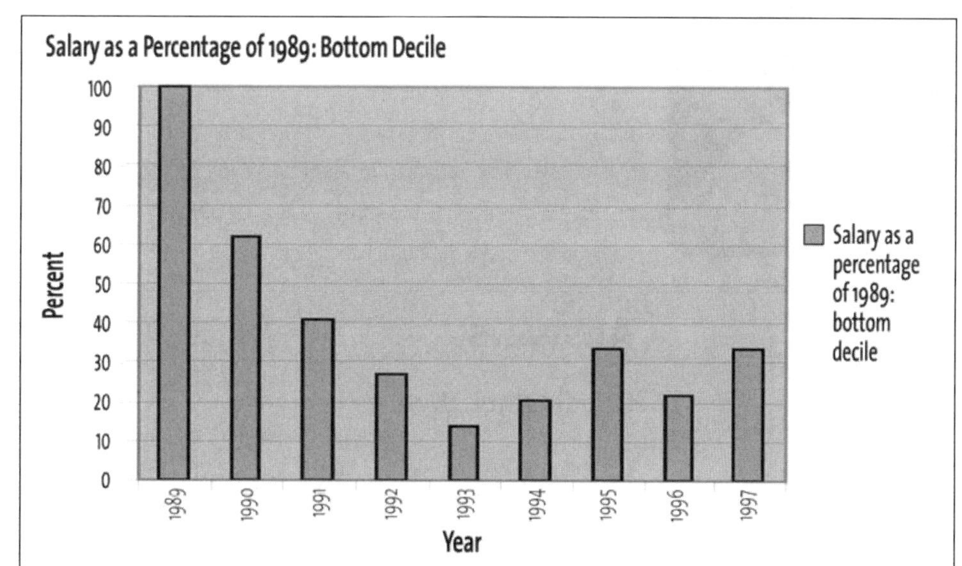

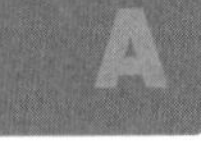

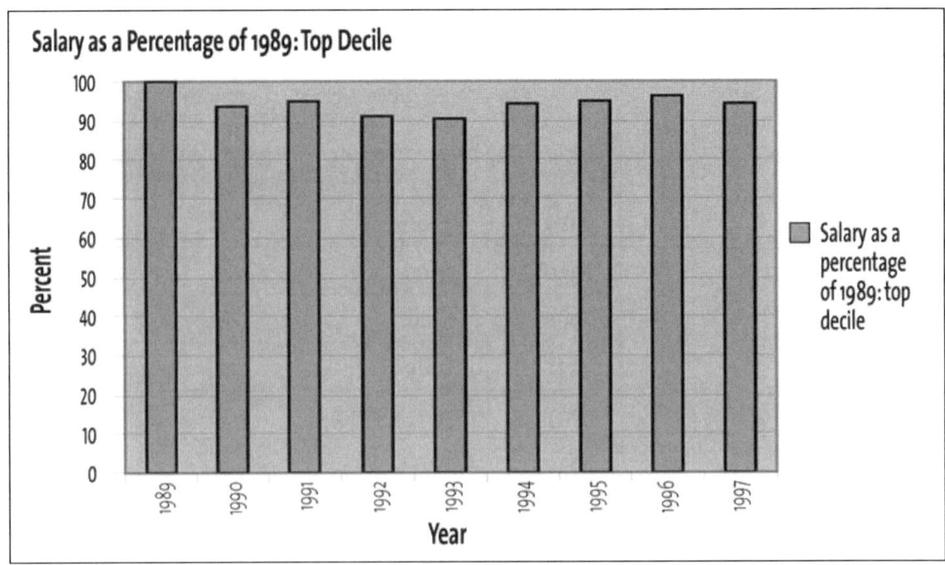

2.d.

2.e. The impact of the drop in salary is significantly different for both groups: the wealthiest never dip below 91% of their 1989 salary levels (the shape of the graph changes very little) while the poorest decile drops to as little as 14% of their 1989 salary levels (the best fit line drops sharply). Presumably, that would have devastating consequences for families living in the bottom group.

2.f. If you made the Y-axis include all values for salary and plotted both sets of data on the same graph you'd see the same results (and you'd see a huge gap between the two groups.)

3. Six of the nine provinces listed show a lower ratio in 1993 than in 1989, indicating that even through the recession, the gap between the top and bottom deciles was able to decrease.

4. Six of the nine provinces listed show a larger gap in 1997 than in 1994 meaning that even as they were recovering economically from the recession, the poorest Canadians did not benefit equally - the gap between the richest and the poorest grew.

What Big Feet You Have - Answers

Suggested Activity...

A Medicins Sans Frontiers fact sheet says that a person in a refugee camp uses about 18 litres of water a day. The typical Canadian resident uses 326 litres per day. Put out 25 mL of water in a beaker. If that represents 18 litres ask the students how much water would represent the water used by the typical Canadian per day. Fill another beaker with that amount of water to compare.

Answers

Opening question:

The energy transnational companies that currently profit on oil, and any of the associated technologies and businesses that profit in an oil-based economy and would stand to lose profit if alternative sources of energy and technologies were used.

Understanding using math:

1. One hectare of land in a square has side lengths that are 100 metres long. That's equivalent to 0.1 kilometres, 10,000 centimetres and 100,000 millimetres.

2. The side length would be 141 metres. Two hectares is just under three times the area of an international soccer field.

3. Four full hectares would make a square with a side length of 200 metres.

4. 9, 16 and 25 hectares will give side lengths of 300, 400 and 500 metres.

5. For example, a rectangle 500 metres by 20 metres is one hectare of land. So is a rectangle 400 metres by 25 metres. A triangle with a base of 400 metres and a height of 50 metres is one hectare.

6. The perimeter of the above rectangles and triangles are 1040 m^2, 850 m^2 and 853.1 m^2. The perimeter of a perfect square would be 400m^2. You may want to ask your students how low they can get the perimeter and what shape would it be?

7.

	Hectares	Square meters	Side length of perfect square of land
United States	10.3	10,300	101.5 m
Australia	9	9000	94.9 m
Canada	7.8	7,800	88.3 m
Germany	5.3	5,300	72.8 m
India	0.8	800	28.3 m
Fair eco-footprint	2	2,000	44.7 m

8.

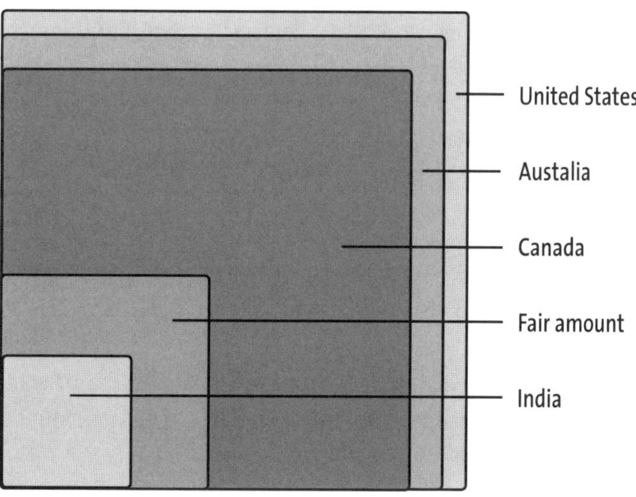

9. 4 additional planets

10.a. 14.9 times

10.b. 4500 L

10.c. 11.7 times and 37.7 times respectively

Blunt Force Trauma - Answers

Suggested Activity...

The correlation between teacher expectation and student achievement is higher than almost any predictive IQ or achievement measure, ranging in numerous studies from correlations of 0.5 all the way to an almost perfect 0.9. Discuss with the class what this means.

Answers

Opening question:

Students who come from wealthy families can afford additional services like private tutoring. These students may also have access to expensive educational products like computers. Family outings may be more frequent, and may involve educational experiences that families with less money cannot afford. Students from wealthy families may benefit from fewer time demands (for example, with housecleaning) that increase time spent on schooling.

Understanding using math:

3. The trend shows that increased family income leads to increased scores on SAT tests.

4. The range considered is now smaller than the first graph and what that does is highlight the increase, or in other words, make the increase look bigger than in the first graph.

5. The range considered is now greater than the first two graphs and what that does is condense the data, making the increase in test scores with increased family income seem very sharp.

6. The second or third graphs highlight the relationship between income and test scores, making the link seem significant. Although the last graph is the steepest, it seems less persuasive with the line squeezed to one side. The second graph could be more persuasive in convincing people that the tests are classist. If I was trying to say that the tests were not classist, I'd use the first one, which makes the data show only a marginal increase in test scores with family income.

7. All of the graphs are biased because they all select a different way of looking at the data. The first is biased in favour of diminishing the correlation between family income and test scores. The second and third graphs are biased in favour of highlighting the correlation between family income and test scores. All presentation of data is biased in some way, either in its selection or its focus.

8.

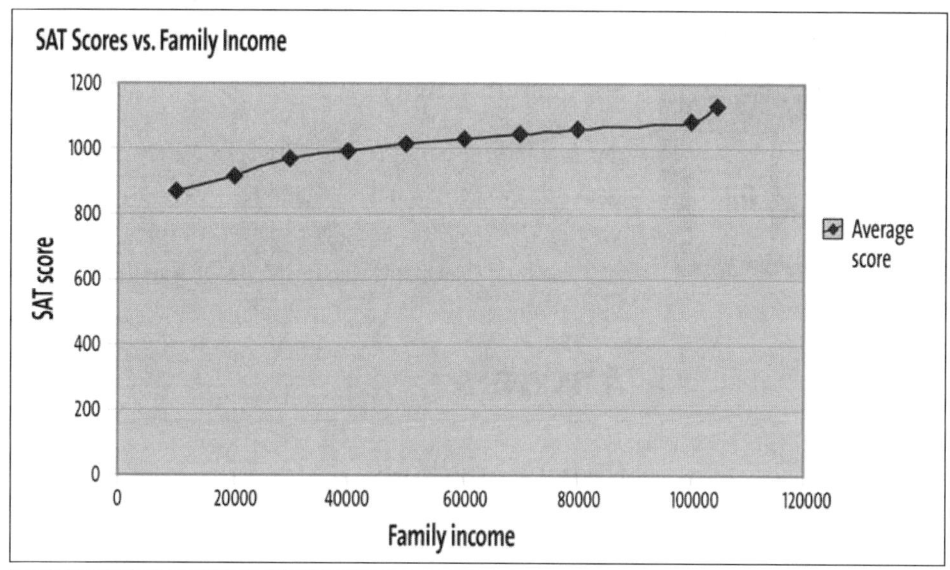

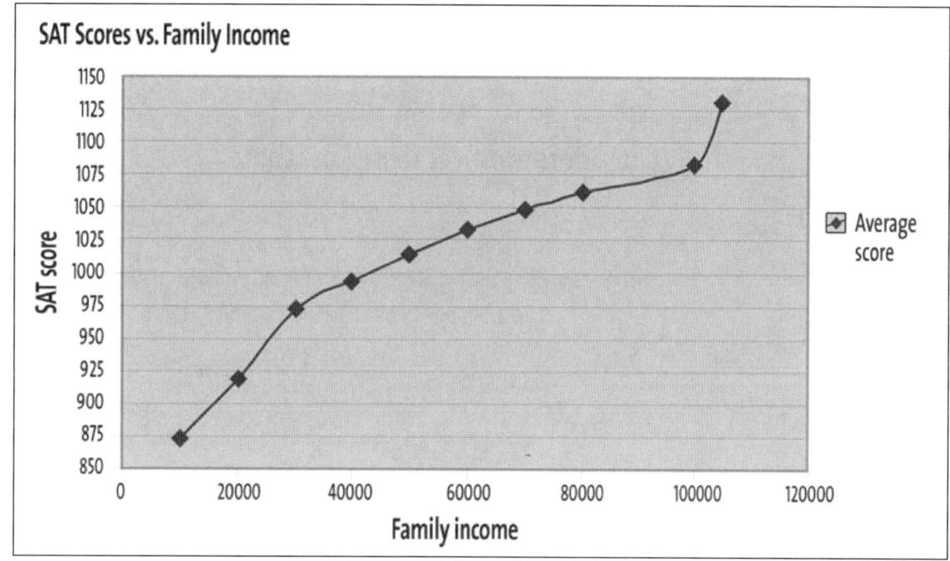

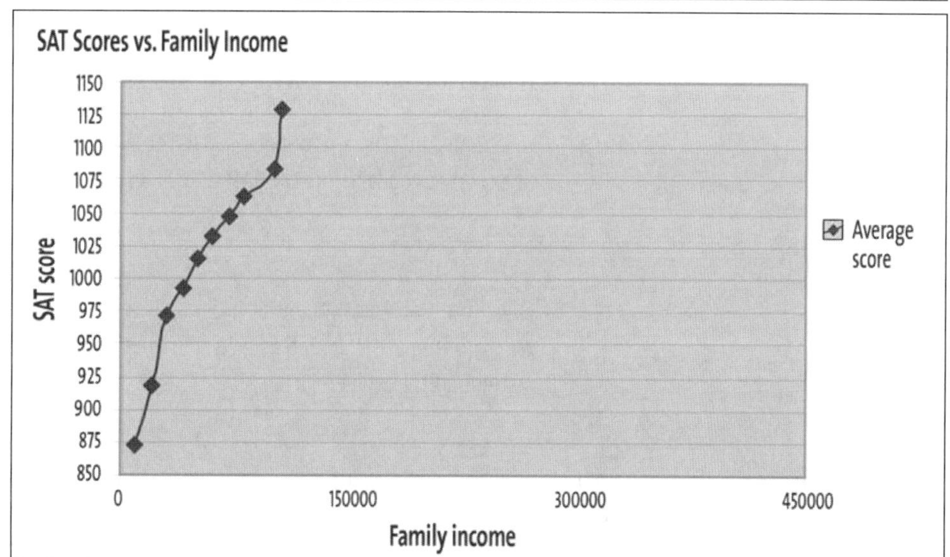

9. Publishing test scores of schools may simply be pointing out an economic issue, while suggesting its really an academic issue.

Totally SAP-ped - Answers

Suggested Activity...

Countries that rely on one or two cash crops and have little economic diversity have greater than a one in five chance of civil war in any given year. Countries with no dominant products have a one in 100 chance of civil war.[378] Create the two spinners with your students and have them spin to see how often their country is thrown into war. Tie this into the questions from this lesson.

Answers

Opening question:

The world markets become flooded with cash crops, which means that the prices for those crops will fall (too much product means the product is less valuable). The poorer countries that make the product get less and the wealthy countries that buy the products get a bargain.

Understanding using math:

1.a. 157

1.b. The United States holds enough votes to ensure that even if all of the other 183 countries voted for a big policy change they would still fall short of the 85% of the votes required.

2.

Number of people visiting the hospital	Increase or	**(Decrease)**
Number of people dying	**(Increase or)**	Decrease
Number of hospital worker layoffs	**(Increase or)**	Decrease
Amount of labour advancements/unions	Increase or	**(Decrease)**
Number of hospital closures	**(Increase or)**	Decrease

3.a. If 'D' represents the amount of exported goods during the SAP and 'B' represents the amount of exported goods before the SAP, then $D = 1.22B$.

3.b. 20,045 kg/week

3.c. Of course it depends on the situation, but there is enough environmental degradation currently to suppose that increasing a countries' output of raw materials by 22% would further compound the problem.

4.a. 50% loss

4.b. An increase of 38% from during the user fee levels. People may not return at the same rate because they don't understand whether or not they need to pay to get into the hospital. People may have also died in the meantime.

---

378 Fishman, Ted. "Making a Killing: The Myth of Capitals' Good Intentions". Harpers Magazine. Aug. 2002, p.35.

4.c. Approximately 17,024 students.

4.d. That is a 52.6% increase. Girls are likely the ones kept home if there is only the financial option to send fewer children and boys are available to go.

5. If 'D' represents the amount of debt payment and 'H' represents the amount of money spent on health, then D = 5.67H.

6. If H = $5,000,000 then D = $28,350,000

7. $64,856,230,030

What's A Gerrymander? - Answers

Suggested Activity...

An excellent mathematical way to prevent gerrymandering has been suggested.[379] You may want to try this activity at the end of the lesson, but it works just as well at the start. Have students draw different voting shapes on big graph paper- a square, a rectangle (both reasonable shapes), and then some irregular shapes (but keep them rectangular-based if you want to keep this easy). A "crookedness number" or CN of the region is found by CN = Perimeter squared divided by the area. The value is independent of the size of the region. A square will always have a CN of 16. A hexagon will be about 13.87. Have the class discuss what CN value a region should be below to be reasonable.

Extensions: What shape will have the lowest CN? What will it be? (Prove that it will be 4pi). Have students draw regions with diagonal lines, requiring the Pythagorean theorem in order to find the perimeter.

Answers

Opening question:

For example, a party may run on 'getting tough on crime' or 'making sure rural water supply is adequately monitored'.

---

379 www.halfbakery.com/idea/Anti-Gerrymandering October 17, 2002

Understanding using math:

1.

Region	Area (km2)	Party A Support Before/ After		Party B Support Before/ After		Party C Support Before/After		Region currently won by Party ...	Newly formed region can be Party...
1	85	14		20		26		C	
2	105.5	7		48		5		B	
3	84	39		15		6		A	
4	39	19		32		9		B	
5	60	43		12		5		A	
6	72	7		20		33		C	
7	52.5	22		30		8		B	
8	35	42		16		2		A	
9	21	14		30		16		B	
10	25	37		21		2		A	
11	16.5	20		17		23		C	
12	29	2		42		16		B	
13	21	5		43		12		B	
	Overall Area: 643	Totals Before/ After 273		Totals Before/ After 344		Totals Before/After 163		Current Overall Party Winner: B	New Overall Winner

2. Party B

3. 60

4. Their population density is less so they enclose more area to make up for fewer people.

5. Solidly controlled: Party B regions 2, 4, 9, 12 and 13. Party A regions 3, 5, 8, and 10. Party C region 6. Regions that have parties that are close are 1, 7 and 11.

7. It is possible.

8. The government wants better diversity in the region to better represent the population of the province. The region has too many or too few people due to immigration or emigration of people.

9. Absolutely! By any of the ways of gerrymandering, you can dilute or concentrate an opposition party's votes, allowing your party to win without popular support. Even without gerrymandering, political parties win the leadership at the provincial and federal level without popular support.

Coming Clean? - Answers

Suggested Activity...

Have students bring in advertising demonstrating gender stereotyping that they do not like and have them write a letter to the CEO of the company expressing their concerns.

Answers

Opening question:

Various answers are possible, but if stereotypes do sell product what implication does that have for reducing them?

Understanding using math:

3. & 4. For example,

Number of women doing the cleaning	Number of men doing the cleaning	Number of children/ youth doing the cleaning	Total number of cleaning ads
5	2	0	7
71.4%	28.6%	0	100%

5. $5\text{ cm} \times 5\text{ cm} \times 7\text{ cm} \times 0.85 = 148.75\text{ cm}^3$

6. Radius = 2.5 cm so area = $\prod r^2 = 19.6625\text{ cm}^2$. Volume = 19.6625×7 cm (height) = 137.6375 cm^3. 85% of volume is 116.99 or 117 cm^3 . So the designer is incorrect (the scoop is in fact smaller than the original).

7. Scoop design #1: $2500 \div 148.75 = 16.8$ scoops

   Scoop design #2: $2500 \div 117 = 21.4$ scoops

   The new design is less profitable because it takes longer to go through the box, which means for the same volume of detergent it will take the consumer longer before needing to go out and buy more.

8. $117 \div 148.75 = 78.7\%$. The small scoop is 78.7% of the larger scoop. By the time the big scoop has finished a full box and created $1.78 of profit, the smaller scoop will have created 0.787×1.78 or $1.40 profit. Per box, the smaller scoop is 38 cents less profitable.

9. $5^2 + 5^2 = 50$, and the square root of 50 is 7.07, the new diameter of the scoop. The radius is then half of that, or 3.54 cm. The area of the bottom of the scoop is $\prod r^2 = 39.37\text{ cm}^2$ so the volume is found by multiplying by the height (7 cm): 275.6 cm^3.

10. 85% of the volume of scoop #3 is 234.3 cm^3.

11. Scoop #3: 2500 ÷ 234.3 = 10.7 scoops. Scoop three is more profitable than both other designs because it uses up the product faster.

12. This technique depends on trying to fool the customer into thinking that they are using the same amount of laundry detergent per load of laundry when in fact they are not.

A Little Goes A Long Way -Answers

Suggested Activity...

After the Exxon Valdez oil spill in 1989 a lot of research was done on the toxicity of oil to the marine animals along the Alaskan and British Columbia coastline.[380] A study by Auke Bay laboratory found that "crude oil in water is toxic to fish at concentrations of 1-4 ppm (part per million)". Give a postage stamp to each table group and tell them that it's area will represent 1 ppm. Ask them to figure out (and tape out on the floor if they can) the area that would represent the 'million' in relation to the stamp. Discuss.

New research now shows that oil is much more toxic to fish than previously believed. Toxicity to pink salmon eggs is being found at 1 ppb (part per billion). Ask the students to take the same stamp and see if they can represent 'a billion' if the stamp represent s one part of a billion parts. Compare to 1 ppm and discuss.

Answers

Opening question:

Drilling in the bush requires putting in roads to get the machinery and the workers into the bush, which costs money. Drilling closer to existing roads won't be as expensive for the business.

Understanding using math:

1. 0.0005 grams, or 0.5 milligrams. A triple beam balance is not able to measure these small amounts accurately.

2. 0.005 kg, 5 grams, or 5000 milligrams.

3. 14% which is much higher than before (more than 4.5 times greater)

4. If 'M' represents metres from the spill and 'T' represents the toxicity level, then T = 5.34 – 0.0007M

5. If T is 4.5 mg/L or more, M is 1200 m or 1.2 km or closer.

6. The area, using a radius of 1.2 km, is 4.52 km^2. The number of people in that area (which will be a circle) is 113,000.

7.a. If 'P' stands for accumulated profit in millions and 'Y' is the number of years, then P = 9Y.

380 www.afsc.noaa.gov/Quarterly/jfm99/rptABL_ifm99.htm

7.b. If Y = 25 years, then P is $225,000,000

8.a. The accumulated profit is shown without regard for the fines.

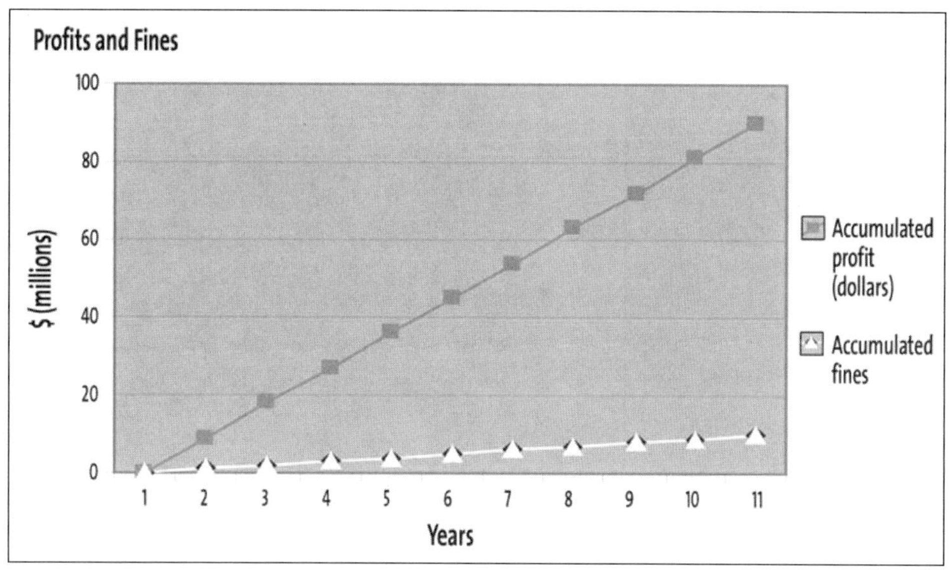

8.b. P = 8Y

9.a. Again, the profit is shown prior to fines or other costs.

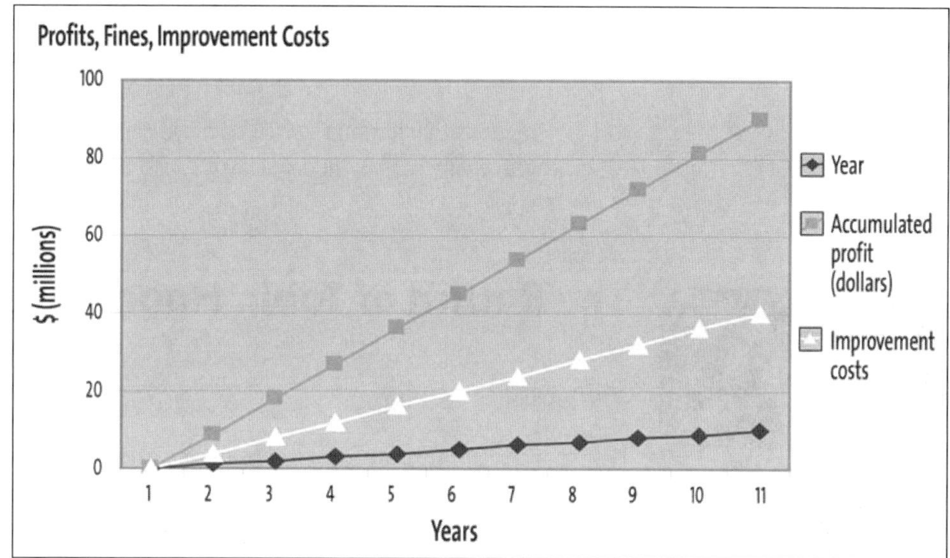

9.b. If the company just takes its chances and pays a fine each year, its profits are P= 8Y. If it does all of the improvements, its profits are P = 5Y. So it makes more economic sense to destroy the environment and maximize profits.

10.a.

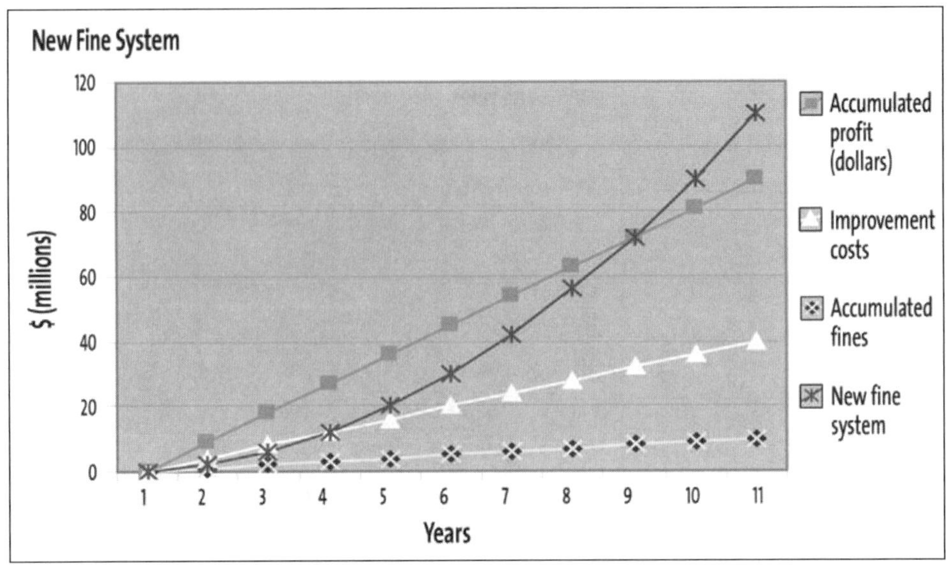

10.b. The first fines were linear, which meant that as long as profit was greater than the fines, the fines would never 'catch up' to the profit and deter the behaviour. The new fine system is non-linear, which means that over time, the fines get bigger and eventually surpass profit. That's important because if the system isn't profitable, it'll need to be changed.

10.c. Year nine

10.d. It's likely that it would be well before year nine however, because the profit margin at that year would be zero. The company if it was smart would implement the changes as soon as possible.

The Return of Tobin Hood - Answers

Suggested Activity...

Have your students try currency speculation in preparation for the lesson: there's an excellent simulation at www.waronwant.org/game/ .

Answers

Opening question:

The people who are speculating on the currency will be opposed to the tax because it cuts into their profits.

Understanding using math:

1.a. 2,196,000 metres, or 2,196 km

1.b. Everest is 8,850 metres so it's equivalent to just over 248 times the height of the mountains.

2.a. 549,000 km high.

2.b. This is 1.43 times the distance to the moon (345,000 km average).

3.a. One fiftieth the amount

3.b. When profit is made off of speculative currency trading it's not based on actual goods and services which are the things that people need to use in their lives.

4.a. $12,500

4.b. None

5.a. $62,500 Canadian dollars

5.b. You have an extra 2.5 million Yen or $20,833 Canadian dollars

6.a.

Roll	1	2	3	4	5	6
1	2	3	4	5	6	7
2	3	4	5	6	7	8
3	4	5	6	7	8	9
4	5	6	7	8	9	10
5	6	7	8	9	10	11
6	7	8	9	10	11	12

6.b. There are 36 different rolls, 11 different sums

6.e. 3 out of 36, or P(0.083). In the real world, you could research as many of the factors within a country that affect the value of its currency so that your prediction will be based on facts rather than luck.

6.f. What is profitable is the change in value of the currency, so if there's little change you can't make the profit like you did in question #5.

7. 0.005 seconds, or 5 thousandths of a second

Buying Your Eyes - Answers

Suggested Activity...

Have the students first guess and then find out how much revenue on average a pop machine in a school generates for the school and how much goes to the pop company.

Answers

Opening question:

Responses will vary.

Understanding using math:

1.

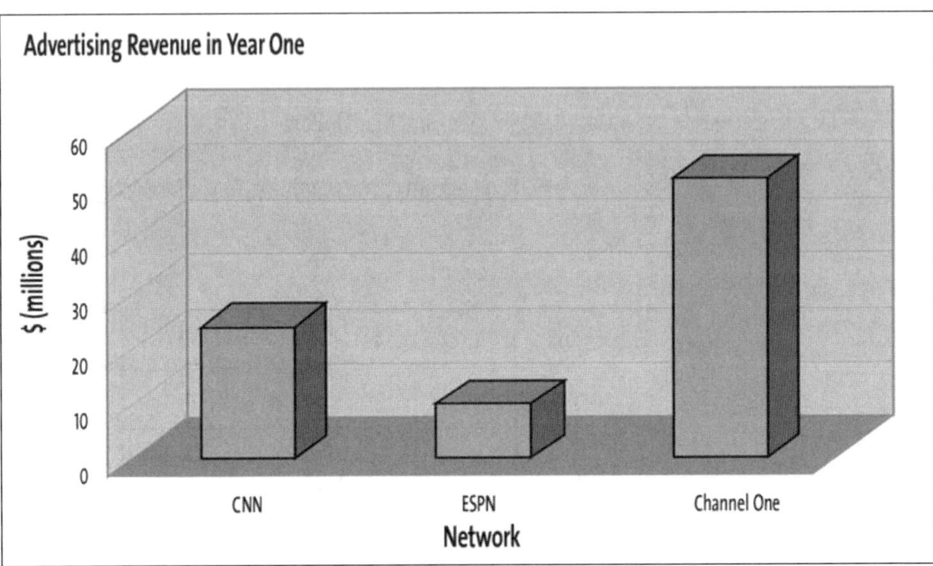

2. Advertisers pay a lot of money when they believe that they can influence their market to buy product. Perhaps advertisers were confident that the captive (the commercials couldn't be turned down or off) youth audience would be profitable.

3. 400 minutes of commercials

4. \$150,000 ÷ \$1000 = 150 thirty second advertising segments required. Number of advertising segments 'N' = 4D, where D is the number of days. 150 = 4D, so the number of days of YNN would be 37.5 days to break even.

5. \$150,000 ÷\$9000 = 16.7 thirty second advertising segments required to break even. Number of advertising segments 'N' = 4D, where D is the number of days. 16.7 = 4D, so YNN would break even in 4.2 days.

6. 30 thirty second advertising segments required to break even. 7.5 days to break even. 192.5 school days remain, each with 4 thirty second commercial slots for a total of 770 slots. 770 x \$5000 = \$3,850,000 revenue after breaking even.

7. 40%

8. Captive audience 37°; a market for product 54°; public recognition for philanthropy 73°; teachers add credibility to business 102°; and corporations in schools are normalized 99°.

Oink, Oink! - Answers

Suggested Activity...

Sometimes people don't realize that in the creation of products, natural resources are used that we never see. For example, it takes 18 litres of water to produce 1 litre of gasoline. At the beginning of the lesson, fill a 2L bottle of pop and ask the students to pretend that it represents 2L of gasoline. Then have them guess how much water (how many 2L pop bottles) was required to make that gas in the production process. Save the answer for the end of the lesson.

Answers

Opening question:

North Americans are bombarded with thousands of advertising messages each day encouraging us to buy things that we probably don't need. Even our reduce, reuse, recycle campaigns have focused on the recycling rather than the reduction of our buying behaviour. That means we're trekking out to the store more often.

Understanding using math:

1. For each one kilogram of resources someone in Mexico uses, a person in North America uses five kilograms of resources.

2. If 'N' represents the amount of resources used by the average North American and 'M' represents the amount used by the average person in Mexico, then N = 5M.

3. N = 5M N = 5 x 23 = 115 kg of resources

4. For each one kilogram of resources someone in China uses, a person in North America uses 10 kilograms of resources.

5. If 'N' represents the amount of resources used by the average North American and 'C' represents the amount used by the average person in China, then N = 10M.

6. N = 10C N = 10 x 23 = 230 kg of resources

7. For each one kilogram of resources someone in India uses, a person in North America uses 30 kilograms of resources.

8. If 'N' represents the amount of resources used by the average North American and 'D' represents the amount used by the average person in India, then N = 30D.

9. N = 30D N = 30 x 23 = 690 kg of resources

10.

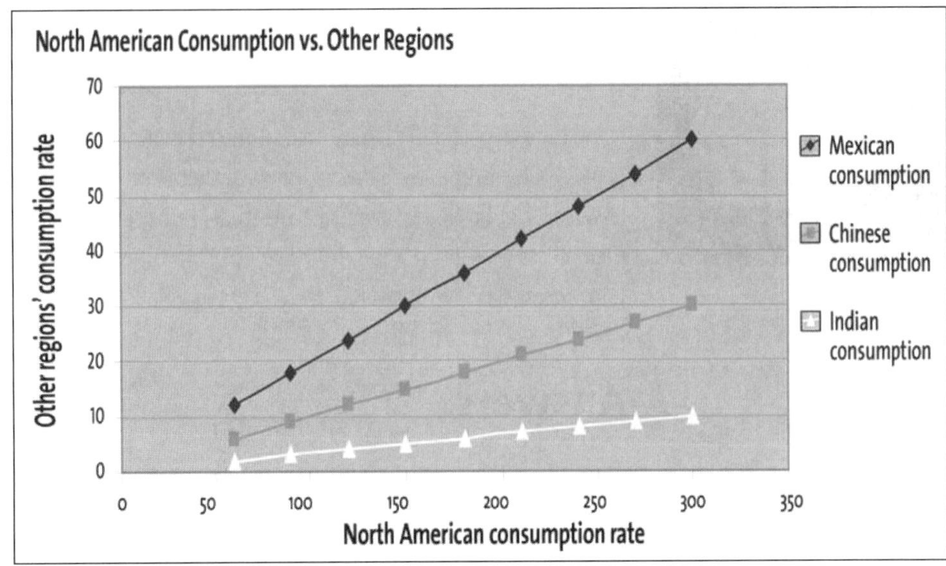

11. The scale of the X-axis is larger because it has to accommodate the North American consumption rate. The Y-axis, which is the consumption of other regions can be small because they don't consume anywhere near the amount that we do.

12. North American vs. Indian consumption: slope is 1/30.

North American vs. Chinese consumption: slope is 1/10.

North American vs. Mexican consumption: slope is 1/5.

13. The graph would extend lengthwise by quite a bit.

14.a. In this scenario an SUV uses three times as much gas as a compact car.

14.b. If 'S' represents the amount of gas an SUV uses and 'C' represents the amount of gas a compact car uses, then S = 3C. If an SUV used 144L of gas for a particular trip, a compact car would require 48L for that same trip.

14.c. 1,944L, 5,832L

The Winner Takes It All...? - Answers

Suggested Activity...

Try a vote in your classroom, voting on how to spend $10,000. Have the students put up and discuss their options on the board. Then vote using first past the post where the winning option gets all of the $10,000 and compare it to proportional representation where each option gets money in proportion to the votes it received.

Answers

Opening question:

In a high stakes competition with one winner per riding, parties put forward the one candidate that is most likely to win. But when you can elect a number of people (for example, in larger ridings or electoral districts) each party brings forth more candidates and "are more likely to attract votes by presenting a diverse list of candidates that reflects all people in that region."[381]

Understanding using math:

1.a.

Party	First Past the Post System: Number of Wins	Proportional Representation System
A	5 regions or 100%	42%
B	0	38%
C	0	20%

1.b. No, they only have 42% of the popular vote.

1.c. 38% which is more fair because the 38% of the population that voted are proportionately represented.

1.d. If, for example, the voter did not want Party A to be in power again, but really preferred the policies of Party C, they could be reluctant to vote for Party C because in an all or nothing race, it looks like Party B will be the only one that has a chance of beating Party A. By voting for C, she or he may actually help Party A to stay in power, by diluting Party B's support. The voter who votes for Party C is casting what is called a 'wasted vote' because it won't count.

2.a. Bloc Quebecois, Liberals, and Progressive Conservatives. The Bloc benefited most by taking about 40% more seats than the percentage of votes it received.

2.b. NDP, and the Other parties. The Other parties lost out the most as a percentage of the votes they received.

3. You need 301 votes, or 50.2%

4. You can win with as few as 201 votes, or 33.5% of the voting population.

5. You can win with as few as 224 votes, which is 22.4% of the country. People may feel that the party has no right to lead the country because they have the support of less than one quarter of the people.

6. 58%

7. Voter participation is down about 14% between 1988 and 2000.

   In no province has voter participation increased between those years.

   The province with the lowest percentage of voter turnout is Northwest Territories.

381 Fair Vote Canada, "Make Every Vote Count" www.fairvote.ca p.2

8.

Country	Rank options	Rank (your guess)
Cuba	1	7
Sweden	2	2
USA	3	58
Canada	7	36
Argentina	10	10
Rwanda	36	1
Denmark	58	3

"GATS Terrible!! - Answers"

Suggested Activity...

There is a card game available from the Polaris Institute in Ottawa that can be ordered for $5 online at www.polarisinstitute.org. The game is played much like the card game 'War' except that goods and services are at stake. Each set is for two or more players.

Answers

Opening question:

A service that is run for profit can increase the fee that you pay for that service. While some people in our society can afford to pay for the increase, others are disadvantaged. When the service is health care or education many people feel that these are human rights that shouldn't be dependant on your ability to pay for them.

Understanding using math:

1. 6,000,000 cm

2. Kilometres would probably be best (60 km)

3. 52,500,000 cm, 525,000 m, and 525 km

4. One possible activity could be to take a map and draw the circle that represents a 525 km radius from the school, looking at the different places that are within or equal to 525 km.

5. 44,000 protestors

6. The budget for the police and the fence was approximately 160 times more than the budget for the protestors. That limits the things that the protestors are able to do.

7. 9,800,000

8.a. If 'P' represents the cost of water during privatization and 'B' represents the cost of water before privatization then $P = 3.5B$

8.b. There were mass protests.

9.a. The cost to do a c-section is greater so when that amounts to more profit for the doctor, they may be more likely to recommend it.

9.b. Tests costs the patient money- more tests mean more profit for the people providing the tests.

9.c. Over prescribed medications mean patients are using drugs that they don't necessarily need, or don't need as often as they have been prescribed. Each sale represents profit for the pharmacies though.

9.d. Preventative measures, like getting enough exercise and eating healthy foods, doesn't put money in the pockets of the people who treat illnesses once they have appeared.

Breaking the Silence - Answers

Suggested Activity...

Hand out and discuss a Street Guide document for your community and discuss where students can go to find help when they need it.

Answers

Opening question:

There are many possible answers: question number one outlines the reasons from a Canadian Red Cross study. Certainly though, fewer symptoms does not mean less impact.

Understanding using math:

1.

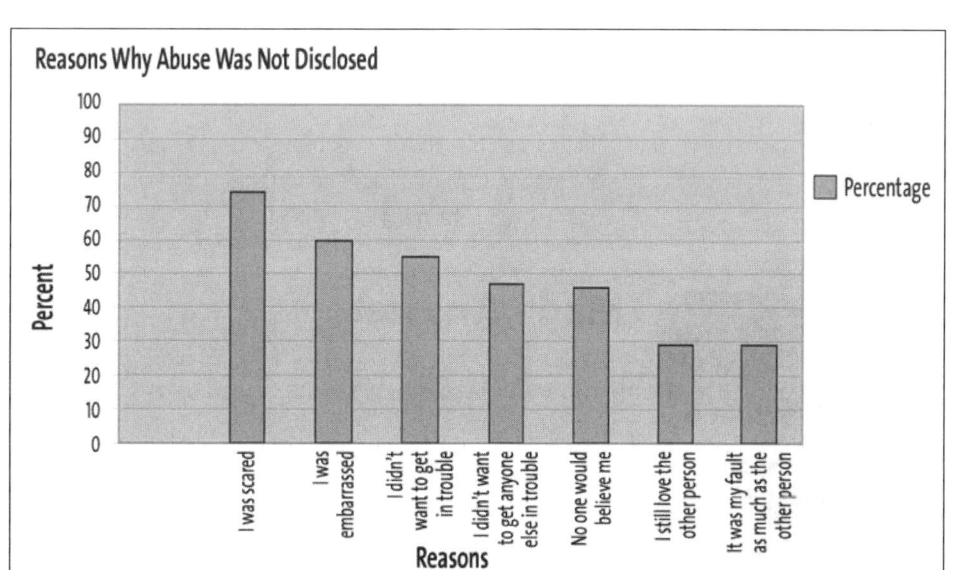

2. Many possible responses.

3. All of the responses add up to more than 100% because the respondents must have been allowed to choose as many replies as were applicable.

4.

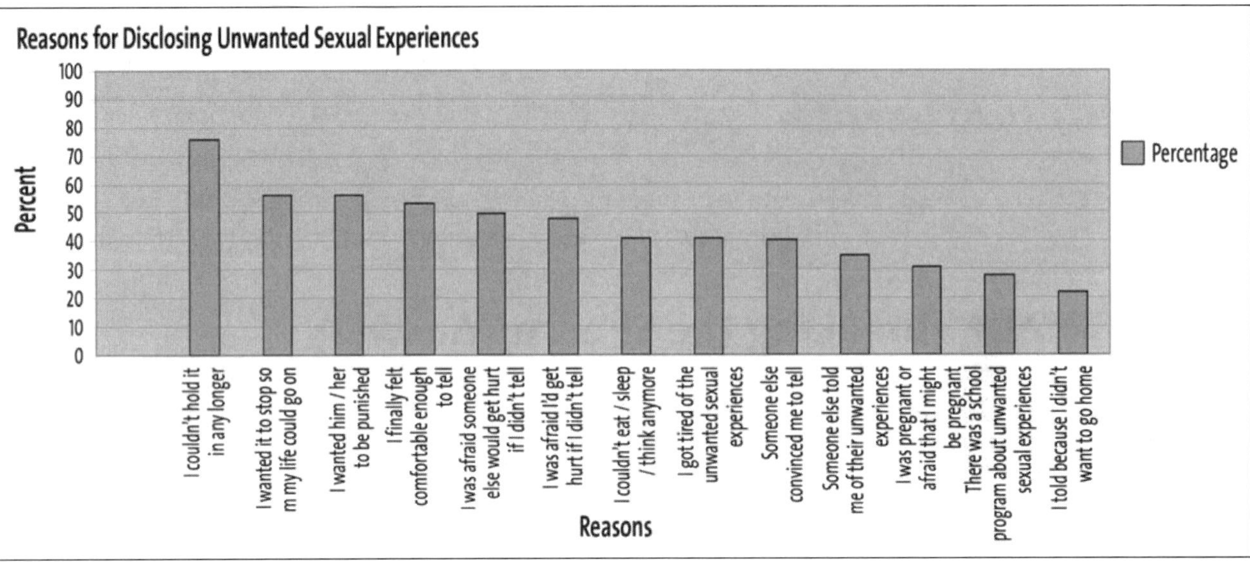

5. Many possible answers.

6. One possible example:

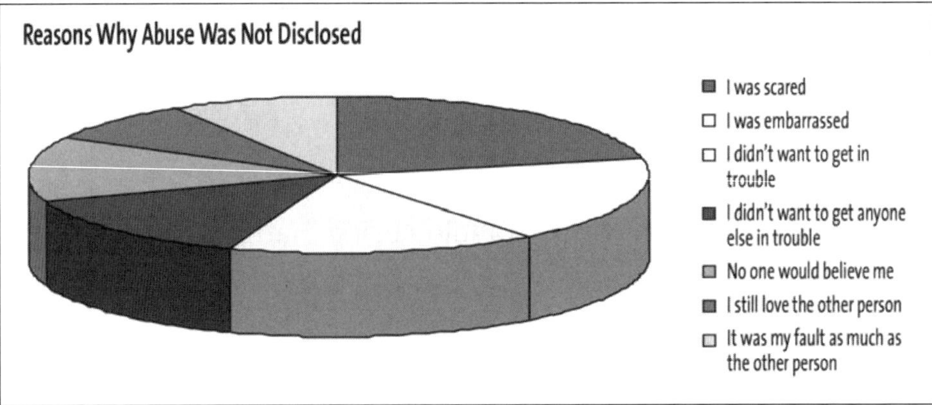

In this case, the student might suggest that reading a circle graph is more difficult than a bar graph because transferring back and forth between the pie and the legend is more difficult, or making relative comparisons is more difficult.

Mad - Answers

Suggested Activity...

Brainstorm a list of stereotypes people have about people with a mental illness. In the Make It Better section there is a website discussing the myths that you could read to prepare yourself for the discussion. Where do we get these ideas? How are they barriers?

Answers

Opening question:

People may be afraid to seek help because they don't want to be associated with something that our society stigmatizes.

Understanding using math:

1. Statement one and three are correct. Statement two is correct if you assume that there are roughly the same number of men as women in Canada. And statement four is not correct (both numbers are about half of the actual numbers).

2. General hospitals may not be adequately equipped to effectively treat people who have a mental illness.

3. Approximately 28,571. In advertising, women's bodies tend to be extremely thin, and the focus on dieting and the fear of being 'fat' in our society may be more targeted to women than men. Bulimia shows the greater disparity between the sexes (15 times greater in women, compared to anorexia, which is 3.5 times greater in women than men).

4. If 'T' represents the total cost of mental illness in Canada and 'N' represents the number of people, then T = 244N and the total cost of mental illness is $7,320,000,000.

5. T = 480N, and the total cost is $14,400,000,000. By addressing the stigma of mental illness, perhaps more people would seek treatment sooner, leading to better outcomes and fewer costs.

6. The probability that a top ten cause of disability in Canada is a form of mental illness is 0.40.

7. 7.9:1 which supports the social causation theory.

8. Social causation. The fact that anxiety and depression did not change much after the move out of poverty could mean that they have a greater genetic link, or simply that anxiety and depression take longer to disappear. Follow up studies years later could give you a clearer picture.

9. One out of fifteen- not nearly enough.

10. 1,350. Article 25 of the Universal Declaration of Human rights states that everyone has the right to a "standard of living adequate for the health and well being of oneself...including housing and medical care and necessary social services.... The existence of supportive housing and community mental health services has been shown to reduce hospitalization by 80%".[382]

---

382 www.thedreamteam.ca/dreamteam_facts.htm

Media Monopoly - Answers

Suggested Activity...

On Election Day 2004 a student vote was held across Canada by Elections Canada, an arm's length government agency. Can-West (a conservative media empire that owns most of Canada's daily newspapers) teamed up with Dominion Institute and Nokia (a cell phone company) and also did a student vote (where students could use their handsets to vote). Here are the stats on the votes:[383]

Pollster:	Elections Canada	Can-West
# youth participating:	>265,000	1,992
Elected:	Liberal minority government, with 50 seats to the NDP (in the adult election they got 19 seats) and fewer seats to the Conservatives than the adult election gave them.	Conservatives win poll "in a landslide".

Discuss the chart with your students- what do they notice? How can the results be so different? Which poll do you think was printed in the papers (the Can-West poll was)?

Answers

Opening question:

3% of 2,620 staff amounts to almost 79 people, far more than the four that the study found. The problem becomes a cycle: rich white men write to "the masses" on topics they do not know much about, which makes these same opinions more 'sale-able' and perpetuates them.

Understanding using math:

1. As is now apparent, the vast majority of people there were the police and soldiers, making the "violent" First Nations people seem different.

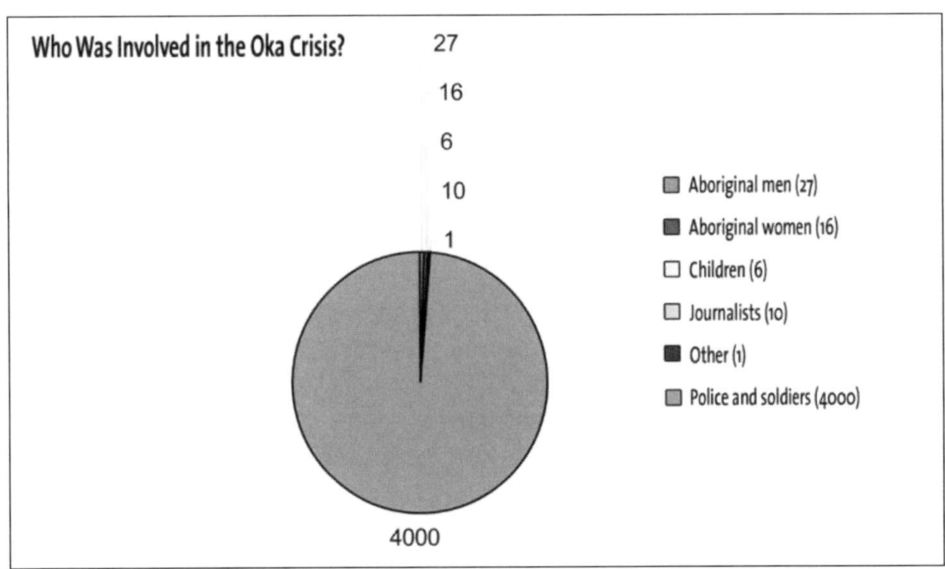

383 Robertson, Heather-jane. "The young and the voteless". *Our Schools Our Selves.* V. 14 N. 2 Winter 2005, pp. 31-33.

2.a. 18%

2.b. 10%

2.c. Women have important stories to tell that benefit us all. To silence the perspectives of half of the people on the planet is to miss the opportunity to learn from them.

3.

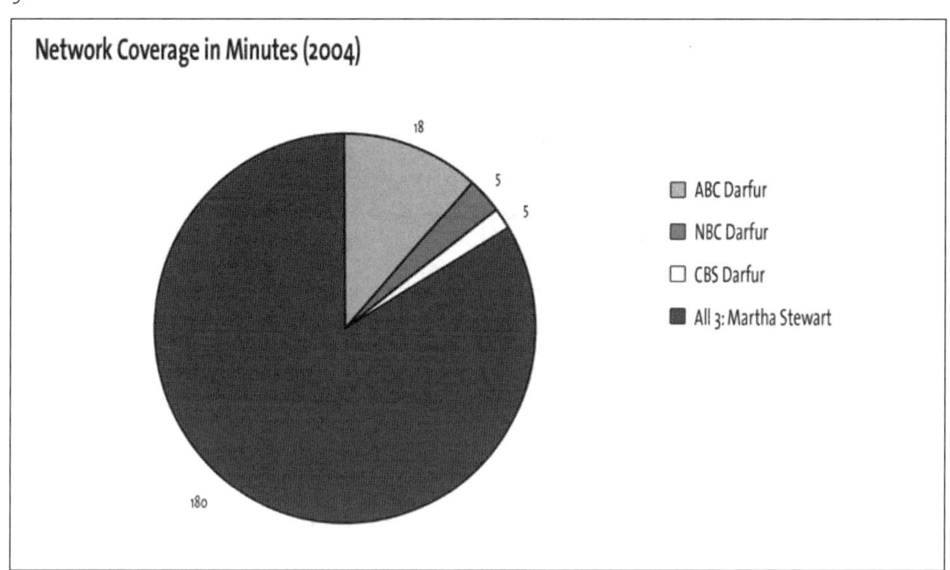

People watching the television hear a disproportionate number of stories about the upper class and miss out on the issues most important to the working class.

4.a. Three jumbo jets a day for a full year.

4.b. 0.001% and 0.1% respectively.

4.c. Money should be allocated where it is most needed. Numbers can help us decide where the money would be best used.

5. Discuss the statistics with the class- which ones seem credible to them and why?

6.

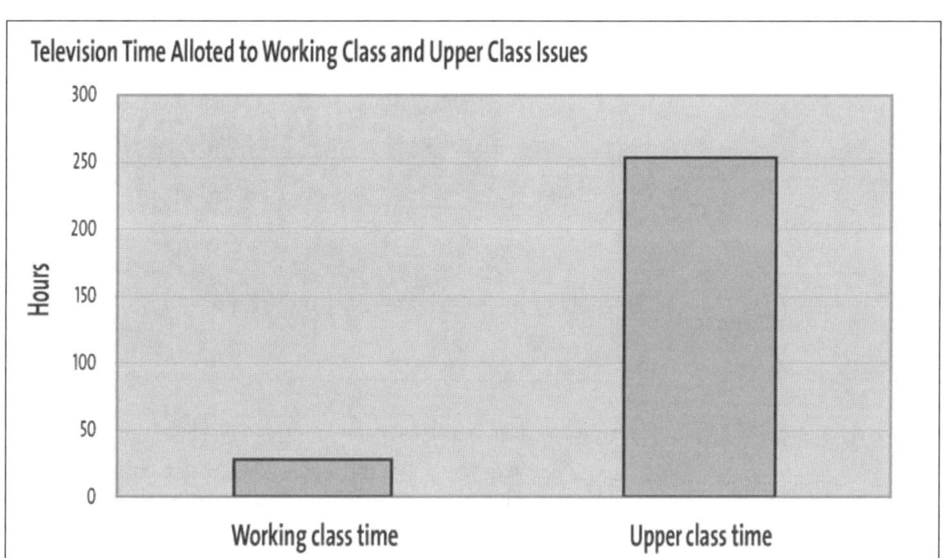

Sick and Tired - Answers

Suggested Activity...

Have students bring in an article about a drug company associated with a conflict over public concerns. Have them share what they learned about it.

Answers

Opening question:

One possible answer is that drug companies will look to produce new drugs that have a market, with people who will buy them. That means making drugs for people who have money. In today's image obsessed culture, that could mean drugs for baldness, wrinkle reduction, skin moisturizers: none of which are life threatening conditions.

Understanding using math:

1.a. 97% is the same as 97/100.

1.b. 97% of 14,000,000 is 0.97 x 14,000,000 = 13,580,000

1.c. 3% of 14,000,000 is 0.03 x 14,000,000 = 420,000

1.d. 97/100 is 0.97 and 3/100 is 0.03.

2.

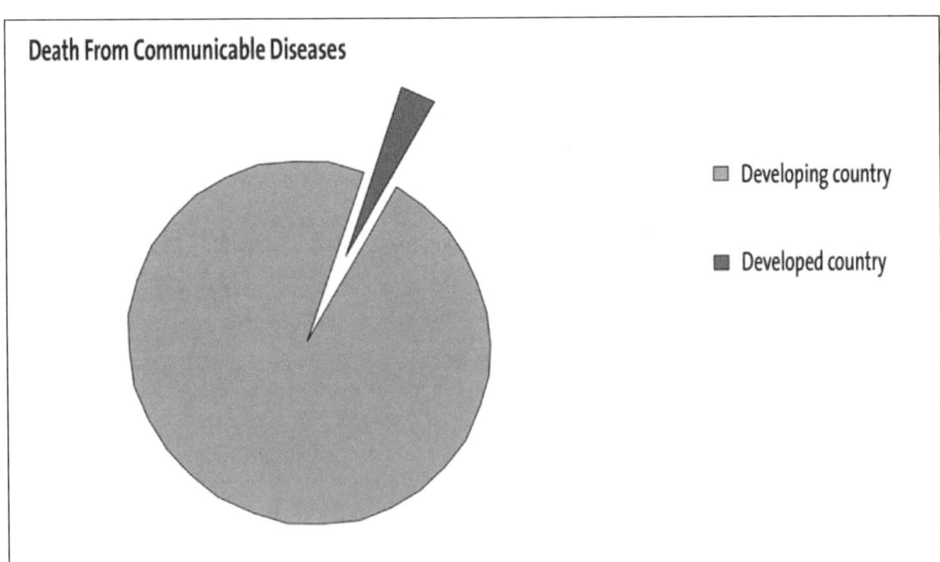

3. People in developing countries don't have the same access to public health systems that people in developed countries do. Clean water, public education and access to affordable drugs are crucial to good public health.

4. Possible root causes of poor health could be poverty, which can come from civil war, capitalism, dictatorship governments, to name a few. If the bottom line in a capitalist system is profit, drug manufacturers will only produce profitable drugs, which aren't necessarily the ones people need.

5. 11/1223 = 0.009 which is almost 1%.

6.

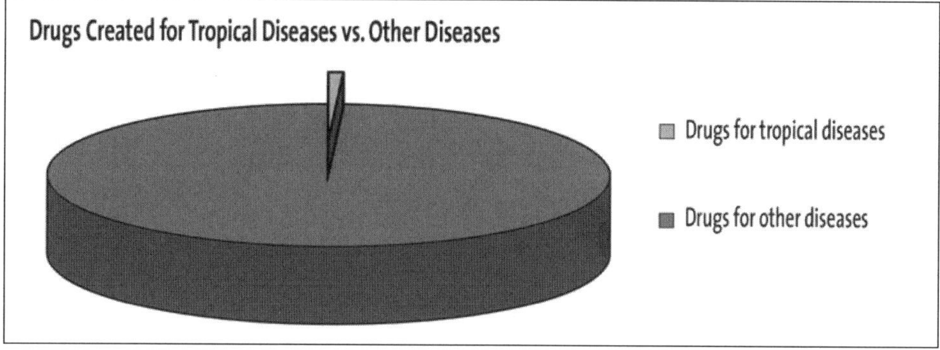

7. The market follows the money, so people with money are probably concerned with baldness. People with tuberculosis probably have a lot less money in general to spend on drugs to cure tuberculosis.

8. You could involve changing the laws to permit generic drugs to be sold for humanitarian reasons. You might suggest reducing the number of years a patent is valid.

9. Marketing. Profit.

10. 1.4 %

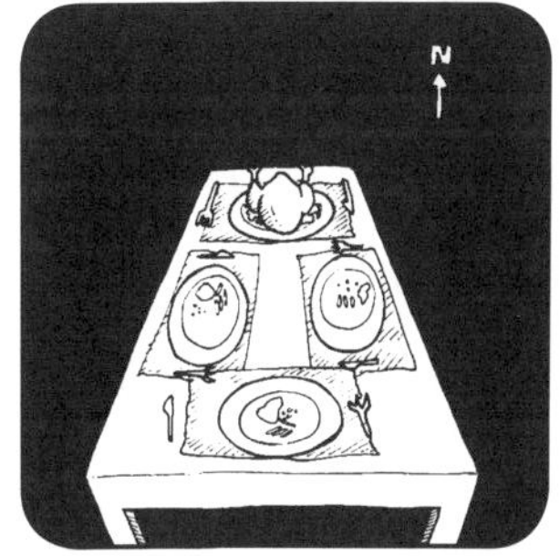

The Poverty of Distribution - Answers

Suggested Activity...

Use the following chart[384] to set up a simulation of a) protein distribution in the world or b) wealth distribution and then discuss. You could distribute the proportionate amount of bread or candy to represent protein and pennies to represent wealth.

Region	Area (%)	People (%)	Protein Distribution (%)	Wealth Distribution (%)
Africa	24	10	10	3
Asia	35	60	5	19
Europe	8	16	25	38
Latin and South America	17	8	15	5
North America	16	6	45	35

384 Church Women United. "The Widening Gap". www.churchwomen.org.

Answers

Opening question:

The new technology may not be made for the place in which it is being introduced. Different climates can cause problems. When new technology breaks, how easy is it to get the replacement parts and the technical expertise required to have it fixed?

An interesting Canadian blunder happened when, in 1971, the Canadian government provided technical advice to the Tanzanian government to grow wheat. It turned out that the soil was too light (it blew away when ploughed), the rainfall necessary to grow the wheat was insufficient, and the local qulea-qulea birds (that of course do not call the Praries home), devoured the crops. John Stackhouse's book *Out of Poverty* (Vintage Canada, 200) has other interesting stories.

Understanding using math:

1. For each one hour, 400 people die from hunger.

2. If 'N' represents the number of people who have died from hunger and 'H' represents the number of hours, then N = 400H.

3. H = 720 hours for a 30 day month so N = 288,000 people.

4. 38,356 per day, 1598 per hour and almost 27 per minute. Kids.

6. To openly and aggressively publish this tragedy would mean that something would need to be done about it. It would take political and economic support.

7.a. If your children may not live very long, larger families ensure support for the family- children will be able to go out and work to bring back money so the family can survive.

7.b. Birthrates in both countries dropped significantly when people had access to healthcare and education and wealth was distributed more fairly.

Just Desserts - Answers

Suggested Activity...

Show part or all of the movie *The Take* by Avi Lewis and Naomi Klein, which is a documentary about how workers in South America take control of their factories and run businesses as cooperatives, without managers and CEOs.

Answers

Opening question:

In a capitalist free market economy, people are free to make as much money as they like, and when governments do not intervene, or intervene in minimal ways, a few people get very, very rich while many people struggle to get by.

Understanding using math:

1.a. 2

1.b. 6

2. About 511 years ago, or just after Columbus had 'discovered' America.

3.a. Corporations, because they hope that government policies will favour their businesses.

3.b. Trade unions, perhaps because they felt that the money would be better spent on union organizing and activity.

3.c.

Type of Contributor	Number of Contributors	% of Contributors	Contributions	% of Total Contributions
Corporation	2,002	61.5	$9,925,033	82.8
Individual	1,219	37.5	$1,919,117	16
Trade Union	33	1	$146,200	1.2
Total	3,254	100	$11,990,370	100

The changes increase the corporate contributions to over 82% and shrink the individual contributions to 16%. This new way of looking at the numbers shows the overwhelming contributions of the corporations.

4. $4,225,000. The government doesn't collect the money, so in the end it has less money to put toward social programs like healthcare and education.

5.a. $1,384.15 per hour

5.b. Almost 269 workers

5.c. 7

5.d. Almost 3,944 people

6.a. $13,925 per hour, or $232.08 per minute

6.b. 2,704 years ago. This is before the birth of Christ.

7. 14.4 hours, almost 145 houses

8.a. $8,296.13 per hour, or $138.27 per minute

8.b. 605,897 kits

8.c. 66,369,042

8.d. 53,924,847

9. One hundredth of one percent or 0.01%

If Syrup Costs 2 Cents A Cup...- Answers

Suggested Activity...

"In Canada close to 40,000 women work at home sewing for big companies. These women are often mistreated and make as little as $2/hour. Sweatshops exist in Canada too." www.cbc.ca/streetcents/guide/2001/16/s02_01.html. Check out the "Why do they do it?" section of this website.

Answers

Opening question:

You might ask the students who would gladly pay the full ticket price what they appreciate about the services offered, and those who would not their reasons why.

Understanding using math:

1.a.

Paid to:	Percentage Breakdown:	Actual cost:
Factory	Wages: 0.4%	52 cents
	Materials: 8 %	$10.40
	Profit: 2%	$2.60
	Other: 1.6%	$2.08
Transport and Tax	5%	$6.50
Shoe Company	Research: 11%	$14.30
	Publicity: 8.5%	$11.05
	Profit: 13.5%	$17.55
Retail Store	50%	$65.00
	Total: 100%	Total: $130

1.c. For example, the shoe company's profit per pair of shoes is almost 34 times the amount of money the worker gets in wages per pair of shoes. And publicity (advertising) per pair of shoes is about 21 times greater than wages.

2. If S = popcorn sold and P = profit, P= 0.9S. If the theatre sold $9780 worth of popcorn, they made a profit of $8802.

3.a. The amount of money spent on packaging is one eleventh the amount spent in the store.

3.b. If 'P' represents the amount spent on packaging and 'T' represents the amount spent in the store, then T = 11P.

3.c. The total spent was $10,501, and the amount spent on packaging was $954.64.

4.a. The amount of money spent in the store is two and a half times greater than the amount spent on marketing those goods.

4.b. If 'T' represents the total amount spent in the store, and 'M' represents the marketing dollars that went into the goods purchased, then T = 2.5M.

4.c. $4200.40

5.

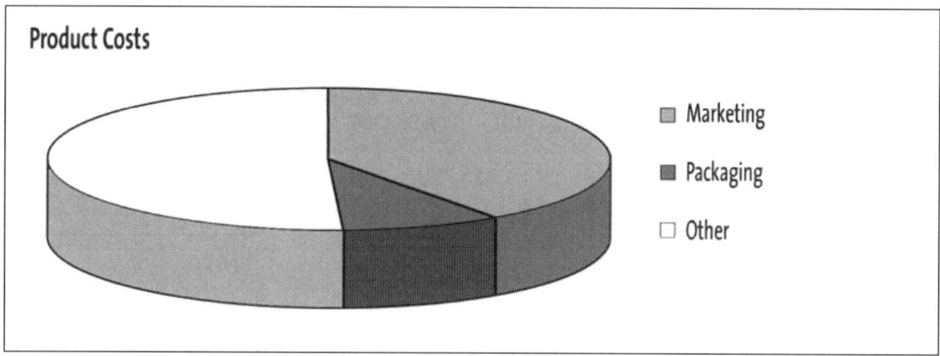

6. Advertising is a business's way of being known. If all of the other businesses are aggressively advertising and you aren't, consumers may not frequent your store as often, putting you out of business.

Healthcare For The Masses - Answers

Suggested Activity...

Have students visit www.healthcoalition.ca and bring in one fact that they did not previously know to share with the class.

Answers

Opening question:

A for-profit system is meant to benefit share holders by maximizing profit. Many things that maximize profit cause a loss of services. For example, a for-profit education system could increase its profit by firing music teachers and getting rid of caretakers. Of course this isn't good for the people who live in schools, the students. With the privatization of hospitals the people who benefit are banks, financiers, for-profit health corporations and private developers.[385]

Understanding using math:

3. In a for-profit system, it is less profitable to insure people who are not healthy, because they will end up making claims for services (which the insurance company pays and which come out of insurance company profit). It is also less profitable if doctors are recommending high priced treatment options (even if those happen to be the treatments that should be taken). Scenario four is the most profitable scenario for the insurance companies.

385 Ontario Health Coalition information sheet

4.a. If 'S' represents the savings in administrative costs between the American system and the Canadian system per dollar and 'D' represents the amount of dollars spent on administration of the system, then S = 0.14D. If Canada spent $28 million, the US would pay $31.92 million.

4.b. If 'S' represents the amount of savings per person and 'P' represents the number of people then S = 3,702P. If all of our 30 million people used the system like the U.S. we'd need an additional $111,060,000,000.

4.c. Employers end up paying 8.2 times the amount in healthcare premiums for their employees using the American system rather than the Canadian system.

Sheltered From The Storm? - Answers

Suggested Activity...

In the shelter system, sometimes staff members prevent homeless people from staying because they are unmanageable, violent or drug dependant. Let's say the trend seems to be that more people are being turned away for these reasons. Ask your students to look at the following graph and use the numbers to argue for a solution to the problem that responds to the systemic, rather than the personal, reasons to the problem.

Year	Staff to Client Ratio	Hours of Staff Training	Number of Harm Reduction Services	Funding
3 years ago	1:5	10 hours	15	$150,000
2 years ago	1:7	8 hours	12	$126,000
1 year ago	1:10	8 hours	11	$112,000
This year	1:15	6 hours	10	$110,000

Answers

Opening question:

People living on the street cost the medical system more money- they have more, and longer, stays in hospitals. Since it's harder to find jobs when you live on the street, you also need to consider the tax money lost when people who are homeless aren't working. Some people who are desperate may resort to crime, which has associated costs as well.

Understanding using math:

1.a. 20,000 per year multiplied by 13 years is 260,000 housing units.

1.b. Since the general trend had been downward, using the average of 20,000 might lead to a higher result than the pattern predicted.

1.c. The average is approximately 12,000 housing units per year. 12,000 multiplied by 13 years is 156,000 housing units since 1993.

1.d. People turn to family and friends for financial support or for a place to live. Some people become homeless and use the shelter system. People try to make due with less, by using food banks and other support services.

2. Just over 13%

3. The ratio is approximately 2:1

4. In five years the number of shelter beds has increased dramatically, from 9,200 to 20,000. That's more than double!

5.a. In order, the ratios are approximately 2:1; 5:1; 3:1; 6:1; 6:1; 9:1; and 48:1

5.b. What these ratios mean is that the homeless population will require the use of the medical system more often (which costs money).

6. Not only does it cost more to shelter someone in the shelter system ($10.50 more per night), but for every one person that has a home and has to use a hospital for a night ($3000) there are five people who don't have homes staying three times as long in the hospital ($45,000).

7. The average length of stay in the hospital is three times as long a person who has shelter ($9000 compared to $3000). Likely this is because the person's ability to fight off disease is weakened by living on the street.

8.a. 208 m^2.

8.b. Add approximately 20 squares (or 79 square metres).

8.c. 11 m^2 or almost 3 squares

Clear Sight - Answers

Suggested Activity...

Collect a number of advertisements and bring them into class. Then play the game John Allen Paulos calls "Spot the Sleight."[386] You play by examining the numbers used in the advertising and trying to point out how they are being used to make things seem more attractive than perhaps they really are.

Answers

Opening question:

Marketing claims are meant to convince consumers to buy the product, so they may stretch the truth or distort it completely if they believe a profit can be made (and it doesn't break any laws with respect to advertising codes).

Understanding using math:

1. After taking the first 20% off of the original price, the second 20% off is a percentage of the reduced price. The actual final price is $9.76 which is 36% off of the original price, not 40% off.

386 Paulos, John Allen. *A Mathematician Reads the Newspaper* Doubleday New York p. 87

2. The first question to ask would be "Better in what way?" because if it's a way that isn't important to the consumer it may mislead. For example, if one product is considered better because it's packaged in easy to open pouches perhaps that's not a quality that really matters. Perhaps also it is better in a useful way but only in limited circumstances.

3. The two variables may be correlated but not causally related. Drinking milk may be a symptom of something else that is causing the problem of cancer. For example, the ability to consume milk is partially dependent on one's wealth- you have to be able to afford it. But perhaps wealthy people use barbeques more often and char their food (creating carcinogens) than do people without wealth.

4. Heart disease and cancer are more common in older people, so someone might argue that although they kill more people, those people have less time to live, and the resources put into saving younger people are more cost effective. Of course, this argument is problematic: how do we choose to value one life over another?

5. According to the chart, students have two days for school. The fallacy of the argument is that several of the categories overlap, and so data is counted more than once when it shouldn't be (weekends include sleeping, and also occur during summer vacations).

Activity	Proportion of the year	Actual Time (Days)
Sleeping	1/3	121.7 days
Eating	1/8	45.6 days
Summer vacation and holidays	1/4	91.3 days
Weekends	2/7	104.3 days
		Total: 363 days

6. In a population of 3 million young people and with a rate of 12 suicides per 100,000 you would expect 360 suicides annually. 28 teenagers is well below that number- which is not to say that the game was not causally linked to suicide for some young people.

7. "How much does it reduce it by?" 75%? 1% Who knows?

8. The loss leader is getting the people into the store, so that even if the store owner takes a loss on the one product, it's making up for it with a greater quantity of shoppers who tend to buy other things while in the store.

	With no loss leader	With a loss leader
Average number of customers per day	152	196
Average profit per customer	$3.24	$2.95
Average daily profit	$492.48	$578.20

9. $16.84. A shirt sold for $20.20 could be put on sale 20% off. So by marking the original $12.95 up 156% it will work.

10. One of the items in the store could be 80% off while the other 500 items could be marked at much lower reductions.

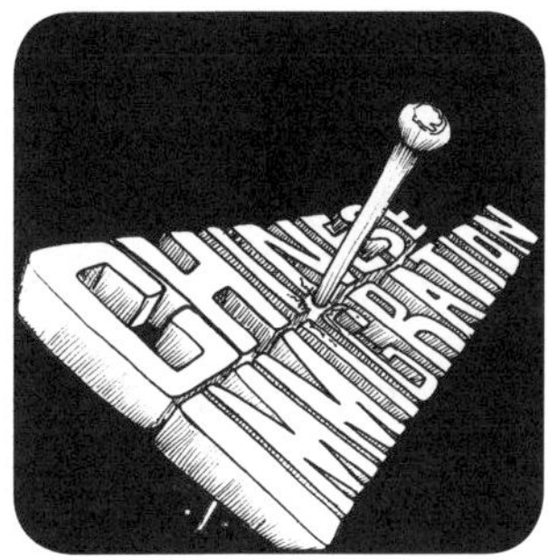

The Last Spike - Answers

Suggested Activity...

Read the storybook *Ghost Train* by Paul Yee to the students. It's an award winning story about Choon-yi, who lives in China and whose father has gone to North America to find work building the railway.

Answers

Opening question:

Few descendants came from the Chinese rail workers because they didn't bring women with them as they crossed the Pacific for work. White Eurocentric society, many who considered the Chinese workers 'evil,'[387] made life very difficult for the Chinese men.

Understanding using math:

1. For 127 years between 1880 and 2006, and an inflation rate of 3%, $50 in 1880 would be the same as paying $2,134.50.

2. For 104 years between 1903 and 2006, $500 in 1903 is the same as $10,815.37.

3. For the 84 years between 1923 and 2006, 18 million dollars in 1923 would be worth $215,575,489.20.

4. 700 out of 17,000 amounts to 4.1%.

5.a.

	Racialised Group	Percentage of Total	Total Workers
Fire fighters	335	1.50%	22,333
Police Officers	1,850	3%	61,667
Judges	90	3.66%	2,459
Elementary/Kindergarten Teachers	9465	4%	236,625
Secondary School Teachers	8,385	5%	167,700
Lawyers	2,885	5%	57,700
University Professors	6,500	14%	46,429
Food Service Counter Attendants and Food Preparers	22,995	17%	135,265
Light Duty Cleaners	26,505	19%	139,500
Kitchen and Food Service Helpers	26,945	24%	112,271
University Educated		34%	
Harvesting Labourers	4,410	40%	11,025

387 The ARTSPAPER, Summer 2001, p. 15.

5.b. The jobs where racialised groups are underrepresented are positions of authority and power, and higher paying jobs as well, for example, judges and lawyers.

5.c The jobs where racialised groups are overrepresented are in positions that pay low wages: cleaners and labourers for example.

5.d If 11% of Canadians are racialised and yet they make up 34% of the university educated, it's harder to argue that the group as a whole is under qualified.

6. Although visible minority immigrants who have been in Canada for longer tend to have higher annual salaries, immigrants who are not visible minorities in all year categories except one have higher annual salaries (sometimes by as much as 38%).

7.a. Yes. It's possible because older people tend to earn more, on average, than younger people. But the differences in full and part time employment between the two groups need to be seen in light of the "discriminatory nature of work attainment".[388]

7.b. Systemic biases could be preventing racialised Canadians from securing full time employment.

8.a. If there were other variables that were different, they could have explained the differences in the results and you would be unable to conclude that the wearing of the hijab had anything to do with the results.

8.b. Again, unless all participants approach the potential employer in the same way, they will add confounding variables and be unable to draw conclusions.

8.c. In this study, the garment factories are the most discriminatory toward women who wear the hijab. The least discriminatory is the fast food industry. Campaigns to raise awareness about worker's rights could be targeted to industries where the problem was greatest.

8.d.

	Total Sites	Fast Food	Retail Stores	Garment Factories	General Factories
Applicant without hijab immediately asked and applicant with hijab not immediately asked	10	1	2	4	3
Applicant without hijab not immediately asked and applicant with hijab immediately asked	2	1	1	0	0
Both applicants immediately asked or both not immediately asked	4	1	2	0	1

With such a tiny sample size the results are interesting but not reliable. To get a reliable result you need a sample size of about 1000 (which takes a lot of time and money)

388 Galabuzi, Grace-Edward. *Canada's Creeping Economic Apartheid.* Centre for Social Justice, 2001, p.66.